The
Canadian Writer's
Workplace

Eighth Edition

The **Canadian Writer's** Workplace

Eighth Edition

by Gary Lipschutz, Sandra Scarry, and John Scarry

NELSON

NELSON

The Canadian Writer's Workplace, Eighth Edition
by Gary Lipschutz, Sandra Scarry, and John Scarry

VP, Product and Partnership Solutions:
Anne Williams

Publisher, Digital and Print Content:
Laura Macleod

Executive Marketing Manager:
Amanda Henry

Content Development Manager:
Jacquelyn Busby

Photo and Permissions Researcher:
Courtney Thorne

Production Project Manager:
Jaime Smith

Production Service:
MPS Limited

Copy Editor:
Sheila Wawanash

Proofreader:
MPS Limited

Indexer:
Christine Hoskin

Design Director:
Ken Phipps

Managing Designer:
Franca Amore

Interior Design:
Liz Harasymczuk

Cover Design:
Trin Truong

Cover Image:
Paper Boat Creative/Getty Images

Compositor:
MPS Limited

Library and Archives Canada Cataloguing in Publication

Lipschutz, Gary, 1964-, author
    The Canadian writer's workplace /
by Gary Lipschutz, Sandra Scarry, and
John Scarry. — Eighth edition.

Includes index.
ISBN 978-0-17-658254-8 (paperback)

    1. English language—Rhetoric—
Textbooks. 2. English language—
Rhetoric—Problems, exercises, etc.
3. English language—Grammar—
Problems, exercises, etc. I. Scarry,
Sandra, 1946-, author II. Scarry,
John, author III. Title.

PE1413.C355 2015
808'.042   C2015-904465-0

ISBN-13: 978-0-17-679519-1
ISBN-10: 0-17-679519-7

Why Am I Here?

Welcome to the eighth edition of *The Canadian Writer's Workplace!*

At this point, you may be asking yourself questions like these:

- Why am I here (in an English course)? After all, I received 95 in high school English, and I thought I would never have to take an English course again.
- Why am I learning how to write a paragraph when I've already written essays that I've gotten 90's on?
- Why am I required to take English when it doesn't seem relevant to my program?
- Why do I need more English than I already have? I already speak English. It's my first and only language, and I speak it well enough to get by. There are so many students whose first language is something other than English; they are still learning it, but I already know it.

These are all legitimate concerns. Here are some responses:

If you plan to practise your career in an English-speaking country, no course is more relevant than English. How well you communicate what you know will determine, more than anything else, how far you go.

You might have gotten 90's in high school English, but a postsecondary education is going to focus on different aspects of the subject. High school English may have concentrated more on the generation of ideas, for example, while college places more emphasis on clarity, style, sentence structure, document formatting, and textual analysis to prepare you for success in the workplace.

English is made up of several complex skills: writing, speaking, and comprehension based on reading and listening. Everybody has strengths and weaknesses. The course into which you've been placed might be perfect for dealing with your particular weaknesses. See it as an opportunity, not a problem. Grab the opportunity to learn something. Make yourself stronger!

It doesn't matter if English is your only language or your third. One never stops learning a language. Luckily, you can apply your language skills to everything in your life—professional and personal. Everyone knows how important first impressions are. Imagine the value of using language effectively in making a powerful first impression.

Better language skills will also help you to think more clearly, to focus more quickly, to articulate more precisely and intelligently, and to argue more effectively. How can such skills not be relevant to your career?

Become a more powerful and effective communicator. Give the course, your professor, this book, and yourself a chance; you will get back more than you expect. Improving your English will help you to get what you want. Change your language. Change your life!

Gary Lipschutz

Brief Contents

Online Appendices

Go to **www.nelson.com/student** and see the Student Companion site for *The Canadian Writer's Workplace,* Eighth Edition.

Contents

andresr/istockphoto.com

Christopher Futcher/istockphoto.com

anucha maneechote/shutterstock.com

OJO_Images/istockphoto.com

EXCUSES, EXCUSES **378**

Student excuses are getting more sophisticated. But so are the investigative tactics of teachers. Adrian Lee of *Maclean's* magazine explores the excuses used today and the proof students may need to back them up.

HOW TO GET HAPPILY MARRIED **381**

Using a book by an experienced divorce lawyer and a marriage psychotherapist—and best friends—Julia McKinnell discusses both the reasons behind a bad marriage and the ways to ensure a better one.

CANADA, MY CANADA **384**

Tomson Highway, who was born and raised in and around the Barren Lands First Nation reserve near Brochet, in northern Manitoba, paints a proud and vibrant picture of the country he calls home.

I LOST MY TALK **387**

Mi'kmaq poet Rita Joe writes from the perspective of a First Nation child who asked to be sent to a residential school. What she found was not what she may have expected.

A MATTER OF POSTAL CODES **389**

In sci-fi movie *Gattica*, starring Uma Thurman and Ethan Hawke, a person's success in life could be predicted with a simple eye scan. *Maclean's* writer Ken MacQueen points out that such predictions are already being made, not with eye scans, but with people's postal codes.

A TOUGH APPROACH THAT MIGHT WORK **393**

How often do you hear someone say building more prisons is the solution to Canada's problem of repeat offenders in the area of petty theft? Canadian lawyer and activist James C. Morton asks readers to consider an alternative to incarceration.

merzzie/shutterstock.com

Preface

It's been said that the first casualty of war is truth. Well, the first casualty of writing is often clarity. Writing without clarity is bad writing. *The Canadian Writer's Workplace,* Eighth Edition, is an easy-to-use textbook that aims to inspire and guide students on the road to achieving clarity in their writing. With this book, students are expected to develop the solid paragraph- and essay-writing skills needed not only in English courses, but also in many other courses taken in college and/or university and, subsequently, wherever written communication is required. *The Canadian Writer's Workplace* can help students get the most out of any endeavour that calls for the ability to write clearly and effectively.

EVERYTHING YOU NEED BETWEEN TWO COVERS

The Canadian Writer's Workplace is a **three-in-one textbook of sentence skills, rhetoric (writing steps and strategies), and readings**. When you use this book, there is no need to look for a supplemental book containing work on grammar or a book to teach writing skills or a reader providing material that inspires students to generate thoughtful and well-written composition. Everything you need is already between two covers.

STRUCTURE OF THE TEXTBOOK

The Canadian Writer's Workplace is made up of six units:
   Unit I: Sentence Skills
   Unit II: The Reading-Writing Connection
   Unit III: The Writing Process
   Unit IV: Writing Strategies for the Paragraph and Essay
   Unit V: Major Readings
   Unit VI: Appendices

EIGHT TYPES OF EXERCISES, QUESTIONS, AND ASSIGNMENTS

With examples and figures, *The Canadian Writer's Workplace* offers constant reinforcement of every definition stated and every writing technique taught at every step of the way. Numerous practice exercises and writing assignments throughout the entire book offer further reinforcement of what is being learned. The format of *The Canadian Writer's Workplace* features flexibility in that the book enables an instructor to work on different exercises with an entire class, gives individual students opportunities to work by themselves or with a tutor in a lab, and encourages students to work in groups. Certain sections can be skipped if the material is not needed for a particular class—or a class might begin with a later section, with the earlier chapters being used as a review. Eight types of exercises, questions, and assignments in this textbook are as follows:

1. Quick Quiz

Each chapter in Unit I begins with a Quick Quiz, designed to assess students' skills in the material in that chapter. Based on the results of this quiz, the instructor can choose either to skip over the material in the chapter, or to spend extra time on the material in question if the students' skills in this area are shown to be weak.

2. Practices

The answers for these are provided in the Answer Key at the back of the textbook. Practices enable students, therefore, to work independently by checking their work without having to consult an instructor.

3. Exercises

Answers to the Exercises are not at the back of the textbook. The main reason for the deliberate absence of these answers is so that instructors can assign these exercises for in-class testing or homework. Answers to the Exercises are provided, however, in the Instructor's Manual that accompanies the eighth edition of *The Canadian Writer's Workplace*.

4. Review Practices and Exercises

These are often found at the end of each chapter in Unit I. They are cumulative so that they test the students not only on a particular point of grammar, but also on a number of points discussed within the chapter at hand. Similar to the Practices and Exercises earlier in the chapter, the Practices in the Review section have their answers in the back of the book, while the Exercises in the Review section do not.

5. Working Together

A valuable and popular feature, Working Together can be found at the end of every chapter in the book. This feature promotes group work, an approach that provides opportunities for the peer-mediated activities that many instructors use to make their classes more fun and at the same time to reinforce concepts from a chapter they have already discussed in their classes.

6. Questions for Analysis

Several questions for analysis follow every model essay found in Unit IV: Writing Strategies for the Paragraph and Essay. They prompt the student for short answers on either content or form. Sample questions include "Is the author's argument effective? Why or why not?"

7. Assignments

Throughout Unit IV, the reader will find chapters on the various rhetorical modes, or writing strategies, such as description, comparison and/or contrast, and process. For each chapter, there are Assignments listing several topics relating to the chapter from which the student can choose to write a paragraph or essay on something the student finds of interest to him or her.

8. Four Types of Questions Following Major Readings in Unit V

Every major reading in Unit V is followed by four sets of questions. The four sets are: (1) Comprehension Questions, (2) Questions about Form, (3) Questions for Discussion, and (4) Writing Ideas. Often students ask professors if they can do practice writing in preparation for major writing assignments done in class. The questions in the fourth category in particular can be used for this purpose, and sometimes so can questions from the third. Regardless, all of these questions are designed to foster further understanding and appreciation for the reading they follow and the issues, in general, under discussion.

THE READINGS

Students often require inspiration to help motivate them to learn how to write better. In the interest of further inspiration and stimulation, the readings in this edition have been expanded to include more cutting-edge essays with particular appeal to postsecondary students. Overall, the readings throughout the text are extremely varied: they include a sample research paper in Chapter 24, model paragraphs and essays in Unit IV, and twelve new major readings in Unit V. Some of the works in Unit IV are by student writers; others are taken from a wide range of novels, essays, short stories, and books of nonfiction by world-famous authors. Unit V contains mostly nonfiction and some short fiction and poetry—all carefully chosen to evoke thoughtful and well-structured written responses from students. The writers of the major readings in Unit V are exclusively Canadian, and they are all seasoned writers and/or academics. The strong Canadian flavour of the text offers the postsecondary student in Canada an insight into various aspects of Canadian culture.

NEW FEATURES OF THE EIGHTH EDITION

Many features of the first seven Canadian editions of the book have been retained. As mentioned earlier, they include the comprehensive package of sentence skills, rhetoric, and readings. This eighth edition, however, offers some exciting and innovative changes:

- In response to feedback from across the country, a brand new unit (Unit II) has been dedicated to connections between reading and writing. This unit features strategies to help students more easily understand what they are reading and strategies for how to respond better in writing.
- A brand-new chapter in Unit III: "The Writing Process" is entitled "Style." This chapter features the qualities of writing that often go beyond grammar and mechanics. Many colleges are requiring the use of more formal language, for example, because of their mandate to prepare students for the workforce. Formal language is a featured section of this new chapter, while other items include tone, active and passive voice, sentence variety, and word economy.

- Twelve new pieces appear in Unit V, which houses the book's major readings. The new readings have been chosen with the intent to engage the reader. Among the new readings is "Excuses, Excuses" by Adrian Lee, which is a humorous look at the evolving nature of student excuses for not doing homework and ways in which professors are responding. And two professionals have written a book in which they claim that a happy marriage depends on making the right life choices. Find out what they are in Julia McKinnell's "How to Get Happily Married."

ANCILLARIES

Instructor Resources

The **Nelson Education Teaching Advantage (NETA)** program delivers research-based instructor resources that promote student engagement and higher-order thinking to enable the success of Canadian students and educators. Visit Nelson Education's **Inspired Instruction** website at http://www.nelson.com/inspired/ to find out more about NETA.

The following instructor resources have been created for *The Canadian Writer's Workplace*, Eighth Edition. Access these ultimate tools for customizing lectures and presentations at www.nelson.com/instructor.

NETA Test Bank

The Test Bank for *The Canadian Writer's Workplace,* Eighth Edition, contains an extensive selection of exercises corresponding to every point of grammar discussed in Unit I and Appendices A, C, and D.

Enriched Instructor's Manual

This resource was written by Frances Sparano, Humber College. It is organized according to the textbook chapters and contains chapter overviews, learning outcomes, suggested classroom activities, and answers to exercises contained in the core text.

NETA PowerPoint

Microsoft® PowerPoint® lecture slides for every chapter have been created by Frances Sparano, Humber College. There is an average of 20 slides per chapter, many featuring key figures, tables, and photographs from *The Canadian Writer's Workplace*. NETA principles of clear design and engaging content have been incorporated throughout, making it simple for instructors to customize the deck for their courses.

Image Library

This resource consists of digital copies of figures, short tables, and photographs used in the book. Instructors may use these jpegs to customize the NETA PowerPoint or create their own PowerPoint presentations.

MindTap

MindTap

Offering personalized paths of dynamic assignments and applications, **MindTap** is a digital learning solution that turns cookie-cutter into cutting-edge, apathy into engagement, and memorizers into higher-level thinkers. **MindTap** enables students to analyze and apply chapter concepts within relevant assignments, and allows instructors to measure skills and promote better outcomes with ease. A fully online learning solution, **MindTap** combines all student learning tools—readings, multimedia, activities, and assessments—into a single Learning Path that guides the student through the curriculum. Instructors personalize the experience by customizing the presentation of these learning tools to their students, even seamlessly introducing their own content into the Learning Path. The MindTap to accompany *The Canadian Writer's Workplace* was written by Sarah Duffy, Centennial College.

Aplia

Aplia™ is a Cengage Learning online homework system dedicated to improving learning by increasing student effort and engagement. **Aplia** makes it easy for instructors to assign frequent online homework assignments. **Aplia** provides students with prompt and detailed feedback to help them learn as they work through the questions, and features interactive tutorials to fully engage them in learning course concepts. Automatic grading and powerful assessment tools give instructors real-time reports of student progress, participation, and performance, while **Aplia**'s easy-to-use course management features let instructors flexibly administer course announcements and materials online. With **Aplia**, students will show up to class fully engaged and prepared, and instructors will have more time to do what they do best—teach.

STUDENT ANCILLARIES

MindTap

MindTap

Stay organized and efficient with **MindTap**—a single destination with all the course material and study aids you need to succeed. Built-in apps leverage social media and the latest learning technology. For example:

- ReadSpeaker will read the text to you.
- You can highlight text and make notes in your MindTap Reader. Your notes will flow into Evernote, the electronic notebook app that you can access anywhere when it's time to study for the exam.
- Self-quizzing allows you to assess your understanding.

Visit http://www.nelson.com/student to start using **MindTap**. Enter the Online Access Code from the card included with your text. If a code card is *not* provided, you can purchase instant access at NELSONbrain.com.

Online Appendices

Students can access the two online Appendices, "Solving Spelling Problems" and "Irregular Verbs," on the Student Companion site for *The Canadian Writer's Workplace,* Eighth Edition. Please visit www.nelson.com/student.

Aplia

Founded in 2000 by economist and Stanford professor Paul Romer, **Aplia**™ is an educational technology company dedicated to improving learning by increasing student effort and engagement. Currently, **Aplia** products have been used by more than a million students at over 1300 institutions. **Aplia** offers a way for you to stay on top of your coursework with regularly scheduled homework assignments that increase your time on task and give you prompt feedback. Interactive tools and additional content are provided to further increase your engagement and understanding. See http://www.aplia.com for more information. If **Aplia** isn't bundled with your copy of The *Canadian Writer's Workplace, Eighth edition* you can purchase access separately at NELSONbrain.com. Be better prepared for class with **Aplia!**

ACKNOWLEDGMENTS

For their advice and/or personal support, the author is indebted to John Artibello, Tamina Basarab, Maxine Beale, Shawn Brake, Denvil Buchanan, Sarah Duffy, Dan Gaze, Andrea Jacobs, Ben Labovitch, Karen Naidoo, Sofia Phillips, Ron Schafrick, Martha Shephard, Emilda Thavaratnam, George Thomas, and Susan Whitzman.

Kudos and thanks go to the winning team at Nelson—Laura Macleod, Jacquelyn Busby, and Jaime Smith—and freelance editor Sheila Wawanash. Their hard work and dedication have helped make this edition what it is.

The comments and advice from the following reviewers were invaluable:

Lisa Alward, University of New Brunswick
Diana Barrie, Loyalist College
Dina Chipouline, Seneca College
Sandy Dorley, Conestoga College
Aicha Gaboune, Northern Lakes College
Kathleen Oliver, Langara College
Clayton Rhodes, Durham College
Stephanie Samboo, Sheridan College
John Stilla, Humber College
Antoinette Zichy, Seneca College

To the student essayists who have generously given permission to publish their work in this edition of *The Canadian Writer's Workplace*, the author and editors wish to extend most sincere thanks. They are Margo Fine, Zack Goodman, Donald Pianissimo, Leila Sayeed, Akis Stylianou, Cara Watters, and Jenny Yuen.

Your Feedback or Questions Are Invited

If you have any feedback or questions you would like to send regarding this edition of *The Canadian Writer's Workplace,* please do so via the following email address:

glips@centennialcollege.ca.

I welcome your comments. In the meantime, I hope you enjoy reading and using the 8th edition.

Gary Lipschutz

Unit I **Sentence Skills**

andresr/istockphoto.com

andresr/istockphoto.com

Chapter 1 **Parts of Speech: Overview**

The Canadian Writer's Workplace begins with an overview of sentence skills to ensure that you have an understanding of basic terms. Such an understanding will help you succeed with the rest of this text.

Words can be divided into nine categories called **parts of speech.** Understanding these categories will help you work with language, especially when it comes to revising your own writing.

QuickQuiz Test your knowledge of the various parts of speech. Determine the correct part of speech for the underlined words in the following sentences. There is no need to actually write the answers in the blanks; this Quick Quiz is primarily for self-assessment. The answers to the questions are upside down beside the quiz.

1. By installing the <u>service</u>, you <u>agree</u> to <u>the</u> following conditions.

2. <u>Follow</u> the instructions <u>on</u> the screen to uninstall the <u>older</u> version <u>of</u> the <u>program</u>.

3. <u>Running</u> the program is <u>easily</u> handled if <u>you</u> pay attention to the <u>next</u> part of the video.

4. <u>Everything</u> you need <u>to do</u> is explained <u>in</u> <u>ten</u> easy steps.

5. <u>If</u> you have any <u>questions</u>, <u>call</u> our <u>toll-free</u> number.

Answers:
1. noun, verb, article
2. verb, preposition, adjective, preposition, noun
3. gerund (*-ing* word acting as a noun), adverb, pronoun, adjective
4. pronoun, infinitive (*to* + a verb), preposition, adjective
5. conjunction, noun, verb, adjective

Parts of Speech		
1. Nouns	4. Verbs	7. Conjunctions
2. Pronouns	5. Adverbs	8. Interjections
3. Adjectives	6. Prepositions	9. Articles

1. What Are Nouns?

> **DEFINITION**
>
> A **noun** is a word that refers to a person, place, or thing.
> **Example:** The *student* is doing her *homework*.
> (Both *student* and *homework* are nouns.)

Types of Nouns

There are two types of nouns: common nouns and proper nouns.

Types of Nouns	
Common Nouns	**Proper Nouns**
officer	Michael Johnson
station	Union Station
magazine	*Canadian Geographic**
university	Centennial College
*When a title is that of a major publication such as a book or a magazine, the title should be italicized or underlined (underlining in a handwritten text is the equivalent of italics in a printed text).	

Common nouns are nouns that are not names or titles. For this reason, common nouns do not begin with a capital letter (unless, of course, the word begins a sentence):

> I plan to attend *university* next fall.

The word *university* is a common noun in this sentence because it is not part of a specific name or title. The *u* must not be capitalized.

Proper nouns are names or titles. Every significant word of a proper noun must start with a capital letter.

> Carleton University is in Ottawa, our nation's capital. The University of Cape Breton, on the other hand, is in Sydney, Nova Scotia.

In the above two sentences, the *U* in University (the word immediately following *Carleton* and the second word in the second sentence) must be capitalized because the word *University* in both cases is now a proper noun; it is part of the title of a specific university. (See Chapter 12: "Capitalization.") The University of Cape Breton includes the word *of*, whose first letter is not capitalized because *of* is a *preposition* (see p. 7) and a preposition is not considered a significant word in a title.

Concrete vs. Abstract Nouns

Nouns are said to be **concrete** if they represent things you can see or touch.

window	river
paper	finger

Nouns are said to be **abstract** if they represent things you cannot see or touch. These words can be concepts, ideas, or qualities.

meditation	carelessness
honesty	fearlessness

To test for a noun, it may help to ask these questions:

- Can I put the article *the* in front of the word?
- Is the word used as the subject or object of the sentence?

A noun may be the subject of the sentence it is in (the performer of the action). But it may not be. All subjects are nouns, but not all nouns are subjects. For example, a noun might be an object (the receiver of the action) instead.

> *Marissa* gave a book to her daughter.

The noun *Marissa* is the subject of the sentence. The noun *book* is a direct object (it receives the action directly). The noun *daughter* is an indirect object (it receives the action indirectly).

Countable vs. Non-countable Nouns

Countable nouns, quite simply, can be counted.

> There are three *marbles* on the floor.

Non-countable nouns, just as simply, cannot be counted.

> The *water* spilled onto the floor.

Do not put an indefinite article (*a* or *an*) in front of a non-countable noun. For example, the following is not correct: A water spilled onto the floor.

2. What Are Pronouns?

> **DEFINITION**
>
> A **pronoun** is a word that takes the place of a noun. Like a noun, it can be the subject or object of a sentence. Pronouns come in several cases (*see next page*).
> **Example:** *He* is dating the girl next door.
> (The pronoun *he* can replace a noun such as *Johnny* or *the boy*.)

Pronoun Cases

Depending on how it is used in a sentence, a personal pronoun will be in one of three cases: subjective, objective, or possessive. Possessive adjectives (last column) are not pronouns because they do not replace nouns; they modify them instead.

| | Personal Pronouns | | | Possessive |
	Subjective	Objective	Possessive	Adjectives
Singular				
1st person	I	me	mine	my
2nd person	you	you	yours	your
3rd person	he	him	his	his
	she	her	hers	her
	it	it	its	its
Plural				
1st person	we	us	ours	our
2nd person	you	you	yours	your
3rd person	they	them	theirs	their

Relative Pronouns	**Demonstrative Pronouns**	**Indefinite Pronouns**
who, whom, whose	this	all, both, each, one
which	that	nothing, nobody, no one
that	these	anything, anybody, anyone
what	those	something, somebody, someone
whoever, whichever		everything, everybody, everyone

3. What Are Adjectives?

> **DEFINITION**
>
> An **adjective** is a word that modifies a noun or pronoun.
> **Example:** The *red* car is hers.

An adjective usually comes before the noun it modifies, but it can also come after a verb.

> The *unusual* letter was delivered to my house.
> It felt *heavy*.

4. What Are Verbs?

> **DEFINITION**
>
> A **verb** is a word that indicates an action, state, or occurrence; its form also indicates the time at which the action, etc., takes place.
> **Example:** The Montreal Canadiens *advanced* to the second round of the Stanley Cup Playoffs in 2015.

Verbs can be divided into three classes: action verbs, linking verbs, and helping verbs.

Action Verbs

An action verb tells us what its subject is doing. Most verbs are action verbs.

> The athlete *cycles* 20 km every morning.
> (The action takes place in the present.)
>
> The crowd *applauded* the sax player.
> (The action took place in the past.)

Linking Verbs

A linking verb joins the subject of a sentence to one or more words that describe or identify the subject.

> She *is* a jazz musician in her twenties.
> He *seemed* excited about getting married.

Common Linking Verbs		
act	become	look
appear	feel	seem
be (am, is, are, was, were, have been)	grow	taste

Helping Verbs (also called Auxiliary Verbs)

A helping verb, or auxiliary, is any verb used before the main verb.
It could show the tense of the verb:

> It *will* rain tomorrow.
> (shows future tense)

It could show the passive voice (see pp. 38–40 for more on active and passive voice):

> The new concert hall *has been* finished.

It could give a special meaning to the verb:

> Avril Lavigne *may be* singing at that concert.

The most common auxiliary verbs are forms of the irregular verbs *do*, *have*, and *be*.

A *modal* auxiliary is a helping verb that comes before the main verb and expresses probability, obligation, ability, or necessity.

Common Modal Auxiliary Verbs
can, could
may, might, must
shall, should
will, would

See Appendix C online at www.nelson.com/student (see Student Companion site for *Canadian Writer's Workplace*, Eighth Edition) for more on irregular verbs.

5. What Are Adverbs?

She is sure to succeed *eventually*.

- The adverb *eventually* answers the question "When?"
- It ends in -*ly*, and it modifies the verb *succeed*.

It will be *very* cold tomorrow.

- The adverb *very* answers the question "How?"
- It modifies the adjective *cold*.

Winter has come *too* early.

- The adverb *too* answers the question "How?"
- It modifies the adverb *early*.

Here are some of the more common adverbs:

Common Adverbs		
Adverbs of Frequency	**Adverbs of Degree**	
always	even	quite
ever	extremely	surely
never	just	too
often	more	very
seldom	much	
sometimes	only	

6. What Are Prepositions?

Common Prepositions			
about	below	in	since
above	beneath	inside	through
across	beside	into	to
after	between	like	toward
against	beyond	near	under
along	by	of	until
among	down	off	up
around	during	on	upon
at	except	outside	with
before	for	over	within
behind	from	past	without

7. What Are Conjunctions?

DEFINITION

A **conjunction** is a word that joins or connects other words, phrases, or clauses.

Examples: I was sick, *but* I still came to work.

She had eggs *and* pancakes for breakfast.

Connecting two words

Sooner *or* later, you will have to pay.

Connecting two phrases

The story was on the radio *and* in the newspaper.

Connecting two clauses

Dinner was late *because* I had to work overtime at the office.

> Since one word can have several meanings, and words can function differently depending on their forms, you must study the context in which a word is found to be sure what part of speech it is.

The parent makes sacrifices *for* the good of the children.

In the sentence above, *for* is a preposition.

The parent made sacrifices, *for* the child needed a good education.

In the sentence above, *for* is a conjunction meaning "because."

Conjunctions		
Coordinating Conjunctions	**Subordinating Conjunctions**	
and	after	provided that
but	although	since (meaning "because")
nor	as, as if, as though	unless
or	because	until
for (meaning "because")	before	when, whenever
yet	how	where, wherever, whereas
so	if, even if	while
Correlative Conjunctions	**Adverbial Conjunctions** (also known as "conjunctive adverbs")	
either ... or	To add an idea: furthermore	
neither ... nor	moreover	
both ... and	likewise	
not only ... but also	To contrast: however	
	nevertheless	
	To show a result: consequently	
	therefore	
	To show an alternative: otherwise	

TIP

You can use the acronym FANBOYS as a way to remember the coordinating conjunctions: *F* for *for*, *A* for *and*, *N* for *nor*, *B* for *but*, *O* for *or*, *Y* for *yet*, and *S* for *so*.

For
And
Nor
But
Or
Yet
So

8. What Are Interjections?

DEFINITION

An **interjection** is a word that expresses a feeling (often a strong one) and is not connected grammatically to any other part of the sentence.
Example: *Darn!* I lost my wallet. *Well,* that means I'll have to borrow cash from a friend.

9. What Are Articles?

DEFINITION

An **article** is a word that identifies a noun in a general sense.
Example: *The* dogs were mistreated for years by *a* previous owner.

Articles are considered to be adjectives. There are two types of articles: definite (*the*) and indefinite (*a, an*).

> She read *the* magazine (a particular magazine).
> She read *a* magazine (some magazine not identified).

Do not use *a* or *an* with non-countable nouns (things that can't be counted separately, such as *water*).

> Water leaked under my roof during the rainstorm.

Use an indefinite article (*a* or *an*) before countable nouns when you don't specify the particular thing referred to.

> *An* open window allowed the fresh air in (any one of a number of windows).

Use *a* before a noun that begins with a consonant or with a *u* pronounced as *y*. Use *an* before a word that begins with a vowel or a silent *h*.

> *a* vacation
> *a* unit, *a* eulogy (*u* and *eu* in these words are pronounced "*yu*")
> *an* automobile
> *an* hour

Working Together: Puzzle Pieces and Sentence Parts

Review the names for sentence parts by doing this crossword puzzle. Feel free to look back through the chapter for the answers.

Grammatical Terms Crossword Puzzle

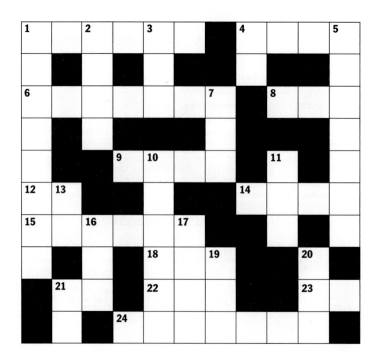

Across

1. Verbs like *hop*, *sing*, and *play* are called _____ verbs.

4. A helping verb

6. Every sentence has a _____ and a verb.

8. A helping verb

9. Which of the following is a preposition?
   must, upon, they

12. A preposition

14. *Word*, *witch*, *wall*, and *willow* are examples of this part of speech.

15. Most nouns are _____ nouns. They are not capitalized.

18. In the following sentence, which word is an adjective?
    His pet theory was disproved.

21. A preposition

22. In the following sentence, which word is an abstract noun?
    The era was not economically successful.

23. A preposition

24. A word that can take the place of a noun

Down

1. *Joy*, *confidence*, *and peace* are examples of this kind of noun, which is the opposite of a concrete noun.

2. Which word is the subject in the following sentence?
   Here is the tube of glue for Toby.

3. An indefinite pronoun

4. A plural pronoun

5. *Look*, *appear*, *feel*, and *seem* are examples of _____ verbs.

7. Which word is the object of the preposition in this sentence?
   He made sure to call her before ten.

10. The opposite of a common noun

11. A pronoun

13. A preposition

16. A helping verb

17. Which of the following is a proper noun?
    king, Nero, hero, teen

19. Which of the following is an adjective?
    net, tan, Nan, man

20. Which word is the verb in the following sentence?
    Run down to the car for our bag.

21. A common linking verb

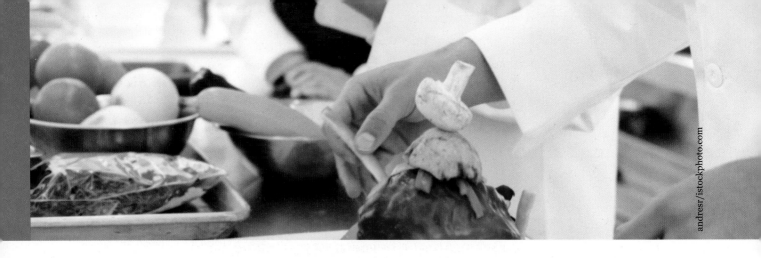

Chapter 2 **Recognizing Subjects and Verbs**

QuickQuiz   Test yourself on your knowledge of subjects and verbs. In each of the following sentences, find the subject of the sentence and the verb that goes with it. Write your answers in the spaces provided. The answers are upside down beside the quiz.

Subject	Verb

_____ _____ 1. The definition of marriage has become a major issue in Canada.

_____ _____ 2. Studies show that many people are getting married later than their parents did.

_____ _____ 3. In Quebec, a large proportion of people have chosen to live in common-law relationships.

_____ _____ 4. Researchers have given more attention to divorces than to successful marriages.

_____ _____ 5. A positive attitude toward the partner appears to be the most important quality in a successful marriage.

Answers:
1. Subject: *definition*
   Verb: *has become*
2. Subject: *studies*
   Verb: *show*
3. Subject: *proportion*
   Verb: *have chosen*
4. Subject: *researchers*
   Verb: *have given*
5. Subject: *attitude*
   Verb: *appears*

Why Should We Use Complete Sentences When We Write?

If you walk up to a friend at noon and say "Lunch?" you are expressing only part of a complete thought. Your friend probably understands your meaning: "Would you like to join me for lunch?" Even though we do not always use complete sentences in daily conversation, we usually have complete thoughts in mind. We say and hear words and phrases such as "Lunch?" every day, and these words and phrases seem to be complete thoughts because both the speaker and the listener supply the missing words in their own minds.

You are free to use language in this way when you speak casually with friends, but you must use a different approach in more formal speaking and writing situations. When writing down your thoughts, you cannot assume that another person will finish your thoughts for you. Each of your written thoughts must be a complete expression of what is in your mind.

The purpose of writing is to communicate something that is of value to a reader. Once you understand how the parts of a complete sentence work, you will be able to focus as much attention on *what* you are saying as on *how* you are saying it. You can take control of the sentence. You will have the power to make words work for you.

What Is a Complete Sentence?

> **DEFINITION**
>
> A **complete sentence** must contain a subject and a verb, as well as express a *complete thought*.
> **Example:** The cat drank.
>   (*Cat* is the subject; *drank* is the verb. You need not know what the cat drank for the sentence to be complete.)

A *complete thought* is difficult to describe. It may be best understood by means of an example:

1. If you want an "A" in this course.
2. If you want an "A" in this course, you should do all your assignments and homework, attend all your classes, and communicate to your professor any difficulties you're having.
3. You want an "A" in this course.

The first thought is incomplete. The second thought is complete. So is the third. Obviously, length does not determine completeness.

How Do You Find the Subject of a Sentence?

The subject of a sentence is the person or thing about which the rest of the sentence makes an assertion. Any sentence must be about someone or something; therefore, every sentence must have a subject. To find the subject of any sentence, ask yourself this question: Who or what is the sentence about? When you have answered this question, you have found the subject of the sentence. Try to zero in on one word that is the subject—sometimes this is not possible, but it is possible most of the time. The subject in sentence #3 on page 13 is *you*. The words "*A*" and *course* are also nouns, but neither is the subject of the sentence.

 Exercise 1   Recognizing Subjects

Examine each of the following sentences and ask yourself who or what it is about. (Choose only one word where possible.) Underline the subject. Answers and explanations are provided below.

1. The student graduated in the spring.
2. The unemployed Rick Daniels spent the summer looking for work.
3. He took a job as a security guard.
4. The building was near the waterfront.
5. The warehouse grew bitterly cold.
6. Cowardice was not the issue.
7. Tina and Margot listened to his complaints whenever they got together.

Since the subject of a sentence is made up of one or more nouns (or a word, phrase, or clause that functions as a noun), it is helpful to learn some of the terms used in traditional grammar to describe different kinds of nouns.

1. The student graduated in the spring.

The sentence is about the *student*. In this case, the subject is a common noun.

 DEFINITION

Nouns refer to people, places, and things. Most nouns are common nouns.
Common nouns are the general terms for all the people, places, and objects around us. They are not specific names; therefore, they are not capitalized.
Examples: woman, city, cola

2. The unemployed Rick Daniels spent the summer looking for work.

The sentence is about *Rick Daniels*. In this case, the subject *Rick Daniels* is made up of the two words in his name, both of which are proper nouns.

 DEFINITION

Proper nouns name particular persons, places, or things. Proper nouns are always capitalized.
Examples: Juanita, Calgary, Pepsi

Notice that words such as *unemployed* can be put in front of nouns to describe them further. These words are called **adjectives.** *The, a,* and *an* are called **articles.** An article is also a form of adjective because it modifies a noun (**Example:** *the* cat).

3. He took a job as a security guard.

The sentence is about *he*.

DEFINITION

Words that can be used in place of nouns are called **pronouns.**
Examples: she, he, it, we, I, you, and they

4. The building was near the waterfront.

The sentence is about the *building*, a common noun. Can you replace this noun first with a proper noun and then with a pronoun?

_____ was near the waterfront.
_____ was near the waterfront.

5. The warehouse grew bitterly cold.

The sentence is about the *warehouse*. Here the common noun is not a person or place but a thing. What pronoun could take the place of *warehouse*?

_____ grew bitterly cold.

6. Cowardice was not the issue.

The sentence is about *cowardice*, another common noun.

7. Tina and Margot listened to his complaints whenever they got together.

The sentence is about *Tina* and *Margot*. The subject is made up of two proper nouns joined by *and*. This sentence provides an example of a compound subject.

DEFINITION

A **compound subject** is made up of two or more nouns joined together by *and, or, either/or,* or *neither/nor.*
Example: Neither the *teacher* nor the *students* know the answer.

Not every noun or pronoun functions as a subject. Nouns and pronouns can also function as **objects.** Can you find a noun in the following sentence that is not the subject of the sentence?

Marc bought a ticket.

The word *ticket* is a noun, but not a subject. It does not perform the action of the verb, *bought*—it receives the action. It is an object. (The subject, *Marc*, does the action.)

Guide to Finding the Subject of a Sentence

Definition: The subject of a sentence is who or what the sentence is about.

How to find the subject: Ask yourself, "Who or what is this sentence about?" or "Who or what is doing the main action?"

- Subjects usually come early in the sentence.
- Subjects can be modified by adjectives.
- Subjects can be compound.

Look for these two kinds of words as your subjects:

1. **Nouns:** the names of persons, places, or things

Common	or	Proper		Concrete	or	Abstract
aunt		Aunt Giselle		face		loneliness
country		Ghana		people		patriotism
watch		Timex		jewellery		time

2. **Pronouns:** words that take the place of nouns

Personal	Indefinite	Relative	Demonstrative
I	one	who	this
you	each	that	that
he, she, it	some, someone, somebody, something	what	these
we	any, anyone, anybody, anything	which	those
they	nobody, nothing everyone, everybody, everything all many several		

 Practice 1 **Finding the Subject of a Sentence**

Underline the subject in each of the following sentences. An example has been done for you. Check your answers against those in the Answer Key on page 454.

The seat belt <u>sign</u> switched on.

1. The plane landed.
2. Michelle Bates gathered her bags.
3. She was so excited.
4. Strange sounds filled her ears.
5. A mother and her three children shared a lunch.
6. The battered red taxi idled outside.
7. A light rain had fallen recently.

Finding the Subject in Sentences
with Prepositional Phrases

The sentences you worked with in the Practice on page 16 were short and basic. If we wrote only such sentences, our writing would sound choppy. Complex ideas would be difficult to express. One way to expand a simple sentence is to add a prepositional phrase.

> He put his suitcase on the seat.

On is a preposition. *Seat* is a noun, used here as the object of the preposition. *On the seat* is a prepositional phrase.

DEFINITION

A **prepositional phrase** is a group of words containing a preposition and an object of the preposition with its modifiers. Prepositional phrases contain nouns, but these nouns are never the subject of the sentence.
Example: The dog buried the bone *under the porch*.

In sentences with prepositional phrases, the subject may be difficult to spot. Consider the following sentence:

> In the young woman's apartment, paintings covered the walls.

In the sentence above, what is the prepositional phrase? Who or what is the sentence about?

To avoid making the mistake of thinking that a noun in a prepositional phrase could be the subject, it is a good practice to cross out any prepositional phrases in a sentence where you are looking for the subject.

> ~~In the young woman's apartment~~, paintings covered the walls.

With the prepositional phrase crossed out, it now becomes clear that the subject of the sentence is the noun *paintings*.

TIP

When you are looking for the subject of a sentence, do not look for it within a prepositional phrase.

You can easily recognize a prepositional phrase because it always begins with a preposition. Study the following list so that you will be able to quickly spot all of the common prepositions.

Common Prepositions			
about	below	in	since
above	beneath	inside	through
across	beside	into	to
after	between	into	toward
against	beyond	near	under
along	by	of	until
among	down	off	up
around	during	on	upon
at	except	outside	with
before	for	over	within
behind	from	past	without

In addition to these common prepositions, English has a number of prepositional combinations—groups of words that function together as prepositions.

Common Prepositional Combinations		
ahead of	in addition to	in reference to
at the time of	in between	in regard to
because of	in care of	in search of
by means of	in case of	in spite of
except for	in common with	instead of
for fear of	in contrast to	on account of
for the purpose of	in the course of	similar to
for the sake of	in exchange for	with regard to

TIP

Notice that when a prepositional phrase begins a sentence, a comma usually follows the phrase. (Sometimes, if the prepositional phrase is short, the comma is omitted.)

Examples: In the corner, the dog buried its bone.

Before lunch they left.

 Exercise 2 Creating Sentences with Prepositional Phrases

Use each of the prepositions in the list below to write a prepositional phrase. Then write a sentence containing that prepositional phrase. Two examples have been done for you.

Preposition	Prepositional Phrase	Sentence
before	before breakfast	My cousin called before breakfast.

Preposition	Prepositional Phrase	Sentence
between	between the two barns	Between the two barns, the old Buick lay rusting.

Preposition   **Prepositional Phrase**

1. in   _____

   Sentence _____

2. with   _____

   Sentence _____

3. of   _____

    Sentence _____

4. from   _____

    Sentence _____

5. during   _____

    Sentence _____

6. by   _____

    Sentence _____

 Exercise 3   **Finding Subjects in Sentences with Prepositional Phrases**

Remember that you will never find the subject of a sentence within a prepositional phrase. In each of the following sentences, cross out any prepositional phrases. Then underline the subject. An example has been done for you.

~~On the circus grounds,~~ <u>Lisa</u> wandered ~~among the elephants, horses, and camels.~~

1. Young people in the circus search for travel, adventure, danger, and romance.
2. However, after a few weeks of pulling cages and sleeping on hay, most of these people get tired of the circus and go back home.
3. The art of clowning, for instance, is very serious work.
4. Today, a circus clown must graduate from Clown College in Venice, Florida.
5. The staff of Clown College looks across the country for applicants.
6. Admission to the college is not easy.
7. Only 60 people out of 3000 applicants are admitted.

What Are the Other Problems in Finding Subjects?

Sentences That Are Questions

Some sentences begin with words indicating that a question is being asked. These words, such as *why, where, how,* and *when,* give the reader the signal that a question will follow. This kind of sentence-opening question word is not the subject. The subject will be found later on in the sentence.

The following sentences begin with question words. The subjects are italicized:

Why is *he* going away?

How did *he* find his sister in the city?

Notice that the subject is not found in the opening part of either sentence. To make the subject in a question easier to spot, try answering the question or changing it into a statement.

He is going away ...

He found his sister ...

Using *here* and *there*

The words *here* and *there* can never be the subject of a sentence.

> There is a new teacher in the department.

Who or what is this sentence about? It is about a teacher. *Teacher* is the subject of the sentence.

> Here is the book.

The subject of this sentence is *book*.

Commands

Sometimes a sentence contains a verb that gives an order:

> Go to Halifax.
> Help your sister.

In these sentences, the subject *you* is not written, but it is understood. This is the only case where the subject may be left out when you write a sentence.

Sentences That Contain Appositive Phrases

> **DEFINITION**
>
> An **appositive phrase** is a group of words in a sentence that gives us extra information about a noun in the sentence.
> **Example:** Don Koyama, *the retired chemist*, sat at his desk.

In the example above, the words *the retired chemist* make up the appositive phrase because they give you extra information about Don Koyama. Notice that commas separate the appositive phrase from the rest of the sentence. If you leave out the appositive phrase when you read the sentence, the thought will still be complete.

> Don Koyama sat at his desk.

Now the subject is clear: *Don Koyama*.

> **TIP**
>
> When you are looking for the subject of a sentence, you will not find it within an appositive phrase.

The word *chemist* in the example in the box above cannot be the subject because it is in an appositive phrase.

Subjects That Look Like Verbs

Words that end in -*ing* but have no helping verb in front are called *gerunds*. They act as nouns, not verbs. A gerund, therefore, can be the subject of a sentence.

Jogging is good for your health.

 Practice 2 Finding Hidden Subjects

Each of the following sentences contains an example of a special problem in finding the subject of a sentence. For each sentence, first cross out any prepositional phrases and appositive phrases. Then underline the subject. An example has been done for you. Check your answers against those in the Answer Key on page 454.

What can <u>we</u> learn ~~from the study of an ancient civilization~~?

1. Look at a map of South America.
2. Where is the ancient city of Chan Chan?
3. Here on the coastal desert of northern Peru stand the remains of this city of the kings.
4. Chan Chan, once the fabulously wealthy centre of the Chimor, is situated in one of the driest, bleakest regions in the world.
5. It was the largest pre-Columbian city in South America.
6. In the ruins of this city, scientists have found fragments to piece together the mystery of the past.
7. How could this civilization have survived this hostile environment and become so advanced?

How Do You Find the Verb of a Sentence?

Every sentence must have a verb. Verbs can be divided into three classes:

1. Action: An **action verb** tells what the subject is doing.
   Christine Sinclair *played* soccer in the FIFA Women's Soccer Cup in Canada in 2015.
2. Linking: A **linking verb** indicates a state of being or a condition.
   The crowd *seemed* exhausted during the triathlon.
3. Helping: A **helping verb** combines with a main verb to form a verb phrase; it indicates the time of the main verb or gives it a special meaning.
   Canadians *can* expect strong performances from their Olympic athletes in the future. The gold medal *might* become a tradition.

Verbs tell time. Use this fact to test for a verb. If you can put a word into different tenses, it is a verb.

Present:	(Today,) he runs.
Past:	(Yesterday,) he *ran*.
Future:	(Tomorrow,) he *will run*.

Action Verbs

> **DEFINITION**
>
> **Action verbs** tell us what the subject is doing and when the subject does it.
>
> **Example:** The woman *studied* ballet.

Look at the example in the box above.

> What was the woman doing? studying
>
> What is the time of the action? the past (*-ed* is the past tense ending)

Action Verbs			
Most verbs are action verbs. Here are a few examples:			
arrive	learn	open	watch
leave	forget	write	fly
enjoy	help	speak	catch
despise	make	teach	wait

Practice 3 Finding Action Verbs

Find the action verb in each of the following sentences. First, cross out any prepositional or appositive phrases; then underline the subject of the sentence. Finally, circle the verb (the word that tells what the subject is doing). Also, note the time of the action: is it past, present, or future? An example has been done for you. Check your answers against those in the Answer Key on page 454.

> Many <u>people</u> (begin) hobbies ~~in childhood~~. (present)

1. Some people collect very strange objects.
2. One man saved the fortunes from fortune cookies.
3. A group of people in Alberta often met to discuss their spark plug collections.
4. People in Brandon will gather many types of barbed wire.
5. Collectors take pride in the possession of unusual items.
6. A collection, such as odd rocks or unique automobiles, will let a person express his or her individuality.
7. Collections keep us entertained from childhood to old age.

Exercise 4 Finding Action Verbs

Each of the following sentences contains an action verb. Find the action verb by first crossing out any prepositional or appositive phrases and underlining the subject of the sentence. Then circle the verb (the word that tells what the subject is doing). Note also the time of the action: past, present, or future. An example has been done for you.

> <u>Attitudes</u> ~~toward medical practices~~ (will change.) (future)

1. Traditional Chinese medicine harnessed ancient healing techniques in the practice of "qigong" (pronounced *chee gong*).

2. Masters of this Chinese practice claimed the ability to cure many diseases.

3. The master will project a mysterious force into his students.

4. The hands of the Chinese qigong practitioner will pound at the air above a patient.

5. Many patients respond to this invisible force.

6. Some patients sway their bodies with the power of the force.

7. Some doctors conducted research in China in hopes of finding the secrets of this ancient art.

Linking Verbs

DEFINITION

A **linking verb** is a verb that joins the subject of a sentence to one or more words that describe or identify the subject.

Examples: The <u>girl</u> (is) a constant dreamer.

<u>She</u> (seems) distracted.

<u>We</u> (feel) sympathetic.

In each of the examples above, the verb links the subject to a word that identifies or describes the subject. In the first example, the verb *is* links the noun *girl* with the noun *dreamer*. In the second example, the verb *seems* links the pronoun *she* with the adjective *distracted*. Finally, in the third example, the verb *feel* links the pronoun *we* with the adjective *sympathetic*.

Common Linking Verbs	
act	feel
appear	grow
be (am, is, are, was, were, have been)	look
become	seem
	taste

 Exercise 5 Finding Linking Verbs

Find the linking verb in each of the following sentences. First, underline the subject of the sentence. Then, draw an arrow to the word or words that identify or describe the subject. Finally, circle the linking verb. An example has been done for you.

<u>Dreams</u> (are) very important to the Aboriginal peoples of Canada.

1. My dream last night was wonderful.

2. I had become middle-aged.

3. In a sunlit kitchen with a book in my hand, I appeared relaxed and happy.

4. The houses were empty and quiet.

5. In the morning light, the kitchen felt cozy.

6. I seemed to have grown calmer.

7. The ice cream tastes very chocolatey.

 **Exercise 6** **Finding Linking Verbs**

Each of the following sentences contains a linking verb. Find the linking verb by first underlining the subject of the sentence. Then draw an arrow to the word or words that identify or describe the subject. Finally, circle the linking verb. An example has been done for you.

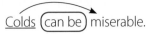

Colds (can be) miserable.

1. Monica is afraid of catching a cold.
2. She felt healthy.
3. Everyone in her family became sick.
4. Her brother looked horrible.
5. She seemed immune to the cold.
6. Soon Monica's head grew stuffy.
7. The chicken soup from the deli down the street tasted delicious.

Helping Verbs (Also Called Auxiliary Verbs)

Helping verbs (verbs that come before the main verb) can help the main verbs express a particular time and/or a special meaning.

Sentence Using Helping Verb	Time and/or Meaning Expressed
He *is* sleeping.	right now
He *might* sleep.	maybe now or in the future
He *should* sleep.	ought to, now or in the future
He *could have been* sleeping.	maybe in the past

A **modal auxiliary verb** is a helping verb that comes before the main verb and expresses probability, obligation, ability, or necessity.

Modal Auxiliary Verbs
can, could
may, might, must
shall, should
will, would

Be, *do*, and *have* are the most common auxiliary verbs. Remember that *be*, *do*, and *have* can also be used as main verbs of sentences. (When used as a main verb, *be* is a linking verb while *do* and *have* are action verbs.) All other helping verbs are usually used only as helping verbs.

Watch out for **adverbs** that may come in between the helping verb and the main verb.

 DEFINITION

Adverbs are words that can modify verbs, adjectives, or other adverbs.
Example: Dreams can *often* frighten young children.

The word *often* is an adverb that comes between the two words in the verb phrase *can frighten*. For a list of common adverbs, see page 7.

Exercise 7 Finding Helping Verbs

Each of the following sentences contains a helping verb in addition to the main verb. In each sentence, first underline the subject. Then circle the entire verb phrase. An example has been done for you.

> In some writing classes, <u>students</u> (must keep) a diary of their work.

1. Keeping a diary could have several advantages.
2. In a journal, a person can safely express true feelings without fear of criticism by family or friends.
3. You will be able to capture your memories before they fade.
4. Important, too, would be the development of a writing style and the improvement of language skills.
5. A journal might awaken your imagination.
6. It may unexpectedly bring pleasure and satisfaction.
7. You should seriously consider the purchase of one of those lovely fabric-bound notebooks.

Chapter Review Exercises

Practice 4 Finding Subjects and Verbs in Simple Sentences

In each of the following sentences, cross out any prepositional phrases or appositive phrases. Then underline the subject and circle the complete verb. An example has been done for you. Check your answers against those in the Answer Key on page 454.

> The modern <u>family</u> (has been disrupted) ~~by many negative outside influences~~.

1. Mother and Dad always blame me for any trouble with my sister.
2. My sister, the most popular girl in her class, is two years older than I.
3. Yesterday, for instance, she was trying on her new graduation dress.
4. Helpfully, I took out her new shoes and purse for her.
5. Margaret instantly became furious with me.
6. I was only sharing Margaret's excitement about her new clothes.

Exercise 8 Finding Subjects and Verbs in Simple Sentences

In each of the sentences in the following paragraph, cross out any prepositional or appositive phrases. Then underline the subject and circle the complete verb.

> Go West! Western Australia, one of the remaining great boom areas of the world, constitutes one-third of the Australian continent. Why did people by the tens of thousands go to western Australia in the late 1800s? In 1894,

Leslie Robert Menzies jumped off his camel and landed in a pile of gold nuggets. In less than two hours, this man gathered over a million dollars in gold. He eventually took five tonnes of gold to the bank by wheelbarrow! Kalgoorlie and Boulder, the two boom towns that grew up there, boast the richest golden mile in the world. With all the gold seekers, this surface gold did not last very long. Now the only bands of rich ore lie more than 1200 meters down under the ground. There are many ghost towns with their empty iron houses and rundown chicken coops.

 Exercise 9 Composing Complete Sentences

Below are two lists, one of subjects and one of verbs. Compose ten complete sentences, each one using any subject from one list and any verb from the other list. Use each subject and each verb only once. Try to vary the position of the subject in the sentence. An example has been done for you. (Do not use it as one of your own sentences.)

The dentist looks very tired today.

1.	dogs	is
2.	nose	chased
3.	she	are
4.	dentist	was
5.	Saskatchewan	singing
6.	fishing	has
7.	problems	screams
8.	obeying	see
9.	mailbox	approaches
10.	storm	looks

1. _____

2. _____

3. _____

4. _____

5. _____

6. _____

7. _____

8. _____

9. _____

10. _____

Working Together: Singling Out Subjects

Student Profile: On a separate piece of paper, answer the five questions about yourself that are listed below. Write on every other line to make your writing more readable. Write freely for twenty minutes. Then exchange papers with another student. Using a pencil, circle the subject in every sentence in your classmate's writing (you should be able to narrow it down to one word in most cases). Try not to confuse subjects (nouns that do the action) with objects (nouns that receive the action). Be prepared to share examples with the class.

1. Tell about the first book you remember looking at or reading.
2. Who was your most memorable teacher in elementary school? What is it about this teacher that you remember?
3. What person outside of school has taught you the most?
4. What magazines do you subscribe to or would like to subscribe to, and why?
5. When you have a day or half a day to yourself, how do you spend that time?

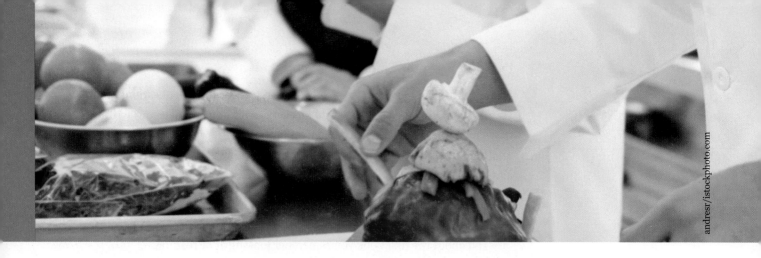

Chapter 3 **Solving Verb Problems**

Note: For problems involving subject-verb agreement, see Chapter 4.

QuickQuiz Test yourself on your knowledge of verb forms. In each of the following sentences, choose the correct form for the verb in parentheses. Answers to the questions are upside down beside the quiz.

1. The soccer game will continue only after the lightning and rain _____. (stop)

2. Since he was poor and unappreciated by the music world when he died in 1791, Mozart did not realize the importance that his music _____ (have) in the twenty-first century.

3. My aunt told me yesterday that she _____ (buy) a new condo the day before that.

4. Hemingway wrote only about subjects that he _____. (like)

5. I _____ (see) the woman buy the purple hat yesterday.

Answers:
1. have stopped, OR stop
2. would have
3. had bought
4. liked
5. saw

Since every sentence contains at least one verb, and verbs can take many forms, it is worth taking some time and effort to understand these forms and their uses. In Chapter 2, you learned to recognize verbs. In this chapter, you will study several other aspects of verbs that often cause difficulty for writers:

Irregular verbs
Verb tense consistency
Sequence of verb tenses
Present perfect and past perfect tenses
Active and passive voice
Subjunctive mood

What Are the Principal Parts of the Irregular Verbs?

The English language has more than 100 irregular verbs—that is, ones that do not form the past tense or past participle with the usual *-ed* ending. When you listen to young children, you often hear them utter expressions such as "Yesterday I cutted myself." Later on, they will learn that the verb *cut* is unusual and calls for the irregular form: "Yesterday I cut myself." The best way to learn these verbs is to listen to how they sound. Say the irregular forms out loud over and over until you have learned them. If you find that you don't know a particular verb's meaning, or you cannot pronounce a verb and its forms, ask your instructor for help. Most irregular verbs are very common words that you will use often in both writing and speaking. You will want to know them well.

For more on this topic, see Appendix D, "Irregular Verbs," online at www.nelson.com/student (see Student Companion site for *The Canadian Writer's Workplace*, Eighth Edition).

> **DEFINITION**
>
> An **irregular verb** forms its past tense and/or past participle in a different way from the usual *-ed* ending of regular verbs.
>
> **Example:** Yesterday, he cut himself.
>
> (The word *cut* is the past tense form of the irregular verb *to cut*.)

Practising 50 Irregular Verbs

These are the three principal parts of irregular verbs:

Simple Form (also called **Bare Infinitive Form**)	Past Form	Past Participle (used with perfect tenses after *has*, *have*, or *will have*, or with passive voice after the verb *to be*)

I. The following verbs do not change their forms:
(Notice they all end in *-t* or *-d*.)

Simple Form	Past Form	Past Participle
bet	bet	bet
cost	cost	cost
cut	cut	cut
fit	fit	fit
hit	hit	hit
hurt	hurt	hurt
quit	quit	quit
spread	spread	spread

II. The following verbs have the same simple present form and past participle:

Simple Form	Past Form	Past Participle
come	came	come
become	became	become

Exercise 1 **Using Irregular Verb Forms**

Fill in the correct form of the verb in the following sentences.

(cost)   1. Last year the tuition for my education _____ 7 percent more
                 than the year before.

(quit)   2. I have _____ trying to guess my expenses for next year.

(spread)   3. The message has _____ that college costs continue to spiral.

(hit)   4. Most parents have been _____ with large tax increases.

(become)   5. Financing a child's higher education has _____ a difficult task.

III. The following verbs have the same simple past form and past participle:

Simple Form	Past Form	Past Participle
bend	bent	bent
bleed	bled	bled
bring	brought	brought
buy	bought	bought
catch	caught	caught
creep	crept	crept
feed	fed	fed
fight	fought	fought
keep	kept	kept
lead	led	led
lend	lent	lent
seek	sought	sought
send	sent	sent
sleep	slept	slept
speed	sped	sped
spend	spent	spent
sweep	swept	swept
teach	taught	taught
think	thought	thought
weep	wept	wept

 Exercise 2 **Knowing the Irregular Verb Forms**

Fill in the correct form of the verb in the following sentences.

(buy)   1. Last year the school district _____ new chemistry texts.

(spend)   2. Some parents felt they had _____ too much money on
                 these new books.

(bleed)   3. They claimed the taxpayers were being _____ dry.

(keep)   4. These parents argued that the school should have _____ the
                 old books.

(think)   5. The teachers _____ the old books were worn out.

IV. The following verbs all have different forms:

Simple Form	Past Form	Past Participle
begin	began	begun
bite	bit	bitten (or bit)
blow	blew	blown
drink	drank	drunk
drive	drove	driven
fly	flew	flown
grow	grew	grown
hide	hid	hidden (or hid)
know	knew	known
ride	rode	ridden
ring	rang	rung
rise	rose	risen
shrink	shrank	shrunk
sing	sang	sung
sink	sank	sunk
spring	sprang	sprung
strive	strove	striven
swim	swam	swum
throw	threw	thrown
write	wrote	written

 Exercise 3 Knowing the Irregular Verb Forms

Fill in the correct form of the verb in the following sentences.

(grow)   1.   Adventure holidays _____ in popularity during the last decade.

(fly)   2.   Years ago, travellers _____ to Spain to see bullfights.

(throw)   3.   Today, some clients dream of <u>being</u>_____ by the bull.

(ride, swim) 4.   As part of adventure trips, people <u>have</u>_____ horseback, <u>have</u>_____ across rivers, and have walked for days to get to their destinations.

(shrink)   5.   Clients of a new trend called "reality tours" do not even _____ from visiting jails.

 Exercise 4 Using Irregular Verb Forms

Supply the past form or the past participle for each verb in parentheses.

Ever since people _____ to write, they <u>have</u>_____ about the great
                    (begin)   (write)
mysteries in nature. For instance, no one _____ why the dinosaurs
                                            (know)
disappeared. Scientists now <u>have</u>_____ on one strong possibility.
                                (bet)

That possibility is that 65 million years ago, a chunk of rock 10 km wide _____
                                                                                              (hit)
the earth and _____ up a thick cloud of dust. The dust _____ the
                              (throw)   (keep)
sunlight from the earth; therefore, certain life forms disappeared. Some

scientists have _____ that this could also have _____ the earth's
                        (think)   (shrink)
animal population by as much as 70 percent. Other scientists are not so sure

that this is the answer. They believe time has _____ the real reason for the
                                                              (hide)
disappearance of the dinosaurs.

Exercise 5   Using Irregular Verb Forms

Supply the past form or the past participle for each verb in parentheses.

Medical researchers have _____ a cure for the common cold,
                                    (seek)
but so far they have _____ without success. The cold virus has _____
                            (fight)   (spread)
throughout the world, and the number of cold victims has _____ every
                                                                          (rise)
year. Past experience has _____ us that people who drink plenty of
                                  (teach)
liquids and take aspirin get over colds more quickly than those who do not,

but this remedy is not good enough. People have also believed that

you _____ a fever and starved a cold, but recent research has _____
          (feed)   (lead)
to a refutation of this belief. It has _____ a lot of time and effort to search
                                              (cost)
for a vaccine, but so far the new knowledge has not _____ a cure.
                                                                      (bring)

Avoiding Unnecessary Shifts in Verb Tense

Do not shift verb tenses (move from past to present, for example) as you write
unless you intend to change the time of the action.

Shifted tense: The customer asked (past tense) for the prescription,
                    but the pharmacist says (present tense) that the
                    ingredients are being ordered (present tense).

Revised: The customer asked (past tense) for the prescription,
              but the pharmacist said (past tense) that the
              ingredients were being ordered (past tense).

Practice 1 **Correcting Unnecessary Shifts in Verb Tense**

Each of the following sentences has an unnecessary shift in verb tense. Revise each sentence so that the tense remains consistent. There may be more than one correct answer for each sentence. Check your answers against those in the Answer Key on page 455.

1. After I complete that writing course, I took the required history course.

   _____

   _____

2. In the beginning of the movie, the action was slow; by the end, I am sitting on the edge of my seat.

   _____

   _____

3. The textbook gives the rules for writing a Works Cited page, but it didn't explain how to use parenthetical references.

   _____

   _____

4. I was walking in the park when all of a sudden I see her running toward me.

   _____

   _____

5. The encyclopedia gave several pages of information about astronomy, but it doesn't give anything about black holes.

   _____

   _____

6. The invitation requested that Juan be at the ceremony and that he will attend the banquet as well.

   _____

   _____

7. That website gives you excellent information, but it was too cluttered.

   _____

   _____

 Practice 2 **Correcting Unnecessary Shifts in Verb Tense**

The following paragraph contains unnecessary shifts in verb tense. Change each incorrect verb to past tense. Check your answers against those in the Answer Key on page 455.

Doctor Norman Bethune grows up in Gravenhurst, Ontario. He was educated in Toronto and serves as a stretcher bearer in World War I. He contracted tuberculosis and thereafter devotes himself to helping other victims of the disease when he practises surgery in Montreal. He also invents or redesigned twelve medical and surgical instruments. Bethune travelled to Russia in 1935, joined the Communist Party, and goes to Spain in 1936, where he organized the first mobile blood transfusion service during the Spanish Civil War. After returning to Canada, he shortly left for overseas again, this time to China, where he helped the Chinese Communists in their fight against Japan. "Spain and China," he writes, "are part of the same battle." While there, he contracted an infection and died. Mao's essay "In Memory of Norman Bethune," prescribed reading during China's Cultural Revolution, urges all Communists to follow Bethune's example of selfless dedication to others. Bethune is the best-known Canadian to the Chinese, and many Chinese visit his Canadian birthplace.

What Is the Sequence of Tenses?

Sentences often contain two or more verbs that carry different tenses according to the times at which the actions take place. The type of sentence in which this happens is a complex sentence: one that contains both an independent clause and a dependent clause. (Note that the dependent clause might come before the independent clause.)

Before explaining the **sequence of tenses,** which refers to the proper order of verb tense when a sentence contains more than one action, it is first necessary to introduce the terms **independent clause** and **dependent clause.**

> ### DEFINITION
> An **independent clause (IC)** is a group of words that can be a simple sentence. *Independent* means that the words can stand alone as a sentence, and *clause* means there is a subject and a verb. An *Independent clause* is a **complete thought.**
> **Example:** The students worked on their papers all night long.

> ### DEFINITION
> A **dependent clause (DC)** cannot stand alone as a simple sentence. It is an **incomplete thought.** Even though it has a subject and a verb, it depends on the rest of the sentence for completeness.
> **Example:** Because their assignments were due in the morning
> The word *assignments* is the subject of the verb *were*, so this group of words is a *clause.* But it is not a complete sentence. It is a **dependent clause (DC).**

> ### DEFINITION
> The term **sequence of tenses** refers to the proper use of verb tenses in complex sentences (sentences that have both an independent clause and a dependent clause).
> **Example:** The students had worked on their papers all night long because their assignments were due the following morning.
> The verb *had worked* in the independent clause is in the past perfect tense, and the verb *were* in the dependent clause is in the past tense. The first action (the students working) takes place before the second one (the papers being due).

The verb tense in the independent clause determines the tense of the verb in the dependent clause. The guide below shows the relationship between the verb in the independent clause (IC) and the verb in the dependent clause (DC).

Sequence of Tenses

Independent Clause	Dependent Clause	Time of the DC in Relation to the IC
If the tense of the independent clause is in the **present** (he *knows*), here are the possibilities for the dependent clause:		
He knows	that she *is right.*	same time
	that she *was right.*	earlier
	that she *will be right.*	later
If the tense of the independent clause is in the past (he *knew*), here are the possibilities for the dependent clause:		
He knew	that she *was right.*	same time
	that she *had been right.*	earlier
	that she *would be right.*	later
If the independent clause is in the future (he *will tell*), here are the possibilities for the dependent clause:		
He will tell us	if she *goes.*	same time
	if she *has gone.*	earlier
	if she *will go.*	later

Practice 3   Using the Correct Tense

In each of the following sentences, choose the correct tense for the verb in the dependent clause. Use the guide above if you need help. Check your answers against those in the Answer Key on page 455.

1. The golf tournament <u>will continue</u> only after the thunder and lightning _____.
   (stop)

2. Since he thought that he was buying a well-maintained car, Enzo <u>did not realize</u> the problems that this car _____ in the months to come.
   (have)

3. I <u>will know</u> when I get my next paycheque whether or not I _____ a stereo next week.   (buy)

4. Albert Einstein <u>failed</u> the entrance exam at the Swiss Federal Institute of Technology because he _____ a very disciplined student.
   (be) + never

5. Jacob <u>ate</u> only those foods that he _____.
   (like)

6. Sasha <u>believes</u> that with a lot of hard work and a little luck, she _____ successful.   (be) + soon

7. I <u>know</u> that my best course of action _____ to tell the truth.
   (be)

How Do You Use the Present Perfect and the Past Perfect Tenses?

Forming the Perfect Tenses

Present perfect tense: has or have + past participle of the main verb

has worked

have worked

Past perfect tense: had + past participle of the main verb

had worked

What Do These Tenses Mean?

> **DEFINITION**
>
> The **present perfect tense** describes an action that started in the past and continues to the present time.
>
> **Example:** Elena *has worked* at the hospital for ten years.

The example in the box above indicates that Elena began to work at the hospital ten years ago and is still working there now.

Examine the following timeline. What does it tell you about the present perfect tense?

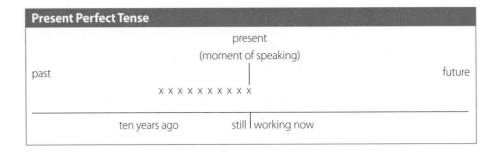

The following sentences include examples of the **present perfect tense:**

She *has studied* French since 2004.

I *have* always *despised* that television show.

> **DEFINITION**
>
> The **present perfect tense** can also describe an action that has just taken place, or an action whose exact time in the past is indefinite.
>
> **Examples:** *Has* Elena *found* a job yet?
>
> Elena *has* (just) *found* a new job in Moncton.
>
> *Have* you ever *been* to Kapuskasing?
>
> Yes, I *have been* there three times.

If the time were definite, you would use the simple past:

Elena *found* a new job yesterday.

Yes, I *was* there last week.

DEFINITION

The **past perfect tense** describes an action that occurred before another activity or before another point in the past.

Example: Elena *had worked* at the hospital for ten years before she *moved* away.

In the example in the definition above, there are two past actions: Elena *worked*, and Elena *moved*. The action that took place first is in the past perfect (*had worked*). The action that took place later, but was also completed in the past, is in the simple past (*moved*).

Past Perfect Tense

	present (moment of speaking)	
past		future
first action second action in the past in the past x x x x x x x x x x		
had worked moved		

The following sentences include examples of the **past perfect tense:**

> I *had* just *arrived* when the alarm *rang*.
> She *said* that Marty *had told* the class about the essay deadline.
> He *had provided* the report long before last week's meeting.

Exercise 6 **Exercise Using the Correct Verb Tense**

Complete the following sentence by filling in each blank with either the present perfect tense or the past perfect tense of the verb given.

1. Yolanda told us that she _____ in Fort Smith before she moved to Mexico City.   (live)

2. Mexico City _____ visitors for many years.
       (fascinate)

3. This city _____ the largest Spanish-speaking city in the world, and
       (become)
people _____ it grow larger every year.
       (watch)

4. The suburbs of the city _____ old villages that _____ peacefully
           (overwhelm)   (exist)
since the days of the Aztecs.

5. Today, Mexico City _____ a computer-controlled subway system to deal
        (build)
with its huge transportation problem.

What Is the Difference between Active and Passive Voice?

In the active voice, the subject does the acting. In the passive voice, the subject is acted upon. (See examples in the box below.) But which one is usually better to use? And does this mean the other should never be used at all?

Active Voice Is Generally Best

Stylistically speaking, using the active voice most often produces a stronger sentence:

Active: The dog buried its bone.

Passive: The bone was buried by the dog.

The first sentence is stronger not only because it is shorter, but because the subject does the action, so more focus is placed on the subject in this sentence. In the second sentence, *the bone* is the subject. But the bone does not do the burying. The dog has still done the burying, but *the dog* is not the subject. (In fact, it is part of a prepositional phrase, so it cannot be the subject. See the definition of a prepositional phrase on p. 17.) So the focus is taken away from the action and its doer.

The Place for Passive Voice

Although active voice is generally better than passive voice, there are situations in which passive voice is more appropriate:

1. You are in a position of authority and, in an official capacity, you are required to give bad news to someone. In such a case, it is sometimes advisable to speak deliberately vaguely about what the cause of the bad news is. Using the passive rather than the active voice helps to do this.

   > Unfortunately, it was decided that the job go to an internal candidate.

   The above sentence is in the passive voice. The person who made the decision is not mentioned. This wording might have been chosen to protect whoever did the deciding. Since the passive voice takes the focus away from the performer of the action (deciding), the recipient of the bad news is less likely to ask specific questions that the employer would prefer not to discuss.

2. It is also better to use the passive rather than active voice when the subject that has been acted upon is more important than the doer of the action.

   > The Conservatives have been given more seats than the Liberals in the House of Commons.

   Who is the doer of the action here? Who actually gave more seats to the Conservatives? The answer is *the people of Canada who voted in the election.* So why aren't these people mentioned at all? Well, it's obvious, since that's how elections work. What isn't obvious is who won, so that's why the word *Conservatives* becomes the subject of the sentence even though it does not refer to the doer of the action. The sentence, therefore, is better in the passive voice, which places the focus on the most relevant information.

3. Putting a sentence in the passive voice is also a good idea when the action itself is more important than the doer of the action. People in the sciences and in legal affairs often report events this way.

> Ice was found on Mars today.
> Michael Jackson was acquitted today.

In the first sentence above, there is no need to report that scientists found the ice. Nor is there need to mention, in the second sentence, that Jackson was acquitted by a jury of his peers.

Active and Passive Voice

In the **active voice**, the subject does the acting:

> The committee made the decision.

Choose the active voice generally in order to achieve direct, economical, and forceful writing. Most writing, therefore, should be in the active voice.
In the **passive voice**, the subject is acted upon:

> The decision was made by the committee
> or
> The decision was made.

Notice in these passive sentences that the actor is de-emphasized since it is not the subject. In fact, it may be omitted entirely from the sentence.

Choose the passive voice to de-emphasize the actor or to avoid naming the actor at all.

Study the two sentences below. The first is in the active voice and the second is in the passive. Which one is more appropriate in this case and why? What are the disadvantages of each?

> Canadian astronaut Chris Hadfield took his third trip to space in 2013.
> A third trip to space was taken by Canadian astronaut Chris Hadfield in 2013.

How Do You Form the Passive Voice?

The passive voice of a verb consists of a form of *be* (*am, is, are, was, were, being, be,* or *been*) plus the past participle of the main verb.

> Cars and trucks *are built* in Oshawa.

1. Use the past participle, not the base form or past tense of a verb, to form the passive voice.
2. Identify the subject, and make sure the form of the auxiliary verb *be* agrees with it.
3. Use only transitive verbs (verbs that can take a direct object) in the passive voice.

Subject Acted Upon	+ Verb *to be*	+ Past Participle	+ *by* Phrase (Optional)
The race	was	won	(by the runner)
The fish	was	cooked	(by the chef)
The books	are	illustrated	(by the artists)

Practice 4 Choosing the Right Voice

Rewrite the following sentences, changing the active voice to the passive and the passive voice to the active. Then decide in each case which one is best and why. Check your answers against those in the Answer Key on page 455.

1. No policy or funding announcements were made by the Canadian health minister at the International AIDS Conference in Toronto.
2. Six hundred and fifty million dollars (U.S.) was given by Microsoft founder Bill Gates to the war against HIV/AIDS.
3. Canadian authorities allowed the foreign minister of Zimbabwe into Canada for the international conference despite a ban on visits by senior officials from that African country.
4. The audience was told by former U.S. president Bill Clinton that many mistakes were made during his presidency, but that underfunding AIDS research was not one of them.
5. The International AIDS Conference in Toronto in 2006 was attended by 22 000 delegates and 8000 journalists, exhibitors, volunteers, and staff.
6. The impact that poverty has on HIV and AIDS in developing countries was discussed in great detail at the conference.
7. Actor and activist Richard Gere stressed the importance of the role of media in spreading the word about HIV/AIDS.

Exercise 7 Choosing the Right Voice

Fill in the following chart by making all sentences on the left active voice and all sentences on the right passive voice. Then discuss with your classmates and instructor why you might choose the active voice or the passive voice in each case.

Active Voice	**Passive Voice**
1. _____ _____ _____	1. The wrong number was dialled by the child by mistake.
2. _____ _____ _____	2. We went to the store where many shoes were available to be purchased.
3. The tornado struck Cherry Creek last spring.	3. _____ _____
4. The wind blew the leaves across the yard.	4. _____ _____
5. _____ _____ _____	5. In the 1970s, platform shoes were worn by many fashionable young men and women.

What Is the Subjunctive?

> **DEFINITION**
>
> The **subjunctive** is a verb form used to express untruths, desires, or demands. It is found in some dependent clauses.
>
> **Examples:** If I *were* a millionaire, I would travel around the world.
>
> She demanded that he *arrive* on time.
>
> (Verbs in italics are in the subjunctive form.)

Recognize these three situations that call for the subjunctive:

1. Unreal conditions using *if*, *wish*, *as if*, *as though*

   > *If he were* my teacher, I would be pleased.
   > He *wishes he were* in France.
   > Try to act *as though you were* proud.

   Note that *as if* and *as though* don't always call for the subjunctive. It is correct to say, "It looks as if it is snowing." In this case, the speaker is simply describing what is very likely true. The difference is in the degree of doubt.

   The subjunctive of the verb *be* has the form *were* whether the subject is plural or singular. Use it to show that what is being wished for or considered is not (or not yet) a fact. For example:

   > If I *were* you . . . (I can't be you.)
   > I wish I *were* rich. (I'm not.)
   > He acts as if *he were* the boss. (He's not.)

2. Clauses starting with *that* expressing demands, resolutions, or requests (after verbs such as *ask*, *command*, *demand*, *insist*, *move*, *order*, *recommend*, *suggest*, or *urge*)

   > I demand that she work harder.
   > Sullivan insisted that Jones report on Tuesday.

   The subjunctive uses the simple form of the verb (see p. 31) whether the subject is singular or plural.

3. Clauses starting with *that* after adjectives expressing urgency (as in *it is necessary*, *it is imperative*, *it is urgent*, *it is important*, and *it is essential*)

   > *It is necessary* that *she wear* a net covering her hair.
   > *It is essential* that Robert *understand* the concept.

   Again, the subjunctive always uses the simple form of the verb.

Other Problems with Verbs

Do not use more than one **modal auxiliary** (*can, may, might, must, should, ought*) with the main verb.

> **Incorrect:** Ethan *shouldn't ought* to drop that course.
> **Correct:** Ethan *ought* not to drop that course.
>
> or
>
> Ethan *shouldn't* drop that course.

Do not use should of, would of, or could of to mean should have, would have, or could have.

> **Incorrect:** Alana *would of* helped you if she *could of.*
> **Correct:** Alana *would have* helped you if she *could have.*

See more on helping verbs in Chapter 1, pages 6–7.

Chapter Review Exercises

 Practice 5 **Solving Problems with Verbs**

Revise each of the following sentences to avoid problems with verbs. Check your answers against those in the Answer Key on page 456.

1. He hadn't ought to drive so fast.

   _____

2. It is essential that Lynn takes her dog to the vet.

   _____

3. I wish I was a chef.

   _____

4. She sung for a huge crowd Saturday night.

   _____

5. I was shook up by the accident.

   _____

6. The hill was climbed by the skiers.

   _____

7. My father ask me last night to help him build a deck.

   _____

Exercise 8 **Solving Problems with Verbs**

Some of the verbs in the following paragraph are incorrect. Find the errors and correct them.

> I knowed I was in big trouble in chemistry when I took a look at the midterm exam. My semester should of been a lot better. The first day I had my new textbook, I put it on the back shelf of a taxi and forgot it when I got out. Then I catched a cold and miss the next two classes. When I finally start off for class, I missed the bus and walked into the classroom half an hour late. The teacher scowls at me and ask to speak to me after class. I use to always sit in the front row so I could see the board and hear the lectures, but now that I am late I have to take a seat in the last row. I wish I was able to start this class over again the right way. No one had ought to have such an unlucky start in any class.

Working Together: Verbs, Not Verbiage

Student Profile: On a separate piece of paper, answer the following five questions about yourself. Double space or write on every other line to make your writing more readable. Write freely for twenty minutes. Then exchange papers with another student. Using a pencil, circle each verb in your classmate's writing. Are any of the verbs incorrect in their form or in their tense? Be prepared to share examples with the class.

1. Tell about the first car you remember owning or driving.
2. Who was the first person you were ever attracted to? What is one thing about this person that you remember?
3. Who was the person in school who taught you the most?
4. What is one television program you enjoy and why?
5. When you go away for the weekend, where is one place you like to go?

Chapter 4 **Subject-Verb Agreement**

QuickQuiz Test yourself on your knowledge of subject-verb agreement. On the line before each sentence below, write the correct form of the verb. Answers to the questions are upside down beside the quiz.

_____ 1. The history of humankind's attempts to fly (goes, go) back hundreds of years.

_____ 2. An ancient myth that describes men trying to fly with wings made of feathers and wax (has, have) been passed on.

_____ 3. The famous inventor Leonardo da Vinci made designs for a helicopter that (was, were) very detailed.

_____ 4. Every aviator who set a new flying record in the early years of flight (was, were) treated as a hero.

_____ 5. Not only helicopters but also the jet engine (was, were) among the advances that occurred during the Second World War.

Answers:
1. goes
2. has
3. were
4. was
5. was

For your sentences to be logical, all parts of each sentence must agree. Agreement is the correspondence between words in number, gender, or person. Subjects and verbs agree in number (singular or plural) and person (first [*I* or *we*], second [*you*], or third [*he, she, it,* or *they*]).

Since many students have problems with agreement in their writing, you should work through this chapter carefully so that you will be able to identify and deal effectively with these trouble spots in your own writing.

Subject-Verb Agreement within the Sentence

DEFINITION

There is subject-verb agreement in a sentence when a verb agrees with its subject in **number** and in **person.**

Examples: The girl plays.

The girls play.

I am here on Thursdays.

(The verb *plays* in the first sentence is singular. It agrees with the singular subject *girl*.)

(The verb *play* in the second sentence is plural. It agrees with the plural subject *girls*.)

(The verb *am* in the third sentence is in the first person. It agrees with the first-person subject *I*.)

If the subject is singular, the verb must also be singular. Notice how singular and plural subjects are handled in the following chart:

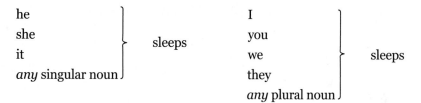

he
she
it
any singular noun ⎬ sleeps

I
you
we
they
any plural noun ⎬ sleeps

Example: The baby *sleeps*.   ***Example:*** The babies *sleep*.

TIP

Remember that a singular verb (in the present tense) that goes with a singular noun or pronoun (except I or you) needs a final s.

Practice 1   Making the Subject and Verb Agree

Underline the correct verb in the following sentences. Check your answers against those in the Answer Key on page 456.

1. My uncle (cycle, cycles) 30 km a day.
2. He (amaze, amazes) the family.
3. His routes (varies, vary) with his mood.
4. Friends (cheers, cheer) him on.
5. I (hopes, hope) I'm that energetic at his age.

Special Problems in Making Verbs Agree with Their Subjects

RULE 1

The subject is not always the noun closest to the verb. Remember, you will not find the subject of the sentence within a prepositional phrase.

In the example that follows, the subject is underlined, the prepositional phrase is crossed out, and the verb is circled.

The hairline <u>cracks</u> ~~in the engine~~ (present) a serious threat to passengers' safety.

Chapter 4   Subject-Verb Agreement   **45**

Practice 2 **Making the Subject and Verb Agree**

Underline the correct verb in the following sentences. Check your answers against those in the Answer Key on page 456.

1. The rules of the game of chess (is, are) very complicated.
2. The pawns on the board (moves, move) only one square at a time except on the first move, when they can move up to two squares.
3. The rooks on the four corners of the board (moves, move) in straight lines, not diagonally.
4. Several versions of the musical about the game and with the same name—*Chess*—(is, are) being performed throughout the world.
5. If all the pawns on, for example, the white side (is, are) gone from the board, no white pieces can any longer be retrieved.

 Exercise 1 **Making the Subject and Verb Agree**

Underline the correct verb in the following sentences.

1. The marbles from the box (is, are) multicoloured.
2. The box of soup cans in the kitchen (was, were) delivered from the charity.
3. The fees for riding public transportation (has, have) been lowered for the first time in the city's history.
4. The three students from English class (go, goes) to Tim Hortons together every day.
5. Over the bridge, through the tunnel, and across the meadow, the cats from the farm (travel, travels) daily.

 RULE 2

Many indefinite pronouns take a singular verb.

Indefinite Pronouns

Indefinite Pronouns Taking a Singular Verb:

–one	everyone	someone	anyone	no one
–body	everybody	somebody	anybody	nobody
–thing	everything	something	anything	nothing
	each	another	either	neither

Everyone is expecting a miracle.

Indefinite Pronouns Taking a Plural Verb:

both	few	many	several

The talks between the two countries failed.
Both were to blame.

Indefinite Pronouns Taking a Singular or Plural Verb Depending on the Meaning in the Sentence:

any	all	more
none*	some	most

The books are gone.   All were very popular.
The sugar is gone.   All of it was spilled.

*in informal usage

The English language is constantly evolving. The word *none*, for example, is in transition. The letters *one* inside the word *none* suggest that this indefinite pronoun should be singular. In formal usage, this is so, and *none* takes a singular verb in accordance with the subject-verb agreement rule:

> None of my pens *is* working.

In general (less formal) usage, *none*, like the other indefinite pronouns listed with it in the box above, can be either singular or plural depending on the noun that it refers to (this noun usually follows the preposition *of* after the word *none*).

> None of the sugar *is* wasted.
> None of the people *are* here yet.

This may be a case where you, the individual, have to make a decision. Do you go with formal or general usage? Your decision might depend on the audience for your composition and on its purpose (see p. 245 in Chapter 21: "Style"). You might also want to ask your instructor what he or she prefers.

 Practice 3 **Making the Subject and Verb Agree**

Underline the correct verb in the following sentences. Check your answers against those in the Answer Key on page 456.

1. Everyone in the four classes (is, are) studying for exams.
2. Neither book (has, have) the answer to her question.
3. Everybody in all programs (is, are) expected to bring a student card to the exam.
4. Each question on all exams (specifies, specify) how many marks the question is worth.
5. No one, except for emergency purposes, (is, are) allowed to leave the exam until it is over.
6. Both the English exam and the math exam (is, are) on Tuesday.
7. None of these pencils (is, are) sharp enough for the Scantron portion of the math exam.

> **RULE 3**
> **When a pair of conjunctions is used, the verb agrees with the subject closer to the verb.**

> *Neither* the textbook *nor* my lecture <u>notes</u> (explain) the meaning of the term "tidal wave."

Textbook and *notes* together make up the compound subject. Since *notes* is closer to the verb, the verb agrees with *notes*.

Pairs of Conjunctions		
neither … nor	either … or	not only … but also

Practice 4 **Making the Subject and Verb Agree**

Underline the correct verb in the following sentences. Check your answers against those in the Answer Key on page 456.

1. Neither the students nor the teacher (is, are) smoking on the patio.
2. It was obvious that not only the automotive students but also their dean (was, were) noticeably outraged by the college president's decision to shut the campus down.
3. Neither the police officer nor the firefighters (seems, seem) afraid in spite of people's continuous screams.
4. Not only the children but also their mother (takes, take) the bus every day.
5. Either the buses or the subway (has, have) resumed service, but not both.

 RULE 4

In some sentences, the subject can come after the verb. In these cases, be sure that the verb agrees with the subject.

Here (is) the <u>surprise</u> I promised you.

Who (were) the <u>people</u> with you last night?

 Practice 5 **Making the Subject and Verb Agree**

Underline the correct verb in the following sentences. Check your answers against those in the Answer Key on page 456.

1. In the room, there (is, are) two windows.
2. If they are ever late, there (is, are) always a good reason.
3. Who (is, are) her real friends, as opposed to those who just want things from her?
4. There (is, are) plenty of marbles on the floor.
5. Here (is, are) some salt for your fries.

 RULE 5

A group noun in Canadian English usually takes a singular verb if the group is acting as a unit. (The test is to substitute the word *it* in place of the group noun.)

The town <u>council</u> (is planning) a Canada Day celebration.

In this sentence, the council is acting as a unit. *It* is planning a celebration. Therefore, the verb is singular.

 RULE 6

A group noun takes a plural verb if the members of the group are acting as individuals. (The test is to substitute the word *they* for the group noun and see if it sounds right.)

The town <u>council</u> (are preparing) their speeches for this event.

In this sentence, the council members are individually preparing speeches. *They* substitutes for the group noun in this sentence. Since the individuals are acting separately, the verb is plural.

Common Group Nouns			
audience	class	committee	council
crowd	family	group	jury
management	number	team	staff

Practice 6 Making the Subject and Verb Agree

Underline the correct verb in the following sentences. Check your answers against those in the Answer Key on page 456.

1. The class (is, are) performing their presentations this week.
2. The family (is, are) all eating at separate times throughout the week.
3. The committee (has, have) decided to go ahead with the construction of the public swimming pool.
4. The group (has, have) voted 5–4 in favour of joining forces with their opponents.
5. The crowd (claps, clap) whenever the "applause" sign lights up.

RULE 7

The verbs *do* and *be* are often troublesome. Remember that standard English uses *s* for the third person singular in the present tense (*he, she,* or *it does*) and for the verb *to be* in the past tense (*he, she,* or *it was*).

Verbs *do* and *be*			
The verb *to do*		**The verb *to be* (past tense)**	
I do	we	I was	we
you do	you (plural) ⎱ do	you were	you ⎱ were
he ⎱	they ⎰	he ⎱	they ⎰
she ⎰ does		she ⎰ was	
it		it	

She *does* the signage for the Christmas pageant every year.

They *do* everything they can to help others.

You *were* at the scene of the crime.

He *was* elected to the position.

Practice 7 Making the Subject and Verb Agree

Underline the correct verb in the following sentences. Check your answers against those in the Answer Key on page 456.

1. The boy and his date (does, do) the samba every time they go to a Latin dance club.
2. She and he (was, were) the first ones to arrive.

3. It (does, do) feel like 40 degrees outside today.
4. Jake and Amelia (does, do) their homework together every weekend.
5. Cameron and she (was, were) here for three hours before they talked to each other.

Chapter Review Exercises

 Practice 8 Making the Subject and Verb Agree

Underline the verb that agrees with the subject. Check your answers against those in the Answer Key on page 457.

1. He (doesn't, don't) study in the library anymore.
2. We (was, were) hoping to find him there.
3. The library (doesn't, don't) close until eleven o'clock.
4. (Was, Were) you late tonight?
5. Ann (doesn't, don't) care if you stay until closing time.

 Practice 9 Making the Subject and Verb Agree

In the blanks next to each sentence, write the subject of the sentence and the correct form of the verb. An example has been done for you. Check your answers against those in the Answer Key on page 457.

	Subject	Verb
The eleven proposals for the development of a new building at Laurier Circle (has, have) been submitted to the city.	proposals	have
1. The price of airline tickets to England (has, have) remained fairly reasonable.		
2. His decision (requires, require) much thought.		
3. She (doesn't, don't) know the answer to any of the test questions.		
4. Either the guide or the security guard (see, sees) every visitor.		
5. The committee (agree, agrees) to the fundraising projects for this year.		
6. Potato chips and cola (is, are) most of her diet.		
7. One of the people in the audience (is, are) my brother.		

Exercise 2 **Making the Subject and Verb Agree**

In the blanks next to each sentence, write the subject of the sentence and the correct form of the verb.

	Subject	Verb
1. Included in the price of the trip (was, were) five nights in a lovely hotel and all meals.	_____	_____
2. None of the members (wants, want) to go.	_____	_____
3. Jerry and Aldo (works, work) well together.	_____	_____
4. The number of essay questions on the apprenticeship exam (seems, seem) to be increasing.	_____	_____
5. When (does, do) your parents return from their holiday?	_____	_____
6. In the whole town there (is, are) only two good restaurants.	_____	_____
7. Neither a piano nor Jim's guitar (was, were) available.	_____	_____

 Exercise 3 **Making the Subject and Verb Agree**

Take your answers from the blanks in Exercise 2, and use them as the main subjects and verbs in your own sentences. For example, if the subject in the first column is *cars*, and the verb in the second is *perform*, your own sentence might look something like this:

Cars from Japan generally perform better than cars from the United States.

Note that the sentence *I prefer cars from Japan because they perform better than cars from the United States* would not work in this exercise because in this sentence, the subject is not *cars* but *I* and the main verb is *prefer*.

 Exercise 4 **Making the Subject and Verb Agree**

The following paragraph may have several occurrences of subject-verb disagreement. Rewrite the paragraph making sure all verbs agree with their subjects.

Going to the movies are a favourite thing for me to do on the weekends. If I don't have someone "special" in my life, I still go to the movies either with friends or even by myself. I like all kinds of movies: horror flicks, comedies, drama, adventure film, etc. And not all the movies I watch comes from Hollywood. I also like independent film, foreign films with subtitles, and Bollywood movies. When I go with my friends, they often want to see something I've already seen. They can't believe I see so many on a regular basis. But because I like movies so much, I sometimes sees them twice, especially since sometimes it's more fun to see the same movie with friends than a brand new one by myself. Except for the astronomically high prices the cinema charge for popcorn, pop, and candy, there's not many more exciting things to do than go to a great movie on a weekend night. For two hours or so, the problems of the world disappears and I'm very content to be lost in a world outside of myself.

 ### Working Together: Magazine Mayhem

To the Instructor: Bring a magazine (that you don't mind destroying) to class. If your class is made up of students from one particular program, you might want to bring a magazine in which there is related subject matter. Circulate the magazine among your students along with a pair of scissors. Announce to the students how much time they have for the following activity. Students may use their text if they think it can help.

To the Students: Cut out any one paragraph of at least five sentences long that looks interesting to you, then pass the magazine and scissors on to the next person.

In your paragraph, underline the subject of every sentence, and circle the verb that goes with each subject. Then rewrite the paragraph on a separate sheet of paper, but deliberately make every verb that you have circled disagree with its subject. Write as legibly as possible and double space your work, so that someone else can easily read it.

Now trade your rewritten paragraph with that of someone else who is sitting close to you. Keep your original paragraph with the underlined subjects and the circled verbs. On the separate sheet of paper you now have from someone else, underline the subject of every sentence and circle the verb that goes with each one, correct or incorrect. Write in corrections above the incorrect verbs, making sure all verbs now agree with their subjects. Trade the sheets of paper back with your classmate when you're finished.

Now compare the subjects and corrected verbs on the separate sheet of paper your classmate gave you to the answers on the original paragraph you cut out. Discuss any discrepancies with your classmate.

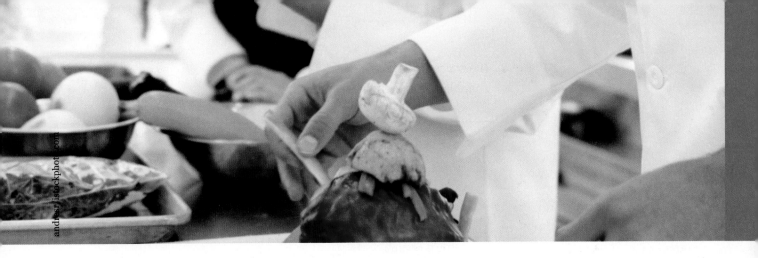

Chapter 5 **Coordination and Subordination**

QuickQuiz 1 Test yourself on your knowledge of combining sentences using **coordination** (a comma and a coordinating conjunction). The following pair of sentences could be combined into a single sentence. Among the four choices given, place a check mark in front of the example that joins them correctly using coordination. The answer to the question is upside down beside the quiz.

Chocolate became a popular drink throughout Europe. It was thought to be good for your health.

_____ 1. Chocolate became a popular drink throughout Europe, it was thought to be good for your health.

_____ 2. Chocolate became a popular drink throughout Europe because it was thought to be good for your health.

_____ 3. Chocolate became a popular drink throughout Europe, for it was thought to be good for your health.

_____ 4. Chocolate became a popular drink throughout Europe and good for your health.

Answers:
Sentence 3 is correct.
Sentence 1 is a run-on and sentence 4 is not parallel.
Sentence 2 is grammatically correct, but it shows subordination rather than coordination.

QuickQuiz 2 Test yourself on your knowledge of combining sentences using **subordination** (a subordinating conjunction or a relative pronoun). Combine each of the following pairs of sentences using either a subordinating conjunction or a relative pronoun. More than one correct answer is possible. Sample answers are upside down beside the quiz.

1. I live alone with two cats.
   They sleep on the braided rug in my bedroom.

   _____

2. The police stood by the door.
   They blocked our entrance.

   _____

3. She wore high heels.
   They made marks in the wooden floor.

   _____

4. My aunt is my favourite relative.
   Her name is Bharati.

   _____

5. He wore expensive designer clothes.
   He claimed to be struggling financially.

   _____

Reading the above sentences, you can see that writing only simple sentences would result in a choppy style. Also, it would make it difficult to express more complicated ideas.

You will, therefore, want to learn how to combine sentences. You can do this by using particular marks of punctuation and special connecting words called **conjunctions.** The two major ways of joining sentences together are called **coordination** and **subordination.**

What Is Coordination?

> **DEFINITION**
>
> The pairing of similar elements—words, phrases, or clauses—to give equal weight to each pair is called **coordination.** Coordination can link two independent clauses to form a compound sentence.
>
> **Example:** I was sick. I went to work anyway.
>
> I was sick, but I went to work anyway.

Combining Sentences Using Coordination

You can use coordination whenever you have two sentences that are related and that contain ideas of equal importance. There are three ways to combine such sentences. All three ways result in a new kind of sentence called a **compound sentence.** Before you study these three methods, however, it is important to understand the term *independent clause.* The **independent clause** is a group of words that can be a simple sentence. We can say that a compound sentence combines simple sentences, or we can say we that it combines independent clauses. Don't let this term confuse you. *Independent* means that the words could stand alone as a sentence, and *clause* means a group of words that includes a subject and predicate (what is said about the subject). IC will mean *independent clause* in the work that follows.

Use a Comma Plus a Coordinating Conjunction

> **TIP**
>
> The first way to combine independent clauses (or complete thoughts) is to use a comma plus a coordinating conjunction. A conjunction is a connecting or joining word.

IC	, and	IC
He spoke forcefully	, and	I felt compelled to listen.

Connectors: Coordinating Conjunctions

For easier remembering, spell FANBOYS.

Conjunction:	**Logical use:**
For	to introduce a reason
And	to add an idea
Nor (negative of "or")	to add an idea when the first clause is in the negative
But	to contrast two opposing ideas
Or	to show a choice
Yet	to contrast two opposing ideas (like but)
So	to introduce a result

Used in Pairs (correlative conjunctions)

either … or

neither … nor

not only … but also

> **TIP**
>
> Whenever any of the above coordinating conjunctions ("FANBOYS") is used to separate two independent clauses, always place a comma before it.

When the sentence is short, the comma before the coordinating conjunction becomes less necessary, but to be safe, it is wise to leave the comma in every time.

I arrived late, and most people had already finished the exam.

 Practice 1 Recognizing the Comma and Coordinating Conjunction

Each of the following compound sentences contains two independent clauses. Draw a single line under the subject and two lines under the verb of each independent clause. Then circle both the coordinating conjunction and the comma. An example has been done for you. Check your answers against those in the Answer Key on page 457.

The <u>speaker</u> <u>rose</u> to his feet (, and) the <u>room</u> <u>became</u> quiet.

1. The audience was packed into the room, for this was a man with an international reputation.

2. He could have told about all his successes, but instead he spoke about his disappointments.
3. His words were electric, so the crowd was attentive.
4. I should have brought a tape recorder, or at least I should have taken notes.

Did you find a subject and verb for both independent clauses in each sentence?

Now that you understand the structure of a compound sentence, you need to think about the meanings of the different coordinating conjunctions and how they can be used to show the relationship between two ideas, with each idea given equal importance.

 Exercise 1 Combining Sentences Using Coordinating Conjunctions

Each of the following examples contains two simple sentences. In each case, join the sentences to form a new compound sentence. Use a comma and one of the seven coordinating conjunctions. There can be more than one correct answer for each example. Be sure the conjunction you choose makes sense in the sentence. An example has been done for you.

Two simple sentences: Many farmers are desperate. They are going bankrupt.

Compound sentence: Many farmers are desperate, for they are going bankrupt.

1. The farmers in Canada want to work.
   Some are experiencing severe financial difficulty.

   _____

   _____

2. Some people are losing their farms.
   The banks are refusing to make further loans.

   _____

   _____

3. Many government programs have not been effective.
   The public cannot do anything.
   (Use *nor*. You will have to change the word order in the second sentence.)

   _____

   _____

4. The farmers feel neglected.
   They are protesting against the government.

   _____

   _____

5. There is an increased need for farm products.
   The government pays farmers not to grow food.

   _____

   _____

6. Everyone needs what the farmers produce.
   We should be concerned about their problems.

   _____

   _____

7. In the future, fewer people will become farmers.
   The problem is likely to become increasingly serious.

   _____

   _____

Coordinating Conjunctions That Do Not Combine Two Independent Clauses

Remember that a coordinating conjunction such as *and* is not always used to combine two independent clauses. Often, it is used simply to combine two items. When this is the case, do not place a comma before the coordinating conjunction.

> I had bacon *and* eggs for breakfast.

The word *and* does not separate two independent clauses, so there is no comma before it.

> I had bacon and eggs for breakfast, *and* then I had a salad for lunch.

In this sentence, the second *and* does combine two independent clauses. Therefore, the comma is required.

The coordinating conjunction *but* is the exception here. It is sometimes a good idea to put a comma before *but* regardless of whether it combines two independent clauses or not. This is because *but* is a strong indication of an opposite point of view. The comma gives the reader a chance to focus on this abrupt shift in thinking.

> He is short, *but* powerful.
> He is short, *but* he exudes a powerful aura.

Use a comma for both situations involving the word *but*.

Use a Semicolon, an Adverbial Conjunction, and a Comma

TIP

A second way to combine independent clauses (or complete thoughts) is to use a semicolon, an adverbial conjunction, and a comma.

IC	; adverbial conjunction,	IC
I had worked hard	; therefore,	I expected results.

Adverbial conjunctions (also called **conjunctive adverbs**) are another set of connecting words. They have similar meanings to the common coordinating conjunctions, but give the compound sentence more emphasis. They may also sound slightly more formal to you than the shorter conjunctions *and* and *but*. If an adverbial conjunction connects two independent clauses, place a semicolon before it. If it does not, use a comma before it instead.

> **TIP**
>
> Unlike the combination of a comma and a coordinating conjunction, the combination of a comma and an adverbial conjunction *cannot* connect two independent clauses.

    Incorrect: I had worked hard, therefore, I expected results.

The above is a run-on sentence (see Chapter 7.)

    Correct: I had worked hard, so I expected results.
    Correct: I had worked hard; therefore, I expected results.

Connectors: Common Adverbial Conjunctions		
Addition (and)	**Alternative (or)**	**Result (so)**
in addition	instead	accordingly
also	otherwise	consequently
besides		hence
furthermore		therefore
likewise		thus
moreover		
Contrast (but)	**Emphasis**	**Time**
however	indeed	meanwhile
nevertheless	in fact	
nonetheless		

 Practice 2 **Recognizing the Semicolon, Adverbial Conjunction, and Comma**

The following compound sentences each contain two independent clauses. Draw a single line under the subject and two lines under the verb of each independent clause. Then circle the semicolon, adverbial conjunction, and comma. An example has been done for you. Check your answers against those in the Answer Key on page 457.

    The <u>jet</u> <u><u>was</u></u> the fastest way to get there (; moreover,) <u>it</u> <u><u>was</u></u> the most comfortable.

1. The restaurant is always too crowded on Saturdays; nevertheless, it serves the best food in town.
2. The land was not for sale; however, the house could be rented.

3. The lawsuit cost the company several million dollars; consequently, the company went out of business a short time later.
4. The doctor told him to lose weight; furthermore, she insisted he also stop smoking.

 Practice 3 **Combining Sentences Using Adverbial Conjunctions**

Combine each pair of sentences below to make a compound sentence. Use a semicolon, an adverbial conjunction, and a comma. Be sure the conjunction you choose makes sense in the sentence. There can be more than one correct answer for each pair of sentences. An example has been done for you. Check your answers against those in the Answer Key on page 457.

> **Two simple sentences:** Our family would like to purchase a computer. We must decide on which computer best serves our needs.
>
> **Compound sentence:** Our family would like to purchase a computer; however, we must decide on which computer best serves our needs.

1. People once preferred to write with a pen or pencil.
   The computer has now become a favourite writing tool. (Show contrast.)

   _____

   _____

2. Computers provide a powerful way to create and store pieces of writing.
   They make the editing process fast and efficient. (Add an idea.)

   _____

   _____

3. Computers have revolutionized today's offices.
   No modern business is without them. (Show result.)

   _____

   _____

4. Computers have become relatively inexpensive.
   Most people own a computer. (Show result.)

   _____

   _____

5. Many children know more about computers than many adults.
   Many children are teaching adults how to operate computers. (Add an idea.)

   _____

   _____

6. Professional writers have become enthusiastic about the use of computers. There are still some writers who will use only a ballpoint pen. (Show contrast.)

_____

_____

7. We have many technological aids for writing. Let us not forget that the source of all our ideas is the human brain. (Show contrast.)

_____

_____

Exercise 2   Combining Sentences Using Adverbial Conjunctions

To each independent clause below, add the suggested adverbial conjunction and another independent clause that makes sense. Remember to punctuate correctly. An example has been done for you.

> **Adverbial conjunction + Simple sentence:** (in fact) I was early for the exam
> **Compound sentence:** I was early for the exam; in fact, I was able to study for an extra half hour.

1. (however) I'll be at the library for a few hours

_____

_____

2. (therefore) James asked to borrow my notes

_____

_____

3. (otherwise) I'm thinking about taking a part-time job

_____

_____

4. (instead) Marcus is not going home for reading week

_____

_____

5. (in fact) They haven't won a game this year

_____

_____

6. (furthermore) Suzie has given up coffee and cigarettes

_____

_____

7. (consequently) My computer keeps crashing

_____

_____

Use a Semicolon

> **TIP**
>
> The third way to combine two independent clauses is to use a semicolon by itself (that is, without an adverbial conjunction).

Remember, do not capitalize the first word after a semicolon (unless the word is one that is always spelled with a capital letter).

IC	;	IC
He arrived at ten	;	he left at midnight.
He arrived at ten	;	I left at midnight

This third method of combining sentences is used less often. No connecting word is used. The semicolon takes the place of the conjunction.

Two independent clauses: I used to watch the Toronto Blue Jays play baseball at Exhibition Stadium. Tonight, I'm going to see them play at Rogers Centre.

Compound sentence: I used to watch the Toronto Blue Jays play baseball at Exhibition Stadium; tonight, I'm going to see them play at Rogers Centre.

The semicolon was used in this example to show that the content of the two clauses is closely related and, therefore, belongs together in one sentence.

When sentences are combined by using a semicolon, the grammatical structure of each independent clause is often similar:

Gasoline prices increased; **_vacations_** became less frequent.

Both independent clauses above begin with a subject. (See Chapter 8: "Parallel Structure.")

Exercise 3 Combining Sentences Using the Semicolon

To each of the independent clauses below, add another independent clause that expresses a related idea with a similar grammatical structure. Join the two clauses with a semicolon. An example has been done for you.

Independent clause: He wrote the speech.
Compound sentence: He wrote the speech; she gave it.

1. The apartment was light and airy.

   _____

   _____

2. Many students decorate their rooms wonderfully.

   _____

   _____

3. I plan to learn two foreign languages.

   _____

   _____

4. I tried to explain.

   _____

   _____

5. This rain will never stop.

   _____

   _____

What Is Subordination?

When you use coordination to combine sentences, the ideas in both of the resulting clauses are given equal weight. However, ideas are not always equally important. Subordination allows you to show which idea is the main idea.

DEFINITION

Subordination is the method used to combine sentences whose ideas are not equally important. It is a combination of an independent clause and a dependent clause.

Example: I stayed home today   because I was sick.

          Independent Clause   Dependent Clause

Combining Sentences Using Subordination

When you combine sentences using subordination, you make the more important idea an independent clause and the less important idea a dependent (subordinate) clause. The sentence that results is called a **complex sentence.** Each idea contained within a complex sentence is called a **clause.** Various methods of subordination are discussed on the next page; the method you choose shows the relationship between the main idea and the secondary one.

In a complex sentence, the main idea is called the **independent clause** because it could stand alone as a simple sentence. The less important idea is called the **dependent clause** because, even though it has a subject and a verb, it is dependent on the rest of the sentence for its meaning. Consider the following clauses:

> **Independent clause:** That girl leaves.
> **Dependent clause:** If that girl leaves

Notice that each clause in the example above has a subject and a verb. (In both cases, the subject is *girl* and the verb is *leaves*.) The difference is that the dependent clause has an additional word, *if,* which is an example of a special kind of connecting word (a subordinating conjunction—see below) that makes the clause "dependent" on an additional idea. A dependent clause contains a thought that is not complete; it cannot stand on its own. Here is the same dependent clause presented above but with an independent clause added to it:

> If that girl leaves, then I can finish my homework.

Now the thought is complete.

In your writing, you will want to be comfortable creating sentences with dependent clauses. For this, you will need to practise using two kinds of these special "connecting" words: **subordinating conjunctions** and **relative pronouns.** First, let's look at subordinating conjunctions.

Use a Subordinating Conjunction to Create a Complex Sentence

Following is a list of the most common subordinating conjunctions. These connecting words signal the beginning of a dependent clause. It is a good idea to memorize them, especially for the purpose of preventing fragments (see Chapter 6: "Correcting Fragments").

Connectors: Common Subordinating Conjunctions		
after	if, even if	unless
although	in order that	until
as, as if	provided that	when, whenever
as long as, as though	rather than	where, wherever, whereas
because	since	whether
before	so that	while
even though	though	

You might have had teachers in elementary school who told you never to begin a sentence with *because*. If so, they might have said this because they were afraid you wouldn't finish the sentence.

> **Incomplete:** Because the child was sick
> **Complete:** Because the child was sick, she stayed home yesterday.

With the addition of an independent clause to the dependent clause, the sentence is now complete.

Function of Subordinating Conjunctions

To introduce a <u>condition</u>: if, even if, as long as, provided that, unless

> I will go *as long as* you go with me.
> I won't go *unless* you go with me.

To introduce a <u>contrast</u>: although, even though, through

> I will go *even though* you won't go with me.

To introduce a <u>cause</u>: because, since

> I will go *because* the meeting is very important.

To show <u>time</u>: after, before, when, whenever, while, until

> I will go *whenever* you say.
> I won't go *until* you say it is time.

To show <u>place</u>: where, wherever

> I will go *wherever* you send me.

To show <u>purpose</u>: in order that, so that

> I will go *so that* I can hear the candidate for myself.

You can choose between two ways of writing the complex sentence. You can begin with either the dependent clause (DC) or the independent clause (IC).

First way:	DC	,	IC
Example:	If Barbara leaves	,	we can finish our homework

Second way:	IC		DC
Example:	We can finish our homework		if Barbara leaves.

TIP

Use a comma when you begin a sentence with a dependent clause. Do not use a comma when the independent clause comes first.

From the above examples you can see that when a sentence begins with an independent clause, a comma may not always be needed. For example, the comma is omitted if the dependent clause is essential to the main idea of the speaker.

 Practice 4 **Recognizing Dependent and Independent Clauses**

In the blank to the left of each group of words below, write the letters *IC* if the group is an independent clause (a complete thought) or *DC* if the group is a dependent clause (not a complete thought, even though it contains a subject and a verb). Check your answers against those in the Answer Key on page 457.

_____ 1. while the photographer was getting ready

_____ 2. before the guests arrived

_____ 3. I've been a bridesmaid for two of my friends

_____ 4. even though we're all in our teens

_____ 5. this one was more fun than most

_____ 6. whenever I see you

_____ 7. since I did not take the subway

Practice 5 Combining Sentences Using Subordination

Combine each pair of sentences below using subordination. Look back at the list of subordinating conjunctions if you need to. There may be more than one correct answer for each of these exercises. Check your answers against those in the Answer Key on page 457.

1. He was eating breakfast.
   The results of the election came over the radio.

   _____

   _____

2. Simon gave up his plan to launch a dot-com company.
   He felt it was too risky.

   _____

   _____

3. I will see my teacher tonight.
   She is speaking at the university this evening.

   _____

   _____

4. The designer hoped for a promotion.
   Not one person in the department was promoted last year.

   _____

   _____

5. The designer hoped for a promotion.
   She made sure all her work was done accurately and on time.

   _____

   _____

Exercise 4 Combining Sentences Using Subordination

Below are three pairs of sentences. Combine each pair by using the subordinating conjunction given. Write each new complex sentence two different ways: first,

Chapter 5 Coordination and Subordination

begin the sentence with the dependent clause and use a comma; second, begin the sentence with the independent clause and use a comma only if necessary.

1. (Use *since.*) Wildlife habitats are being destroyed.
   Many species are in danger.

   a. _____

   _____

   b. _____

   _____

2. (Use *after.*) He won the wrestling match.
   He went out to celebrate.

   a _____

   _____

   b _____

   _____

3. (Use *when.*) Halyna returned from Europe this spring.
   The family was excited.

   a _____

   _____

   b _____

   _____

 Exercise 5 Combining Sentences Using Subordination

Rewrite the following paragraph using subordination to combine some of the sentences wherever you feel it would be effective. Be prepared to discuss the reasons for your choices. You may also want to discuss places where coordination might be a good choice. More than one correct answer is possible.

Many Canadian communities collect refuse from its source. Waste is delivered to a waste disposal site. Very little waste is recycled. Very little waste is burned. Many smaller towns and villages cannot afford a waste collection service or a proper waste disposal site. Smaller communities are prevalent in Canada. Improperly operated dumps outnumber the better-operated facilities used by larger communities. Over the next few years, many of our landfills will close. They are getting full. Some places in Ontario already truck their trash to the United States. The garbage continues to pile up. The newspapers print stories about it every week. Trash is not a very glamorous subject. People in every town talk about the problem.

Here is a summary so far of how clauses (dependent and independent) can be combined to form complete sentences.

Remember: IC stands for *independent clause* (complete thought).

DC stands for *dependent clause* (incomplete thought).

IC	, coordinating conjunction	IC
IC	; adverbial conjunction,	IC
IC	;	IC
DC	,	IC
IC		DC

Note the absence of any comma when an independent clause comes before a dependent clause, as in the last row above.

Use a Relative Pronoun to Create a Complex Sentence

Often, two sentences can be combined using a relative pronoun.

Common Relative Pronouns		
who whose whom that	refers to people	**Note:** "whose" can also refer to things. **Example:** They performed a play whose two acts were only fifteen minutes each.
which that whose	refers to things	**Note:** "that" can also refer to people when a class or type of person is meant. **Example:** The teacher I prefer is one that offers help outside of class.

Two simple sentences: The researcher had a breakthrough.

He was studying diabetes.

These sentences are short and choppy. To avoid this choppiness, a writer could join these two related ideas using a relative pronoun.

Combining sentences with a relative pronoun: The researcher who was studying diabetes had a breakthrough.

Now join a third idea to the sentence (use *which*).

Third idea: He reported the breakthrough to the press.

TIP

Remember to put the relative pronoun directly after the word it refers to.

Incorrect: The researcher, which he reported to the press, had a breakthrough who was studying diabetes.

Correct: The researcher who was studying diabetes had a breakthrough, which he reported to the press.

The relative pronoun *who* and its clause *who was studying diabetes* refers to *the researcher,* not to *a breakthrough.* See more on the relative pronoun *who* (vs. *whom*) on page 108. The relative pronoun *which* and its clause *which he reported to the press* does refer to *a breakthrough,* so this clause should follow the noun *breakthrough.* (See Chapter 10 for more on modifiers.)

 Practice 6 **Combining Sentences Using a Relative Pronoun**

Combine each of the pairs of sentences below into one complex sentence by using a relative pronoun. Do not use commas. More than one correct answer is possible for each pair of sentences. An example has been done for you. Check your answers against those in the Answer Key on page 458.

That woman created the flower arrangement.
She visited us last weekend.

Combined: That woman who visited us last weekend created the flower arrangement.

1. The chemistry lab is two hours long.
   I attend that chemistry lab.

   Combined: _____

   _____

2. The student assistant is very knowledgeable.
   The student assistant is standing by the door.

   Combined: _____

   _____

3. The equipment was purchased last year.
   The equipment will make possible some important new research.

   Combined: _____

   _____

How Do You Punctuate a Clause with a Relative Pronoun?

Punctuating relative clauses can be tricky because there are two types of relative clauses.

1. One type of relative clause is basic to the meaning of the sentence:

> Never eat fruit that hasn't been washed first.

The basic meaning of the sentence is not "never eat fruit." The relative clause is necessary to restrict the meaning. This clause is called a **restrictive clause** and does not use commas to set it off. *Note:* Clauses beginning with the pronoun *that* are usually in this category.

2. The other type of relative clause is not basic to the meaning of the sentence:

> Kim's famous salad, *which included spinach and almonds,* was delicious.

In this sentence, the relative clause is not basic to the main idea. In fact, if the clause were omitted, the main idea would not be changed. This clause is called a **nonrestrictive clause.** Commas are required to indicate that the information is nonessential. *Note:* Clauses beginning with the pronoun *which* are usually in this category. Remember, the relative pronoun *which* always refers to things.

Note: While *which* refers to things in a nonrestrictive clause and *that* refers to things in a restrictive clause, the relative pronouns used to refer to people (*who, whom,* and *whose*) are used for both nonrestrictive and restrictive clauses. Remember, restrictive clauses do not take commas to separate them from the rest of the sentence, while nonrestrictive clauses do. (For more on commas, see Chapter 11: "Punctuation.")

 Practice 7   Recognizing Restrictive and Nonrestrictive Clauses

Choose whether or not to insert commas in the sentences below. Two examples have been done for you. Check your answers against those in the Answer Key on page 458.

> The man who is wearing the Hawaiian shirt is the bridegroom.
> (The relative clause is essential. There are no commas.)

> Al, *who was wearing a flannel shirt,* arrived late to the wedding.
> (The relative clause is nonessential. Commas, therefore, are necessary.)

1. Canada's first census which was taken in 1667 showed 3215 non-Native inhabitants in 668 families.
2. Most of the families who lived near the St. Lawrence River were French Canadians.
3. By the time of Confederation, the population of the country had risen to 3 463 000 which was an increase of 1077 percent over 200 years.
4. If the population of Canada which is about 30 000 000 persons now increases by a similar percentage over the next 150 or so years, we'll have a population of 280 200 000 by the year 2167.
5. Where do you think we will we put everyone who lives in Canada then?

Exercise 6 **Combining Sentences Using Relative Pronouns**

Add a clause that begins with a relative pronoun to each of the sentences below. Use each of these possibilities at least once: *who, whose, whom, which, that.* Be sure to punctuate correctly. An example has been done for you.

Simple sentence: The leader was barely 1.5 metres tall.

Complex sentence: The leader, who was always self-conscious about her height, was barely 1.5 metres tall.

1. The figure skaters _____ began their program.

2. The music _____ had a Latin beat.

3. Their first figure _____ was a triple toe loop.

4. The crowd _____ cheered wildly.

5. Even the judges _____ seemed impressed.

6. Her triple Axel _____ was a little ragged.

7. Their coach _____ was thrilled by the final score.

Exercise 7 **Combining Sentences Using Relative Pronouns**

Combine the following pairs of sentences using a relative pronoun. There may be more than one correct answer for each example.

1. Stress can do a great deal of harm.
   We experience stress every day.

   _____

   _____

2. People often use food to help them cope.
   Some people work long hours at demanding jobs.

   _____

   _____

3. The practice of eating to cope with stress is often automatic.
   The practice of eating to cope often goes back to childhood.

   _____

   _____

4. Foods can actually increase tension.
   People turn to foods in times of stress.

   _____

   _____

5. One of the biggest mistakes people make is to use alcohol as an aid to becoming calm.
Alcohol is really a depressant.

_____

_____

6. People should eat three light meals a day and two small snacks.
People want to feel a sense of calm.

_____

_____

7. Eat a good meal at regular intervals to help reduce stress.
Binge eating puts on pounds, drains you of energy, and increases your stress level.

_____

_____

Chapter Review Exercises

 Practice 8 Combining Sentences Using Coordination and Subordination

Look over the following paragraph, which is made up of simple sentences. Then rewrite the paragraph, combining sentences where you think it would improve the meaning and style. Be creative, and don't be afraid to alter the wording to accommodate the changes you want to make. Check your answers against those in the Answer Key on page 458. (The Answer Key will give you one possible answer, but there are many ways of revising this passage.)

> The wind is strong. The waves are choppy. They are growing larger. I paddle my kayak harder. My arms are getting tired. The energy is draining from them. They grow limp and heavy. The other side of the harbour seems distant. The glow of the setting sun is behind me. It spreads orange and purple fingers across the sky. A wall of rocks lies offshore. It picks up the last light of the setting sun. It is a silver beacon. I focus on that wall and paddle harder. The sea smashes against my bow. It seems to push me away from shore. Flecks of spray hit my face. I taste the salt on my lips. With that taste of the sea, the beauty of the sea and shore strikes me. I am distracted from my labour and absorbed by the world around me. My kayak finally glides past the rocks to the sheltered beach beyond. I am exhilarated and exhausted.

 Exercise 8 Combining Sentences Using Coordinating and Adverbial Conjunctions

Combine each pair of sentences below to make a compound sentence. Use a coordinating, subordinating, or adverbial conjunction, but be sure that the conjunction clearly shows the relationship between the ideas. There can be more than one correct answer for each example.

1. For many people, mathematics is a necessary evil.
   To a few, mathematics provides a lifetime of challenge and fun.

   _____

   _____

2. Most Canadians have studied math only to Grade 12.
   This limits their ability to understand new scientific developments.

   _____

   _____

3. Their knowledge extends to little more than basic arithmetic.
   People in the seventeenth century knew as much about math as most Canadians today.

   _____

   _____

4. Few Canadians study math at the university level.
   Many promising mathematics graduates are offered employment in the United States.

   _____

   _____

5. Many schools form math teams to compete in area contests.
   Other schools encourage interest in math with math clubs.

   _____

   _____

6. Some schools suffer from a lack of science and math teachers.
   Mathematicians can find well-paid employment in industry.

   _____

   _____

7. It is important to increase the number of mathematics graduates.
   Canadian students may continue to trail behind those of many other countries in math and science ability.

   _____

   _____

Exercise 9 Combining Sentences with a Subordinating Conjunction or a Relative Pronoun

Combine each of the following pairs of sentences using either a subordinating conjunction or a relative pronoun. Be sure that the word you use makes sense in the sentence. There can be more than one correct answer for each example.

1. People have been fascinated for centuries by the problem of stuttering. Modern science is only beginning to understand some of the underlying causes of the problem.

   _____

   _____

2. For some people, stuttering disappears by itself. For others, stuttering continues into adulthood.

   _____

   _____

3. Stutterers usually keep their condition. They seek professional help.

   _____

   _____

4. It is true that there is some psychological basis for stuttering. It is true that psychologists have not been able to solve the problem.

   _____

   _____

5. All kinds of scientists have looked at the problem from all different angles. There is no single answer to stuttering.

   _____

   _____

6. Stuttering runs in families. Children of such families have a greater chance of becoming stutterers.

   _____

   _____

7. You often hear someone say he or she knows the causes of stuttering. You know that person cannot be speaking scientifically.

   _____

   _____

Working Together: Practising Coordination and Subordination

A controversial issue today concerns the wide gap between the wages earned by people in some professions and the wages earned by people in other professions. For instance, some sports figures and entertainers earn millions every year. How are wages determined in our society? How do you think wages should be determined? Should there be a minimum wage in Canada? Should everybody earn the same salary? Divide into groups and discuss the subject for fifteen minutes.

Following the general discussion, practise using coordination by writing ten compound sentences on the subject of wage differences. If you like, you may try to summarize the ideas of your group. Try to use each of the following ten coordinating conjunctions to combine two independent clauses:

> **F**or, **A**nd, **N**or, **B**ut, **O**r, **Y**et, **S**o (FANBOYS)
> either/or, neither/nor, not only/but also (correlative conjunctions)

Now, revise each sentence you've written so that the two independent clauses are combined with a subordinating conjunction instead. Consult the list of subordinating conjunctions on page 63.

After working on these sentences for fifteen minutes, exchange papers with another student and answer the following questions about the sentences on the paper you have:

1. In each case, has the writer combined two independent clauses?
2. In each sentence, does the coordinating or subordinating conjunction carry the correct meaning for the sentence?
3. Is the punctuation correct?

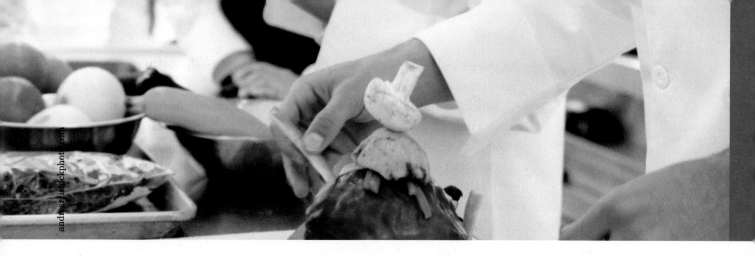

Chapter 6 **Correcting Fragments**

QuickQuiz Test yourself on your knowledge of fragments. Some of the examples below are complete sentences; some are fragments (only parts of sentences). Write *C* if the example is a complete sentence. Write *F* if the example is a fragment. The answers to the questions are upside down beside the quiz.

_____ 1. Whale watching is a popular tourist activity in British Columbia.

_____ 2. Although its effects are being studied.

_____ 3. Whales coping with heavy boat traffic.

_____ 4. The noise from engines can disturb the whales' communication.

_____ 5. Which may be changing their habitat.

Answers:
1. C
2. F
3. F
4. C
5. F

Recognizing and Correcting Sentence Fragments

Once you have learned that a sentence must have a subject and a verb, and that a sentence must also express a complete thought, you are on your way to correcting one of the most frequent errors in student writing: the fragment. A fragment is an incomplete sentence. Although many of our daily conversations are informal and sometimes contain fragments, standard writing is always more formal and requires complete sentences.

Although you will occasionally spot incomplete sentences in professional writing, such as newspaper writing, advertising, novels, and so on, it is hoped that the writer is using these fragments intentionally. In such cases, the fragment may capture the way a person thinks or speaks, or it may create a special effect. A student developing his or her writing skills should be sure to use only standard sentence form (complete sentences) so that thoughts will be communicated effectively. Most of the writing you will do in your life—papers in school, business correspondence, or reports in your job—will demand standard sentence form.

Fragments will be looked upon as a sign of poor writing skills rather than an indicator of creative style!

The fragment is a major problem for many student writers. In the writer's mind, a thought may be clear; however, on paper the idea may turn out to be incomplete, missing a subject or a verb. In this chapter, you will improve your ability to spot incomplete sentences (fragments), and you will learn how to correct them. This practice will prepare you to avoid such fragments in your own writing.

Remember the definition of a sentence:

> **DEFINITION**
>
> A **complete sentence** has a subject and a verb and expresses a complete thought.
> **Example:** The cat drank.

Notice that it is not necessary to know *what* the cat drank in order for the sentence to be grammatically complete.

A Typical Casual Conversation

The following conversation is one that a couple of students might have at the start of their English class.

> JOHN: Early again.
> LESIA: Want to get a front-row seat.
> JOHN: Your homework done?
> LESIA: Nearly.
> JOHN: Think he'll give a quiz today?
> LESIA: Hope not.
> JOHN: Looks like rain.
> LESIA: Better not. Haven't got a bag for these new books.
> JOHN: Going to the game Saturday?
> LESIA: Probably.

Remember, when you write in complete sentences, this writing is likely going to be quite different from the way you would express the same idea in everyday conversation with a friend. In the conversation above, not one sentence is complete. There is at least one fragment on every line. If this dialogue were to appear in a novel, punctuated correctly with quotation marks, it would be perfectly acceptable. But using fragments in texts that call for standard English form is, quite simply, an example of poor writing skills.

What Is a Fragment?

> **DEFINITION**
>
> A **fragment** is a piece of a sentence.
>
> **Examples:** Which is not what the teacher wanted to hear.
>
> Because the bus was late.
>
> Whereas she was better at math.
>
> Fragments often begin with the relative pronoun *which* or the subordinating conjunctions *because* and *whereas*.

A group of words is a fragment, not a sentence, if any one of the following is true:

a. The subject is missing.

> delivered the plans to my office

b. The verb is missing.

> the architect to my office

c. Both the subject and verb are missing.

> to my office

d. The group of words is a dependent clause. In other words, a subject and a verb are present, but the words do not express a complete thought.

> when the architect delivered the plans
> which the architect identified as her favourite design
> because the bus was late
> the reason being the bus was late

Sometimes a fragment might look like a complete sentence because it is fairly long, starts with a capital letter, and ends with a period. Obviously, these criteria are not enough to identify a complete sentence.

Practice 1 Understanding Fragments

Each of the groups of words on the next page is a fragment. In the blank to the right of each fragment, write *a, b, c,* or *d* to identify what change would make the fragment into a sentence. An example has been done for you. Check your answers against those in the Answer Key on page 458.

> a. Add a subject.
> b. Add a verb.
> c. Add a subject and a verb.
> d. Add or delete words to express a complete thought. (A subject and a verb are present, but the group of words is a dependent clause.)

Fragment	Change Needed
the red fox	b. Add a verb.
1. returned to the river	_____
2. a bird on the oak branch	_____
3. between the island and the mainland	_____
4. the hawk in a soaring motion	_____
5. the fishing boats on the lake	_____
6. dropped like a stone into the water	_____
7. because the fisherman put the net away	_____

How Do You Correct a Fragment?

You can eliminate fragments in two ways:

1. Add the missing part or parts to develop the fragment into a complete sentence:

> *Fragment:* along the coastal road
> *Add:* subject and verb
> *Sentence:* He drove along the coastal road.

2. Join the fragment to another sentence. In order to do this, you may need to make use of the comma, the colon, or the dash, or you may not need to use punctuation. For example:

a. Using the comma

> *Fragment:* including a stop at the shoe store
> *Other sentence:* He has to make a number of purchases.
> *Fragment eliminated:* He has to make a number of purchases, including a stop at the shoe store.

b. Using the colon

> *Fragment:* action, science fiction, and comedy
> *Other sentence:* I like three types of movies.
> *Fragment eliminated:* I like three types of movies: action, science fiction, and comedy.

c. Using the dash

> *Fragment:* more often than she should
> *Other sentence:* She goes to the casino every day.
> *Fragment eliminated:* She goes to the casino every day—more often than she should.

d. Using no punctuation

> *Fragment:* on top of the mountain
> *Other sentence:* We planned to plant the flag.
> *Fragment eliminated:* We planned to plant the flag on top of the mountain.

Practice 2 Turning Fragments into Sentences

Change the fragments of Practice 1 into complete sentences by adding the missing part or parts that you identified. Check your answers against those in the Answer Key on page 458. (The Answer Key will give you sample answers, but there are many ways of correcting these fragments.)

1. returned to the river

   _____

2. a bird on the oak branch

   _____

3. between the island and the mainland

   _____

4. the hawk, in a soaring motion

   _____

5. the fishing boats on the lake

   _____

6. dropped like a stone into the water

   _____

7. because the fisherman put the net away

   _____

Practice 3 Turning Fragments into Sentences

The following groups of words may or may not be fragments. If the group of words forms a complete sentence, write *complete*. Otherwise, rewrite it, adding whatever is necessary to correct the fragment. Check your answers against those in the Answer Key on page 458. (The Answer Key will give you sample answers, but there are many ways of correcting these fragments.)

1. As long as it's a windy day.

   _____

2. Into the forest, armed with a machine gun.

   _____

3. It's great.

   _____

4. Along a deserted and dusty road.

_____

5. Where the deer and the antelope play.

_____

6. The groundhog run over by three different cars.

_____

7. A jeep has parked.

_____

 Exercise 1 **Turning Fragments into Sentences**

Each of the following passages contains one or more fragments. First read each passage. Then locate the fragments in it. Correct the fragments by joining them to other sentences using a comma, a colon, a dash, or no punctuation. There can be more than one correct answer for each passage.

1. Fishing is one of the oldest sports in the world. And can be one of the most relaxing. Someone with a simple wooden pole and line can have as much fun as a professional angler. With expensive equipment. For busy executives, overworked teachers, and even presidents of nations. Fishing can be a good way to escape from the stress of demanding jobs.

2. The first electric car was built in 1887. Six years later, it was sold commercially. At the turn of the century, people had great faith in new technology. In fact, 300 electric taxicabs were operating in New York City by 1900. However, electric cars soon lost their popularity. The new gasoline engine became more widely used. With our concern about pollution. Perhaps electric cars will become desirable once again.

3. Most sports evolve over many years. But not basketball. A Canadian-born teacher invented basketball in December 1891. Working at a YMCA training school in Massachusetts. The coach needed an indoor game to keep his students fit over the winter. Dr. James Naismith created goals. By nailing two peach baskets to the gym balcony.

Don't Confuse Phrases with Sentences

Fragments are usually made up of phrases. These phrases are often mistaken for sentences because they are groups of words. However, they do not fit the definition of a sentence.

What Is a Phrase?

DEFINITION

A **phrase** is a group of words that go together but lack one or more of the elements necessary to be classified as a sentence.

Example: In the barn at the back of the house

In the example above, two prepositional phrases have been put together (see #3, below). It is another example of a fragment.

How Many Kinds of Phrases Are There?

In English, there are a number of types of phrases that you should learn to recognize. Some of them you have already studied in the previous chapter. Remember, a phrase is not a complete sentence; it is a sentence fragment, and as such must be either joined to another sentence or made into a complete sentence.

1. **Noun phrase:** a group of words that functions as a noun

   Noun phrase: large square bricks
   Complete sentence: The garage is built out of large square bricks.

2. **Gerund phrase:** a type of noun phrase; a group of words beginning with a gerund (an *-ing* word that looks like a verb, but functions as a noun)

   Gerund phrase: jogging every morning at 6:00
   Complete sentence: Jogging every morning at 6:00 is something I cannot miss.

3. **Prepositional phrase:** a group of words beginning with a preposition (For a list of common prepositions, see p. 18.)

   Prepositional phrase: on the porch
   Complete sentence: Many of our neighbours are sitting on the porch.

4. **Verb phrase:** a group of words that functions as a verb

   Verb phrase: is walking
   Complete sentence: My best friend is walking to my house.

5. **Infinitive phrase:** a group of words beginning with an infinitive

   Infinitive phrase: to have a good job
   Complete sentence: I think it's important to have a good job.

 Practice 4 Identifying Phrases

Identify each of the underlined phrases in the following sentences. Check your answers against those in the Answer Key on page 459.

1. <u>To visit Montreal</u> is a thrill for most Canadians.
2. Many people love <u>to see the French culture</u>.

3. Museums, restaurants, shopping, and the varied night life offer endless possibilities <u>for the tourist</u>.
4. <u>On the subways,</u> tourists experience one of the cleanest underground transit systems in North America.
5. <u>My brother Don</u> rode the subway under the St. Lawrence River.
6. <u>A landowner from the country,</u> he enjoyed the continental atmosphere of Quebec's largest city.
7. Montreal's continual fascination is its rich mix <u>of cultures and lifestyles</u> from all over the world.

 Practice 5 Identifying Phrases

In the following sentences, identify what kind of phrase each numbered group of underlined words is. Check your answers against those in the Answer Key on page 459.

<u>In Canada,</u>[1] crime seems <u>to be increasing</u>[2] <u>at an alarming rate</u>.[3] Stories about <u>many major crimes</u>[4] <u>can be seen</u>[5] almost daily <u>in the newspapers</u>.[6] <u>To avoid</u>[7] the issue will not solve the problem. Citizens <u>should be concerned</u>[8] and try <u>to make their views known</u>[9] <u>to their elected officials</u>.[10]

1. _____
2. _____
3. _____
4. _____
5. _____
6. _____
7. _____
8. _____
9. _____
10. _____

Making a Complete Sentence from a Fragment That Contains a Verbal

DEFINITION

Verbals are words that look like verbs, but that function as nouns, adjectives, or adverbs. There are three types of verbals: **infinitives, participles,** and **gerunds.** All three of these types of verbals appear in phrases. These phrases by themselves are not complete sentences. They are fragments.

Infinitive phrases: to kill a mockingbird
                          to tour the West
Complete sentences: It is a sad thing to kill a mockingbird.
                          He began to tour the West.

Participial phrases: beaten to a pulp
                          running like the wind
Complete sentences: I was afraid I would be beaten to a pulp.
                          Running like the wind, he's never looked more afraid in his life.

Gerund phrases:	working on the car
	sitting on the bench
Complete sentences:	Working on the car can wait until she's finished her supper.
	All players hate sitting on the bench.

Participial phrases function as adjectives. Gerund phrases can look like (present) participial phrases (because both end in *-ing*), but when they appear in complete sentences, gerund phrases function as nouns.

> ### TIP
>
> For those of you with a tendency to include fragments in your writing, avoid starting sentences with the following words or types of words or constructions. Fragments often begin with them. People who are inclined to have a problem with fragments seldom complete their sentences when their sentences start with these constructions:
>
> **Because**
> **Fragment:** Because he was sick.
> **Complete sentence:** Because he was sick, he was absent from work.
> **Which**
> **Fragment:** Which is why he was absent.
> **Complete sentence:** He was sick, which is why he was absent.
> **-ing word**
> **Fragment:** Jogging in the morning.
> **Complete sentence:** Jogging in the morning is something she loves to do every day.
> **Fragment:** The reason being the bus was late.
> **Complete sentence:** The reason is the bus was late.
> **Whether**
> **Fragment:** Whether or not school shuts down because of snow.
> **Complete sentence:** Whether or not school shuts down because of snow, the students decided they would not attend today.
> **Although, though, even though**
> **Fragment:** Although, the chocolate cake was cheaper.
> **Complete sentence:** Although the chocolate cake was cheaper, her father bought the cake with vanilla ice cream and chocolate swirls.

You can form a sentence from a fragment that contains a participle in any of the following ways.

Fragment: he talking in his sleep

1. Add a helping verb to the participle:

   He *is talking* in his sleep.

2. Change the participle to a different form of the verb:

   He *talks* in his sleep.

3. Use the participle as an adjective, being sure to provide a subject and verb for the sentence:

   Talking in his sleep, he muttered something about his boss.

4. Use a gerund phrase (which has the same form as the present participle) as a subject:

> *Talking in his sleep* got him into trouble.

 Practice 6 **Correcting a Fragment That Contains a Participle**

Make four complete sentences from each of the following fragments. An example has been done for you. Check your answers against those in the Answer Key on page 459. (The Answer Key will give you sample answers, but there are many ways of correcting these fragments.)

Fragment: using the back stairway

a. He *is using* the back stairway.
b. He *uses* the back stairway.
c. *Using the back stairway,* he got away without being seen.
d. *Using the back stairway* is not a good idea.

1. climbing in the Rockies

   a. _____

   b. _____

   c. _____

   d. _____

2. playing video games

   a. _____

   b. _____

   c. _____

   d. _____

3. going clubbing on Tuesdays

   a. _____

   b. _____

   c. _____

   d. _____

 Practice 7 **Recognizing Fragments**

The paragraph below contains fragments. Read the paragraph. Then write *complete* after each example that is a complete sentence. Write *fragment* after each example that is a phrase or piece of a sentence. Keep in mind that a sentence must have a subject and verb as well as express a complete thought. Check your answers against those in the Answer Key on page 459.

That summer, she cycled through the backcountry of southern France. Discovering early that her bike was ideal. The perfect mode of transportation. Because they are cycling fanatics. The French almost always treated her with respect and kindness. In spite of her halting attempts at the language. They would shout encouragement. As she puffed up a hill. The waitress in a café where she stopped to rest. Urged her to eat more, slipping an extra portion onto her plate.

1. That summer, she cycled through the backcountry of southern France. _____
2. Discovering early that her bike was ideal. _____
3. The perfect mode of transportation. _____
4. Because they are cycling fanatics. _____
5. The French almost always treated her with respect and kindness. _____
6. In spite of her halting attempts at the language. _____
7. They would shout encouragement. _____
8. As she puffed up a hill. _____
9. The waitress in a café where she stopped to rest. _____
10. Urged her to eat more, slipping an extra portion onto her plate. _____

 Practice 8 Editing for Fragments

The paragraph below may contain fragments. Rewrite the paragraph, correcting any fragments that appear. You may use any method you have learned to make the corrections, but change the content as little as possible. Circle any changes you have made. Check your answer against the Answer Key on page 459. (The Answer Key will give you one possible answer, but there are many ways to revise this paragraph.)

Soccer's World Cup in 2006 was won by Italy for the first time in 24 years, but it is a public disgrace for which the game will be remembered by the world. By halftime, the final game between Italy and France was tied 1–1. After 120 minutes, the game was still tied. The final victory depended on the penalty shootout. Which took the game to 5–3 for Italy. But 10 minutes before the end of extra time. France's illustrious captain, Zinedine Zidane, was expelled. For head-butting Marco Materazzi. Apparently, Marco had called him a terrorist. And had insulted both his mother and his sister. Was this a deliberate, desperate, and cheap attempt to achieve final victory in what had become a gruelling final game? Celebrations by Italians around the world were unstoppable. Partying with abandon. But soccer scandal continues to loom over the Italian team. Zinedine Zidane exited from his last World Cup under an umbrella of shame. Because he didn't take the moral high road. While millions of fans watched his every move.

Exercise 2   **Correcting a Fragment That Contains a Participle**

The following passage includes four fragments containing participles. Circle the fragments and correct them in one of the four ways shown in Practice 1. There can be more than one correct answer.

At last taking the driving test. I felt very nervous. My mother was sitting in the back seat. All my papers sitting on the front seat. The inspector got into the car and sat on my insurance form. He looked rather sour and barely spoke to me. Trying not to hit the curb. I parallel parked surprisingly well. I managed to get through all the manoeuvres. Now tensely waiting for the results.

Chapter Review Exercises

 Exercise 3   **Correcting the Fragment**

Rewrite each fragment so that it is a complete sentence. There can be more than one correct answer.

1. early morning a time of peace in my neighbourhood

    _____

2. the grey mist covering up all but the faint outlines of nearby houses

    _____

3. the shapes of cars in the streets and driveways

    _____

4. to sit and look out the window

    _____

5. holding a steaming cup of coffee

    _____

6. the only sound the rumbling of a truck

    _____

7. passing on the highway a kilometre away

    _____

 Exercise 4   **Correcting the Fragment**

Revisit the paragraph in the exercise "Correcting a Fragment That Contains a Participle" above. Rewrite the paragraph, correcting each of the fragments you identified in one of the following ways:

- Join the phrase to the sentence preceding it.
- Join the phrase to the sentence that follows it.
- Add a subject, a verb, or both so that the sentence is complete.

There can be more than one correct answer.

 Exercise 5 **Correcting a Fragment**

Each of the following passages contains a fragment. Underline the fragment, and on the lines beneath each passage, rewrite the passage so that it is composed of complete sentences. There can be more than one correct answer.

1. The moon rose high in the sky. All of us worked quickly to pitch the tent. Then making a fire.

   Revised passage: _____

   _____

   _____

2. Raising the drinking age to 21 improves the safety of all drivers. The drinkers and nondrinkers. Every province should raise the drinking age to 21.

   Revised passage: _____

   _____

   _____

3. Companies do a great deal of research before they name a new product. Based on the results of a market research team. The company makes its final selection.

   Revised passage: _____

   _____

   _____

4. The day of my eighteenth birthday, the reservations made at a fine restaurant. My father came home early from work.

   Revised passage: _____

   _____

   _____

5. In 1930, Clint Benedict of the Montreal Maroons donned professional hockey's first face mask. It was a crude leather device intended to protect his broken nose. During the game, an opponent jammed the mask into Benedict's face. Causing further injury. Benedict tore off the mask and quit the game forever.

   Revised passage: _____

   _____

   _____

Working Together: Editing Ad Copy

Read the Pure Michigan (destination brand of the U.S. state of Michigan) advertisement illustrated below. Notice that this advertisement contains several fragments. The writing we must produce for academic or professional purposes is often very different from the kind of writing we find in advertisements and other kinds of popular writing. Why do you think the advertiser would choose to include fragments? Rewrite the entire advertisement using only complete sentences. In your small group, choose a representative to read the two versions out loud. Discuss with people in your group which one is more effective. Why?

We go this way to school.
That way to work. One way home.
And before we know it, we get stuck in a routine.

So let's take a left instead of a right.
Instead of the direct route, let's take the scenic route.

To a place where something new and exciting
is waiting for us just around the corner.

Right this way to Pure Michigan.

PURE MICHIGAN®
Your trip begins at michigan.org

Photo courtesy of the Michigan Economic Development Corporation/Travel Michigan

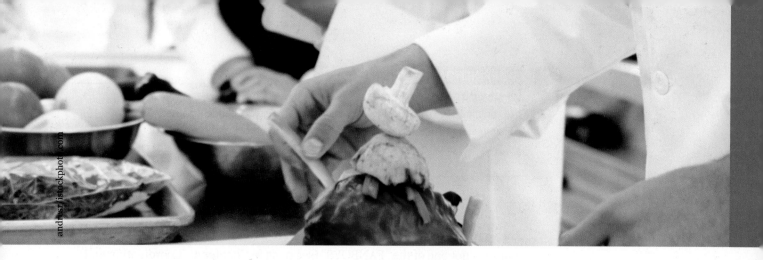

Chapter 7 **Correcting Run-Ons**

QuickQuiz Test yourself on your knowledge of run-ons. Some of the examples below are complete sentences; some are run-ons (two or more independent clauses inadequately separated). Write *C* if the example is correct. Write *R* if the example is a run-on. Answers are upside down beside the quiz.

_____ 1. Strong competition exists among computer companies, each carefully guards its new software designs.

_____ 2. Last year, newspapers carried the story of the great video game design robbery, in fact, it sounded like a spy movie.

_____ 3. A young worker for a California company wanted money to buy a sports car, so he tried to sell the secret company designs to an Asian competitor.

_____ 4. The worker thought the designs were safely hidden on a disk in an airport locker, however, the police caught him and recovered the disk.

_____ 5. The company pressed charges, the worker was given a suspended sentence.

Answers:
1. R
2. R
3. C
4. R
5. R

Run-Ons Are Not "Long Sentences"

Many people think that a run-on is simply a sentence that "runs on and on and on." This is not the definition of a run-on. The question of whether a sentence is a run-on or not does not depend on length. The following is a run-on sentence even though it is quite short: *I did, he didn't*. A run-on is simply two or more independent clauses without adequate separation. There are many ways to provide this separation. It is important that you be able to recognize runs-ons in your writing and separate the clauses properly to solve the problem.

A **run-on** is two or more complete thoughts without adequate separation.
(A comma alone is NEVER adequate separation between independent clauses.)

Examples: Everyone watched silently as the bus pulled into the school parking lot, then each
person stepped onto the bus in a very orderly fashion.

I came to school, however, I was late.

Both examples in the definition box above are run-ons. In the first sentence, the word *then* is used incorrectly as if it were a coordinating conjunction. It is not. It is not one of the "FANBOYS" (see p. 55 in Chapter 5: "Coordination and Subordination"). In the second sentence, the adverbial conjunction *however* separates two complete thoughts. It, therefore, requires a semicolon before it, not just a comma.

What Kinds of Run-Ons Are There?

The Different Kinds of Run-On Sentences

1. The *fused run-on:* two or more independent clauses that run together without any punctuation

   Example: I met Diana again we were happy to see each other.

2. The *comma splice:* two or more independent clauses that run together with only a comma

   Example: I met Diana again, we were happy to see each other.

   (The comma splice is the most common type of run-on sentence.)

3. The *"and" run-on:* two or more independent clauses that run together with a coordinating conjunction but no punctuation

   Example: I met Diana again and we were happy to see each other and we talked for hours.

Note: A long sentence is not necessarily a run-on. The following sentence might be considered long, but it is not a run-on:

> I met Diana again, and despite the fact that we hadn't seen each other in years, we both felt as if we hadn't parted at all, as strange as that may seem to everyone.

How Do You Make a Complete Sentence from a Run-On?

Guide for Correcting Run-Ons

There are three different ways to correct a run-on.

1. Make two simple sentences with end punctuation:

   Example: I met Diana again. We were happy to see each other.

2. Make a compound sentence using one of the three methods of coordination:

   Examples: I met Diana again, and we were happy to see each other.

   I met Diana again; furthermore, we were happy to see each other.

   I met Diana again; we were happy to see each other.

   (For more on using the semicolon correctly—either with adverbial conjunctions or alone—see pp. 57–62 in Chapter 5: "Coordination and Subordination.")

3. Make a complex sentence using subordination:

   Examples: When I met Diana again, we were happy to see each other.

   We were happy to see each other when I met Diana again.

 Exercise 1   Recognizing and Correcting Run-Ons

The following story is written as one sentence. Rewrite the story, breaking it up so there are no run-ons. Put a period at the end of each complete thought. You may have to omit some of the words that loosely connect different ideas, or you may want to use coordination and subordination (see Chapter 5). Remember to start each new sentence with a capital letter. More than one correct answer is possible.

My best friend is accident-prone if you knew her you'd know that she's always limping, having to write with her left hand, or wearing a bandage on her head or ankle, last week for example, she was walking down the street minding her own business when a shingle from someone's roof hit her on the head and she had to go to the emergency ward for stitches, then this week one of her fingers is purple because someone slammed the car door on her hand, in fact, sometimes I think it might be better if I didn't spend too much time with her, you know her bad luck might be catching!

 Practice 1   Correcting Run-Ons

Each of the following examples is a run-on. Supply four possible ways to correct each one. Check your answers against those in the Answer Key on page 460. Refer to the guide above if you need help.

1. Five-year-old Davie asked Grandpa for an iPod for his birthday, he started crying because Grandpa didn't know what that was.

Two simple sentences (sentences with a single subject, a verb, and one complete thought):

a. _____

_____

Two kinds of compound sentence (two simple sentences connected with either a comma and a coordinating conjunction, a semicolon and an adverbial conjunction, or just a semicolon):

b. _____

_____

c. _____

_____

Complex sentence (an independent clause and a dependent clause connected using subordination):

d. _____

_____

2. Many people are opposed to gambling in all its forms, therefore, they will not even buy a lottery ticket.

Two simple sentences:

a. _____

_____

Two kinds of compound sentence:

b. _____

_____

c. _____

_____

Complex sentence:

d. _____

_____

3. Hockey may be Canada's national sport, the game can be quite brutal.

Two simple sentences:

a. _____

_____

Two kinds of compound sentence:

b. _____

_____

c. _____

_____

Complex sentence:

d. _____

_____

4. Many young people manage to travel, they find ways to do it cheaply.
   Two simple sentences:

   a. _____

   _____

   Two kinds of compound sentence:

   b. _____

   _____

   c. _____

   _____

   Complex sentence:

   d. _____

   _____

5. The need for a proper diet is important in any health program, however, all
   the junk food on the grocery shelves makes it hard to be consistent.

   Two simple sentences:

   a. _____

   _____

   Two kinds of compound sentence:

   b. _____

   _____

   c. _____

   _____

   Complex sentence:

   d. _____

   _____

Practice 2 **Correcting Run-Ons**

Each of the following examples is a run-on. Supply four possible ways to revise each one. Check your answers against those in the Answer Key on page 460. Refer to the guide on page 91 if you need help.

1. The airline has begun its new route to the islands everyone is looking forward to flying there.

   Two simple sentences:

   a. _____

   _____

   Two kinds of compound sentence:

   b. _____

   _____

   c. _____

   _____

   Complex sentence:

   d. _____

   _____

2. The movie begins at nine o'clock, therefore, let's have dinner before the show.

   Two simple sentences:

   a. _____

   _____

   Two kinds of compound sentence:

   b. _____

   _____

   c. _____

   _____

   Complex sentence:

   d. _____

   _____

3. The studio audience screamed at the contestant, after all, they wanted her to try for the big prize.

Two simple sentences:

a. _____

_____

Two kinds of compound sentence:

b. _____

_____

c. _____

_____

Complex sentence:

d. _____

_____

4. Maya needs new shoes, she is running in the marathon.

Two simple sentences:

a. _____

_____

Two kinds of compound sentence:

b. _____

_____

c. _____

_____

Complex sentence:

d. _____

_____

5. My actor friend grabbed my arm, she wanted to tell me about her new part in the movie.

Two simple sentences:

a. _____

_____

Two kinds of compound sentence:

b. _____

_____

c. _____

_____

Complex sentence:

d. _____

_____

 Practice 3 **Editing for Run-Ons**

Rewrite the following paragraph, correcting the run-on sentences using any of the methods you have learned. Check your answers against those in the Answer Key on page 461. (The Answer Key will give you one possible answer, but there are many ways of revising this passage.)

Mythology is the study of myths and myths are known as the oldest form of literature and the oldest myths are creation myths. Cultures from around the world have their own creation myths all of them are amazingly similar despite the vast geographical distances between these cultures and the fact that there are no known ways in which communication could have taken place between certain ones. The details of these myths change from one culture to the next, however, various themes of the myths remain the same. For example, although characters (most of the time, but not all of the time) take on new names from one culture to another, every culture refers to the existence of a creator, also the number of gods differs from one mythology to another, nevertheless, every mythology has at least one god or one heroic figure in it. All in all, myths are incredible stories that, in many cases, have lasted thousands of years no matter where they come from and what they are about, they bear striking similarities from one culture to another, and they all share a wisdom about something that never changes: our human nature.

 Practice 4 **Editing for Run-Ons**

Rewrite the following paragraph, correcting the run-on sentences using any of the methods you have learned. Check your answers against those in the Answer Key on page 461. (The Answer Key will give you one possible answer, but there are many ways of revising this passage.)

Sigmund Freud and Carl G. Jung were both psychiatrists, they have had a great deal of influence on the study of psychology to this day, for example, each was famous for his own model of the human psyche. In Freud's model, there are three main parts, they are the ego, the id, and the superego. In

Jung's model, there are also three main parts, they are the conscious, the personal unconscious, and the collective unconscious. Freud (Jung's teacher and subsequent collaborator until they parted due to a major disagreement in 1912) and Jung both believed that dreams come from the unconscious part of our psyche (for Freud, this meant the id and superego), nevertheless, they disagreed a great deal in the area of dream interpretation.

Chapter Review Exercises

 Exercise 2 Editing for Run-Ons

Rewrite the following paragraph, correcting all run-on sentences. There is more than one correct answer.

Commercial farming in Atlantic Canada is concentrated in the dairy, poultry, and horticultural sectors, the most important crop in the region, particularly in New Brunswick and Prince Edward Island, is potatoes. In Ontario and Quebec, farming is highly diversified and includes specialty crops such as soybeans, tobacco, fruit, and vegetables. In the Prairie region, most of the country's wheat, oats, barley, rye, flaxseed, canola, mustard, and sunflowers are grown livestock raising is also very important in Canada with the majority of ranches being located in the three Prairie provinces.

 Exercise 3 Editing for Run-Ons

Rewrite the following paragraph, correcting all run-on sentences. There is more than one correct answer.

Although the metric system was legalized in Canada in 1871, the British Imperial system of units, based on yards, pounds, gallons, etc., continued to be used until the 1960s, with rapidly expanding technology and worldwide trade, the need for an international measurement system became apparent. Britain decided to convert to the system the United States was studying a similar move. A number of Canadian businesses favoured the metric system in January 1970 the government passed legislation stating that a single, coherent measurement system based on metric units should be used for measurement purposes in this country.

 Exercise 4 Editing for Run-Ons

Rewrite each of the following run-ons in two different ways using the different methods you have learned. There is more than one possible answer for each example.

1. I had to buy a new DVD, I gave my only copy to my brother.
2. I'm taking guitar lessons, four of us want to start a band.
3. It was hot outside, I wanted to get some exercise.
4. The storm came on suddenly, we were lost.

5. There were no right answers to the questions, we tried to answer them.
6. He is a politician, he serves his community well.
7. Where is Kanata, I think it's near Ottawa.
8. When did Canada last win the World Junior Hockey Championship, it was in 2015.
9. Our tour was interesting, four of us became lost in Edmonton.
10. We tried our hardest, the exam was too difficult.

 Exercise 5 Editing for Run-Ons

Rewrite any run-ons below in at least two ways using any of the different methods you have learned. If a sentence is already correct, write *C* beside it.

1. The right answer was not at the end of the chapter, it was at the beginning of the next one.
2. I was late for school, however, the teacher wasn't in class today.
3. The pizza was cold, then again, it was still good.
4. At the edge of the table, the marble slowed down and began to roll the other way.
5. The time was right, it was now or never.
6. Listening to the radio at dawn, I found myself singing the words to every song.
7. My teacher is dedicated to her profession, furthermore, she's the best teacher I've ever had.

 Working Together: Operation "Plot without Run-Ons"

Choose a movie or book you have seen or read recently, and retell the plot. In about twenty minutes, write as much of the story as you can remember. (Be careful to write only on every other line, separating words clearly, and write neatly so your classmates can read what you have written.) Exchange papers and read the paper you receive in order to check for run-ons. If you find what you believe to be a run-on, put a mark beside that sentence, and be ready to read the sentence, or put it on the board for class discussion.

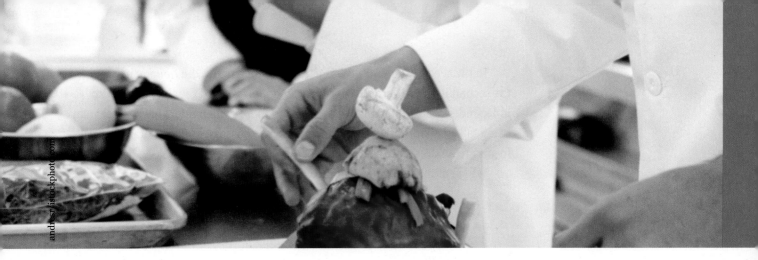

Chapter 8 **Parallel Structure**

QuickQuiz Test yourself on your knowledge of parallel structure. In each of the sentences below, the underlined portion is not parallel with the rest of the sentence. Revise these underlined groups of words as needed to make the sentences parallel. Answers are upside down in the margin.

1. While the men go out in their boats, the women and children stay in camp, cook meals, and <u>to take care of the dog teams</u>.

2. The weather on the East Coast is often wet, windy, and <u>the temperatures are low</u>.

3. His office is without windows, on the fourth floor, and <u>you have to go down a dark hallway to get there</u>.

4. Carmelita does her work quickly, accurately, and <u>with cheerfulness</u>.

5. The mayor promised lower taxes, less crime, and <u>the number of jobs would be higher</u>.

Answers:
1. take care of the dog teams
2. cold
3. down a dark hallway
4. cheerfully
5. more jobs

What Is Parallel Structure?

DEFINITION

Parallel structure is balance in a sentence that contains a list. The list might consist of words, phrases, or clauses. Balance occurs when all the items in the list are in the same grammatical form: all nouns, all adjectives, and so on.

Example: Parallel: She went out with him because of the twinkle in his eye, the swagger in his step, and his love for movies.

Unparallel: She went out with him because of the twinkle in his eye, swaggering, and he loves movies.

In the first sentence above, at the heart of each of the three items in the list is a noun: *twinkle*, *swagger*, and *love*. They are all nouns (with modifiers), so the sentence is parallel.

In the second sentence, the first item is still a noun, the *twinkle* in his eye; the second item is a verbal (a gerund), *swaggering*; and the third item is an independent clause starting with the pronoun *he* (which refers back to the man being talked about rather than the qualities he possesses). These grammatical forms are all different. This sentence, therefore, is not parallel.

Which of the following sentences is better balanced?

> Her favourite pastimes are reading novels, listening to jazz, and to go to films.
>
> Her favourite pastimes are reading novels, listening to jazz, and going to films.

If you selected the second sentence, you made the right choice. The second sentence uses parallel structure (all three items in the list begin with *-ing* words (gerunds): *reading*, *listening*, and *going*). By giving each first word of the items in the list the same *-ing* structure, you make the sentence easier to understand and more pleasant to read. Any list of words, phrases, and even clauses should be parallel.

RULE 1

Words in a list should be the same part of speech.

Incorrect: The town was small, quiet, and the atmosphere was peaceful.
(The list is composed of two adjectives and one clause.)

Correct: The town was small, quiet, and peaceful.
(*Small*, *quiet*, and *peaceful* are all adjectives.)

RULE 2

Phrases in a list should be the same kind of phrase (infinitive phrases, prepositional phrases, verb phrases, noun phrases, participial phrases).

Incorrect: Her lost assignment is in her closet, on the floor, and the clothes are hiding it.
(two prepositional phrases and one clause)

Correct: Her lost assignment is in her closet, on the floor, and under a pile of clothes.
(three prepositional phrases beginning with *in*, *on*, and *under*)

RULE 3

Clauses in a list should be parallel.

Incorrect: One clerk polished the antique spoons; they were placed into the display case by the other clerk.

Correct: One clerk polished the antique spoons; the other clerk placed them in the display case.

Practice 1 Making Sentences Parallel

Each of the following sentences has an underlined word, phrase, or clause that is not parallel. Make the underlined section parallel. There may be more than one correct answer for each sentence. Check your answers against those in the Answer Key on page 461.

1. My favourite armchair is lumpy, worn out, and <u>has dirt spots everywhere</u>.

   _____

   _____

2. She enjoys reading novels, studying the flute, and also <u>sews her own clothes</u>.

   _____

   _____

3. He admires teachers who make the classroom an exciting place and <u>willingly explaining material more than once</u>.

   _____

   _____

 Practice 2 Making Sentences Parallel

The following sentences all lack parallel structure. In each one, underline the word, phrase, or clause that is not parallel with the other items in the pair or series and revise it so that the sentence is balanced. An example has been done for you. There may be more than one correct answer for each sentence. Check your answers against those in the Answer Key on page 461.

Incorrect: The best leather comes from Italy, from Spain, and is imported from Brazil.

Correct: The best leather comes from Italy, from Spain, and from Brazil.

or: The best leather comes from Italy, Spain, and Brazil.

1. Winter in Edmonton is very windy and has many bitterly cold days.

   _____

   _____

2. I would prefer to fix an old car than watching television.

   _____

   _____

3. Alex is a talented athlete, a top student, and even generous to her friends.

_____

_____

4. The apartment is crowded and without light.

_____

_____

5. The dancer is slender and moves gracefully.

_____

_____

6. The trees were tall and had a lot of leaves.

_____

_____

7. My friend loves to play chess, to read science fiction, and working out at the gym.

_____

_____

Practice 3 Making Sentences Parallel

Each of the following sentences lacks parallel structure. Underline the word, phrase, or clause that is not parallel, and revise it so that its structure balances with the other items in the pair or series. There may be more than one correct answer for each sentence. Check your answers against those in the Answer Key on page 462.

1. The dog had to choose between jumping over the fence, or he could have dug a hole underneath it.

_____

_____

2. She was great at swimming, canoeing, and as a rock climber.

_____

_____

3. As I looked down the city street, I could see the soft lights from restaurant windows, I could hear the mellow sounds of a nightclub band, and carefree moods of people walking by.

_____

_____

4. The singers have been on several road tours, have recorded for two record companies, and they would also like to make a movie someday.

_____

_____

5. They would rather order a pizza than eating homemade cooking.

_____

_____

6. I explained to the teacher that my car had broken down, my books had been stolen, and I left my assignment pad at home.

_____

_____

7. That night the prisoner was sick, discouraged, and filled with loneliness.

_____

_____

To help you with the chapter review exercises, here is a reminder of all the rules for parallel structure. (For further explanation of these rules, refer back to page 100.)

RULE 1

Words in a list should be the same part of speech.

RULE 2

Phrases in a list should be the same kind of phrase (infinitive phrases, prepositional phrases, verb phrases, noun phrases, participial phrases).

RULE 3

Clauses in a list should be parallel.

Chapter Review Exercises

Exercise 1 Making Sentences Parallel

Each of the following sentences has a part that does not work with the rest of the sentence; therefore, the sentences lack parallel structure. Find the errors and correct them. There may be more than one correct answer for each sentence.

1. Now that he was retired, he started tending to his garden, drank his latte at his favourite café every day, and a new book project was something he was eager to launch.

_____

_____

2. The dancer was used to eating her banana, stretching for an hour, and then rehearsal for the next performance kept her busy for the rest of the day.

_____

_____

3. The car wasn't in the garage, nobody could find it on the street, and we found out the police hadn't towed it.

_____

_____

4. After volunteering at a seniors' residence, doing his chores for his parents, and once his homework was finished, he had no time left for his girlfriend.

_____

_____

5. He had to put salt on the ice, food in the dog's dish, and he had to make sure that the driveway was shovelled.

_____

_____

Exercise 2 Making Sentences Parallel

Revise each sentence below to make it parallel. There may be more than one correct answer for each sentence.

1. Most of the neighbours are friendly, considerate, and they give help.

_____

_____

2. She is charming and has beauty.

_____

_____

3. I enjoy reading, writing, and to conduct laboratory experiments.

_____

_____

4. Either going for a ride or to lie in the sun is my idea of a good time.

_____

_____

5. She got a new job with a higher salary, increased benefits, and she also works fewer hours than before.

_____

_____

 Working Together: Practise Making Sentences Parallel

Read the following paragraph. Look for places that lack parallel structure, then write a corrected version of the paragraph. When you're finished, check your answers with another student in the group or class, preferably someone with whom you would not normally sit.

> I've had several great summer jobs. They include desk clerk for a student residence, cashier for a busy convenience store, and I even worked as an assistant janitor in an elementary school where my boss and I had some of the best conversations I've ever had. The best summer job, however, was organizing the Miss Glace Bay Pageant. The titillation factor associated with a beauty competition was certainly one reason. Other reasons for enjoying the job included auditioning talent for the entertainment component, I wrote the script for the emcee, and meeting a young woman among the contestants whom I'd already met six months earlier. First, because I love music, having a say as to who performed on the big evening was exciting beyond description. Second, I've always enjoyed writing. And writing what the emcee would say that evening gave me experience with a kind of writing I'd never tried before. But most important, when I saw Sherry with her long golden hair among the contestants on the first day of rehearsals, I knew this second meeting was no coincidence. And about a week later when she sat down next to me, laid her head on my shoulder, and "Hello, there," was whispered into my ear, I knew we'd be dating before too long. She didn't win the pageant, but she definitely won my heart. I'd had some great summer jobs, but organizing the pageant was the one that etched that summer onto the wall of my memory storehouse forever.

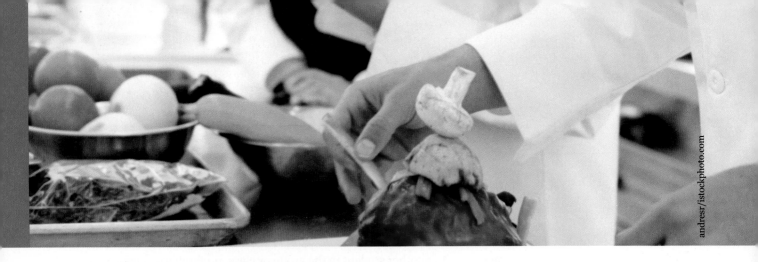

andresr/istockphoto.com

Chapter 9 **Pronouns**

QuickQuiz   Test yourself on your knowledge of pronouns. In each of the following sentences, choose the correct pronouns. Answers are upside down beside the quiz.

1. Between you and (me, I), the reason I can't go is that I lost my ticket.

2. The girl I'm dating is taller than (I, me).

3. (We, Us) students are going to Cancun for the spring break.

4. Would you spare some change for my son and (I, me)?

5. (Him, He) and (me, I) spent lots of money on the weekend.

Answers:
1. me
2. I
3. We
4. me
5. He, I

A discussion of pronouns never fails to be interesting because of the potential controversy surrounding usage. Even well-educated people disagree sometimes on what is acceptable. Those who tend to support a particular usage, even if it's not grammatically correct, will argue that it's acceptable because that's what they hear everyone else saying. But what everyone seems to be saying is not always correct, and what is not correct is still unacceptable in most situations. In the final analysis, the more correct grammar you know, the safer you'll be.

Most people acquainted with a basic knowledge of English grammar know, for example, that it is improper to say, "Me and him are going downtown." But not everyone knows that it is also improper to say, "Between you and I …" (the correct usage is "Between you and me …"). Some English instructors accept "Everyone has their own way of doing things," while fewer instructors accept "To who should I give this book?" In any event, this textbook is still partial to the correct way. If there is widespread movement toward acceptance of certain pronoun usage that was once and might still be considered incorrect, you might simply have to make a personal decision. But don't do this before considering the rules of grammar.

Pronouns and Case

Guide to Pronoun Case			
Pronouns Used as Subjects (Subjective Case)	**Pronouns Used as Objects (Objective Case)**	**Pronouns Used as Possessives (Possessives Case)**	**Possessive Adjectives**
I	me	mine	my
you (sing.)	you (sing.)	yours	your
he	him	his	his
she	her	hers	her
it	it	its	its
who	whom	whose	whose
whoever	whomever	whosever	
we	us	ours	our
you (pl.)	you (pl.)	yours	your
they	them	theirs	their

Use the guide to choose the correct answers in the following examples:

1. (She, Her) is singing at the concert tonight.
2. He bought those tickets for Jan and (I, me).

3. He sold (us, we) the best seats in the house.
4. To (who, whom) should I address the letter?
5. Her voice is much stronger than (he, him, his).

6. (Who, Whom, Whose) music was left on the piano?

7. She is dating a man who is shorter than (she, her) is.

> **DEFINITION**
>
> **Possessive adjectives,** technically speaking, are not pronouns; they do not replace nouns. They are adjectives because they modify nouns. But both the possessive adjective and the noun it modifies can be replaced by a possessive pronoun.
>
> **Example:** He returned *my* book.
>
> He returned *mine.*
>
> (The word *my* is a possessive adjective. The word *mine* in the second sentence is a possessive pronoun. See the chart "Guide to Pronoun Case" on p. 107).

Who vs. Whom

Who is the subjective form; *whom* is the objective form. Use *who* whenever *he, she, they, I,* or *we* could replace who. Likewise, use *whom* when *him, her, them, me,* or *us* could replace *whom.* (You might need to mentally rearrange the word order as shown in parentheses after the following examples.)

1. To *whom* were you talking? (Were you talking to him?)

> **TIP**
>
> Keep in mind the rule that the subject of the sentence is not ever part of a prepositional phrase.

In sentence 1 above, *to* is a preposition (see pp. 7–8). So the objective form of *who,* which is *whom,* must be used after it.

However, the following two examples show the exception to the rule.

2. I get angry when I have to listen to people who talk on cellphones in a movie theatre. (*People* talk on cellphones.)

3. The matter of *who* should pay was not decided. (*He or she* should pay.)

The rule that a subject never follows a preposition is broken in sentences 2 and 3 because the word *who,* on the one hand, is the object of a preposition, but is also a subject (the doer of an action). **Choose the *subjective* form of the relative pronoun (*who* or *whoever*) when it is both an object and a subject in a sentence.**

Exercise 1 Choosing Correct Pronoun Forms

Circle the correct pronoun in each of the sentences below.

1. Matthew and (she, her) presented the project today.
2. Between you and (I, me), I think it was outstanding.
3. Their visual materials will help (whoever, whomever) will study the project later.
4. He is usually a better speaker than (she, her).
5. (Whoever, Whomever) heard them agreed that it was an impressive presentation.

6. (Who, Whom) do you think made the best points?

7. I am not as deeply involved in my project as (they, them).

8. Their research was much more detailed than (us, our, ours).

9. The professor gave both Carolyn and (he, him) A's

10. My partner and (I, me) will have to work harder to reach this standard.

 Exercise 2 Choosing Correct Pronoun Forms

Circle the correct pronouns to complete the following paragraph.

When my mother and (I, me) decided to care for my very ill father at home, some of our friends objected. My sister and (they, them) said we would be exhausted and unable to handle the stress. To (who, whom) could we go for help in the middle of the night? My father, (who, whom) we believed would be happier at home, had been our first consideration. Of course, we would have benefited if my mother or (I, me) had been a nurse. However, we did have a visiting nurse available at times. We were more confident than (they, them) that we could handle the situation.

Pronoun-Antecedent Agreement

 RULE

A pronoun must agree in number (singular or plural) and in gender (masculine, feminine, or neutral) with any other word to which it refers.

 DEFINITION

The word to which the pronoun refers is known as the **antecedent** of the pronoun. Most errors in pronoun number agreement occur when a plural pronoun is used to refer to a singular noun, and vice versa.

> **Incorrect:** The school has their own way of doing things.
> **Correct:** The *school* has *its* own way of doing things.

The *antecedent* in the sentence above is *school*. Because *school* is singular and neutral (neither masculine nor feminine), use *its* as the pronoun that refers back to it.

The following sentences contain pronoun-antecedent disagreement in **number**—in both cases, the pronoun is plural, while its antecedent is singular:

> The *company* changed *their* name last month.
> *Everyone* worked on *their* final draft.

In the first sentence, the antecedent *company* is singular in number and neutral in gender. Therefore, the pronoun (or possessive adjective) referring back to it must be singular and neutral as well. Here is the corrected version:

> The company changed its name last month.

(The possessive adjective *its* is both singular and neutral. Notice there is no apostrophe in a possessive adjective.)

The problem in the second sentence is that *everyone* is a singular word (even though it refers to many people—see the discussion of **indefinite pronouns** below), but *their* is a plural pronoun. You may often have heard people use the plural pronoun *their* to refer to a singular subject. In fact, the second sentence above may sound correct, especially when it is heard during casual conversation, but it is still a mistake in formal writing. Here are two approaches a writer might take to correct this sentence:

Everyone worked on *his* final draft.

This approach is currently unpopular because it is widely considered a sexist construction.

Everyone worked on *his* or *her* final draft.

This form is technically correct, but if it is used several times, it sounds awkward and repetitious.

The best solution for this kind of construction is often to revise it so that the antecedent is plural:

All the students worked on *their* final drafts.

Everyone is an **indefinite** pronoun. It may look plural, but actually, it is singular. For more on indefinite pronouns, see pages 46–47 in Chapter 4: "Subject-Verb Agreement."

Many other indefinite pronouns are singular, too (any pronoun with *-one, -body,* or *-thing* in it).

Indefinite Pronouns That Are Singular				
-one	everyone	someone	anyone	no one
-body	everybody	somebody	anybody	nobody
-thing	everything	something	anything	nothing
	each	another	either	neither

Another problem with pronoun-antecedent agreement in number occurs when a **demonstrative** pronoun *(this, that, these, those)* is used with a noun (such as *kind* or *type*). A demonstrative used this way is technically an adjective, although some will still call it a pronoun when it is used alone in a sentences such as "*This* is what I am talking about." The demonstrative must agree with the noun it modifies.

Singular: this, that

Incorrect: *These kind* of shoes hurt my feet.
Correct: *This kind* of shoe hurts my feet.

Plural: these, those

Incorrect: *Those type* of cars always need oil.
Correct: *Those types* of cars always need oil.

Exercise 3 **Pronoun-Antecedent Agreement in Number**

Rewrite each of the following sentences so that the pronoun agrees with its antecedent in number.

1. Everybody should believe they have choices.

   _____

   _____

2. Each of the children brought their own toys.

   _____

   _____

3. There was no one who invited us to their homes.

   _____

   _____

4. If the birdwatchers hope to see anything, one must get up early.

   _____

   _____

5. The association sent a memo to all their members about the special meeting.

   _____

   _____

6. Please pass the tissues; those kind of movies make me cry.

   _____

   _____

7. These type of shoes are "so yesterday."

   _____

   _____

 RULE 2

Pronouns must also agree with their antecedents in person.

"Person" refers to the doer of the action—first person (I); second person (you); third person (e.g., *he, she, it* in the singular; *they,* among others, in the plural). First-person pronouns highlight the writer and are suitable for personal writing. Second-person pronouns focus on the reader and are useful for giving instructions. Third-person pronouns emphasize the topic of the text and are useful in professional and academic writing.

The following **incorrect** sentence contains a pronoun-antecedent disagreement in **person:**

> When mountain climbing, *one* must maintain *your* concentration at all times.

The sentence could be correctly rewritten in a variety of ways, including the following:

> When mountain climbing, *one* must maintain *one's* concentration at all times.
> When mountain climbing, *you* must maintain *your* concentration at all times.
> When mountain climbing, *I* must maintain *my* concentration at all times.
> When mountain climbing, *we* must maintain *our* concentration at all times.

 Exercise 4 Pronoun-Antecedent Agreement in Person

Rewrite each of the following sentences so that the pronoun agrees with its antecedent in person.

1. I enjoy math exams because you can show what you know.

   _____

   _____

2. When people take geometry, you discover that frequent review of past assignments helps make the course seem easy.

   _____

   _____

3. People always need to practise your skills in order not to forget them.

   _____

   _____

4. When you study for exams, one should not watch television at the same time.

   _____

   _____

5. Math is a subject we often neglect in school, but later you use it all the time.

   _____

   _____

Missing, Ambiguous, or Repetitious Pronouns

RULE

The antecedent of a pronoun should not be missing, ambiguous, or repetitious.

The following is a sentence with a missing antecedent:

Missing antecedent: In British Columbia, *they* have many challenging hiking trails.

Possible revision: British Columbia has many challenging hiking trails.

In the first sentence, who is meant by *they?* If the context has not told us that *they* refers to government departments or to tourist companies, for instance, then the antecedent is missing. The sentence should be rewritten in order to avoid *they.*

In the next sentence, the antecedent is ambiguous.

Ambiguous antecedent: Margaret told Lin that *she* needed to earn $1000 during the summer.

Possible revision: Margaret said that Lin needed to earn $1000 during the summer.

In the first example, *she* could refer to either Margaret or Lin. The sentence should be revised in a way that avoids this confusion.

The next example illustrates a repetitious antecedent.

**Repetitious pronoun
and antecedent:** The newspaper article, *it* said that Earth Day, 1993, reestablished humankind's commitment to the earth.

Possible revision: The newspaper article said that Earth Day, 1993, reestablished humankind's commitment to the earth.

The subject should be either *article* or, if there is already an antecedent, *it.* Using both the noun and the pronoun results in needless repetition.

 Exercise 5 **Sentences with Proper Antecedents**

Each of the following sentences features a missing, ambiguous, or repetitious antecedent. Revise the sentences as necessary to correct their use of pronouns. There may be more than one correct answer for each sentence.

1. The biologist asked the director to bring back his microscope.

   _____

   _____

2. In the report, it says that the number of science and engineering students seeking doctoral degrees has fallen considerably since the mid-sixties.

_____

_____

3. At the laboratory, they said the research had run into serious difficulties.

_____

_____

4. The testing equipment was accidentally dropped into the aquarium, and it was badly damaged.

_____

_____

5. You can't believe anything they say in that newspaper.

_____

_____

Chapter Review Exercises

Practice 1   Making Pronouns and Antecedents Agree

Each of the following sentences contains an error in pronoun use. Revise each sentence so that all pronouns agree with their antecedents and there are no missing or ambiguous antecedents. There may be more than one correct answer for each sentence. Check your answers against those in the Answer Key on page 462.

1. His father mailed him his high school yearbook.

_____

_____

2. No one wants their income reduced.

_____

_____

3. When a company fails to update its equipment, they often pay a price in the long run.

_____

_____

4. The graduate today has many more options open to them than ever before.

_____

_____

5. Everybody knows their own strengths best.

_____

_____

6. Each of the soccer players put effort into their game.

_____

_____

7. If the campers want to eat quickly, each one should help themselves.

_____

_____

Exercise 6 Making Pronouns and Antecedents Agree

Read the following sentences carefully, watching for errors with pronouns. Revise the sentences as necessary so that pronouns agree with their antecedents and there are no missing or ambiguous antecedents. There may be more than one correct answer for each sentence. If a sentence is correct, simply write *C*.

1. The manager told Karen she was responsible for the mix-up in orders.

_____

_____

2. The county submitted their proposal for the bridge repairs.

_____

_____

3. We rushed away from the trees to our cars because you had to wait for the thunderstorm to stop.

_____

_____

4. A young person does not receive enough advice on how they should choose their career.

_____

_____

5. These type of watches are very popular.

_____

_____

6. People were taken forcibly from our homes.

_____

_____

7. No one ate their lunch in the cafeteria.

_____

_____

 Working Together: Practise with Pronouns

Pair up with someone else in the class, preferably someone with whom you do not normally sit. Together, come up with ten sentences, each with at least three pronouns in it (including possessive adjectives). Each of the three pronouns should be in a different case: subjective, objective, and possessive. Come up with at least one sentence that is of a type that often has incorrect pronoun-antecedent agreement, and at least one where there is potential for pronoun ambiguity. Between the two of you, make sure all pronouns are correct. If you disagree on any, give the other student an explanation as to why you think yours is correct. Here is an example of a sentence that complies:

Jacquie and **I** are faster than **they,** so **they** have to not only pay **our** way to the festival, but also give **us** spending money once **we**'re there.

I, they, they, we:	subjective case
our:	possessive adjective
us:	objective case

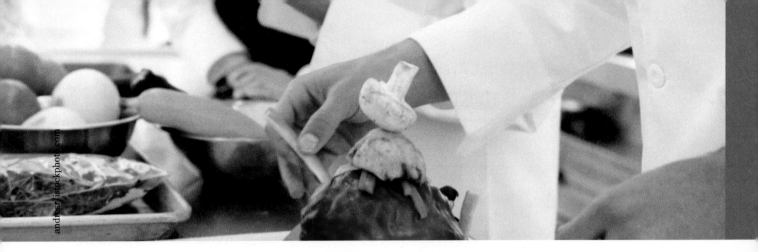
andreas/istockphoto.com

Chapter 10 Modifiers: Misplaced and Dangling

QuickQuiz Test your knowledge of dangling and misplaced modifiers by selecting the correct sentence in each pair below. Answers are upside down in the margin.

1. a. Sweeping the dust in the attic, the dead bugs numbered in the thousands.
   b. Sweeping the dust in the attic, I noticed that the dead bugs numbered in the thousands.

2. a. Reduce speed when wet.
   b. Reduce speed when roads are wet.

3. a. While shaving in the bathroom, Grant accidentally cut his ear with his razor.
   b. While shaving in the bathroom, the razor cut Grant's ear.

4. a. To make a good impression on your employer, ensure you have a neat and clean appearance.
   b. To make a good impression on your employer, a neat and clean appearance is advisable.

5. a. Though old and shoddy, Uncle Jake made the room in the back of the house look new again.
   b. Though the room in the back of the house was old and shoddy, Uncle Jake made it look new again.

Answers:
1. b
2. b
3. a
4. a
5. b

What Are Modifiers?

Modifiers describe or modify other words in the sentence. If a modifier is put in the wrong place or in an ambiguous or awkward place in the sentence, the meaning will be unclear. If the modifier has no word at all to modify, the result might be confusing or even unintentionally humorous (as in #2a above).

This chapter shows how to solve two types of modifier problems—misplaced modifers and dangling modifiers—in order to make the intended meaning clear. Study the examples carefully. Once you are able to recognize these problems in the exercises that follow, you will begin to recognize them in your own writing as well.

What Are Misplaced Modifiers?

There are three types of misplaced modifiers:

1. The modifier in the wrong place

   > ***Wrong:*** The salesperson sold the used car to the customer that needed extensive bodywork.

   Who or what needs bodywork—the car or the customer?

   > ***Revised:*** The salesperson sold the customer the used car that needed extensive bodywork.

   The following was found in a personals ad:

   > If you are tired of meeting the wrong people like me, please leave me a message.

Does this make sense? If the person who made up the ad is an example of "wrong people," why would anyone respond? Perhaps what the person meant was this:

> If you, like me, are tired of meeting the wrong people, please leave me a message.

Be especially careful to put each of the following words closest to the word, phrase, or clause it modifies.

Common Modifiers				
almost	exactly	just	nearly	scarcely
even	hardly	merely	only	simply

Notice how the meaning of each of the following sentences changes with the placement of the modifier *only*.

> *Only* Charlene telephoned my brother yesterday.
> Charlene *only* telephoned my brother yesterday.
> Charlene telephoned *only* my brother yesterday.
> Charlene telephoned my *only* brother yesterday.
> Charlene telephoned my brother *only* yesterday.

2. The awkward modifier that interrupts the flow of the sentence

> *Awkward:* Cheryl planned to only call my sister.

The adverb *only* could be better placed so that it would not split the infinitive *to call*.

> *Revised:* Cheryl planned to call only my sister.

3. The "squinting modifier"—a modifier placed ambiguously so that it could describe a word or words on either side of it

> *Squinting:* Anyone who can write clearly should have a blog.

Is the meaning here that only people who write clearly should have blogs, or that anyone who can write at all should, clearly, have a blog?

> *Revised:* If you can write clearly, you should have a blog.

What Are Dangling Modifiers?

DEFINITION

A dangling modifier is a modifier in a sentence that has no word, phrase, or clause that the modifier can describe.
Example: Riding the bicycle, the countryside seemed different.

In the above example, it sounds like the countryside is riding the bicycle. *Riding the bicycle* is the dangling modifier. It has nothing in the sentence to modify.

> ***Dangling:*** Working on the engine of the car, the dog barked all afternoon.

Who worked on the engine? Was it the dog?

> ***Revised:*** Working on the engine of the car, I heard the dog barking all afternoon.
>
> ***Or:*** The dog barked all afternoon while I was working on the engine of the car.

Chapter Review Exercises

 Practice 1 Revising Misplaced or Dangling Modifiers

Revise each sentence to correct a misplaced or dangling modifier. There can be more than one correct answer for each sentence. Check your answers against those in the Answer Key on page 462.

1. Victor fed the dog wearing his tuxedo.

   _____

   _____

2. Visiting the Vancouver Aquarium, the otters entertained us.

   _____

   _____

3. The toddler that ate her breakfast cheerily started singing.

   _____

   _____

4. A band was playing in the park that we had heard earlier.

   _____

   _____

5. After running over the hill, the farm was visible in the valley below.

   _____

   _____

6. The truck caused a traffic jam, which was broken down on the highway, for kilometres.

   _____

   _____

7. Hanging from the ceiling in my bedroom, I saw three spiders.

   _____

   _____

Exercise 1 **Revising Misplaced or Dangling Modifiers**

Revise each sentence so there is no misplaced or dangling modifier. There may be more than one correct answer for each sentence.

1. Leaping upstream, we fished most of the day for salmon.

   _____

   _____

2. At the age of ten, my family took a trip to Fredericton.

   _____

   _____

3. Skimming every chapter, my biology textbook suddenly made more sense.

   _____

   _____

4. Waiting at the airport, every minute seemed endless.

   _____

   _____

5. Working extra hours last week, my salary increased dramatically.

   _____

   _____

6. We watched a movie in the theatre for which we had paid five dollars.

   _____

   _____

7. Dressed as Tinkerbell, he thought she looked charming.

   _____

   _____

 Working Together: Modifiers Making the Difference

Form groups of four or five. Look back at the list of common modifiers in the box on page 119. As a group, pick one modifier and create a sentence that includes it. Then move the modifier to as many different positions as possible while making sure the sentence still make sense. (See the example of five sentences using the modifier *only* below the box on page 119.) Then, figure out exactly what each sentence means based on the location of the modifier. Discuss what these changes in meaning suggest about the importance of word placement.

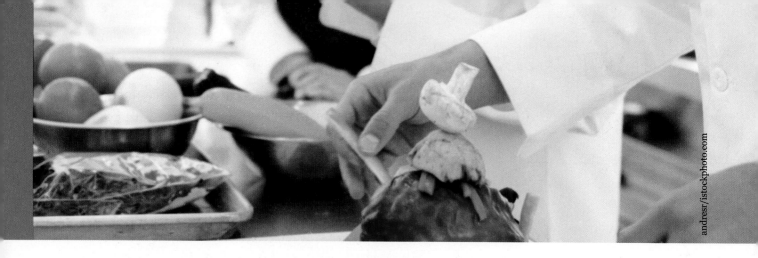

Chapter 11 **Punctuation**

QuickQuiz Test yourself on your knowledge of commas. In each of the following sentences, place commas wherever they should go. Answers are upside down beside the quiz.

1. White-collar criminals dishonest company executives are being exposed in growing numbers.

2. White-collar criminals are found in industrial plants government offices and banks.

3. For example manufacturers have been caught cheating the government and well-known banks have been caught laundering money.

4. In the past white-collar criminals have not been prosecuted very vigorously by the law.

5. However some executives are now being given jail sentences for their white-collar crimes.

Answers:
1. criminals, executives,
2. plants, offices, [second comma is optional]
3. example, government,
4. past,
5. However,

Correct Punctuation: A Strong Indicator of a Writer's Competence

Many people put commas in "where it feels right." Sometimes their feelings are absolutely correct, but sometimes they're not. Others use the dash when they are not quite sure what other punctuation mark to use instead. Like most aspects of writing, correct punctuation is a strong indicator of a writer's competence. Periods, commas, colons, semicolons, dashes, hyphens, quotation marks—all these tiny marks have incredible power over the meaning and ultimate effectiveness of the words and messages they accompany.

The Eight Basic Rules of the Comma

Many students feel very uncertain about when to use the comma. The starting point is to concentrate on a few basic rules. These rules will cover most of your needs.

The tendency now in English is to use fewer commas than in the past. There is no one perfect set of rules on which everyone agrees. However, if you learn the eight basic rules explained in this chapter, your common sense will help you figure out what to do in other cases. Remember that a comma usually signifies a pause in a sentence. As you read a sentence out loud, listen to where you pause. This is often your clue that a comma is needed. Notice that in each of the examples for the following eight rules, you can pause where the comma is placed.

RULE 1

Use a comma to separate parallel words, phrases, and clauses in a list.

> The sky was cloudy, grey, and ominous.
> I was dreaming of running in the race, finishing among the top ten, and collapsing happily on the ground.

With respect to Rule 1, note the following points:

- A list means more than two items.
- Some writers omit the comma before the *and* that introduces the last item.

  > The sky was cloudy, grey and ominous.

- When an address or date occurs in a sentence, each part is treated as a separate item in a list. A comma follows each item even if there are only two items (as in the second example below):

  > I lived at 14 Tartan Avenue, Halifax, Nova Scotia, for many years.
  > He was born on August 17, 1980, on the same street where his father was born.

- A comma does not follow the last item in a list unless that last item is part of an address or a date.
- A group of adjectives may not be regarded as a list if some of the words "go together." You can test this by putting *and* between the items. If it doesn't work, then don't use commas.

  > I carried my *torn, dusty* coat.
  > In the yard was a *battered old maple* tree.
  > I rode in his *new red sports* car.

Practice 1 **Insert Necessary Commas**

In each of the following sentences, insert commas wherever they are needed. Check your answers against those in the Answer Key on page 462.

1. Problems with the water supply of Canada the United States Europe and other parts of the world are growing.
2. Water is colourless tasteless odourless and free of calories.
3. You will use on an average day 90 litres of water for flushing 120 litres for bathing and washing clothes and 95 litres for other uses.
4. It took 450 litres of water to create the eggs you ate for breakfast 13 250 litres to obtain the steak you might eat for dinner and over 200 000 litres to produce the steel used to make your car.
5. The English-Wabigoon river system runs through Grand Narrows Ontario and had become polluted with mercury.

RULE 2

Use a comma before a coordinating conjunction that joins two independent clauses (complete thoughts). (See Chapter 5: "Coordination and Subordination.")

> The house was on fire, but I was determined not to leave my place of safety.
>
> The bees are dying, and one theory is that microwaves from cellphones are killing them.

With respect to Rule 2, note the following points:

- Be careful to use the comma before the conjunction only when you are combining independent clauses. If you are combining only words or phrases, no comma is used.

  > The weather was hot and dry.
  > He grabbed the ball and sent it flying.
  > Larry was neither at third base nor at home plate.

- When clauses joined by a coordinating conjunction are short and closely connected, the comma is often omitted.

  > Let's sit down and I'll dish out the food.

 Practice 2 Insert Necessary Commas

In each of the following sentences, insert commas wherever they are needed. Check your answers against those in the Answer Key on page 462.

1. The most overused bodies of water are our rivers but they continue to serve us daily.
2. Canadian cities often developed next to rivers and industries followed soon after in the same locations.
3. The people of the industrial age can try to clean the water they use or they can watch pollution take over.
4. The Great Lakes are showing signs of renewal yet the struggle against pollution in them must continue.
5. Most people have not been educated about the dangerous state of our water supply nor are all our members of Parliament fully aware of the problem.

RULE 3

Use a comma to follow introductory material—words, expressions, phrases, or clauses that come before independent clauses (complete thoughts).

The following are examples of introductory material:

A. Introductory words (such as *yes, no, oh, well*)

> Oh, I never thought he would do it.

B. Introductory expressions (transitions such as *as a matter of fact, finally, secondly, furthermore, consequently*). A list of common transitions appears on the inside back cover of this book.

> Therefore, I will give you a second chance.

C. Introductory phrases. The comma signals the end of the introductory group of words and the beginning of the sentence proper.

> **Long prepositional phrase:** At the beginning of the course, I thought I would never be able to do the work.

> **Short prepositional phrases** don't generally need to be followed by a comma. However, a comma is often used if the phrase ends with a date.

>> At night I like to watch the stars.
>> In 2001, a moderate earthquake hit the West Coast.

> **Participial phrase:** Walking on tiptoe, the young mother quietly peeked into the nursery.
> **Verbal phrase:** By walking daily, I lost weight. (gerund)
>> Confident of her skills, she entered the contest. (participle)
>> To be honest, I don't like it. (infinitive)

D. Introductory dependent clauses beginning with a subordinating conjunction (See Chapter 5: "Coordination and Subordination.")

> When the food arrived, we all grabbed for it.

Practice 3 Insert Necessary Commas

In each of the following sentences, insert commas wherever they are needed. Check your answers against those in the Answer Key on page 463.

1. A total solar eclipse when the moon's shadow blots out the sun completely is an outstanding cosmic event.
2. Once you see your first solar eclipse you start looking forward to the next one.
3. However witnessing this spectacle takes planning and the ability to travel to the best viewing spots.
4. In eastern Turkey on August 11 1999 a crowd of astronomers and "eclipse chasers" watched the last total eclipse of the millennium.
5. At the moment of totality people cheered clapped and even cried.

Use commas to surround words, phrases, or clauses whenever they interrupt the main idea.

Note the following examples of Rule 4:

A. Interrupting word

We will, however, take an X-ray.

B. Interrupting phrase

Prepositional phrase: I wanted, of course, to stay.
Appositive phrase: Ann, the girl with the red hair, has a wonderful sense of humour.

C. Interrupting clause

He won't, I think, try that again.

Words, phrases, or clauses that interrupt the main idea of a sentence can be *restrictive* or *nonrestrictive*.

A **restrictive** word, phrase, or clause is essential to the meaning of the sentence and is not set off by commas from the rest of the sentence.

The man with the red hat is my father.

The phrase *with the red hat* is essential to specifically identify the man with the red hat; otherwise, any number of unidentified men could be the father.

Author Timothy Findley said it takes failure to become a great writer.

Likewise, the name *Timothy Findley* is essential to the meaning of the sentence above.

A **nonrestrictive** word, phrase, or clause is not essential to the meaning of the sentence, and is set off by commas from the rest of the sentence. (See more on nonrestrictive and restrictive clauses on pages 68–69 in Chapter 5: "Coordination and Subordination.")

Ann, who has red hair, has a wonderful sense of humour.

TIP

Some words can have more than one grammatical function.

She came to the dance; however, she didn't stay long.

In the last sentence, *however* is used to combine independent clauses and therefore requires a semicolon before it.

She did, however, have a good time.

In this sentence, *however* interrupts the main idea and therefore requires a comma before it and a comma after it (comma rule #4).

TIP
Some clauses can be used in different ways.

Ann, who has red hair, has a wonderful sense of humour.

In this sentence, *who has red hair* interrupts the main idea of the sentence. It is a **nonrestrictive clause,** so commas are used. The nonrestrictive clause is not essential to the meaning of the sentence.

The girl who has red hair is my sister Ann.

The clause *who has red hair* is used to identify "the girl." This **restrictive** clause does not interrupt the main idea but is necessary to and part of the main idea. Therefore, no commas are used.

Practice 4 Insert Necessary Commas

In each of the following sentences, insert commas wherever they are needed. Check your answers against those in the Answer Key on page 463.

1. Natural disasters I believe have not been historically significant.
2. They have however significantly affected the lives of many Canadians.
3. Canada's worst coal ine disaster at Hillcrest, Alberta occurred on June 19 1914.
4. In Springhill, Nova Scotia furthermore 424 persons were killed in the mines between 1881 and 1969.
5. Avalanches, storms, and floods which are natural disasters have also made their marks on the face of our country.

RULE 5
Use commas to surround a noun in direct address.

Ali, can you help me with this problem?
I wonder, Michaela, if you really know what you're doing.

Practice 5 Insert Necessary Commas

In each of the following sentences, insert commas wherever they are needed. Check your answers against those in the Answer Key on page 463.

1. Honey I hope you're not planning to wear that hat.
2. I wonder Samir if the game has been cancelled.
3. Dad could I borrow five dollars?
4. Can you help me Doctor?
5. Ayesha is that you?

RULE 6

Use a comma in numbers of 1,000 or larger in some styles.

> 1,999
> 1,999,999,999

Note that in the metric system of measurement, spaces are used instead of commas, and numbers of four digits need not be separated. This practice is becoming more widespread in Canada.

> 4000 or 4 000
> 38 622

RULE 7

Use a comma to set off exact words spoken in dialogue.

> "The pen," she said, "is mightier than the sword."

The comma, as well as the period, is always placed **inside** the second quotation mark, as shown in the sentence above.

Practice 6 Insert Necessary Commas

In each of the following sentences, insert commas wherever they are necessary. Check your answers against those in the Answer Key on page 463.

1. "I'm innocent" he cried "of all charges against me."
2. He mumbled "I won't incriminate myself."
3. "I was told" the defendant explained "to answer every question."
4. "This court" the judge announced "will be adjourned."
5. "The jury" said Al Tarvin of *The Star* "was handpicked."

RULE 8

Use a comma where it is necessary to prevent a misunderstanding.

> Before eating, the cat prowled through the barn.

Practice 7 Insert Necessary Commas

In each of the following sentences, insert commas wherever they are needed. Check your answers against those in the Answer Key on page 463.

1. Kicking the child was carried off to bed.
2. To Maria Suzuki was the boss from hell.
3. When you can come and visit us.
4. Whoever that is is going to be surprised.
5. Skin cancer seldom kills doctors say.

Review this summary of the rules for comma usage. Then try the exercises that follow.

The Eight Basic Rules of the Comma

RULE 1: Use a comma to separate parallel words, phrases, and clauses in a list.

RULE 2: Use a comma before a coordinating conjunction that joins two independent clauses (complete thoughts). (See Chapter 5: "Coordination and Subordination.")

RULE 3: Use a comma to follow introductory words, expressions, phrases, or clauses that come before independent clauses (complete thoughts).

RULE 4: Use commas to surround words, phrases, or clauses whenever they interrupt the main idea.

RULE 5: Use commas to surround nouns in direct address.

RULE 6: Use a comma in numbers of 1,000 or larger in some styles (this practice is decreasing in Canada).

RULE 7: Use a comma to set off exact words spoken in dialogue.

RULE 8: Use a comma where it is necessary to prevent a misunderstanding.

 Exercise 1 Insert Necessary Commas

In each of the following sentences, insert commas wherever they are needed.

1. Fog-water collection is a relatively simple way to supply water to certain areas where water is scarce or polluted.
2. The collectors with screens made of a fine polypropylene mesh look like big volleyball nets.
3. Tiny water droplets which are blown sideways by the wind hit the screen and run down into a trough.
4. In El Tofo Chile eighty-eight fog collectors supply clean water to the fishing village of Chungungo.
5. The El Tofo system on a high coastal ridge is the largest project so far.
6. Amazingly these collectors channel 13 000 litres of water per day to the village.
7. Once almost a ghost town Chungungo now boasts homes with running water and lush gardens.

 Exercise 2 Insert Necessary Commas

In each of the following sentences, insert commas wherever they are needed.

1. The first games known as the British Empire Games attracted 400 competitors from eleven countries.
2. The Commonwealth Games were first held in Hamilton Ontario in 1930.
3. By 1978 during the Commonwealth Games in Edmonton nearly 1500 athletes from 41 countries competed.
4. Canada has been a leading supporter of these games which are held every four years.
5. Memorable performances feats by both Canadian and non-Canadian athletes have become a hallmark of the games.

6. In Edmonton Canadian athletes won forty-five gold thirty-one silver and thirty-three bronze medals in 1978.
7. Next to the Olympics the Commonwealth Games are one of the world's best international competitions.

Other Marks of Punctuation

The Apostrophe

The apostrophe has three uses:

1. Possession
2. Contraction
3. Avoiding confusion

> **RULE 1**
>
> **To form the possessive, add 's or just an apostrophe.**

With respect to Rule 1, note the following points and examples.

A. Add *'s* to singular nouns:

> the pen of the teacher = the teacher's pen
> the strategy of the boss = the boss's strategy

Be careful to choose the right noun to make possessive. Always ask yourself *who* or *what* possesses something. In the phrases above, the teacher possesses the pen and the boss possesses the strategy.

> **TIP**
>
> As a rule, nouns that are inanimate things should not be in the possessive. Use a phrase with *of* instead.

> **Examples:** the leg of the table (NOT the table's leg)
> the smell of the sewer (NOT the sewer's smell)
> the noise of the cars (NOT the cars' noise)

In common expressions that refer to time and measurements and in phrases suggesting personification, possessives are generally acceptable:

> a stone's throw
> two weeks' vacation
> New Year's resolution
> winter's final blast

Note these unusual possessives:

> **Hyphenated words:** mother-in-law's advice
> **Joint possession:** Rita and Ashley's television special
> **Individual possession:** John's and Steve's ideas

B. Add *'s* to irregular plural nouns that do not end in *-s*.

> the hats of the children = the children's hats
>
> the harness for the oxen = the oxen's harness

C. Add *'s* to indefinite pronouns:

> everyone's responsibility
>
> somebody's wallet

Indefinite Pronouns			
anyone	everyone	no one	someone
anybody	everybody	nobody	somebody
anything	everything	nothing	something

TIP

Possessive pronouns in English (*his, hers, its, ours, yours, theirs, whose*) do *not* use an apostrophe.

> *Whose* phone is this?
>
> The phone is *his*.
>
> The car is *theirs*.

D. Add only an apostrophe to regular plural nouns ending in *-s*.

> the nests of the hornets = the hornets' nests
>
> the store of the brothers = the brothers' store

TIP

A few singular nouns ending in the *s* or *z* sound are awkward-sounding if another *s* sound is added. You may, in these cases, drop the final *s*. Let your ear help you make the decision, and be consistent with your choice.

> Mr. Jones' car *or* Mr. Jones's car

RULE 2

To show where letters have been omitted in contractions, use an apostrophe.

> cannot (or can not) = can't
>
> should not = shouldn't
>
> will not = won't (the only contraction that changes its spelling)
>
> I am = I'm
>
> she will = she'll
>
> it is/it has = it's

Note: The possessive adjective *its* (meaning "belonging to it") does not take an apostrophe.

> The dog buried its bone.

RULE 3

To form certain plurals, in order to prevent confusion, use *'s*.

Numbers: 100's
Letters: a's and b's
Years: 1800's or 1800s
Abbreviations: Ph.D.'s
Words referred to in text: He uses too many and's in his writing.

Do *not* use the apostrophe to form plurals in any situations other than these.

Here is a reminder of the uses and rules of the apostrophe:

The Three Rules of the Apostrophe

RULE 1: To form the possessive, add *'s* or just an apostrophe.

RULE 2: To show where letters have been omitted in contractions, use an apostrophe.

RULE 3: To form certain plurals, in order to prevent confusion, use *'s*.

 Practice 8 Using the Apostrophe

Fill in each of the blanks below using the rules you have just studied for uses of the apostrophe. Check your answers against those in the Answer Key on page 463.

1. shirts for boys   _____ shirts

2. the house of them   _____ house

3. the bakery of Grandpa Moses   _____ bakery

4. the house of Antony and Maria
   (joint possession)   _____ house

5. the idea of nobody   _____ idea

6. The book belongs to him.   The book is _____.

7. in the century of 1700   in the _____

8. It is their choice.   _____ their choice.

9. the nightlife of Vancouver   _____ nightlife

10. the dress of Wendy   _____ dress

 Practice 9 Using the Apostrophe

Fill in each of the blanks below using the rules you have just studied for uses of the apostrophe. Check your answers against those in the Answer Key on page 463.

1. the voice of Don Cherry   _____ voice

2. the flight of the geese   the _____ flight

3. the jackets of Carol and Tess
   (individual possession)   _____ jackets

4. the CD of somebody   _____ CD

5. The drums belong to her.   The drums are _____.

6. the terrible year of two   the terrible _____

7. cannot leave yet.   We _____ leave yet.

"I can't believe I went out with an apostrophe.
He was so possessive."

www.CartoonStock.com

Exercise 3   Using the Apostrophe

Fill in each of the blanks below using the rules you have just studied for uses of the apostrophe.

1. the ice cream of Ben and Jerry   _____ ice cream

2. the spirit of the class   the _____ spirit

3. the centre for women   the _____ centre

4. the wish of everybody   _____ wish

5. The ideas belong to them.   The ideas are _____ .

6. The student mixes up *b* and *d*.   The student mixes up his

     _____ .

7. I will not leave this house.   I _____ leave this house.

8. the revenue of the company   the _____ revenue

9. the paw of the doggie   the _____ paw

10. the policies of Ridge School and
Orchard School (individual possession)   _____ policies

Quotation Marks

Use quotation marks as follows:

RULE 1

Use quotation marks for a direct quotation (a speaker's exact words).

"Please," he begged, "don't go away."

Do not use quotation marks for an indirect quotation (one person's idea put into someone else's words):

He begged her to stay.

RULE 2

Use quotation marks for material copied word for word from a source.

According to Statistics Canada, "Families or individuals spending 58.5 percent or more of their pre-tax income on food, clothing, and shelter are in financial difficulty."

RULE 3

Use quotation marks for titles of shorter works, such as short stories, one-act plays, poems, articles in magazines and newspapers, songs, essays, and chapters of books.

"A Modest Proposal," an essay by Jonathan Swift, is a masterpiece of satire.
Mavis Gallant wrote the short story "In Youth Is Pleasure" in 1975.

TIP

Titles of longer works, such as novels, full-length plays, and names of magazines or newspapers, are underlined when handwritten. In word-processed or published texts, these titles appear in italics: *Maclean's* magazine, *Country Living*.

RULE 4

Use quotation marks for words used in a special way.

"Duckie" is a term of affection used by the British, the way Canadians would use the word "honey."

Here is a summary of rules for quotation mark usage:

The Four Basic Rules of Quotation Marks
RULE 1: Use quotation marks for a direct quotation.
RULE 2: Use quotation marks for material copied word for word from a source.
RULE 3: Use quotation marks for titles of shorter works, such as short stories, one-act plays, poems, articles in magazines and newspapers, songs, essays, and chapters of books.
RULE 4: Use quotation marks for words used in a special way.

Practice 10 **Insert Necessary Quotation Marks**

In each of the following sentences, insert quotation marks wherever they are needed. Check your answers against those in the Answer Key on page 463.

1. The Hot House is one of the stories contained in Rosemary Sullivan's *More Stories by Canadian Women.*
2. Nellie McClung said I'll never believe I'm dead until I see it in the papers.
3. The prime minister told his caucus that they would have to settle the problem in the next few days.
4. To diss is a slang term meaning to show disrespect.
5. She read the article Whiz Kids in *The Review.*

If the above five sentences were handwritten, which words would have to be underlined?

The Semicolon

Use the semicolon as follows:

> ### RULE 1
> **Use a semicolon to join two independent clauses (or complete thoughts) whose ideas and sentence structures are related.**

He decided to consult the map; she decided to ask the next pedestrian she saw.

> ### RULE 2
> **Use a semicolon to combine two sentences using an adverbial conjunction.**

He decided to consult the map; however, she decided to ask the next pedestrian she saw.

> ### RULE 3
> **Use a semicolon to separate items in a list when the items themselves contain commas.**

I had lunch with Linda, my best friend; Mrs. Zhangi, my English teacher; and Jan, my sister-in-law.

Notice in the last example that if only commas had been used, the reader might think six people had gone to lunch.

Practice 11 **Using Semicolons**

In each of the following sentences, insert a semicolon wherever one is needed. Check your answers against those in the Answer Key on page 464.

1. One of the best ways to remember a vacation is to take numerous photos one of the best ways to recall the contents of a book is to take notes.
2. The problem of street crime must be solved, otherwise, the number of vigilantes will increase.

3. The meal was composed of bruschetta, an appetizer, roast duck, the house specialty, and lemon mousse, a tart dessert.
4. The bank president was very cordial, however, he would not approve the loan.
5. New methods of production are being used in the factories of Japan eventually they will be common in this country as well.

The Colon

Use the colon as follows:

RULE 1

Use a colon after a complete thought (or independent clause) when the material that follows is a list, an illustration, or an explanation.

A. A list

> Please order the following items: five dozen pencils, twenty rulers, and five rolls of tape.

Notice that no colon is used (such as after *are*) when there is not a complete sentence before the colon:

> The courses I am taking this semester are English Composition, Introduction to Psychology, Art Appreciation, and Survey of Canadian Literature.

B. An illustration or explanation

> She was an exceptional child: at 7 she was performing on the concert stage.

RULE 2

Use a colon following the salutation of a business letter.

> To whom it may concern:
> Dear Madam President:

RULE 3

Use a colon between the hours and the minutes when telling time.

> We will eat at 5:15.

RULE 4

Use a colon between the title and subtitle of a book, article, essay, etc.

> *Plain English, Please: A Rhetoric*
> "Hemingway: His Foreshadowed Suicide"

In each of the following sentences, insert colons wherever they are needed. Check your answers against those in the Answer Key on page 464.

1. Two Canadian-born comedians have achieved great success in the United States Jim Carrey and Mike Myers.
2. The official has one major flaw in his personality greed.
3. The restaurant has lovely homemade desserts such as German chocolate layer cake and baked Alaska.
4. The college offers four courses in English literature Romantic Poetry, Shakespeare's Plays, The British Short Story, and The Modern Novel.
5. Arriving at 615 in the morning, Marlene brought me a sausage-and-cheese pizza, some ginger ale, and a litre of ice cream.

The Hyphen

Use the hyphen as follows:

RULE 1
Use a hyphen with two or more words that go together before the noun to act as one adjective.

> I am a second-year student.
> She is a well-known actor.

TIP
If the group of words that describes the noun comes after the noun, do not use a hyphen.

> The actor is well known.

TIP
If the group of words contains an -*ly* adverb, do not hyphenate.

> The dimly lit diner closed every night at eleven.

RULE 2
Use a hyphen at the end of a line to divide a word between syllables.

Make sure you divide the word at the right place. Check a dictionary if you're not sure. Otherwise, avoid splitting words altogether. Never split a one-syllable word.

> When Farah saw her boyfriend kissing another wom-
> an, she walked away from him for good.

Other compound words are not hyphenated. There is no rule to determine which is which. Use a dictionary to make the right decision. Where there is disagreement between dictionaries, pick one spelling and be consistent in your own writing.

The following are word spellings upon which all dictionaries agree:

father-in-law	hairbrush
trade-in	stepmother

RULE 4

Use hyphens with two-word numbers from twenty-one to ninety-nine.

thirty-seven
seventy-three

RULE 5

Use hyphens in words that contain the prefixes *self, ex,* and *all;* prefixes that are followed by proper nouns; and the suffix *elect.*

self-respect, self-confidence
ex-husband, ex-police officer
all-Canadian cast
anti-Catholic
Premier-elect Philippe Couillard

Exercise 4   Inserting Hyphens Where Necessary

In each of the following sentences, insert a hyphen wherever it is necessary.

1. The students in third year weren't in class today, but all the second year students were.
2. Kelly loved her baseball glove despite its war torn appearance.
3. The all American company of actors was scared to come to Canada because of SARS.
4. Her low self esteem caused her to stay with her husband despite the repeated beatings he inflicted on her.
5. The widely acclaimed impressionist painter received a standing ovation before he accepted his 32 thousand dollar cheque.
6. Julia's forty four year old ex boyfriend returned all thirty three compact discs she had borrowed when she was enrolled in her postgraduate university program.
7. Faisal bought the all purpose cleaner that his mother in law recommended when he and his wife were still a happily married couple.

The Dash and Parentheses

Like the comma, both the dash and parentheses can be used to show an interruption of the main idea. The particular form you choose depends on the degree of interruption.

RULE 1

Use the dash for a less formal and more emphatic interruption of the main idea.

> He came—I thought—by car.
> She arrived—and I know this for a fact—in a pink Cadillac.
> I could see you this weekend—for example, Saturday.

RULE 2

Use a dash before such words as *all, these,* and *they* when these words summarize a preceding list of details.

> Periods, commas, colons, semicolons, dashes, hyphens, and quotation marks—all these tiny marks among words have incredible power over the meaning and ultimate effectiveness of the words or sentences in which they appear.

RULE 3

Use parentheses to insert extra information that some readers might want to know, but that is not essential to the main idea. Information within parentheses is de-emphasized.

> Timothy Findley (1930–2002) wrote *The Wars.*
> Plea-bargaining (see p. 28) was developed to expedite court verdicts.

Practice 13 Using Dashes or Parentheses

In each of the following sentences, insert dashes or parentheses wherever they are needed. Check your answers against those in the Answer Key on page 464.

1. Herbert Simon is and I don't think this is an exaggeration a genius.
2. George Eliot her real name was Mary Ann Evans wrote *Silas Marner.*
3. You should in fact I insist see a doctor.
4. Health Canada's website has suggestions to help smokers quit visit www.infotobacco.com.
5. Mass media television, radio, movies, magazines, and newspapers are able to transmit information over a wide range and to a large number of people.

Chapter Review Exercises

Practice 14 Punctuation Overview

Insert any necessary punctuation into the following sentences. Check your answers against those in the Answer Key on page 464.

1. To measure crime, sociologists have used three different techniques official statistics, victimization surveys, and self-report studies.

2. David is one of the best loved poems of Earle Birney.
3. That show uses one thing I hate a laugh track.
4. Farley Mowat wrote numerous books for adults however, he also wrote very popular books for children.
5. Tuberculosis also known as consumption has been nearly eliminated by medical science.
6. The Victorian period 1837–1901 saw a rapid expansion in industry.

 Practice 15 Punctuation Overview

Insert any necessary punctuation into the following sentences. Check your answers against those in the Answer Key on page 464.

1. Many young people have two feelings about science and technology awe and fear.
2. Mr. Doyle the realtor Mrs. Tong the bank officer and Ivan Petroff the lawyer are the three people to help work out the real-estate transaction.
3. The book was entitled *English Literature The Victorian Age.*
4. My computer, she said, has been crashing all day.
5. She brought a bathing suit, a towel, sunglasses, and several books to the beach.
6. The meeting to discuss a pay increase I'll believe it when I see it has been rescheduled for Friday.
7. The complex lab experiment has these two major problems too many difficult calculations and too many variables.

 Exercise 5 Editing for Correct Punctuation

Read the paragraph below, then insert the following punctuation marks into it wherever they are needed:

a. commas to separate items in a series
b. comma with a coordinating conjunction to combine two complete thoughts
c. comma after an introductory word, phrase, or clause
d. commas around words that interrupt the main idea
e. comma to set off spoken words
f. parentheses
g. quotation marks
h. line under the title of a full-length work of art
i. semicolon
j. apostrophe

Tom Thomson 1877–1917 is often remembered as the artist of Canada's North. He was born on August 4 1877 near Leith Ontario. During the twenties Thomson apprenticed as a machinist enrolled in business college then he spent a few years in Seattle working as an engraver. In 1906 he took art lessons and first used oil paint. His first important painting done in 1917 and titled A Northern Lake was sold for $250 a great deal of money in those days. Thomson led the vanguard of a new movement in Canadian art. One reviewer said Thomson paints a world of phenomena of colour and of form which will not be touched by another artist. Thomson drowned at Canoe Lake Algonquin Park July 8 1917. Among his many works are Hot Summer Moonlight, Autumn's Garland and The Jack Pine.

Exercise 6 Editing for Correct Punctuation

Read the paragraph below, then insert the following punctuation marks into it if and when they are needed:

a. commas to separate items in a series
b. comma with a coordinating conjunction to combine two complete thoughts
c. comma after an introductory word, phrase, or clause
d. commas around words that interrupt the main idea
e. comma in a number of 1,000 or larger
f. parentheses
g. quotation marks
h. line under the title of a full-length work of art
i. semicolon
j. colon
k. apostrophe

Albert Schweitzer was a brilliant German philosopher physician musician clergyman missionary and writer on theology. Early in his career he based his philosophy on what he called reverence for life. He felt a deep sense of obligation to serve humanity. His accomplishments as a humanitarian were great consequently he was awarded the Nobel Peace Prize in 1952. Before Schweitzer was 30 he had won an international reputation as a writer on theology as an organist and authority on organ building as an interpreter of the works of Johann Sebastian Bach and as an authority on Bachs life. When he became inspired to become a medical missionary he studied medicine at the university in Strasbourg Germany. He began his work in French Equatorial Africa now called Gabon in 1913 where his first consulting room was a chicken coop. Over the years he built a large hospital where thousands of Africans were treated yearly. He used his $33 000 Nobel Prize money to expand the hospital then he set up a leper colony in fact he even designed all the buildings. One of Schweitzers many famous books which you might like to find in the library is entitled Out of My Life and Thought. His accomplishments were so many music medicine scholarship theology and service to humanity.

Working Together: Designing Punctuation Tests

Work with a group of your classmates. Together, make up an exam to test the other students' knowledge of punctuation. From any book, choose a paragraph that uses a variety of punctuation. Have one person from the group carefully write out or type the paragraph without its punctuation. Then make enough copies so a group or the entire class can take the test. Is your test a fair one? Is it too easy or too hard? Does it cover the material studied in this chapter?

Chapter 12 **Capitalization**

QuickQuiz Test yourself on your knowledge of capitalization. Correct any errors of capitalization in the following sentences. Answers are upside down in the margin.

1. I am hoping to go to the University in British Columbia in the fall, but if I can't, I'll have more money to spend at christmas.

2. My Doctor's appointment this afternoon is with doctor Shari Mohammed.

3. The pacific ocean is beautiful at Sunset.

4. I told the umpire, "you don't know the rules of baseball any more than grandma does!"

5. Sam and i have travelled through the rockies by Train three times now, for they are absolutely breathtaking.

Answers:
1. university, Christmas
2. doctor's, Doctor (or Dr.)
3. Pacific Ocean, sunset
4. You, Grandma
5. I, Rockies, train

Many students are confused or careless about the use of capital letters. Sometimes they capitalize words without thinking, or they capitalize words they feel are "important" words without really understanding what makes a word important enough to deserve a capital letter. The question of when to capitalize words becomes easier to answer when you study the following rules and carefully apply them to your own writing.

Ten Basic Rules for Capitalization

RULE 1

Capitalize the first word of every sentence.

RULE 2

Capitalize the names of specific things and places.

Specific buildings

I went to the Jamestown Post Office.

but

I went to the post office.

Specific streets, cities, provinces, states, countries

She lives on Elam Avenue.

but

She lives on the same street as my mom and dad.

Specific organizations

He collected money for the Canadian Cancer Society.

but

Janice joined more than one club at the school.

Specific institutions

The loan is from the Royal Bank of Canada.

but

The loan is from one of the banks in town.

Specific bodies of water

My uncle fishes every summer on Lake Winnipeg.

but

My uncle spends every summer at the lake.

RULE 3

Capitalize days of the week, months of the year, and holidays. Do *not* capitalize the names of seasons.

The second Monday in October is Thanksgiving Day.

but

I cannot wait until spring.

RULE 4

Capitalize the names of all languages, nationalities, races, religions, deities, and sacred terms.

My friend who is Ethiopian speaks very little English.
The *Qur'an* is the sacred book of Islam.

RULE 5

In a title, capitalize the first word, the last word, and every other word *except* articles, prepositions, and coordinating conjunctions (*for, and, nor, but, or, yet,* and *so*—FANBOYS).

"Recognizing Subjects and Verbs" and "Revising and Editing" are chapters in the textbook *The Canadian Writer's Workplace.*

RULE 6

Capitalize the first word of a direct quotation.

The teacher said, "You have been chosen for the part."

but

"You have been chosen," she said, "for the part."

Note: for is not capitalized in the second sentence because it is not the beginning of the sentence being quoted.

RULE 7

Capitalize historical events, periods, and documents.

the Rebellion of 1837
the Great Depression
the *Canadian Charter of Rights and Freedoms*

RULE 8

Capitalize the words *north, south, east,* and *west* when they are used as places rather than as directions.

He comes from the East.

but

The farm is about 40 kilometres west of Weyburn.

RULE 9

Capitalize people's names.

Proper names

George Hendrickson

Professional titles when they immediately precede the person's proper name

Judge Samuelson	*but*	the judge
Professor Shapiro	*but*	the professor

- Do not capitalize a title if it follows the name:

George Shapiro, professor of English

Term for a relative (like *mother, sister, nephew, uncle*) when it is used in the place of the proper name

> I told Grandfather I would meet him later.

- Notice that terms for relatives are not capitalized if a pronoun, article, or adjective is used with the name.

> I told my grandfather I would meet him later.

RULE 10

Capitalize brand names.

> Band-Aid
>
> Kleenex

Band-Aid and *Kleenex* are product names and therefore are proper nouns.

Here is a summary of these rules:

Ten Rules for Capitalization
RULE 1: Capitalize the first word of every sentence.
RULE 2: Capitalize the names of specific things and places.
RULE 3: Capitalize days of the week, months of the year, and holidays. Do not capitalize the names of seasons.
RULE 4: Capitalize the names of all languages, nationalities, races, religions, deities, and sacred terms.
RULE 5: In a title, capitalize the first word, the last word, and every other word except articles, prepositions, and coordinating conjunctions (FANBOYS).
RULE 6: Capitalize the first word of a direct quotation.
RULE 7: Capitalize historical events, periods, and documents.
RULE 8: Capitalize the words *north, south, east,* and *west* when they are used as places rather than as directions.
RULE 9: Capitalize people's names.
RULE 10: Capitalize brand names.

Chapter Review Exercises

Practice 1 Capitalization

In the following sentences, capitalize wherever it is necessary. Check your answers against those in the Answer Key on page 465.

1. The italian student got a job in the school cafeteria.
2. Our train ride through the canadian rockies was fabulous.
3. The author often made references in his writing to names from the bible.
4. A student at the university of alberta was chosen for the national award.
5. My uncle's children always have a party on hallowe'en.
6. I met the president of bell canada last friday at a convention in winnipeg, manitoba.

7. The cobalt-60 cancer therapy unit was invented by a canadian, dr. donald green.
8. My niece said, "why don't you consider moving farther south if you hate the winter so much?"
9. The canadian auto workers voted not to go on strike over the new contract.
10. The book *women of the klondike* tells the story of the late-1890s gold rush in the north.

 Exercise 1 Capitalization

In the following sentences, capitalize wherever it is necessary and put into lower case any capital letters that are incorrect.

1. Some people think the Cabot trail on Cape Breton island is the most spectacular drive on the North American Continent.
2. I'm taking five courses right now, but math 101 is my favourite.
3. I love the Text called *Canadian Writer's workplace;* I've already read twenty of its thrity-two Chapters.
4. Morris C. Shumiatcher is a Lawyer and Civil Rights Spokesperson who graduated from the University Of Calgary.
5. George Orwell wrote the novel *nineteen eighty-four* about a Government that punishes its people for thinking certain thoughts.
6. Born in Mumbia, India, Writer Rohinton Mistry was raised in that City's Parsi Community.
7. The black honda accord and the white ford escape have collided at the Intersection of Chapel street and Bakersville avenue.
8. "I feel your pain," wrote rabbi Wittstein of Temple Israel of london to the muslim community, "And offer you whatever understanding, sympathy, and anger I possess…."
9. Roman Polanski won an oscar for best director in 2002, but was unable to receive the award in person because if he had entered the United States, he would have been arrested for statutory rape.
10. Socrates was a greek teacher who is considered one of the founders of western philosophy.

 Working Together: Designing Capitalization Tests

Work with a group of your classmates to make up an exam to test the other students' knowledge of capitalization. From any book, choose a paragraph that uses a variety of capitalization. Have one person from the group carefully write out or type the paragraph without any capitalization. Then make enough copies so a group or the entire class can take the test. Is your test a fair one? Is it too easy or too hard? Does it cover the material studied in this chapter?

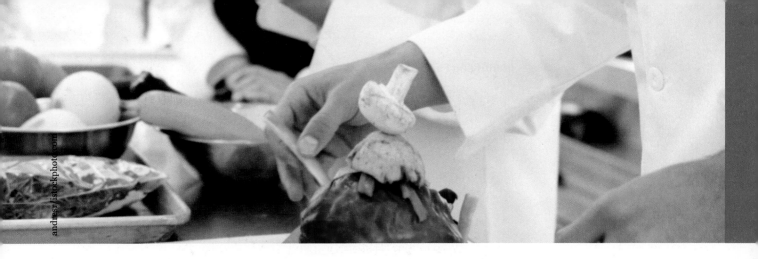

Chapter 13 **Unit I Review:
Using All You Have Learned**

In this chapter of review practices and exercises, you have the opportunity to test yourself on the material in Unit I. Revisit any point of grammar that you know you need to work on a little more. If, for example, you find that you haven't quite understood how to use a semicolon correctly, then it would be a good idea to revisit Chapter 5 ("Coordination and Subordination"), Chapter 7 ("Correcting Run-ons"), and Chapter 11 ("Punctuation"). If you can't find what you're looking for right away, consult the index at the back of the book.

Often we think that if we can already speak the language to the extent that most people seem to understand what we're saying, there is no need to learn to write perfectly. When we speak, especially on informal occasions (which is most of the time), we get away with making mistakes every day. We do not check the grammar of those to whom we speak, nor do they check ours. When someone says, "Lunch?" we know what he or she means, and we don't stop to think, "That wasn't a complete sentence." But when we write, especially in formal situations such as those we encounter in our professional lives, we cannot so easily get away with making the same types of errors. The extent to which we communicate properly will in part determine how far we go in meeting our professional goals.

Mastering a language is an ongoing process. And this textbook certainly doesn't cover everything there is to know about English. Nevertheless, it covers a great deal; you might want to keep it on your shelf as a reference tool even after your course is finished. That way, if ever you forget when you're supposed to use *whom* instead of *who*, or *that* instead of *which*, this book will be there to remind you.

Editing Sentences for Errors

In the following exercises, you will find all the types of grammatical and mechanical problems that you have studied so far:

Fragments	Unparallel structure	Incorrect capitalization
Run-ons	Incorrect punctuation	Misplaced and dangling
Incorrect pronouns	Subject-verb disagreement	modifiers

Practice 1 **Identifying Parts of Speech**

Read the following paragraphs taken from Rosemary Ellen Guiley's book *Dreamwork for the Soul*. Identify the part of speech (as specifically as you can) for each underlined word. Feel free to refer back to Chapter 1 ("Parts of Speech: Overview") for help. The index at the back of the textbook can help for easy reference. Check your answers against those in the Answer Key on page 465.

The first one has been done for you (see below).

(Carl G.) Jung's <u>dreams</u> ① were a <u>constant</u> ② source <u>of</u> ③ creativity <u>and</u> ④ inspiration to <u>him</u> ⑤. Dreams <u>inspired</u> ⑥ his study of archaeology and mythology, and later alchemy. <u>Throughout</u> ⑦ his life, as he developed <u>his</u> ⑧ ideas, Jung <u>was</u> ⑨ aided and guided by dreams. <u>When</u> ⑩ he searched for answers to questions, dreams <u>often</u> ⑪ led him in <u>the</u> ⑫ <u>right</u> ⑬ direction….

Three days before he died, Jung <u>had</u> ⑭ the last of his visionary dreams and a portent of his own <u>impending</u> ⑮ death. In the dream, he had <u>become</u> ⑯ whole. <u>A</u> ⑰ significant symbol was tree roots interlaced with gold, the alchemical <u>symbol</u> ⑱ of completion….

The story of Jung's life can be <u>properly</u> ⑲ understood <u>only</u> ⑳ from his inner experiences. The experiences of the <u>outer</u> ㉑ world were pale and thin by comparison <u>for</u> ㉒ him. <u>He</u> ㉓ said he <u>could</u> ㉔ understand himself only in the light of his inner <u>happenings</u>. ㉕

Answer: 1. *dreams:* common noun

 Practice 2 **Editing Sentences for Errors**

The following sentences contain various types of errors studied in Unit I. If you think a sentence is complete and correct, mark it with a *C.* If it has an error, correct it (you may need to add, delete, or change words, punctuation, and capitalization). There can be more than one correct answer for each sentence. Check your answers against those in the Answer Key on page 465. An example has been done for you.

> ***Incorrect:*** A group of Roma people who now live in Ireland.
> ***Correct:*** A group of Roma people now live in Ireland.
> *or*
> A group of Roma people, who now live in Ireland, make their living by repairing pots and pans.

1. Roma (also known as Gypsies or Romany Gypsies) now living in many countries of the world.

_____

_____

2. The international community of scientists agree that these Roma originally came from India thousands of years ago.

_____

_____

3. After the original Roma people left India they went to Persia there they divided into groups.

_____

_____

4. One branch of Roma went West to Europe the other group decided to go East.

_____

_____

5. In the middle ages (476–1453), some Roma people lived in a fertile area of Greece called little egypt.

_____

_____

6. Roma often found it hard to gain acceptance in many countries because of their wandering lifestyle.

_____

_____

7. Today Roma families may be found from Canada to Chile living much as his ancestors did thousands of years ago.

_____

_____

 Practice 3 Editing Sentences for Errors

The following sentences contain sentence errors studied in Unit I. If you think a sentence is complete and correct, mark it with a *C*. If it has an error, correct it. There can be more than one correct answer for each sentence. An example has been done for you. Check your answers against those in the Answer Key on page 465.

Incorrect: Science fiction writers have imagined magic rays that can destroy entire cities, but in recent years a magic ray in the form of laser beams have become scientific fact.

Correct: Science fiction writers have imagined magic rays that can destroy entire cities, but in recent years a magic ray in the form of laser beams has become scientific fact.

1. The laser beam a miracle of modern science already has many practical uses in today's world.

   _____

   _____

2. Laser beams are narrow, highly concentrated beams of light that burns brighter than the light of the sun.

   _____

   _____

3. Scientists have found many possible military uses for the laser, but they are hoping it can be converted into constructive uses.

   _____

   _____

4. John Polanyi, Canadian winner of the 1986 Nobel Prize for chemistry, conducted early experiments on the use of lasers.

   _____

   _____

5. The possibility of making a laser was first described in 1958 and two years later in California the first laser beam was created.

   _____

   _____

6. Since they are so precise, laser beams are used in medicine to help make a specific diagnosis and to perform operations such as repairing delicate retinas and the removal of cancerous tumours.

   _____

   _____

7. The future uses of the laser seems endless, and it is up to us to decide whether we want to use this invention for war or for peaceful purposes.

   _____

   _____

 Exercise 1   Editing Sentences for Errors

The following sentences contain sentence errors studied in Unit I. If a sentence has an error or errors, correct it. More than one correct answer is possible for each sentence. If you think a sentence is complete and correct, mark it with a *C*. An example has been done for you.

> ***Incorrect:*** Frostbite an injury to the skin and underlying tissues is a serious danger in very cold weather.
>
> ***Correct:*** Frostbite, an injury to the skin and underlying tissues, is a serious danger in very cold weather.
>
> (commas added around a phrase that interrupts the main idea)

1. A common threat to outdoor adventurers frostbite can strike anyone who is not adequately protected against the cold.

   _____

   _____

2. Risk factors are of three types exposure, faulty judgment, and underlying medical conditions.

   _____

   _____

3. Ice crystals in the skin possibly starting to form at −6°C.

   _____

   _____

4. Symptoms of frostbite includes: cold numbness and a feeling of clumsiness or heaviness in the affected part of the body.

   _____

   _____

5. The first thing to do is find a warm shelter and remove any wet clothing.

   _____

   _____

6. Prevention measures includes wearing proper clothing, educating yourself about weather conditions, and awareness of risk factors.

   _____

   _____

7. Frostbite injury which gets worse with time should be treated immediately.

   _____

   _____

 Exercise 2 Making Sentence Parts Work Together

In each of the following sentences, one part does not work with the rest of the sentence. Find the error and correct it. There may be more than one correct answer for each sentence.

1. Two Statistics Canada studies, which have been reported recently on the CBC television network, links stress and obesity now with health problems later in life.

   _____

   _____

2. Suffering from stress and obesity, the researchers found that Canadians will probably suffer major health problems as soon as six years later.

   _____

   _____

3. People who suffer from stress and obesity become a perfect candidate for health problems such as arthritis and rheumatism, chronic bronchitis or emphysema, and stomach or intestinal ulcers.

   _____

   _____

4. One study shows that for men, diseases also include heart disease, and for a woman, asthma and migraine.

   _____

   _____

5. According to one of the studies, stress in men appeared to be worse where economic issues are concerned: job loss, demotions and taking pay cuts, for example.

   _____

   _____

6. An obese adult's chance of suffering from arthritis is 60 percent higher than an adult who is not obese.

   _____

   _____

7. They say stress goes down with age and up in low-income people.

   _____

   _____

Editing Paragraphs for Errors

 Exercise 3 Making Sentence Parts Work Together

Read the following paragraph, looking for errors in agreement, for lack of parallel structure, and for misplaced or dangling modifiers. Rewrite a corrected version. More than one correct answer is possible.

Cowboys became important in the United States after the American Civil War who lived on large ranches in Texas, Montana, and other western states. Canada, too, had its cowboys working on ranches on the prairies. One of the traditional names for cowboys are "cowpokes" although they prefer to be called "cowhands." The equipment for cowboys came into use because of his many practical needs. The wide-brimmed cowboy hat served as a bucket to hold water, as a sort of whip to drive cattle, and waving to other cowboys a few hills away. Cowboys began to wear tight trousers because they did not want loose pants to catch in bushes as they chased cattle. The rope is a cowboy's most important tool since they use it to catch cattle, pull wagons, tie up equipment, and even killing snakes. The famous roundup, which takes place twice a year, are important because cattle are separated, classified, and selected for market. When cowboys get together for such a roundup, they often hold a rodeo as a celebration. Rodeos give cowboys opportunities to compete in riding bareback, wrestling steer, and to rope calves. The Calgary Stampede is the modern result of these rodeos.

 Exercise 4 Editing Paragraphs for Errors

Correct all the punctuation and grammatical errors in the following paragraph. More than one correct answer is possible.

Once upon a time whenever I tried to make my writing interesting and imaginative with all sorts of similes and metaphors and colourful language I forgot about my grammar and spelling my essays were full of sentence fragments comma splices and run-ons moreover my syntax was always scrambled even I had trouble figuring out what I had intended to say originally although I could tell that I had started with brilliant ideas help has finally arrived however since I have done all the exercises in my grammar book I now have perfect command of English grammar whereas one time I bit my nails when I handed in an assignment I worry no more no longer do I need to worry about essays being handed back bleeding to death after being savaged by some mean English teacher wielding his or her red pen no longer will my sleep be curtailed by hours of tedious rewrites moreover from now on I'm expecting straight As all the way.

 Exercise 5 Editing Paragraphs for Errors

Correct all the punctuation, capitalization, and grammatical errors in the following paragraphs. More than one correct answer is possible.

Sleep is one of those things you never think about. As long as you're getting your full forty winks at night. As soon as a bout of insomnia hits though sleep is the only thing on your mind. The ancient greeks had a god of sleep called hypnos who could appear as a bird, child, or friendly warrior those images don't suggest sleep to modern people though we prefer fields of sheep and mr. sandman.

Since the greeks scientists have made much progress in unravelling the secrets of sleep but many mysteries remain. They can't explain for example exactly how we fall asleep. Or wake up. Or what dreams are. However they know a lot about insomnia and other sleep disorder. Such as narcolepsy, sudden attacks of deep sleep, sleep apnea (the sleeper stops breathing for several seconds at a time) and, sleepwalking. Which are more amusing to hear about than to experience.

Millions of people suffer from insomnia either chronically, or from time to time. They will try anything to break the curse and science and folklore offers them a carload of choices everything from warm milk and lavender sachets to sleeping pills and sleep clinics. Not that any of these things help the true insomniac of course. And, how maddening it must be for someone who hasnt slept in weeks to come across a bus passenger fast asleep sitting up. Surrounded by strangers. These innocents are like people who stay skinny without having to diet.

Working Together: Remembering Your Canadian Trip

Work with a group of your classmates. With the other students in your group, discuss your favourite Canadian trips. You might recall a particular landmark such as the Cabot Trail in Cape Breton, Nova Scotia (below, left) or Confederation Bridge (the world's longest bridge over icy waters) joining the provinces of P.E.I. and New Brunswick (below, right). Talk about what your impressions were—what moved you and why? Then take about fifteen minutes to write a paragraph about it.

Paul McKinnon/Shutterstock

V. J. Matthew/Shutterstock.com

Once your paragraph is finished, trade papers with someone else. Check the other student's paragraph for fragments, run-ons, lack of parallel structure, misplaced and dangling modifiers, and errors with pronouns, subject-verb agreement, punctuation, capitalization, and so on. When you are finished, hand it back and discuss the grammatical points mentioned above (and the content if you wish to do so).

Unit II The Reading-Writing Connection

Christopher Futcher/istockphoto.com

Chapter 14 **Understanding What You Read**

It's morning at work. Your boss has put an article on your desk. The article is on some new theory about how to save money in your area of your industry. Your boss asks you to write him a response to this article either proposing to adopt the idea or not and then adds, "By the way, I want this response on my desk before you go home today." What kinds of skills are going to be required to get this job done? Imagine how much information your boss will have about you before you leave today on which to base any future decision to promote you or give you a raise or … not.

Writing is very revealing. It tells the reader if you can spell or not. It gives the reader an idea of how rich your vocabulary is. It demonstrates your command of grammar and your knowledge of punctuation. It reveals whether or not you've got an effective style that goes beyond the mechanics of good writing. But it also suggests whether you understand what you are reading. You will sometimes be required, after all, to write in response to reading. So if you do not have a particularly good grasp of what you have read, your writing will unveil the truth about this, too.

You Are Not Alone

Reading skills have suffered right across the country. Good reading skills, like anything else, come with practice. The electronic age has made it difficult to read books, for example, as much as previous generations were accustomed to doing. There are exceptions, of course. Every so often, a student will be found reading a novel between classes instead of testing or talking on her cellphone. But this is rare. And it's more rare than it's ever been before simply because we have more distractions literally at our fingertips.

We have trouble keeping up with what we have to read, whether it's for homework or for work. But when it comes to our spare time, we'd rather be distracted by the Internet or a movie (or a movie on the Internet) than become engaged in a good book. Reading a book takes too long, or it's not as exciting, or it's just not viewed as the valuable exercise it once proved to be. There's also the possibility that people simply don't know what they're missing. When they're told that reading fiction can teach them just as much about human nature, if not more than any class they can take, it's a little hard to believe until they do it.

Another reason people don't read as much as they used to is that they may not be reading effectively. Reading is an active skill that, for some, requires strategies to help them read more effectively. Here are some reading strategies that can help you understand what you read.

Reading Strategies

1. Previewing
    a. Reading an introduction
    b. Titles (and subtitles, headings, and subheadings)
    c. First and last paragraphs
    d. Information in boxes, charts, captions, etc.

2. Taking notes, annotating, and/or highlighting
3. Reading and answering questions that follow the reading
4. Rereading
5. Journalling
    a. What struck you forcefully?
    b. Writing down questions about what you don't understand

6. Reading topic sentences
7. Looking up words you don't understand
8. Looking up references online that you don't understand

1. Previewing

a. Reading an Introduction

Not every reading has an introduction, but if you look at the major readings in this book, in Unit V you'll see what can best be described as an introduction just before the beginning of every single reading. This introduction is not actually part of the reading. It is not written by the author of the reading, but rather the author of the book.

Excuses, Excuses

Adrian Lee

Student excuses are getting more sophisticated, but so are the investigative tactics of teachers. Adrian Lee is the digital editor of *Maclean's* magazine; he also prides himself on being its resident hip hop expert. In this article, Lee explores the world of the excuses used today and the proof students might need to back them up.

Each introduction in Unit V (like the one above) is meant to give the reader some background on the author of the reading and a glimpse into its meaning without giving too much away. The idea is to lure the reader into reading the article. This introduction can be viewed as a kind of abstract, which can help you understand the reading in general. The author of the book is trying to maximize the reader's experience so that you might not only understand the reading more easily, but also enjoy it more than you would if there were no introduction at all. This is why some teachers are baffled when they hear students claim that they didn't understand the reading that was assigned, but they also chose not to read the introduction or do other things that the preview section of these strategies suggests.

b. Titles (and Subtitles, Headings, and Subheadings)

Have you ever read a newspaper? Chances are you haven't read every word of every story from page 1 to the end. If you did do this every day, there would be no time for anything else.

What most people do is read the story titles and/or the headings. The secondary titles, or kickers—set above the headline—break up the text to make it easier to read the overall piece. They also give small hints as to what is to come, and in this way, hopefully, lure you further into the story in case you were thinking of not going on.

Look up words in the title that you don't understand. With respect to a story called "Transparent Silhouette" on page 372 in Chapter 32, most readers are likely to know what *transparent* means. But why would someone go on to read the story without knowing what *silhouette* means also? There's no need to locate a library or even a hard-cover dictionary. Just look up *silhouette* online, and one of your first hits is likely to be a definition of the word, something like "A silhouette is an image of a person." Now you know the title is suggesting a "see-through image of a person." What does this conjure up in your head? A ghost perhaps? Now you might be starting to get curious as to what the story is about.

Titles are extremely important. Authors and editors usually devote a great deal of time to the formulation of good titles. Titles are used, after all, to sell newspapers and magazines, books, movie tickets, etc. How often have you heard someone say they bought the book because they simply liked the title? This is very often the case. It is also true of professors. If a professor has two essays to read next, and one of them is entitled "Love" while the other is entitled "The Incompatibility of Love and Marriage," which one is the professor likely to read first? Why? The second title is clearly more interesting. The student who wrote it took the time to come up with something more specific and thought-provoking. And why is this particular title more thought-provoking? Well, it suggests that the thesis is original, and not common or weak. The thesis is not going to be about the pros and cons of love, whatever love means. It's going to be a controversial and unique claim that probably goes against social norms. And all of that comes from just a title. So if someone goes to the effort of coming up with a good title, the least a reader can do is try to understand what the title means before starting to read the reading.

c. First and Last Paragraphs

You might have read an entire reading already. Then, later, you see this idea of reading the first and last paragraphs as a reading strategy to help you to understand the reading better. You might say to yourself, "But I've already read it. There's no reason for me to read any part of it again." This is not necessarily true. In fact, it is often the first and last parts of an article that are the most important of all. If the first paragraph is written well, it contains a clearly expressed thesis statement. If the last paragraph is well written, it restates the thesis but in different words. By the time you read both the first and last paragraph in quick succession, it might be crystal clear to you what the author is trying to say, even if the middle of the article did not make it clear at all.

The first and last paragraphs of a reading can be compared to the opening and closing scenes of a movie. Some people are so insistent about the importance of these scenes that if they miss the opening scene for whatever reason, they would rather not see the movie at all. One method of analyzing art requires a comparison and contrast of the first and last parts of any work, such as an essay or movie. The method suggests that once the similarities and differences between the first and last parts are determined, the person doing the analysis is able to arrive at the meaning of the piece, whatever it is. If this is true, it is easier to see why some people would prefer not to see the movie at all if they miss the opening scene.

This is also why reading the first and last paragraphs of the article in front of you can be such a good idea! The method described above for analyzing a work of art suggests that one can actually determine the meaning of the work after simply reading the first and last paragraphs, so think of how valuable this activity is as a previewing exercise whose purpose is to help the reader understand what he or she is about to read.

d. Information in Boxes, Charts, Captions, etc.

Boxes can include anything the writer thinks the reader might be interested in seeing more details on. For example, if the writer mentions a survey whose results are astonishing, the reader might be interested in seeing how the survey questions were worded or the breakdown of the results, etc. A box or sidebar may provide further information on something referred to in the text, and at the same time serves to break up the text on the page so that the reader's eyes are diverted and given a break from the text. Any visual aid is aimed at stimulating the reader's senses so that whatever is being read does not become so overwhelming that the reader doesn't finish the piece. Look, for example, at the following illustration taken from page 219 in Chapter 20: "The Essay."

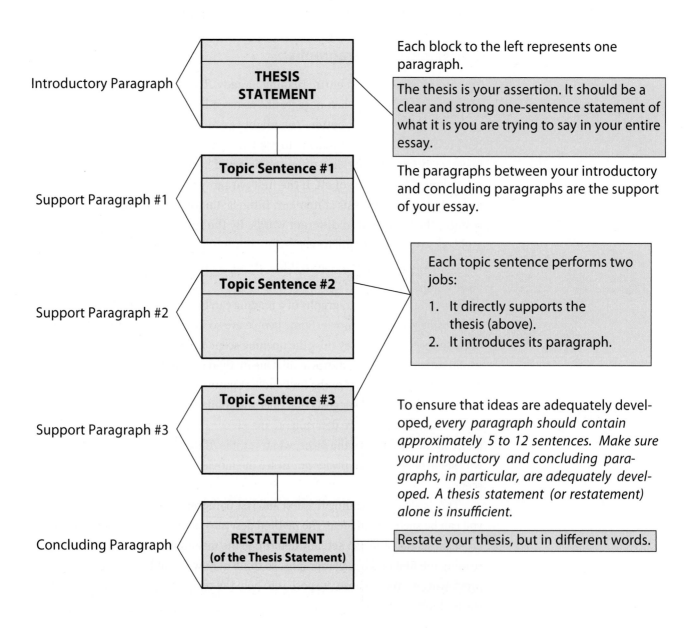

Introductory Paragraph

THESIS STATEMENT

Each block to the left represents one paragraph.

The thesis is your assertion. It should be a clear and strong one-sentence statement of what it is you are trying to say in your entire essay.

Support Paragraph #1

Topic Sentence #1

The paragraphs between your introductory and concluding paragraphs are the support of your essay.

Support Paragraph #2

Topic Sentence #2

Each topic sentence performs two jobs:

1. It directly supports the thesis (above).
2. It introduces its paragraph.

Support Paragraph #3

Topic Sentence #3

To ensure that ideas are adequately developed, *every paragraph should contain approximately 5 to 12 sentences. Make sure your introductory and concluding paragraphs, in particular, are adequately developed. A thesis statement (or restatement) alone is insufficient.*

Concluding Paragraph

RESTATEMENT (of the Thesis Statement)

Restate your thesis, but in different words.

Regardless of the author's or editor's motivation for including boxed information, it can be an excellent way of improving your understanding of the reading. Examine its contents before proceeding to read the article. See if it helps. It may complicate things further, but it may not.

Like the information in boxes, visual elements, charts, and captions can have dramatic effects on the reader. Graphics and photographs are less likely to have "copy," or to use words, so they will add an image to the words already provided in the text. The visual content will either enhance or weaken what the words in the text have already conjured up in the mind of the reader. Sometimes the visual content works. Sometimes the article is better off without it. But it almost always provokes a reaction from the reader. Often the visual content has an emotional effect that is not always the objective of words. But any appeal to the reader's emotions can be quite powerful, which is why most newspapers and television stations have a policy of not showing pictures that are too graphic because of the undesired effects among their readers or viewers. They are fully aware that although visual content can attract temporary attention, it can also result in loss of credibility and, in turn, long-term financial loss.

2. Taking Notes, Annotating, and/or Highlighting

These activities are most often done when students go to class and/or study for exams. They help students understand what they've read or heard. They can also help if you're reading an article for the first time.

Taking notes: The actual act of taking notes, for example, is also a memory technique. Just by quoting the speaker (such as a professor during a lecture) or by paraphrasing something, the student forces himself or herself to focus on something, if only for a moment—long enough to save into memory a fact or idea that will help later on.

Annotating: Annotating simply means explaining or commenting on something. It may be someone else's idea, or it may be your own. Regardless, it is meant to help you later on when you have to study something for an exam or do an assignment that pertains to this article you're annotating now. Annotations are most often written in the margin of the text, or they can be written separately in class notes. It doesn't matter where you make notes. This also applies to annotating for the sake of making it easier to understand a reading. Often, a professor will say something important in introducing an article that has been assigned for reading. Adding an annotation in a strategic location in the reading can be very helpful later on when you're reading the article and trying to gain a better understanding of it.

Highlighting: Highlighting is very popular among students. It helps to point out the important points in a reading, whether their importance has been determined by a professor or by you. Highlighting can be even more helpful if you've been asked to respond to a reading (see the introduction on p. 156), or even if you've been asked to summarize an article or part of one for the sake of identifying the main points that you will be expected to include in your summary.

3. Reading and Answering Questions That Follow the Reading

Look at the main readings in Unit V of this textbook. After every reading, there are four sections of questions: Comprehension Questions, Questions about Form, Questions for Discussion, and Writing Ideas. Without intending to answer these questions, the simple act of reading them can give the reader a better idea of what the reading is about and what it means. And, of course, if you are expected to answer any of these questions eventually, reading them before reading the article can help you know what to look for when you're reading so that you can more easily answer them later. In fact, reading the questions first (if questions are available) can help you with deciding what to highlight or how to annotate while you're reading. After you've done the reading at least once, go ahead and try to answer the questions. This can only help you understand the reading more deeply.

4. Rereading

The first thing that some students might say when this reading comprehension strategy is mentioned is, "What? I hardly have time to read at all, and you want me to read this thing twice?" The problem with this answer is that it suggests that the main objective here might not be optimum learning, but maybe "enough" learning (e.g., to pass a pop quiz). Speed reading is not a skill that most people possess. Many people have to read things more than once to gain a good understanding of anything. This is particularly true if the article is not very well written. If the main objective is optimum learning, then time must be devoted to the process. The more time you devote to the process, whether it's reading, practising, applying, or all three, the better. The adage of "no pain, no gain" applies here as it does to most things that are worthwhile in life.

5. Journalling

a. What struck you forcefully? b. What do you not understand?

Many students will ask their professors, "Do you want me to write anything after I read the assigned reading?" One suggestion is to engage in a kind of journalling after the reading is done. This is a great way to dialogue with the material and with yourself on the subject of the reading. It's also a great way to remember the reading for later assignments.

6. Reading Topic Sentences

The first sentence is supposed to be the topic sentence of a paragraph, if the paragraph is written well. And the topic sentence is charged with two, and maybe three, functions: to introduce the paragraph and to inform you of what the writer will be trying to explain, and if it's written really well, to directly support the thesis of the entire piece as well. In any event, by reading just the topic sentences, you're already getting a good glimpse of the argument the author is trying to develop. Without getting lost in some of the details, just reading the skeletal structure of the argument first might help you understand it better, especially when you read the article in full.

7. Looking Up Words You Don't Understand

When I ask my students if anyone has the time, virtually every student in the room takes out his or her cellphone—unless, of course, it's already on the desk—and tells me the time from the clock on the phone. But when I ask someone to find the definition of a word we've come across in class, no one knows what to do.

"Hasn't anyone thought of looking up the word on Google?" I ask. "Why is it so obvious that you need your phone to tell the time, but you don't even think of the smartphone when it comes to discovering what a word means?" I understand that few people want to carry a hard-copy dictionary around all the time, but considering that most people already carry a smartphone, why not use it to look up the definitions of words to gain a better understanding of a reading and for spelling, etc.?

Gary Lipschutz, lead author of *The Canadian Writer's Workplace*

8. Looking Up References Online That You Don't Understand

Gary Lamphier, author of the reading "The Economic Cost of Depression" in Unit V, refers to a number of people by name. Among them are Winston Churchill, Eric Clapton, Woody Allen, and Ray Charles. If you don't know who these people are, it would no doubt enrich your understanding of the reading if you looked up one or several of them on the Internet.

 Exercise 1   Reading Strategies

Find an article in a newspaper or magazine that you think you actually might not enjoy. Use at least three reading strategies from this chapter to help you understand this article by the time you read it from beginning to end. Write a paragraph on the impact you believe the reading strategies have made on your reading experience.

Working Together: The Best Way to Learn Is to Teach

Assemble a group of four or five and ask every member to find a short article (no more than a couple of magazine pages) that she or he thinks will be of interest to the rest of the group. Ask each person to read his or her own selection to the point where it can be explained to the rest of the group. Then discuss the reading strategies you've used from this chapter that helped you to read the article more easily and effectively. As a group, discuss your experiences with these strategies.

Chapter 15 **Paraphrasing and Summarizing**

Many companies assign reading to their employees, much like instructors do to their students. At a Monday morning staff meeting, for example, each employee might be expected to summarize a booklet, manual, catalogue, or document for the benefit of everyone. If you are that employee, you might also be expected to produce a written summary for everyone who isn't at the meeting.

The ability to **paraphrase and summarize** well is perhaps one of the most useful skills you will learn. Paraphrasing and summarizing are techniques for rewriting something you have read; they require putting in your own words the main idea or ideas of the original text. They are especially useful techniques when studying for tests and exams and writing research essays because they develop and demonstrate your understanding of the material you have read. When writing a research assignment, the techniques of paraphrasing and summarizing are important in making a coherent document out of your various sources. Translating ideas and information into your own words also helps you remember them better because in order to summarize something you have read, you must have a complete understanding of it. The better you understand something, the less likely you are to forget it.

Paraphrasing

 DEFINITION

Paraphrasing is the process of putting another writer's work into your own words. A paraphrase can be as long as or even longer than the original.

An effective paraphrase follows not only the line of reasoning in the original source, but also the sequence of ideas or evidence. You paraphrase in an essay when it is important that every idea of the original work be conveyed to your reader. But, like summarizing, paraphrasing should be done in your own words. Paraphrasing is typically done for shorter passages that are about a paragraph or two in length. Don't worry, your instructor won't ask you to paraphrase a whole book!

Now look at an example to see how a successful paraphrase differs from an unsuccessful one. The sample paragraph below is followed by examples of both unacceptable and acceptable paraphrases.

Original:

"Reality-based" TV programs, which have become very popular recently, appear to capture spontaneous events on film. However, most viewers are not aware that much of the action that transpires on these programs is staged. People who appear on these shows are often selected because producers think they will appeal to the audience, and directors often script important pieces of dialogue at critical moments during production. Therefore, relationships that develop between participants on these shows are often as contrived as those between characters on a TV sitcom or a soap opera.

Unacceptable Paraphrase:

"Reality-based" TV shows, which <u>have become popular recently</u>, seem to depict <u>spontaneous events on film</u>. Most people, however, do not know that a lot of the action that takes place <u>on these programs is staged</u>. The people on shows like these <u>are often selected because the producers</u> believe they will appeal to viewers, and directors frequently write <u>important pieces of dialogue at crucial moments</u> during the filming of the show. <u>Therefore, relationships that develop</u> are frequently as phony as those between personalities on TV sitcoms or soap operas.

This is an unsuccessful paraphrase because the overall structure and the phrasing of the underlined passages are almost identical to the original.

Acceptable Paraphrase:

The popularity of "reality-based" TV shows is founded on the belief that live events are being filmed, but many viewers do not know that much of what they see is made purposely dramatic. Producers of these shows often choose participants because they believe viewers will find them attractive, and the shows' directors often have them acting from scripts to heighten the drama. Thus, participants create relationships that are no more real than those we see on other TV shows, such as sitcoms or soap operas.

This passage is an example of good paraphrasing. The writer has taken the main idea of the original paragraph and restated it using his or her own words. All of the original details and examples appear, but they have been reworded and the sentences restructured.

Writing a Successful Paraphrase

1. **Read the passage and define all unfamiliar or technical terms.**
   Write all unfamiliar terms and their definitions on a separate sheet of paper.

2. **Reread the passage again, paying closer attention to the content and the order in which the ideas develop.** Make sure you have a clear understanding of the passage you are reading before you begin paraphrasing it.

3. **Begin converting the language of the passage into your own words, sentence by sentence.** Look for synonyms of words used in the passage. Alter sentence structure and vocabulary until you are conveying the original ideas in your own voice. If the original uses the first person (*I*), change it to the third person (*he* or *she*).

4. **Write out your paraphrase in full sentences of your own.** Remember not to use more than three words at a time from the original.

5. **Edit for spelling and grammar.**

 Exercise 1 Writing Paraphrases

Use your own words or phrases to express the following. A wide range of correct answers exists for each item.

1. Utterly

_____

2. Every cloud has a silver lining.

_____

3. No pain, no gain.

_____

4. He's like a wolf in sheep's clothing.

_____

5. The apple doesn't fall far from the tree.

_____

 Exercise 2 Paraphrasing a Paragraph

The following passage was excerpted from an article entitled "A Dead End for Humanity," by Wade Davis. Write a paraphrase of this paragraph. The passage contains seventy-nine words, so your paraphrase should be about the same length.

> Of the 6000 languages spoken today, fully half are not being taught to children. Effectively, these languages are already dead. By the end of the twenty-first century, linguistic diversity may be reduced to as few as 500 languages. A language, of course, is not simply vocabulary and grammar; it is a flash of the human spirit, the vehicle by which the soul of a culture comes into the material realm. Each language represents a unique intellectual and spiritual achievement.
>
> *Globe and Mail* (December 28, 2000)

Excerpt from: Wade Davis, "A Dead End for Humanity," *The Globe and Mail* (28 December 2000). Reproduced by permission of the author.

Summarizing

We practise summarizing all the time in our day-to-day lives. When telling friends about a movie, you don't repeat the story or dialogue from beginning to end. Instead, you relate the main points in the plot, or things about the movie that captured your interest.

A summary states the main idea of a passage. The purpose of a summary is to shorten the original piece of writing, providing only important information and eliminating nonessential points. A summary allows the reader to understand the main facts and ideas in the original without reading the entire passage. A summary should be no more than one-third the length of the original passage. The words you use should be your own. To avoid charges of plagiarism, you should not use more than three words at a time from the original. (Plagiarism is discussed in more detail later in this chapter.)

Take a look at this example of a summary. The following passage is taken from a longer piece entitled "Internet Use Continues to Rise" from *The Daily*, published by Statistics Canada on October 28, 2013. Immediately following this excerpt is a summary about a third the length of the original.

> In 2012, 83% of Canadians aged 16 or over used the Internet for personal use from any location, compared with 80% in 2010.
>
> The rise in Canadians using the Internet can be partially attributed to increased use by those who are 65 or older. Internet use by Canadians in this demographic rose from 40% in 2010 to 48% in 2012.
>
> Provincially, the lowest levels of Internet use were found in Newfoundland and Labrador as well as New Brunswick, both at 77%. British Columbia, as in 2010, had the highest proportion of Internet users at 87%, followed by Alberta at 85%.
>
> The census metropolitan areas with the highest rates of Internet use were Kelowna (93%), Regina (90%), and Victoria (90%). Other major metropolitan areas such as Calgary (89%) Vancouver (88%), Toronto (88%) and Montréal (84%) all had rates of Internet use above the national average.
>
> Among individuals living in census metropolitan areas or census agglomerations, 85% used the Internet compared with 75% of those living outside of these areas.*
>
> (approx. 168 words)

Acceptable Summary:

A survey shows that 83% of Canadians over 16 used the Internet in 2012. Newfoundland and New Brunswick are provinces with the lowest levels of usage, while British Columbia and Alberta had the highest. Major cities such as Kelowna

*Statistics Canada, Individual Internet use and e-commerce, 2012. *The Daily*. October 28, 2013. http://www.statcan.gc.ca/daily-quotidien/131028/dq131028a-eng.htm

(93%) and Regina (90%) showed the most usage, while centres outside of large metropolitan areas showed 75%.

(56 words)

Tips on Writing a Successful Summary

1. **Read the passage and identify the topic sentence and controlling idea.** Underline the sentence that you think best expresses the main point of the passage. Rewrite this sentence in your own words.
2. **Identify and eliminate minor supporting ideas.** Specific facts or examples may be important in developing a main idea, but they are not to be included in a summary.
3. **Write out the major supporting details in full sentences in your own words.** Use as few words as possible, and remember not to use more than three words at a time from the original.
4. **Count the words.** Make sure the total is no more than one-third of the original.
5. **Reread your summary.** Make sure that the meaning of the passage is conveyed clearly and that your sentences work together.
6. **Edit for spelling and grammar.**

 Exercise 3 Writing Summaries

Find single words to replace the following phrases. (There can be more than one correct answer in each case.)

1. perform an analysis of _____
2. create a reduction in _____
3. engage in the preparation of _____
4. give consideration to _____
5. is dependent on _____

 Exercise 4 Summarizing a Paragraph

Summarize the following passage, reducing it to approximately one-third of its original length of 216 words.

Canadian society in the twenty-first century is very different from that of early Canadians, and not just because we have smartphones and tablets. Two hundred years ago, people lived half as long as they do today, and families had twice as many children. In general, all Canadians are living longer, which means not only is our working life extended, but we can expect to retire from work and live another fifteen to twenty years to enjoy the fruits of our labours. Canadians born in 1700 had an average life expectancy of thirty to thirty-five years due to poor diet, disease, and accidents. By 1831, four generations had passed, and there had been a slight improvement in life expectancy, with males expecting to live to age 40 and females to 42. During the next four generations, major medical breakthroughs and public health education eliminated a number of infectious diseases and reduced infant mortality, so that Canadians' life spans were almost double what they were a little more than a century previously. But while Canadians can expect a long and healthy life, with many living well into their seventies or eighties, the average life span will not increase indefinitely. While we can expect to live longer than the Canadians of the 1700s, we can't expect to live forever.

 Exercise 5   Summarizing an Article

Summarize the following article, entitled "The Credibility Code," published in *24 Hours Toronto* on April 15, 2013. The final product should be approximately one-third the length of the original. The original is approximately 750 words, so the summary should be approximately 250.

The Credibility Code

A picture is worth a thousand words. It's an old adage, yet for today's professionals, it holds critical new realities, says Cara Hale Alter, author of *The Credibility Code: How to Project Confidence and Competence When It Matters Most* (Meritus, 2012).

A weak economy, along with technology and globalization, has professionals at every level competing at a breakneck pace. In face-to-face interactions, "You have to project confidence and credibility in an instant," declares Alter.

"Business moves at lightning speed, and people make their minds up about you in seconds. Your credentials may get you in the door, but you still have to embody your credibility in the moment."

So what does credibility look like, really? Drawing on two decades of research, Alter identifies 25 specific visual and auditory cues—explicit "codes of conduct" for posture, gestures, vocal skills, and eye contact—that affect the perception of credibility. And unlike countless other cues, such as gender, age, or physical features, these 25 cues are "within your active control," says Alter.

To get started, she recommends trying these five:

1. **Keep your head level.**

   In the dog world, renowned trainer Cesar Millan has exceptional "executive presence." Dogs recognize his alpha status by the way he carries himself.

   In the business world, one of the best ways to project such presence is to keep your head level when speaking—no raising or dropping your chin, which can appear aggressive or submissive. The power of this one skill—literally being levelheaded—can be transformative.

   Practice Tip: Lengthen your spine and level your head. Now, moving only your head, like a camera on a tripod, scan your environment while keeping your torso still. Stillness is an authoritative behaviour, so try not to let your shoulders twist with the movement of your head.

2. **Keep your hands in the gesture box.**

   In poker parlance, a "tell" is a subtle signal revealing the strength or weakness of a player's hand. Similarly, in meetings or presentations, your gestures alone can be telling to others.

The most effective hand gestures happen inside the "gesture box"—no higher than your sternum, no lower than your hips, and no wider than your shoulders. The sweet spot is your navel, where gestures tend to look the most natural.

Practice Tip: A common tell of self-consciousness is when your mouth is engaged but your body language isn't. To appear comfortable, get your hands involved immediately, reaching out to your listeners with interactive gestures. In short, if your mouth is moving … so are your gestures.

3. Speak with optimal volume.

If you're a Seinfeld fan, you surely remember the infamous "low talker." Likewise, in business settings a common problem with volume is speaking too softly or dropping volume at the end of sentences. The good news is that volume is the easiest vocal skill to adjust.

First, however, you must know the difference between adequate volume and optimal volume. Most people err on the side of merely adequate. If you want to be a powerful voice, speak with a powerful voice.

Practice Tip: Your diaphragm, the small muscle separating your chest and abdominal cavity, is your engine for volume. Strengthen this muscle with five minutes of isolated exercises a day. One such exercise: Say the days of the week in a single breath, drawing out the vowels to prevent your diaphragm from resting between words. Later, move on to the months of the year.

4. Hold eye contact for three to five seconds.

"Eye contact is the best accessory," says writer Takayuki Ikkaku. It is also a key indicator of confidence and credibility. Still, there is a difference between making eye contact and holding eye contact. Duration is critical, and in the Western world, holding eye contact for three to five seconds is considered optimal.

Practice Tip: As you converse with co-workers, try speaking one phrase to one person. Then, when you reach a natural pause, speak the next phrase to someone else. Continue in this way, letting the structure of your sentences guide your rhythm. You may look away momentarily, but keep your eyes on the horizon—no looking up or down—and each time you come back, hold eye contact for three to five seconds.

5. Listen actively.

Your credibility can be won or lost when you're simply listening. Do you look bored or disconnected—or respectfully engaged?

Attentive listening means you're an active partner. It's not enough to pay attention; you have to look like you're paying attention. Keep your posture open, your head up, and your navel pointing toward the speaker.

Practice Tip: At your next meeting, imagine that a co-worker is taking notes about your behaviour. What cues are you displaying? Are you following the conversation with your eyes and nose aimed at the speaker? Is your body language open and energized? And are you reacting to others with nonverbal signals that say you're listening?

Source: "The Credibility Code," *24 Hours Toronto* e-edition (15 April 2013). Reproduced by permission of Sun Media Corporation.

Acknowledging the Author (or Attribution)

When paraphrasing or summarizing, even if you are not required to document your sources, it is most often necessary to acknowledge the rightful author or source of the ideas you are expressing. (For times when you do have to document sources, see Chapter 24: "Documentation.") It's easy to do so right in the text. Here is an example acknowledging the author of a reading in Unit V entitled "How to Get Happily Married": *According to Julia McKinnell, the experts say you shouldn't get married in your twenties if you want your marriage to last.* These are not the original words of the author, but it's still the author's idea, and it must be attributed to her when you discuss it in your writing. Along with paraphrasing and summarizing properly, acknowledging other authors appropriately is yet another way to avoid being accused of plagiarism.

Plagiarism: A Serious Offence

Students who write unacceptable paraphrases can be accused of plagiarism. Plagiarism is a form of intellectual theft. It occurs when one person uses the ideas or words of another person *without giving credit to the original source or author*. You can avoid plagiarism by ensuring that credit for work other than your own is cited. (See Chapter 24: "Documentation.") When you paraphrase a passage, be sure to inform your reader about who the original author is and where the original work appeared.

Plagiarism in a school environment often results in a mark of zero on an assignment. If it is a major assignment, one case of plagiarism can result in the overall failure of a course. Plagiarism is not only contrary to school policy (because it is always a clear violation of academic honesty and integrity), but it is also against the law. High-ranking officials have been known to lose their jobs and their reputations because of plagiarism. If you are not sure about how to avoid being accused of plagiarism, ask your professor for advice.

Avoid Unintentional Plagiarism

With so much information at our fingertips today, there may be a tendency and, perhaps, an irresistible temptation to use what is in front of us (such as text on a website) for our papers without even realizing that we might be opening ourselves up to charges of plagiarism. Many instructors consider as few as three consecutive words that are lifted from someone else's text to be plagiarism if these words are not in quotation marks and attributed to their original author. (For a discussion of how to quote properly, See Chapter 16: "Quoting.")

So if you are paraphrasing or summarizing and you want to avoid the plagiarism trap, here is a trick of the trade: read the text closely enough that you understand it thoroughly. Then close the book or the window on the computer (or reduce it so that you cannot see it for now). Write what you remember, or as much as you think you need for the purpose of your paper. Then go back to the original if necessary to check for accuracy. You also might want to check to make sure you haven't, by accident, ended up with phrases three words or longer that are in the original. If you have, change the wording of these phrases. If the original is relatively long, do this one paragraph at a time. In this way, not only will you protect yourself from accusations of intellectual theft, but you will also find yourself absorbing the reading material more efficiently. Developing this good work habit can lead to all sorts of rewards when doing assignments that involve reading and writing.

Of course, if you are writing a research paper, whether it be a review of literature, a report, or an academic essay, you will probably be expected to document your sources. The extent of the documentation required for a particular paper is something that will be determined by your professor. (For more information, see Chapter 23: "The Research Paper," and Chapter 24: "Documentation.")

Analyzing and Critiquing

Paraphrasing and summarizing are useful skills, not just for their own sake but because they are a necessary part of more advanced responses to texts. Eventually, your professor will ask you not only to repeat what someone else has already written, but to agree or disagree and explain the reasons why.

In the major readings unit (Unit V), each reading is followed by several questions, classified into four groups. The first group, "Comprehension Questions," requires some paraphrasing and summarizing. To answer these questions, you will need to recall or look back at what you've read and then repeat, in one way or another, what the author has written.

The questions classified as "Questions for Discussion" and "Questions about Form," on the other hand, call for more thinking on your part. They require analysis and argumentation. To answer them, you will have to support or refute what the author has written. One skill you will develop in this area is usually referred to as *critical thinking*. It is often a requirement in courses across the curriculum at the postsecondary level; it is also a skill that can only help you in any workplace. For more on critical thinking and analysis, see Chapter 25: "Argumentation."

 ### Working Together: Summarizing Opposing Points of View

Form groups of three or four. Look in your local newspaper for feature articles on controversial topics that are of concern to many Canadians, such as the effects of global warming or genetic engineering. Try to find one article that looks at the problem from one perspective and another article that takes an opposing view. For instance, find an article that supports high-speed police chases and another where the author considers them too dangerous. Each group member will then write a summary of one of these articles, making sure that the opposing points of view are clearly indicated. You might use this information to discuss ways in which the media attempt to influence the attitudes of Canadians.

Chapter 16 **Quoting**

Why do students quote? Sometimes it's what they believe the professor wants. When a professor requires text references in a paper, then a student might think this means quoting. A quotation is one type of text reference, but it's not the only type. Another type of text reference is a paraphrase or a summary (see Chapter 15: "Paraphrasing and Summarizing"). But there are also good reasons to quote: (1) to break up the text, and (2) to repeat what someone else says word for word because he or she says it better than most people can.

Text References: Quotations and Paraphrased Ideas

When you're asked to include one or several text references, this usually means you have choices, unless your professor tells you otherwise. A text reference means using an idea from a reading in whatever it is that you're responding to in writing. A text reference can be in the form of a quotation, or it can be a paraphrased idea. A text reference can be used as a piece of evidence to support a point you've just made. Or it can be something you want to respond to in your own piece of writing. When it's used as a piece of evidence, avoid placing it in the topic sentence of a paragraph because this is a place for your own claim, not a piece of evidence in support of it.

Quotations are the exact words of the author. These words must be surrounded by quotation marks unless the quotation is more than two lines. In this case, the quotation is not surrounded by quotation marks but indented, instead. Use a quotation when you can't say in better words what the author has said.

The paraphrased idea is the author's idea, but in your own words. Of course, there are no quotation marks used in this case, but you must still attribute the idea to the author, whether or not you've been asked to document your sources. If there's no documentation required, simply say who said what. For example, *Joseph Campbell said that living authentically means being who you really are (without pretending to be anyone else) and doing what you really want.* By saying *Joseph Campbell said,* you've added "attribution" to your text reference. This suffices if no documentation is required. For more on paraphrasing, see Chapter 15: "Paraphrasing and Summarizing."

How Much Do You Quote?

Quote only as much as you need to in order to support the point you've just made. Do not quote more than that for the sake of filling up space. If part of the quotation is not relevant to your thesis, it's not considered evidence, and if it's not evidence, what's it doing in your paper? Keep another thing in mind. Everything you quote may have to be interpreted. And everything you quote must be analyzed and commented on. These are all reasons to keep quoting to a minimum. You're making it more difficult for yourself if your quotation is longer than it should be.

---

1. YOUR POINT

2. INTRODUCTION TO THE QUOTATION

3. QUOTATION

(EVIDENCE FROM THE TEXT IN SUPPORT OF YOUR POINT)

4. INTERPRETATION

(OF THE QUOTATION IF NECESSARY)

5. ANALYSIS OF THE QUOTATION

(RELATIONSHIP BETWEEN THE QUOTATION AND YOUR POINT)

6. COMMENTARY ON THE QUOTATION

(WHAT DO YOU THINK OF IT?)

Figure 16.1: Giving Meaning to Quotations

A quotation is rarely sufficient on its own. It must be surrounded by items that give it meaning. Without these items, your quotation will make little or no sense. The figure above shows a typical order of items that include the quotation.

Short (Integrated) Quotation

RULE

For a short quotation, four lines or under (some say 40 words or under), place quotation marks around the quotation and integrate the quotation within the regular paragraph. Such a short quotation might be a sentence or two, or even a spot quotation, meaning a partial quoted sentence integrated within a sentence of your own.

Example of a short quotation:

Notice that there is no indentation of the quotation.

Notice the introduction (without quotation marks) of the quotation followed by a comma.

Notice the absence of the word *that* between the word *says* and the quotation. The word *that* is reserved for paraphrases (see Chapter 15: "Paraphrasing and Summarizing").

> The professor said *that* Campbell was a great mythologist.
> The professor said, "Campbell was an accomplished mythologist." (no *that* between the introduction of the quotation and the quotation itself)

A common theme in the study of mythology is that of the hero and the hero's journey. In his most famous book, *The Hero with a Thousand Faces,* Joseph Campbell says, "The battlefield is symbolic of the field of life, where every creature lives on the death of another."

Notice how the final period goes inside the quotation mark. If this is a documented paper, however, there would be no period inside the quotation mark. Instead, a set of parentheses (for the internal documentation) would follow the last quotation mark, and a final period would follow the parentheses. (For examples of internal documentation, see Chapter 24: "Documentation," pp. 267–270 for APA style and pp. 270–273 for MLA style.)

Longer (Block) Quotation

RULE

If your quotation is longer than four lines (or 40 words), you must set it apart from your regular paragraph. When you do this, indent (by a few spaces) the part that is quoted. Do not use quotation marks around or within this quotation at all unless there are quotation marks already within the original quotation.

Example of a block quotation:

The first two lines of the quotation are Campbell's words, so there are no quotation marks yet. But in the third line, there is a set of quotation marks around the words "after long, long years." These words are words that Campbell, himself, has taken from another source (the story by the Grimm Brothers).

In his most famous book, *The Hero with a Thousand Faces*, Joseph Campbell begins to tell the story of "Sleeping Beauty":

Indent the entire quotation

> Little Briar-rose (Sleeping Beauty) was put to sleep by a jealous hag (an unconscious evil-mother image). And not only the child, her entire world went off to sleep; but at last, "after long, long years," there came a prince to wake her. "The king and queen (the conscious good-parent images), who had just come home and were entering the hall, began to fall asleep, and with them the whole estate...."

Note the four periods at the end of the quotation before the final quotation mark. These four periods at the end of a quoted sentence indicate that the original quotation continues, but for the purposes of the quotation by Campbell, this is all that is necessary to support whatever point he is making.

Analyzing the Quotation or Idea

To analyze the quotation or idea is to show the connection between it and the thesis of your paper. Why does the quotation or idea appear here? Do you agree with it or not? How does it support the point that immediately precedes it in your paper? By now, you can see that if the quotation or idea is longer than it should be, you might run into problems with the part that follows.

Exercise 1 Assessing Quotations

Look for a short article in either a newspaper or a magazine. Identify the quotations in this article. Then decide on whether the quotations are appropriate by considering the following questions:

1. Is the quotation a reasonable length? Why or why not?
2. Could the author of the piece have expressed the idea better than the person being quoted? Should the quotation have been paraphrased instead? Discuss.
3. Is everything in the quotation interpreted and analyzed properly? Discuss.

Working Together: Celebrity Canadians

Join a group of four or five. As a group, choose one of the celebrity Canadians pictured below (Drake, Milos Raonic, Kiesza, and Serena Ryder). As an individual, do some research on your smartphone or tablet, or whatever you have access to, on what being Canadian means to the chosen celebrity, then write a five- to seven-sentence paragraph in which you quote something this person has said. Make sure the quotation supports the topic sentence. Read your paragraph aloud to the rest of the group. Then, as a group, discuss the similarities and differences among the paragraphs.

Drake

Milos Raonic

Kiesza

Serena Ryder

Christopher Futcher/istockphoto.com

Chapter 17 **Answering the Question**

More and more often these days, students do not carefully read all the instructions for an assignment. Maybe they think they'll get through the assignment faster if they just go on an assumption. The trouble with this is that they are often wrong. They'll write a paragraph instead of an essay, or an essay instead of a paragraph. Or they will leave out the references. Regardless, this usually results in lower marks. So the first thing to do is read the instructions. And then read them again, if necessary. Reading them a third time before submitting the assignment, making sure nothing was missed, is not a bad idea. This chapter is about understanding exactly what is required when you read the instructions and suggested topics, for instance, so that you can respond as well as possible.

Understanding What Is Asked

What does a question require you to do? Is there more than one part to the question? Does the professor want you to define a term, compare two historical figures, or narrate the story of your search for the right part-time job? Furthermore, how many points is the question worth? How much time can you spend on the question? What is the required format? How long is your answer supposed to be?

Direct Answer to a Direct Question

Often professors say to their students, "Well, you wrote a very thought-provoking paper (or paragraph). But you didn't answer the question." Is it sufficient to write a good paper (or paragraph) if it doesn't answer the question? If what is assigned is a paper on a particular topic without a question being asked, then it might be fine to compose a paper answering your own question. But if a question is asked, or if the topic is very specific—for example, the symbolic meaning of the Holy Grail, as explained by mythologist Joseph Campbell—then you probably don't have the liberty to veer off the path that has been determined for you. In fact, a specific topic, such as the one about the Holy Grail, can be seen as a question that you have to answer. Although not in question form, it can be read this way: What is Joseph Campbell's symbolic interpretation of the Holy Grail? Some professors might even give your paper—no matter how well it might be written—a zero if it doesn't answer the question.

In fact, a direct answer to a direct question makes the best thesis for the first paragraph of an essay (the introduction or introductory paragraph). Again, let's look at the question above.

What is Joseph Campbell's symbolic interpretation of the Holy Grail?

> **Thesis (direct answer to the direct question):** Joseph Campbell says that the Holy Grail is symbolic of a state of mind a human being might have achieved as a result of living his life authentically, that is without lying to himself or anyone else about who he is.

Another thesis in response to the same question might be as follows:

> Joseph Campbell says that the Holy Grail represents the fulfillment of one's spiritual potential.

If you're writing an essay, the rest of the introductory paragraph might be used to expand on the thesis. In the rest of your essay, of course, you would proceed to support your answer with evidence.

Here is another example of a direct question:

> Do you support the idea of bringing capital punishment back to Canada in the most brutal of crimes?

The thesis (direct answer) might look something like this:

> Capital punishment should not return to Canada no matter how brutal the crime.

Notice that there was no need to use the word *I* despite the fact that this thesis is clearly an opinion, which is what a proper argumentative thesis includes. Keep it in third person whenever you can, especially if you're asked for a formal or academic paper.

How to Write Well under Pressure

Most people prefer to do their writing when they have the time to develop their subject, but it often happens that you do not have the chance to write and revise as you would like. Certainly, in your work life after school, you will often be required to write to tight deadlines. Even now, you sometimes have to write under pressure. For example, you may be given a last-minute assignment that must be done right away, or even more likely, you may have to write an exam in-class for a course you are taking.

No matter what the circumstances, you want to be able to do the best writing you can in the time you are given. For example, if you are given an essay question for a final examination in a course, your first step should not be to begin writing. Instead, you should take a few moments to analyze the question you have been given.

Strategies for Answering Timed In-class Essay Questions

1. Understand the question

Read the question twice. If you don't understand it thoroughly, you have at least a couple of choices. Ask the professor for clarification. If he or she, for whatever reason, cannot help make it clear, go on to another question. Usually there's some choice in a test. If not, answer what you understand first; then come back to what you don't understand later. Maximize your chances for high marks.

2. Evaluate the importance of the question

All questions on a test are important as long as they are worth something. But some questions may be worth more than others. Read the instructions associated with individual questions to find out which ones are worth more. Decide, therefore, how much time and writing you should devote to which questions depending on their worth.

3. Figure out precisely what you are being asked to do

See the various methods under "Frequently Used Terms in Essay Questions" on page 182.

4. Answer the question directly

Start with a one-sentence answer, using some words from the question where appropriate before going into detail.

This will force you to focus your thoughts quickly. Once you can do this, you can expand more easily in a way that is more organized.

5. Answer all the parts of the question

This is another reason for reading the question more than once, to make sure that you haven't missed an important part of it.

6. Comply with the length requirements

Sometimes the length requirements change from one question to another. Don't make any assumptions. And don't rely on your memory, especially when you're under pressure to write quickly. Instead of reading instructions just once, try reading them three times: once before you begin, a second time in the middle of your assignment to make sure you're on the right track, and once more after finishing but before submitting the assignment, time permitting, to make sure you haven't missed anything.

> Often I jokingly warn my class that, one day, I will include in the middle of a test's instructions the following sentence: If you write absolutely nothing for this test, you will receive 100 percent. The funny thing is that I would expect no one to qualify because no one seems to read all the instructions anymore. And that's an easy way to throw away marks.
>
> Gary Lipschutz, lead author of *The Canadian Writer's Workplace*

Example of an Essay Question

Study the following essay question to determine exactly what is being asked for:

> Describe the rise of the feminist movement in the 1960s in Canada. Be specific.

If this were one of five short-essay questions on a final examination, the following paragraph would probably be adequate.

The late 1960s saw, in Canada as throughout the Western world, the emergence of a new women's movement. This new feminism rejected all limits to the equality of women's rights and showed that equality in daily life could not be obtained through simple legal, political, or institutional modifications. Discovering that "sisterhood is powerful," women from Vancouver to Halifax began forming groups. The Vancouver Women's Caucus was organized in 1968. The Montreal Women's Liberation Movement was founded in 1969, and the Front de liberation des femmes du Quebec published a feminist manifesto in 1970. At first, some were consciousness-raising groups, but others quickly turned to concrete action—providing access to abortion services, health centres, militant theatre, daycare, shelters for battered women, and rape crisis centres—and they began agitating for equal pay. By the end of the 1960s, Canada had begun to adjust to the rebirth of a major social movement.

Frequently Used Terms in Essay Questions

There are five popular methods of developing an answer to an essay question: definition, comparison and/or contrast, narration, summary, and discussion. The following terms used in essay questions will help you determine which method the professor is asking for.

Define: A definition is the precise meaning of a word or term. When you define something in an essay, you usually write an extended definition in which you select an appropriate example or examples to illustrate the meaning of a term. See more on definition in Chapter 30: "Definition."

Describe: To describe is to give an account of something (such as an accident): to convey the sights, sounds, smells, events, etc., of something or someone; to say what something or someone is like; to paint a mental picture of something so the reader can see it in his or her mind. See more on description in Chapter 29: "Description."

Compare and/or contrast: When you compare two items, you point out the similarities between them. When you contrast two items, you point out the differences. Sometimes you may find yourself using both comparison and contrast in an essay. See more about comparing and contrasting in Chapter 27: "Comparison and/or Contrast."

Narrate: To narrate is to tell a story by carefully relating a sequence of events that are usually (but not always) given in chronological order. See more about narration in Chapter 32: "Narration."

Summarize: When you summarize, you supply the main ideas of a longer piece of writing. A summary is a concise restatement, shorter than the source. When you summarize or paraphrase, avoid copying the actual words and imitating the writer's style or sentence structure. Restate in your own words what the other writer has said. For more on this subject, see Chapter 15: "Paraphrasing and Summarizing."

Discuss: This is a general term that encourages you to write or have a conversation about a subject at length. You might decide to argue both sides of an issue or to investigate something. Asking students to discuss some aspect of a topic is widely used in examination questions.

Explain: To explain is to make clear or understandable, define, or elaborate. You might want to offer reasons for something, such as a person's actions, beliefs, or remarks. (*Example:* The detectives explained their plan to catch the burglars in the act.)

Examine: To examine is to look at, inspect, or scrutinize carefully or in detail—to investigate an issue or situation.

Analyze: When you are asked to analyze something, you must examine it carefully and in detail to identify causes, key factors, and possible results. You might have to separate it into its essential parts to discover the essence of the thing you are analyzing.

Using the Thesis Statement in Essay Questions

Answering a Question in the Form of a Thesis Statement

One of the most effective ways to begin an answer to an essay question is to start with a thesis statement that directly answers the question. Your thesis statement should include the important parts of the question and should also give a clear indication of the approach you intend to take in your answer.

For example, suppose you were going to write an essay in response to the following question:

> Why did the Liberals under Justin Trudeau win a majority of seats in the federal election of 2015?

The following thesis sentence would be an effective beginning:

> Justin Trudeau's Liberals won a majority of seats in the federal election of 2015 for several reasons.

The reader would then know that this was the topic you had chosen and would also know how you intended to approach this topic.

Note: This is not a three-point thesis statement; it does not introduce all the supporting points that will be included in the body paragraphs of the essay. But it is worded in such a way that the reader might expect a few reasons to be introduced immediately following the thesis in the form of a plan of development (POD). For more on plans of development, see Chapter 20: "The Essay."

 Exercise 1 Writing Thesis Statements

Answer each of the following questions in the form of a thesis statement. Read each question carefully and underline the important words or phrases in it. Then formulate a thesis that is a one-sentence direct answer to the question. An example has been done for you.

Essay question: How does one <u>learn another language</u>?
Thesis statement: The process of learning another language is complicated, but usually follows four distinct stages.

1. Essay question: Should the Canadian government support young artists or not?

   Thesis statement:

   _____

   _____

2. Essay question: What is the value of being able to speak two languages in Canada?

   Thesis statement:

   _____

   _____

3. Essay question: Is it harmful or beneficial to adopt a child from one culture and raise this child in another culture?

   Thesis statement:

   _____

   _____

4. Essay question: In what ways can the Canadian government discourage people from smoking?

   Thesis statement:

   _____

   _____

5. Essay question: Are some forms of advertising harmful, and, if so, should harmful advertising be banned?

Thesis statement:

_____

_____

Exercise 2 Methods of Development/Parts of a Question

Each of the following is an example of an essay question. In the spaces provided after each, indicate a) what method of development (definition, comparison and/or contrast, narration, summary, discussion, analysis, description, explanation, etc.) is being called for, and b) how many parts there are to the question. This indicates how many parts there should be in your answer. An example is done for you.

Example: What does the term *sociology* mean? Include in your answer at least four different meanings the term has had since this area of study began.
Method of development: definition
Number of parts to the question: four

1. Compare the reasons Canada entered the Korean War and the reasons it entered World War II.
   Method of development: _____
   Number of parts to the question: _____

2. Briefly trace the history of spacecraft exploration of Mars, from the Viking missions of the 1970s to the successful landing of the rover *Curiosity* on the surface of the red planet in 2012. Include in your answer evidence for and against the presence of water on Mars.
   Method of development: _____
   Number of parts to the question: _____

3. Contrast marriage customs in India with those in Canada.
   Method of development: _____
   Number of parts to the question: _____

4. Explain three effects of high temperatures on space vehicles as they reenter the earth's atmosphere.
   Method of development: _____
   Number of parts to the question: _____

5. What was the process of building the transcontinental railway? Include in your answer six different aspects of the construction, from laying the rails across the Canadian Shield to the effects of the Riel Rebellion.
   Method of development: _____
   Number of parts to the question: _____

Practising Writing in Response to Reading

Unit V in this textbook contains the major readings of the book, after which there are four sections of questions for each reading. Often, when students realize they are going to have to write a paragraph or an essay in response to a reading, they ask if they can do some practice writing. Practice writing is an excellent way to prepare for an English assignment. It's not really considered "studying" for a test or exam. It's better. And most often it's essential if you want to improve your mark.

First of all, find every piece of feedback your professor has already given you on your writing in the course so far, including any diagnostic piece of writing you might have done in the first class. Look for patterns. If your professor has mentioned on three occasions that you have a tendency to include fragments in your writing, then this should become a priority in your preparation for your next assignment. You know that if you don't do anything to learn how to eliminate fragments, there's an excellent chance you will end up including them again and getting a lower mark because of it.

Likewise, if your professor has mentioned more than once that your topic sentences need to be more specific, then work on this also. Once you work on eliminating your fragments and narrowing down your topic sentences, you might be ready for some practice writing as your next step toward preparing for your next writing assignment.

The fourth section of questions after every reading in Unit V is entitled "Writing Ideas." Every writing idea is like a separate writing assignment that requires either a paragraph or an essay to be written in response to the reading that precedes these four sections of questions. Even if your professor asks for a preliminary essay or an extended paragraph rather than either an essay or a paragraph, just assume this is the format being asked for here, too. This an excellent way to practice for the writing assignment you have to do next either in class or at home. Sometimes your professor will encourage you to email your practice assignment to him or her. He or she might also offer some feedback online as long as it is sent a few days before the next assignment is due. If not, then at least show your practice writing to someone whose writing is better than yours for feedback. This is still better than not preparing at all.

Working Together: Formulating Essay Questions

As a class, choose a newspaper or magazine article and distribute copies to everyone. Then form groups of four or five, and ask every member to come up with at least three questions about the article that they think a professor might ask in an exam. As a group, discuss all the questions and decide which five are best. As a class, vote for the group with the best questions.

Unit III The Writing Process

Stephen Coburn/shutterstock.com

Chapter 18 **The Four Stages of Writing for a Paragraph or an Essay**

Few people can go to a desk and write a perfect composition from scratch without giving any of it even a second look. Most people need to go about the writing process in stages. This chapter introduces the writing process (for a paragraph or an essay) in terms of four stages: (1) prewriting, (2) outlining, (3) the rough draft, and finally, (4) postwriting (revising, editing, and proofreading). The chapter begins with some prewriting techniques designed to generate writing ideas and ends with proofreading. Revising and editing (other parts of stage four) are covered in this chapter, but are also examined in more depth in Chapter 22 of this unit.

Stage One: Prewriting

How many times have you heard yourself say, "I don't know what else to write"? Well, what if you really do have plenty to write about and simply don't realize it? The following **prewriting techniques** are designed to retrieve your thoughts and ideas and make sense of feelings you might have so that you can start exploring them on paper. These techniques include brainstorming, freewriting, keeping a journal, and clustering. Use any, all, or none of them—whatever works for you.

Brainstorming

One of the best ways of collecting ideas is through **brainstorming.** Brainstorming is simple—all you need is some time. It is best accomplished in groups of four or more people, but the numbers aren't as important as the generation of ideas.

Here's how brainstorming works:

1. Compile a list of ideas, as many of them as you can.
2. Don't criticize any idea initially. Assessing the ideas will come later. First, just focus on generating several of them.

3. If any ideas generate objections, work on developing alternatives to the ideas rather than simply discarding them.

4. Use ideas to stimulate discussion and to generate other ideas.

5. Make sure that everyone in the group completely understands the ideas generated.

6. Put your list of ideas aside for a while in order to think about them at your leisure. This "back burner" process often generates other ideas.

TIP

When you brainstorm, allow your mind to roam freely around the topic, letting one idea lead to another, even if the ideas seem unrelated or irrelevant. Jot down every word and phrase that pops into your mind when you think about your topic.

Here is what a brainstorming process might look like.

First, identify a topic:

hockey

Then, what things come to mind when you think of this topic?

coaches	referees
Stanley Cup	new drafts
Maple Leafs	Vancouver Canucks

Now, you may want to pick out a couple of these ideas and combine them:

Maple Leafs   and   Stanley Cup

Expand the idea by reflecting on what you know and/or what you believe.

The Maple Leafs can't seem to win the Stanley Cup.

At this point, a question might arise:

Why can't the Leafs win the Stanley Cup?

Use a possible answer to suggest a topic sentence for a paragraph or a thesis statement for an essay:

If they want to win the Stanley Cup, the Maple Leafs should commit to a realistic long-term plan rather than continue to cater to the demands of their short-sighted fans.

Freewriting

In freewriting, you don't have to worry about spelling, grammar, focus, or organization. You just write. Write whatever comes to mind. Let a force beyond your control guide your pen, be it your unconscious, your heart, or the spirit world. The idea here is to generate ideas for writing a composition at a later stage. In the meantime, just have fun letting words explode onto your paper or screen.

Keeping a Journal

When handing in her journal at the end of a semester, a young female college student once said, "The journal was better than any man I've ever known. It listened to absolutely everything I had to say!"

You may have kept some kind of diary in your childhood. Each entry might have started with "Dear Diary" and continued with comments such as "I experienced my first kiss today. It was awkward, but amazing...." Most diaries are logs of what goes on in the daily lives of their writers. As students get older, their diaries may evolve into journals that have a similar format, but content with more depth and other engaging qualities. For example, rather than mention everything you did yesterday in last night's diary entry, you might concentrate on one specific thing that struck you forcefully. It might have been a dream you had that preoccupied you all day, or perhaps something in a conversation you overheard between two other students in front of you in a bus on the way to school. Perhaps this event or thought, whatever it was, made you angry or sad or hopeful or, at the very least, contemplative, causing one of your friends in the cafeteria, or your professor in class, to tell you to snap out of a daze.

Let Your Emotions Serve as a Guide

Think of a teacher from your past whom you remember well. Chances are it was someone who caused you to feel a great deal of emotion, either positive or negative. It might have been a teacher who made you feel stupid—or it might have been one who encouraged you to follow a certain path because of a talent she or he detected in you that your parents never noticed or encouraged. Emotion is often associated with memory. The same can be said for people whom you've dated in the past. You may remember some girlfriends/boyfriends more than others; those with whom you experienced strong emotions are probably the ones you tend to remember the most, no matter how long ago you were with them. Thus, your emotions can be your guide when it comes to choosing the topic of your journal entries and, subsequently, your essays (i.e., if your professor gives you enough choice). What moves you, after all, may cause you to want to write more and will give you more material to write about. You'll experience fewer writer's blocks—fewer occasions on which you're thinking, "I don't know what else to write."

You may be asked to write a response to a piece of writing, either fiction or nonfiction. Does the story you just read remind you of a personal experience? Do you strongly disagree with how the character or writer dealt with his or her own situation because you would have reacted very differently? What should the character or writer have done, and why? If you are asked to respond to a movie, think about what your emotional response to it was. Again, don't try to control the direction of your entry. Let your feelings take you on paper (or on your computer screen) to wherever they seem to want to take you. Regard it as an inner journey into the unknown—a journey into your unconscious or your psyche. (*Psyche,* by the way, is Greek for "soul.")

Buy a Journal That Doesn't Remind You of School

Are you a cat lover? Buy a journal with a hard cover on which there's a picture of a richly exotic Siamese cat! If it's cars you're into, find a journal with a picture of a sexy sports car on the cover. In any event, try to find something that you actually look forward to writing in. Write every day or every night before you go to bed, or take your journal with you in your knapsack so that you can record fresh ideas as they come to mind throughout the day. Between classes, rather than call someone on your cellphone, do some journal writing. Develop a relationship with your journal the same way you would with a good novel that you find hard to put down. Do not allow journal writing to turn into a regular assignment that you feel forced to do just for the marks. Then it turns into meaningless drudgery, like too many things in life already are. It should be, instead, a record of the journey of your mind!

If you prefer to type your entries on a computer screen rather than write them in a paper journal, that's fine, too. Do whatever makes you feel most comfortable and inspired. Do whatever is likely to help you cultivate that relationship, not just the one with your journal, but also the one with yourself that you'll find you are developing as you start to write on a regular basis. Writing regularly in your journal not only can help you get in touch with your feelings and solve your personal problems (for a personal journalling exercise, see Working Together activity #3 on page 198), but it can also help you start writing more quickly and fluently whenever you're asked to complete a task that requires any writing at all.

Clustering (also Known as Diagramming or Mapping)

Many students are visual learners: they learn best by *seeing* something get done rather than by reading or even hearing about it (in a lecture, tapes, etc.). The same can be said for generating ideas. **Clustering** is a kind of brainstorming that makes use of a diagram (see Figure 18.1 for an example). To begin, identify a topic you either have to or want to write about. Label it "main topic" and circle it. This topic becomes the central idea of your clustering activity. Draw a line from that circle up to the left, then another up to the right, etc., and write out other ideas that are related in some way to the central topic. Don't allow yourself to think for too long about what you will add to the diagram next; write down whatever comes to mind first. (Writing something down does not bind you in any way to using it in your final text.) Continue to expand the diagram, building on it in several directions. Eventually, certain ideas will begin to "take hold"—to seem stronger than the others—depending on what is familiar and important to you at the time.

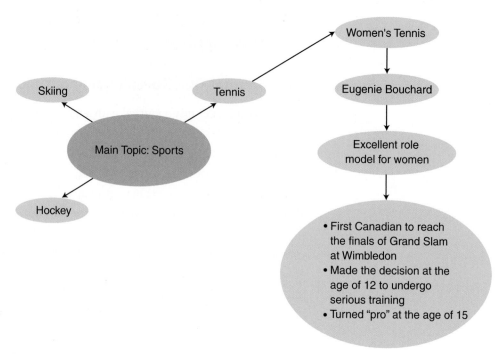

Figure 18.1: Clustering

Clustering is similar to brainstorming (see pages 188–189), except that clustering is more visual. Let one idea generate other more specific ideas based on what you think of next, which may be a result of questions that arise.

Working from the cluster diagram, you could decide that you're interested in women's tennis, specifically in Canada's own Eugenie "Genie" Bouchard. If you feel strongly that Eugenie is an excellent role model for women, this feeling could provide a topic sentence for your paragraph.

Topic sentence: Eugenie Bouchard is an excellent role model for women everywhere.

Then you might ask yourself the following question: Why is Eugenie an excellent role model for women?

The answer to this question might come in several parts, each of which can be used as a supporting point for your paragraph:

Supporting points:

1. She is the first Canadian (not just the first female Canadian) to reach the finals of a Grand Slam in singles at Wimbledon.
2. At the age of 12, she moved to Florida with her mother to be coached by Nick Saviano, proving that long, hard work pays off.
3. In June 2014, she signed a three-year endorsement deal with Coca-Cola, after earlier deals with Rogers Communications, Pinty's, and equipment sponsors Nike and Babolat.

Eugenie Bouchard

Choosing the Topic and the Controlling Idea

Some people have no use for any of the above prewriting techniques. And that's fine. If you can come up with a topic and a controlling idea (your attitude toward the topic) right away, all the better. But remember, even if you can come up with a topic sentence for a paragraph (or a thesis statement for an essay) without prewriting techniques, using them can be helpful for other reasons, too, such as establishing a writing routine, dealing with personal upsets and difficulties, etc.

Jot down two or three different topics that appeal to you; for ideas, look through the lists of topics found throughout Unit IV (look for the heading "Suggested Topics" under "Assignment" for the various writing strategies in each chapter). From one of these lists, select the topic you think would give you the best opportunity for writing. Which one do you feel most strongly about? Which one do you know the most about? Which one is most likely to interest your readers? Which one is best suited to being developed into a paragraph or an essay?

Unit V in this text contains readings that are mostly nonfiction by Canadian writers. Immediately following every reading, there are four sets of questions. Read any piece in Unit V that appeals to you; then practise your paragraph or essay writing by responding to one of the questions. Questions under the headings "Questions for Discussion" and "Writing Ideas" are particularly useful for this purpose. Choose the question you find most interesting.

Every Paragraph or Essay Must Be Persuasive

The word *essay* comes from the French verb *essayer,* which means "to try." What does a writer "try" to do in an essay? A writer tries to persuade the reader of a particular point of view. Even if the essay is considered more expository (writing that explains things) than argumentative, the writer still selects facts that he or she hopes will lead the reader to see things the way the writer does. Any essay—even a single paragraph—is an exercise in *persuasion*. (For more on persuasion, see Chapter 25: "Argumentation.")

Stage Two: Outlining (or Organizing)

Most texts on writing suggest elaborate outlines for paragraphs or essays, some of which seem to be as long as the paragraphs or essays themselves. Here, however, we suggest a very short outline, one that is clear and that saves you time. The pattern of the outline for a paragraph is very similar to that for an essay.

This outline consists of four complete sentences, each of which will appear exactly the same way within the final product.

Outline for a paragraph:

1. The topic sentence
2. The first major supporting sentence
3. The second major supporting sentence
4. The third major supporting sentence

Outline for an essay (of five paragraphs):

1. The thesis statement
2. The topic sentence of the second paragraph
3. The topic sentence of the third paragraph
4. The topic sentence of the fourth paragraph

Of course, by the time you've finished your composition, you may find that the wording of some or all of these sentences has changed because of improvements you've made along the way. The outline is meant to help you ensure that your writing contains persuasive power. If your outline doesn't seem logical, chances are, neither will your composition.

Stage Three: The Rough Draft

After you have applied a prewriting technique and organized the material into some kind of order, the time has come to write a rough draft.

A rough draft is a first attempt at a piece of writing. The first attempt is "rough" because it will undergo many changes before it is finished. Parts may be missing, some paragraphs will probably lack sufficient detail, and some parts may be repetitious or inappropriate. Some sentences will sound awkward, and you will need to rewrite them later. The experienced writer expects all this and does not worry. All that you should try to accomplish in the rough draft is to get down on paper all of your initial ideas according to whatever plan you established in stages one and two. These first ideas will provide the seeds that can be better developed later on.

You may work on a rough draft alone, with a group, with a peer tutor, or directly with your instructor. Below is a list of basic questions you should consider at this most important stage of your work. (If any terms in this list are new to you, see Chapter 19 for terms related to the paragraph, Chapter 20 for those related to the essay, and Chapters 25 to 32 for those related to writing strategies.)

1. Does the rough draft satisfy the conditions for paragraph or essay form? Does it have a topic sentence or thesis statement, adequate support, and a concluding sentence or paragraph? Are there at least five sentences in every paragraph that you've written, but not more than twelve?

2. Does your paragraph or essay contain the writing strategy of your choice, such as narration, cause and effect, or description? Or does your essay combine several strategies, a different one in each paragraph? Does your composition focus on a single event rather than on a general situation? Where does the action take place? Can the reader see it? What time of day, week, or year is it?

3. Have you put the details of the paragraph or essay in a logical order?

4. Does the paragraph or essay seem complete? When you read what you have written, do any questions come to mind that you think should be answered in the text? Is there any material that is irrelevant and should be omitted?

5. Except for what is required in openings and closings, are there sentences or paragraphs that are repetitious?

6. Are there any places where you can substitute better verbs or nouns than the ones you first chose? Can you add adjectives to give the reader better sensory images?

7. Can you think of a better way to begin or end your paragraph or essay?

8. Can you show your draft to at least two other readers and ask them for suggestions?

Once you have a first draft, you have something to work with. No longer is there a blank paper staring you in the face. This accomplishment is a great relief to most writers, but remember, you are far from finished.

Stage Four: Postwriting (Revising, Editing, and Proofreading)

If you have worked hard at revising the rough draft, you will be delighted with the improvements as you write the second draft. For a detailed examination of this part of the writing process, see Chapter 22: "Revising and Editing."

Feedback is an important aid in each of the final stages of writing a paragraph or essay. A good way to help yourself see your own work more clearly is to put the writing aside for a little while, if you can. Then, read aloud what you have written to someone else, or even just to yourself if no one else is available. You may be surprised at the number of places where you will hear the need for a change.

Revising and Editing the Rough Draft

If you have time, put aside your rough draft for a day or two. Then, when you reread it, you will look at it with a fresh eye. In this important revision stage, you should be concerned with how you have organized your ideas. At this point, do not yet worry about grammar, spelling, and punctuation.

Begin this important stage by asking these major questions:

1. Is the paragraph or essay unified? Do you stick to the topic you have announced? Go through the text and take out irrelevant material.

2. Do you repeat yourself? Look back over your paragraph or essay to determine whether you have given any information more than once. Even if you find you have used different words, you should delete the repeated ideas.

3. Does the paragraph or essay make sense? Can a reader follow your logic, your train of thought, and the course of events you describe? (Giving the rough draft to someone else to read will often answer this question for you.) If the paragraph or essay is confusing to the reader, you must find out where it goes wrong and why. Sometimes when you read your writing out loud, you will feel that a sentence has leaped to some point that doesn't follow from the sentence before.

4. For an essay, are the paragraphs roughly the same length? For example, if you see a one-sentence paragraph, you know something is wrong. You may need to develop that paragraph more thoroughly, or the sentence may really belong with the paragraph that comes before or after it. Aim to develop the point of each paragraph using at least five sentences. The first and last paragraphs are usually the shortest in the essay, but they still require approximately five sentences each. Check through your essay. Is each paragraph long enough without being too long? Do you need to change the paragraphing?

5. Do you have all the components essential to a paragraph, or all the types of paragraphs essential to an essay? For an essay, do you have the introduction with its thesis, at least three well-developed body paragraphs with transitional devices used to connect ideas, and a concluding paragraph? For a paragraph, do you have a topic sentence that contains the topic of the paragraph and its controlling idea, several sentences providing strong supporting detail, and a concluding sentence?

6. Can you add more specific details? Most writing instructors agree that nearly every paper they read could be improved by adding more details, more descriptive verbs, and more sensory images to make the writing come alive. You should make sure there is sufficient detail throughout your paper. Remember, however, that in an essay, none of the supporting detail should appear in your introductory or concluding paragraphs.

7. Can you add dialogue or a quotation from someone? A quotation, for example, might make an excellent opening in the introductory paragraph of an essay. (See p. 218 in Chapter 20: "The Essay.") It might also serve as an excellent piece of evidence within a supporting paragraph of an essay.

8. Can you make the introduction, conclusion, or title more creative? These elements of writing are often not taken seriously enough by student writers.

These three items, in fact, are critical components of composition. The title and introduction, in particular, serve to grab a reader's attention. Have you ever tried to read something that hasn't caught your interest? It can be a distressing and agonizing experience. The more time and effort you put into these three elements, the more interesting and effective your writing is likely to be.

Proofreading

An important step still remains. You must check each sentence to see that it is correct, including grammar, spelling, and punctuation. In the rush to get a paper in on time, this step is often overlooked. If you review each sentence by itself, starting with the last and going backwards to the beginning, you will more easily be able to consider the sentence structure and individual words apart from the other aspects of the essay. Taking the time to look over a paper this way usually results in spotting several sentence-level errors.

As a proofreading exercise, you might like to try correcting the errors of grammar, spelling, and punctuation in the rough draft of the student essay on pages 249–250 of Chapter 22: "Revising and Editing."

Note: In many cases, professors will not accept handwritten work and you will be expected to submit a paper produced on a computer. Do not forget to proofread your work after it has been printed out; even if you have your paper typed for you, you are still responsible for errors. If there are not too many errors, you can make corrections neatly in ink on your printed copy before handing it in.

Proofreading

Check your rough draft for
    misspellings
    fragments or run-ons
    incorrect punctuation
    consistency of voice and tense
    verb problems
    agreement
    parallel structure

A checklist for the final preparation of a paragraph or essay follows.

Checklist for the Final Copy

1. Use 8½- by 11-inch (21.5 by 28 cm) paper.
2. Type or write (whichever is required) on one side of the paper only, unless your instructor states otherwise.
3. Double space.
4. Leave margins approximately 1 inch (2.5 cm) wide on all sides of the paper (left, right, top, and bottom).
5. Do not hyphenate words at ends of lines without consulting a dictionary for the correct division of words into syllables.
6. Centre the title at the top of the first page.
7. Put your name, the date, and the title of your paper on a separate title page, unless your professor says otherwise.
8. If you have more than one page, number each one and staple or clip them all together in the upper left-hand corner so they will not be lost.

Working Together: Prewriting Activities

1. Imagine yourself in the following situation: you and your classmates are guidance counsellors in a high school. You have been asked to produce a brochure entitled "When a Young Person Quits School." This brochure is intended for students who are thinking of dropping out. You and the other counsellors meet to brainstorm on the topic.

   Divide into groups. Each group will brainstorm for fifteen minutes or so, then come together again as a class. Make a final grouping of the ideas for this topic on the board, then discuss them.

2. In groups or as a class, construct an outline for an essay to be called "When a Young Person Quits School." (You can use the information gathered in the brainstorming activity if you've done #1 above.) Feel free to follow the suggestion of a brief outline under "Outlining" on page 194 in this chapter.

3. (If you think the following suggestion is too personal, feel free to try #1 or #2 above instead.) As a topic for a journal entry, think of a movie you've seen or a dream you've had that you have found yourself thinking about over and over again. It doesn't matter how long ago you saw the movie or dreamt the dream because your long-term memory can be quite selective and doesn't always work on the basis of time.

   Describe in writing that part of the movie or dream that you seem to be remembering over and over again. It's possible that this part you're remembering may be calling out to you to express it, to explore it, to somehow come to terms with it—and perhaps most important, to learn something from it, something important for you. After all, it's not the movie that's calling out to you. It's something in you that's doing the calling, perhaps something in your unconscious—the part programmed to tell the whole truth about who you are, what you should be doing, where you should be going, and perhaps whom you should be seeing!

   After you write about the part of the movie or dream that you remember the most, adding as much detail as you can, start to discuss how you feel. Then try to explain where these feelings are coming from. Finally, explore what that same place in your unconscious is trying to tell you about what you're supposed to learn from your preoccupation with that part of the movie or dream. You may find yourself the wiser, and the preoccupation with that part of the movie or dream may actually stop.

   Describe the results of your activity to someone else in the class, and allow your partner to ask you questions about it. Then listen and respond as your partner discusses his or her results with you.

Stephen Coburn/shutterstock.com

Chapter 19 **The Paragraph**

What Is a Paragraph?

> **DEFINITION**
>
> A **paragraph** is a group of sentences that develops one main idea. A paragraph may stand by itself as a complete piece of writing, or it may be a section of a longer piece of writing, such as an essay.

No single rule will tell you how long a paragraph should be. An effective paragraph is always long enough to develop the main idea being presented. If a paragraph is too short, the reader will think basic information is missing; if it is too long, the reader will be bored or confused. This textbook suggests, as a rule, that a healthy paragraph should consist of at least five sentences and no more than twelve sentences. You have undoubtedly read paragraphs in newspapers that are only one sentence long, but in academic writing, this is considered unacceptable.

What Does a Paragraph Look Like?

Margins, new-paragraph indication, and complete sentences are essential parts of paragraph form. Study the following paragraph from Elizabeth Pollet's "A Cold-Water Flat" to observe the standard form.

> I got the job. I worked in the bank's city collection department. For weeks, I was like a mouse in a maze: my feet scurried. Every seventh day, I received thirteen dollars. It wasn't much. But, standing beside the pneumatic tube, unloading the bundles of mail that pelted down and distributing them according to their texture, size, and colour to my superiors at their desks, I felt humble and useful.

A margin of adequate width is used on each side of the text (for a manuscript page, this margin should be 1 inch, or 2.5 cm). If another paragraph is added, make sure there is proper indication of the new paragraph. If the first line of the first paragraph is indented (as in the example on the previous page), ensure the first line of the second paragraph is also indented. If you follow the full-block style (no indentation of the first line of a paragraph), then make sure you skip a line between paragraphs. If you're already double spacing, skip two lines between paragraphs. If you neither indent the first line of your paragraph nor skip an extra line between paragraphs, the reader cannot be expected to know where one paragraph ends and the next one begins.

You will note that the layout of this book follows a different format than that suggested for your essays. In this book, the first line of the first paragraph of any section is not indented even if the first line of any subsequent paragraph is. The book industry has its own standards and norms relating to page layout.

Figure 19.1 illustrates the structure of the paragraph.

Note: Any space left over at the end of the last line of a paragraph does not, in itself, properly indicate the end of a paragraph. As mentioned, proper indication of a paragraph means either indenting the first line of each one or skipping a line (or two lines, if you're already double spacing) between paragraphs.

What Is a Topic Sentence?

DEFINITION

A **topic sentence** states the main idea of the paragraph. It contains the topic of the paragraph and a controlling idea (the writer's attitude toward the topic). It is the most general sentence of the paragraph. All the other sentences of the paragraph serve to explain, describe, extend, or support the controlling idea in the topic sentence.

Most paragraphs you read will begin with a topic sentence. However, some topic sentences come in the middle of the paragraph and some come at the end. Occasionally, a paragraph has no stated topic sentence at all; in these cases, the main idea is implied. You are advised to use topic sentences in all your paragraphs in order to be certain that your writing stays focused and develops a single idea at a time. Whether you are taking an essay exam in a history course, doing a research paper for a sociology course, or writing an essay in a composition course, thoughtful use of the topic sentence will always bring better results. Good topic sentences help both the writer and the reader to think clearly about the main points.

The paragraph that follows makes a point, which is stated in its topic sentence. Read the paragraph and notice how the topic sentence is the most general sentence; it presents the main idea of the paragraph. The other sentences explain, describe, extend, or support the topic sentence.

Model Paragraph: Let's Junk It!

We are the great "Let's junk it" society! Mountains of disposable diapers are thrown into garbage cans every day. Tonnes of yogurt containers, pop cans, and plastic items are discarded without so much as a stomp to flatten them out. If the old Chevy is not worth fixing, tow it off to sit with thousands of others on hectares of fenced-in junkyards. Radios, televisions, and toasters

Two Paragraph Types

TOPIC SENTENCE

REGULAR

(About 5–7 sentences including the topic sentence)

CONCLUDING SENTENCE

TOPIC SENTENCE

EXTENDED

(About 8–12 sentences including the topic sentence)

CONCLUDING SENTENCE

Regular and Extended Paragraphs

A **regular paragraph** has about five to seven sentences. An **extended paragraph** is longer (about eight to twelve sentences) because it has more supporting detail. The supporting detail of a paragraph is made up of sentences that directly support the topic sentence (see pp. 205–215). These sentences may be main supporting sentences, or they may be specific examples. Some instructors require a concluding sentence, especially when the paragraph stands alone. See "The Concluding Sentence" on pp. 215–216.

Sample Paragraph (Regular): The Value of Friends

One of the areas in which having choice can be extremely valuable is that of friends. Like leaving home to seek greater knowledge of yourself, picking your own friends from a greater number of people can aid in your journey to seek self-knowledge. After all, if you go out with the same group of small town friends all the time, not because you necessarily like them all that much but because they're the only ones available, this can prove quite limiting when it comes to your growth as an individual. The big city, on the other hand, offers an endless number of opportunities to meet people of like interests. You're much more likely to cultivate relationships with people who help you to grow.

Topic Sentence

A **topic sentence** includes two things: a *topic* and a *controlling idea*. The controlling idea is the attitude or position of the writer of the paragraph toward the topic identified in the topic sentence. The controlling idea gives direction to the paragraph. The topic sentence does not always appear first in a paragraph, but until you are well practised, place the topic sentence first. See "What Is a Topic Sentence?" on pp. 205–215.

Transitions

Transitional words or phrases are used to organize the paragraph better and to make the paragraph flow more smoothly.

Stands On Its Own

Any paragraph, even if it is part of a longer work such as an essay, should be able to stand on its own, just as each movie in a series should.

Paragraph Indication

There are only two ways **to indicate a new paragraph:**

1. **Indent** the first line of the paragraph (see sample paragraph above), or
2. **Skip a line** before starting the next paragraph. If you are already double-spacing your work, skip two lines, instead of one, before starting the next paragraph.

Figure 19.1: Structure of the Paragraph

The sample paragraph (above) is from "City Life Beats the Small Town Blues" (see pp. 321–322).

get the same treatment because it is easier and often less expensive to buy a new product than to fix the old one. Who wants a comfortable old sweater if a new one can be bought on sale? No thought is given to the fact that the new one will look like the old one after two or three washings. After all, what's bad for the environment is probably good for the economy!

All the examples in this paragraph support the topic sentence, which states that we are a "throwaway" society. Although the concluding sentence does not repeat the topic sentence in this case, it gives the paragraph a sense of closure. (For more on concluding sentences, see pages 215–216, later in this chapter.)

 Practice 1 Finding the Topic Sentence of a Paragraph

Each of the following paragraphs contains a topic sentence that states the main idea of the paragraph. Find this sentence and underline it. Check your answers against those in the Answer Key on page 466.

1. Love is a crazy, complicated affair, made trickier by the tangle of superstitions that go along with it. According to the book *Cross Your Fingers, Spit in Your Hat,* you must pull a hair from the head of the one you love to make him or her love you back. Or you can offer your loved one a glass of lemonade in which you have soaked your toenail clippings, or a bowl of soup to which you have added three drops of your blood. Once your sweetheart has devoured either of these concoctions, he or she will love you always.

2. The brain is one of the most remarkable organs, a part of the body that we have only begun to investigate. It will be years before we start to understand all its complex processes. When you remember something, your brain uses more than one method to store the information. You have short-term memory, which helps you recall recent events; you have long-term memory, which brings back items that are further in the past; and you have deep retrieval, which gives you access to long-buried information that is sometimes difficult to recall. Whether these processes are chemical or electrical, we do not yet know, and much research remains to be done before we can say which with any certainty.

How Do You Find the Topic in a Topic Sentence?

To find the topic in a topic sentence, ask yourself this question: What is the topic the writer is going to discuss? Below are two topic sentences. The first topic is underlined. Underline the topic in the second example.

<u>Backpacking</u> in the mountains last year was an exciting experience. College registration can be stressful.

 Practice 2 Finding the Topic in the Topic Sentence

Find the topic in each of the following topic sentences. For each example, ask yourself this question: What is the topic the writer is going to discuss? Then underline the topic. Check your answers against those in the Answer Key on page 466.

1. Remodelling an old house can be frustrating.
2. College work demands more independence than high school work.
3. A well-made suit has three easily identified characteristics.
4. Growing up near a museum had a profound influence on my life.

5. My favourite room in the house would seem ugly to most people.
6. A student who goes to school full time and also works part time has to make careful use of every hour.
7. One of the disadvantages of skiing is the expense.
8. When we met for dinner that night, I was shocked at the change that had come over my friend.
9. According to the report, current tax laws greatly benefit those who own real estate.
10. Greek restaurants, to the delight of many Canadians, can be found in most of our cities.

What Is a Controlling Idea?

Every topic sentence contains not only the topic, but also a controlling idea.

> ### DEFINITION
> The **controlling idea** tells us the position the writer has taken on the topic. It gives the paragraph direction. It is the writer's attitude toward the topic.
> **Example:** Her trip to Kenya was *exciting*.

For example, in the topic sentence "Backpacking in the mountains last year was an exciting experience," the topic is "backpacking" and the controlling idea is that this backpacking trip was "exciting." Another person on the same trip might have had another attitude toward the trip. The person might have found the trip exhausting or boring. A single topic can therefore have any number of possibilities for development, since the writer can choose from a limitless number of controlling ideas, depending on his or her attitude.

How Do You Find the Controlling Idea of a Topic Sentence?

When you look for the controlling idea in a topic sentence, ask yourself this question: What is the writer's attitude toward the topic?

In each of the following examples, the topic is underlined and the controlling idea is circled:

<u>Sealfon's Department Store</u> is my (favourite) store in town.

<u>Sealfon's Department Store</u> is (too expensive) for my budget.

 Practice 3 Finding the Controlling Idea

Below are seven topic sentences. For each sentence, underline the topic and circle the controlling idea. Check your answers against those in the Answer Key on page 466.

1. Vigorous exercise is a good way to reduce the effect of stress on the body.
2. St. John's and Corner Brook differ in four major ways.
3. Many so-called wonder foods are less than wonderful.
4. The number of athletic scholarships available to women is increasing.
5. Caffeine has several adverse effects on the body.

6. Madame Benoît, a famous gourmet cook, had an amusing personality.
7. Computers will make newspapers obsolete by 2020.

Choosing Your Own Controlling Idea

Professors often assign one general topic on which all students must write. Likewise, when writing contests are announced, the topic is sometimes the same for all contestants. But it is much less likely that all papers will have the same controlling idea. There could be as many controlling ideas as there are people to write them. The secret of writing a good topic sentence is to use a controlling idea that strongly and accurately expresses your attitude or feeling toward the topic.

 Exercise 1 Choosing Controlling Ideas for Topic Sentences

Below are two topics. For each topic, think of three different possible controlling ideas, and then write a different topic sentence for each of these controlling ideas. An example is done for you.

Topic: My mother

Three possible controlling ideas:
1. Unusual childhood
2. Silent woman
3. Definite ideas about alcohol

Three different topic sentences:
1. My mother had a most unusual childhood.
2. My mother is a very silent woman.
3. My mother has definite ideas about alcohol.

1. **Topic:** My neighbourhood
   Controlling idea A: _____
   Topic sentence A: _____
   _____
   Controlling idea B: _____
   Topic sentence B: _____
   _____
   Controlling idea C: _____
   Topic sentence C: _____
   _____

2. **Topic:** The Internet
   Controlling idea A: _____
   Topic sentence A: _____
   _____
   Controlling idea B: _____
   Topic sentence B: _____
   _____

Controlling idea C: _____

Topic sentence C: _____

_____

Exercise 2 **Further Practice Writing the Topic Sentence**

Develop each of the following topics into a topic sentence. In each case, the controlling idea is missing. First, decide on an attitude you might take toward the topic. Then use that attitude to write your topic sentence. When you are finished, underline your topic and circle your controlling idea. Make sure your topic sentence is a complete sentence and not a fragment. An example has been done for you.

> **Topic:** My brother's car accident
>
> **Controlling idea:** Tragic results
>
> **Topic sentence:** <u>My brother's car accident</u> had (tragic results) for the entire family.

1. **Topic:** Sending e-mail
   Controlling idea: _____
   Topic sentence: _____
   _____

2. **Topic:** Two years in the armed forces
   Controlling idea: _____
   Topic sentence: _____
   _____

3. **Topic:** Making new friends
   Controlling idea: _____
   Topic sentence: _____
   _____

4. **Topic:** Working as a waiter or waitress
   Controlling idea: _____
   Topic sentence: _____
   _____

5. **Topic:** Going on a diet
   Controlling idea: _____
   Topic sentence: _____
   _____

What Is a Supporting Detail?

DEFINITION

A **supporting detail** is a piece of evidence used by the writer to make the controlling idea of the topic sentence convincing to the reader.

Once you have constructed your topic sentence with its topic and controlling idea, you are ready to move on to supporting your idea with details. These details will convince your readers that what you are claiming in the topic sentence is believable or reasonable.

The Structured Approach

Some instructors require a more structured approach than others when it comes to developing supporting details for a paragraph. This textbook recommends a structured approach. Once you become familiar with the structured approach, you are more likely to be able to take liberties without sacrificing necessary paragraph development.

Two Types

Supporting details can be broken down into two basic types, both of which should be present in every paragraph to make it effective (see Figure 19.2 below):

1. Main supporting sentence
2. Example sentence (or extended example, which is, simply, a longer example—see p. 208)

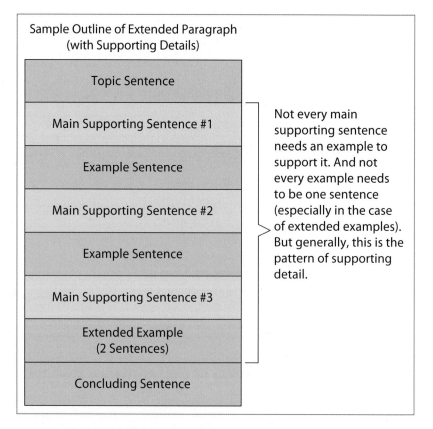

Figure 19.2: Sample Extended Paragraph Outline (with Supporting Details)

For a sample paragraph showing a breakdown of main supporting sentences and their examples, see the section entitled "Examples (Example Sentences)" on pages 208–210.

Supporting Detail Type 1: Main Supporting Sentences

> **DEFINITION**
>
> A **main supporting sentence** contains a main point that directly supports the topic sentence of the paragraph. A paragraph may have only one main supporting sentence or it may have several.

The first type of supporting detail is the main supporting sentence. This type of detail usually follows the topic sentence immediately. The main supporting sentences contain the main points within the paragraph that support the topic sentence directly. They are often distinguished by the fact that they contain not only main points, but also appropriate **transitions**; these include (but are by no means limited to) *first, second, third,* and *finally.* (For a more extensive list of common transitions, see the inside of the back cover.) There is no definitive proper number of main supporting sentences for a paragraph, but instructors generally like the number three, corresponding to three main points per paragraph. A main supporting sentence is often followed by the second type of supporting detail: an **example** that directly supports the main supporting sentence.

The following extended paragraph is taken from page 328 (in Chapter 28: "Process") about what it takes to get a good night's sleep. It begins with a clear topic sentence, which is then followed by several strong supporting details.

> The process of getting a good night's sleep depends on several factors. First, the conditions in your bedroom must be correct. Be sure the room temperature is around 18°C and the room is as quiet as possible. Next, pay attention to your bed and how it is furnished. For example, a firm mattress is best, and wool blankets are better than blankets made of synthetic material. Similarly, a firm pillow is best; after all, one that is too soft can cause a stiff neck and lead to a night of poor sleep. Also, keep in mind that what and how you eat are part of the process of preparing for bed. For example, do not go to bed hungry, but do not overeat, either. And avoid candy bars or cookies; the sugar they contain acts as a stimulant. Finally, do not go to bed until you are sleepy. Do something relaxing until you are tired. In conclusion, everything you do can have an effect on how well you sleep.

Notice that the topic sentence gives us the topic (a good night's sleep) and the writer's attitude toward the topic (that it depends on several factors). Each of the sentences that follow this topic sentence is a supporting detail that convinces us that the controlling idea is a reasonable attitude.

The following shows the breakdown of the topic sentence and the main supporting sentences that support it directly. Example sentences have been omitted for now.

Topic sentence:	The process of getting a good night's sleep depends on several factors.
First main supporting sentence:	First, the conditions in your bedroom must be correct.

Second main supporting sentence:	Next, pay attention to your bed and how it is furnished.
Third main supporting sentence:	Also, keep in mind that what and how you eat are part of the process of preparing for bed.
Fourth main supporting sentence:	Finally, do not go to bed until you are sleepy.

Note the transitions that begin each main supporting sentence: *first, next, also,* and *finally.*

 Exercise 3 Finding the Topic Sentence and Main Supporting Sentences

Read the following paragraph. Write down the topic sentence, then list the main supporting sentences.

> Loneliness comes at any time. It comes in times of sickness or when friends are absent. It comes during sleepless nights when the heart is heavy, during times of failure at work or in relationships. It comes when we lose trust in ourselves and in others. In old age, loneliness can rise up and threaten to overwhelm us. At such times, life can lose its meaning. Loneliness can feel like death.
>
> Jean Vanier, "Heart of Loneliness"

Supporting Detail Type 2: Examples (Example Sentences)

 DEFINITION

An **example** supports (and therefore normally follows) a main supporting sentence. It is a very specific illustration or piece of evidence—more specific than the main supporting sentence it supports. Examples make general ideas more concrete and therefore easier to comprehend and remember. An example may be part of a sentence, it may be an entire sentence on its own, or it may be more than one sentence long.

The same paragraph that was used to illustrate main supporting sentences can be used to demonstrate what examples can look like.

> The process of getting a good night's sleep depends on several factors. First, the conditions in your bedroom must be correct. Be sure the room temperature is around 18°C and the room is as quiet as possible. Next, pay attention to your bed and how it is furnished. For example, a firm mattress is best, and wool blankets are better than blankets made of synthetic material. Similarly, a firm pillow is best; after all, one that is too soft can cause a stiff neck and lead to a night of poor sleep. Also, keep in mind that what and how you eat are part of the process of preparing for bed. For example, do not go to bed hungry, but do not overeat, either. And avoid candy bars or cookies; the sugar they contain acts as a stimulant. Finally, do not go to bed until you are sleepy. Do something relaxing until you are tired. In conclusion, everything you do can have an effect on how well you sleep.

Here is the breakdown of the topic sentence and main supporting sentences again, but this time, the example sentences are also included. Notice how they come after each main supporting sentence, providing even more specific information.

Topic sentence:	The process of getting a good night's sleep depends on several factors.
First main supporting sentence:	First, the conditions in your bedroom must be correct.
Example sentence:	Be sure the room temperature is around 18°C and the room is as quiet as possible.
Second main supporting sentence:	Next, pay attention to your bed and how it is furnished.
Example sentences:	For example, a firm mattress is best, and wool blankets are better than blankets made of synthetic material. Similarly, a firm pillow is best; after all, one that is too soft can cause a stiff neck and lead to a poor night of sleep.

(Note that the above passage actually contains three examples made up of a total of two sentences.)

Third main supporting sentence:	Also, keep in mind that what and how you eat are part of the process of preparing for bed.
Example sentences:	For example, do not go to bed hungry, but do not overeat, either. And avoid candy bars or cookies; the sugar they contain act as a stimulant.

(Note that the third main supporting sentence above is followed by two sentences made up of three examples. The sentence, starting with "For example, do not go to bed" is followed by another sentence that contains a more specific example than those in the first sentence.)

Fourth main supporting sentence:	Finally, do not go to bed until you are sleepy.
Example sentence:	Do something relaxing until you are tired.

Examples may be given in more than one way. They may appear as lists of specific items to illustrate a particular point, or they may be written as extended examples.

> **DEFINITION**
>
> **Extended examples** include lengthy descriptions or stories that are usually several sentences long (or even an entire paragraph long in an extended piece of writing such as an essay).

A good piece of writing is filled with both kinds of examples—specific items and extended examples—that fit together to create a well-developed, convincing whole. Read the following paragraph on the terminology used in weather forecasting. As you read, look for different examples that show how listening to the weather forecast can be a challenge.

> **Model Paragraph: The Shortcomings of Forecasting**
>
> Not only are weather forecasters often wrong with their forecasts, but they speak a language that only the most knowledgeable meteorologist can understand. For the average television viewer or radio listener, a dictionary is a necessity when listening to the weather forecast. "Watch out for the Alberta clipper, folks. It's coming this way!" seems to be part of the forecasters' lexicon in the winter. Or maybe it's the summer. In any case, what is an Alberta clipper? Are we supposed to hide under a table when it approaches? I've never understood the term, nor have I understood the significance of the dew point or a temperature inversion. How could I ever understand these terms when no one has ever defined them for me? Yet they roll off the tongues of weather forecasters as if everyone should know what is happening. The relative humidity mystifies me, as do troughs and ridges of pressure. I know one thing, however: if the forecast is for a sunny day, be sure to take an umbrella.

 Exercise 4 **Finding Examples**

Analyze the model paragraph "The Shortcomings of Forecasting," above. What kind(s) of examples can you find in the paragraph?

 Exercise 5 **Finding Examples**

Find a newspaper or magazine article on a subject that interests you. Examine the article for paragraphs containing lists of examples and paragraphs containing extended examples. How has the writer made the article interesting and memorable through the use of examples?

Qualities of Good Supporting Detail

What makes a good supporting detail? Whether it is a supporting sentence or an example, a supporting detail is stronger if it has these characteristics: it is based on fact, not opinion; it is specific; and it shows respect for other points of view. Your writing will be stronger if, while choosing details to include in your paragraph, you keep these qualities in mind. Each is discussed in more detail below.

State Facts

When you choose your supporting details, focus on facts rather than opinion. Readers do not necessarily have to agree with the point of view you present in your topic sentence or thesis statement, but your supporting details should be accurate and numerous enough to convince your readers to respect your position. You are likely not the only one who has knowledge of a particular subject, so be sure that you don't present vague assertions that leave you open to contradiction. For example, if you have had many problems with a particular make of car and want to write a paragraph detailing its faults, remember to state exactly what happened; don't rely on further opinions to support your initial opinion.

Use Specific Examples

Remember that specific details tend to stay in readers' minds much longer than general ideas. The statement "over 34 600 males died of cancer in Canada in the year 2000" is much more effective and memorable than "cancer has killed many people." Specific details also make a piece of writing more interesting. When the reader has concrete objects, particular people, or recognizable places to hang on to, the contents of the writing become a pleasure to read.

The more precise your examples, the more clearly they will illustrate your points. For example, in the model paragraph "The Shortcomings of Forecasting" (on pp. 210–211), the specific example "Watch out for the Alberta Clipper, folks!" backs up very clearly the statement in the preceding supporting sentence that "a dictionary is a necessity when listening to the weather forecast."

See also the section entitled "How Do You Make Supporting Details Specific?" on pages 213–215, later in this chapter.

Respect Other Points of View

While you hope to convince your reader that what you are saying is true and worthy of belief, remember that no matter how good your supporting sentences and examples are, they might not convince some readers who may have education and experience that you lack. So don't "preach" to the reader or imply in your tone that your point of view is the only one that is valid.

Avoid Restating the Topic Sentence

One of your most important jobs as you write a paragraph is to recognize the difference between a genuine supporting detail (either a main supporting sentence or an example sentence) and a simple restatement of the topic sentence. The following is a poorly constructed paragraph; its sentences merely restate the topic sentence, which has been underlined:

Time Captured in a Picture (I)

My grandmother's photograph dates from a period when she and her family came to live in St. Petersburg. I like to look at the photograph and wonder about how life was in those days. From the clothes that my grandmother is wearing in the old photograph, it looks as if she is ready for a formal occasion. It is difficult to tell, though, because the photograph is old and faded. I don't think she enjoyed formal occasions.

The supporting sentences tell the reader very little about the period in which the photograph was taken. There is no description given of the clothing or why the writer might feel that it was a formal occasion. And even though the photograph is old and faded enough that details can't be seen, the writer assumes that his or her grandmother isn't having a good time.

By contrast, the following paragraph, from Michael Ignatieff's *The Russian Album,* has good supporting details:

Time Captured in a Picture (II)

In the family album there is a photograph of my grandmother, Natasha Ignatieff, that dates from the period when she and her family came to live in St. Petersburg in the dark and cluttered apartment two blocks from the Neva river. She is dressed for a formal winter evening, a fox fur draped over her shoulders. Brussels lace [decorates] the bodice of her velvet gown, her hair [is] swept back in a tight chignon, and a twelve-strand pearl choker [hugs] her stiffly upright neck. She is thin and pale, the cheekbones of her long angular face taking the light, the eyes deep-set and dark. Her expression is guarded, and she seems at odds with the occasion. She was a private soul: in the public glare, she shrank back. She hated Petersburg society: paying courtesy calls on the wives of Paul's superiors, making curtsies and small talk and all the while feeling she was up on a high wire one step from a fall.

Ignatieff's paragraph has vivid illustrations of life in Russia during his grandmother's time. In the first place, naming her gives a personal element to the paragraph. His descriptions of the apartment ("dark and cluttered"), her formal wear ("fox fur," "Brussels lace," "twelve-strand pearl choker"), and her appearance ("hair [is] swept back," "thin and pale," "cheekbones of her long angular face") all support the overall topic: the photograph mentioned in the first sentence. The author provides concrete evidence to back up his statement that she hated St. Petersburg society: her "guarded" expression, the fact that she was a "private soul," and her feeling of being "on a high wire one step from a fall." These details give a clarity and personality to the discussion of the old picture in this paragraph.

 Practice 4   Avoid Restating the Topic Sentence

Each of the topic sentences below is followed by four additional sentences. Three of these additional sentences contain acceptable supporting details, but one of the sentences is simply a restatement of the topic sentence. In the space provided, identify each sentence as either *SD* (if it supplies supporting detail) or *R* (if it is a restatement). Check your answers against those in the Answer Key on page 466.

1. I am surprised at myself when I think how neat I used to be before I started school full time.

    _____ a. In my closet, I had my clothes arranged in matching outfits with shoes, hats, and even jewellery to go with them.

    _____ b. I always used to take great pride in having all my things in order.

_____ c. If I opened my desk drawer, compartments of paper clips, erasers, staples, pens, pencils, stamps, and rulers greeted me without one lost penny or safety pin thrown in out of place.

_____ d. On top of my chest of drawers sat a comb and brush, two oval frames with pictures of my best friends, and that was all.

2. Iceland has a very barren landscape.

_____ a. One-tenth of the island is covered with ice.

_____ b. Not one forest with magnificent trees is to be found.

_____ c. Nature has not been kind to the people of Iceland.

_____ d. Three-fourths of the island is uninhabitable.

Exercise 6 **Distinguishing a Supporting Detail from a Restatement of the Topic Sentence**

Each of the topic sentences below is followed by four additional sentences. Three of these additional sentences contain supporting details, but one of the sentences is simply a restatement of the topic sentence. In the space provided, identify each sentence as *SD* for supporting detail or *R* for restatement.

1. In the last thirty years, the number of people living alone in Canada has increased by 400 percent.

_____ a. People are living alone because the number of divorces has dramatically increased.

_____ b. Many young people are putting off marriage until they are financially more secure or emotionally ready.

_____ c. More and more Canadians are finding themselves living alone.

_____ d. An increasing segment of our population is in the over-65 age group, which includes many widows and widowers.

2. Writing as Sandra Field and Jocelyn Haley, romance author Jill MacLean makes love pay the bills.

_____ a. Her first book, *To Trust My Love,* was published by Harlequin.

_____ b. Jill received a royalty cheque of about $1800 for her first book.

_____ c. She is the author of thirty-six full-fledged romance novels.

_____ d. Jill MacLean writes love stories under two pen names.

How Do You Make Supporting Details Specific?

Students often write paragraphs that are made up of only general statements. When you read such paragraphs, you doubt the author's knowledge and you suspect that the point being made may have no basis in fact. Here is one such paragraph that never gets off the ground.

Don't Trust Doctors (I)

Doctors are terrible. They cause more problems than they solve. I don't believe most of their treatments are necessary. History is full of the mistakes doctors have made. We don't need all those operations. We should never ingest all those drugs doctors prescribe. We shouldn't allow them to give us all those unnecessary tests. I've heard plenty of stories that prove my point. Doctors' ideas can kill you.

Here is another paragraph on the same topic. This paragraph is much more interesting and convincing because the general statements have been changed throughout the essay to supporting details.

Don't Trust Doctors (II)

Evidence shows that "medical progress" has been the cause of tragic consequences and even death for thousands of people. X-ray therapy was thought to help patients with tonsillitis. Now many of these people are found to have developed cancer from these X-rays. Not so long ago, women were kept in bed for several weeks following childbirth. Unfortunately, this cost many women their lives, since they developed fatal blood clots from lying down day after day. One recent study estimates that 30 000 people each year die from the side effects of drugs that were prescribed by doctors. Recently, the Centers for Disease Control reported that 25 percent of the tests done by clinical laboratories were done poorly. All this is not to belittle the good done by the medical profession, but to impress on readers that it would be foolish to rely totally on the medical profession to solve all our health problems.

This second paragraph is much more likely to be of real interest to a reader. Even if someone disagreed with the author's point, it would be very hard to dismiss these supporting details, which are based on facts and information that can be researched. Because the author sounds reasonable, readers can respect her or him even if they have a different position on the topic.

In writing effectively, the ability to go beyond the general statement and get to accurate pieces of information is what counts. A writer who has a statistic, a quotation, a historical example, or a descriptive detail can use these items to clarify the theme. If the examples are well chosen, readers should go away wanting to share with everyone they meet the surprising information they have just learned.

Good writing is filled with supporting details that are specific, correct, and appropriate for the subject. Poor nonfictional writing is filled with generalizations, stereotypes, vagueness, untruths, and/or insults.

 Exercise 7   Creating Main Supporting Sentences

Below are five topic sentences. Supply three main support sentences for each one. Be sure each sentence is specific, not general or vague. Add appropriate transitions.

1. Jim's entire wardrobe should be burned.

   a. _____

   b. _____

   c. _____

2. The Internet is more valuable than television.

   a. _____

   b. _____

   c. _____

3. Dr. Kline is an easy instructor.

   a. _____

   b. _____

   c. _____

4. It is difficult to stop eating junk food.

   a. _____

   b. _____

   c. _____

5. Learning another language will make your life richer.

   a. _____

   b. _____

   c. _____

 Exercise 8 Creating Examples

After completing Exercise 7, in which you were asked to create main supporting sentences, add an example sentence for every main supporting sentence you wrote. Again, add appropriate transitions such as *for example* or *for instance*.

The Concluding Sentence

Some instructors will require that you add a concluding sentence to your paragraph, especially if you're writing a paragraph that stands on its own and not as part of a larger essay. The concluding sentence should give the paragraph a sense of closure. It should be logical and appropriate. It may or may not restate the topic sentence, but it must not introduce new evidence (supporting detail). It should be more general than the sentences that provide supporting detail. It also should be the last sentence in the paragraph. Look back over the two sample paragraphs entitled "Don't Trust Doctors" (I and II) in the previous section (p. 213). Find the concluding sentence in each paragraph. Notice that in one case, the controlling idea of the concluding sentence seems a bit stronger than that of the topic sentence, and in the other case it seems a bit weaker. Either way, however, the concluding sentence reinforces the original controlling idea and does not contradict it.

Concluding Sentences

A concluding sentence

- Does not contain new evidence
- Is more general than any individual supporting detail
- Should be the last sentence in the paragraph
- Restates, or at least reinforces, the controlling idea established in the topic sentence (and, therefore, does not contradict the controlling idea of the paragraph)
- Gives the paragraph closure
- May offer a final commentary on the paragraph

Sample Outline Format

Now that you have learned what all the components of a good paragraph are, it is time to piece them all together. What follows is an outline format that can be used for an **extended paragraph.** How many main supporting sentences to include, how many examples to back up each one, and how many sentences it takes to present each example will depend on the content and on what evidence comes to mind when you are writing. So the following format is merely a suggested one to help you see how everything might fit together. Feel free to use it if it can help guide you as you're practising paragraph development.

For a reminder of the difference between main supporting sentences and examples, review the section entitled "Two Types," earlier in this chapter (p. 206).

Topic sentence: _____

_____

Main supporting sentence #1: _____

_____

Example: (2 sentences) _____

_____

_____

_____

Main supporting sentence #2: _____

_____

Example: (2 sentences) _____

_____

_____

_____

Continued on next page...

Main supporting sentence #3: _____

_____

Example: (1 sentence) _____

_____

Concluding sentence: _____

_____

Total: 10 sentences (extended paragraph)

 Working Together: Controlling Ideas and Supporting Details

1. While doing the various exercises in this chapter, you have written many topic sentences. Choose one of your best sentences and put it on the board. Read the sentences that other students write on the board; choose one, and underline the topics and circle the controlling ideas. If you think the sentence needs improvements, write your own version underneath the original so the class can compare and contrast them.

2. Every topic contains numerous possibilities for controlling ideas. Take, for example, the topic of education. Think for a moment and jot down one or two controlling ideas that come to your mind regarding this topic. Then, as a class, share your ideas (one student could list all the different controlling ideas on the blackboard). Finally, select one of the controlling ideas on the board (it doesn't have to be one you generated) and use it as the basis for a paragraph.

3. Divide into groups. As a group, select one of the topic sentences in the exercise on pages 214–215. Together, make a list of as many supporting details or examples as you can. Then, working individually, write a paragraph selecting details from the list prepared by your group.

Share your paragraph with the other members of your group and read everyone else's. Be sure to give every member enough time to read through all the group's papers. Then discuss the various paragraphs that have been written. Even though each paragraph began with the same topic sentence and supporting details, did all of the paragraphs turn out differently? Why?

Chapter 20 **The Essay**

Writing Is a Skill

Very few writers can "dash off" a masterpiece. We sometimes think that a person is "a born dancer" or "a born writer," but the reality is that anyone with a high level of skill in an area such as these has worked long hours for many years to reach that point. Writing is no exception. Like playing the piano, cleaning a patient's teeth, or managing a restaurant, writing is a skill. It helps to have talent, but talent must still be developed and skills must be mastered, even by talented people.

When you learned to write a well-developed paragraph in Chapter 19, you were creating something that could be a support paragraph for an essay. An essay is a longer piece of writing, usually five or more paragraphs, in which you develop a topic in much more depth than you can in a single paragraph. An essay may also be called a composition, thesis, or paper. In most schools, such writing is an important part of many courses, not only English composition.

Transferability

While writing essays is required in any number of areas of study—law enforcement, business studies, office administration, technology, social sciences, journalism, broadcasting, and more—its purpose goes beyond fulfilling the requirements of a postsecondary-level education. Writing essays also helps prepare students for careers by providing the skills necessary to write corporate reports, evaluations, summaries, research papers, letters, memos, and job applications. Although different jobs call for different kinds of written texts with somewhat different structures, the essay is the basic form at the heart of them all. Spelling, grammar, and logic, which are essential to the composition of an effective essay, remain paramount in all forms of writing, as does the ability to express yourself clearly. In short, the skills you develop when you learn how to write an essay are transferable in countless ways. Contrary to what some people say—that the essay is an outdated exercise—the essay is timelessly practical because of this obvious transferability.

You learned in Chapter 19 that a paragraph, with its topic sentence and supporting details, must have an organization that is both unified and coherent. An essay must also have these characteristics. Furthermore, since an essay develops a topic more thoroughly, making all the parts work together becomes an added challenge. Figure 20.1 illustrates the structure of an essay.

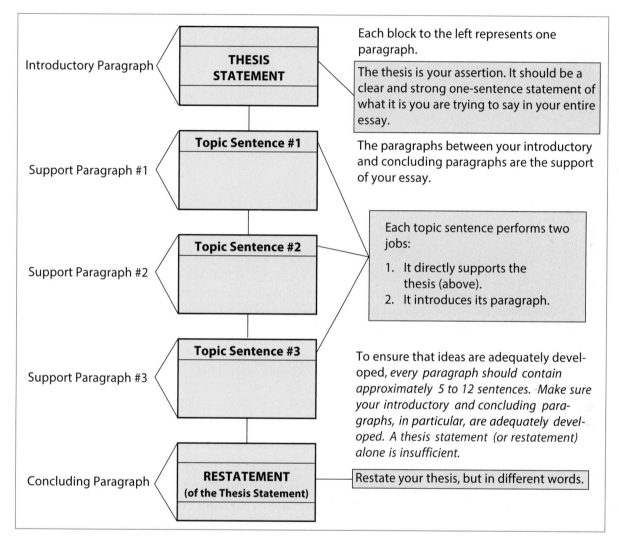

Figure 20.1: The Structure of an Essay

The Components of an Essay

Three types of paragraphs must always be present in an essay: an introductory paragraph, support paragraphs, and a concluding paragraph. (See Figures 20.1 and 20.2.)

1. **The introductory paragraph is the first paragraph of the essay.**
   Its purpose is to be so inviting that the reader will want to continue reading. This introduction must contain a thesis statement.

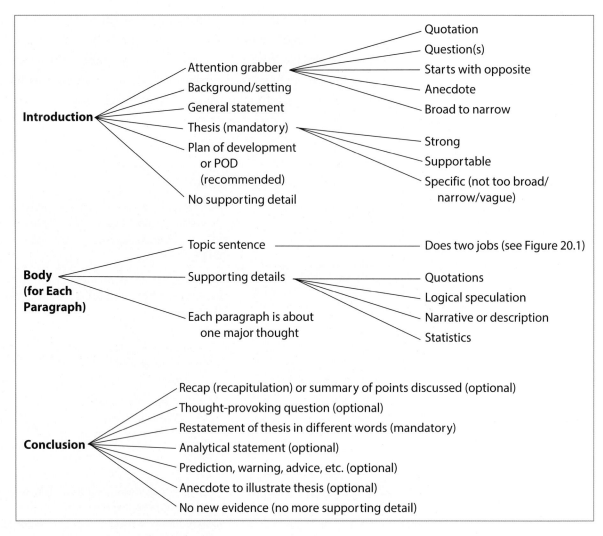

Figure 20.2: Components of the Essay

2. **Support paragraphs (sometimes called body paragraphs) provide the evidence that shows your thesis is valid.** An essay normally has at least three well-developed support paragraphs. (These are the kinds of paragraphs you have studied in Chapter 19.) For an essay, however, one paragraph must flow logically into the next. This flow is accomplished by the careful use of **transitions** or **transitional devices** (discussed later in this chapter).

3. **The concluding paragraph is the last paragraph of the essay.** Its purpose is to give the reader a sense of coming to a satisfying ending—a feeling that everything has been said that needed to be said.

Moving from the Paragraph to the Essay

The paragraph can be considered a mini-essay of sorts. A well-written paragraph includes all the skeletal elements of a full-fledged essay. For it to be transformed, it needs to be expanded and fleshed out. Figure 20.3 shows the relationship between the two structures.

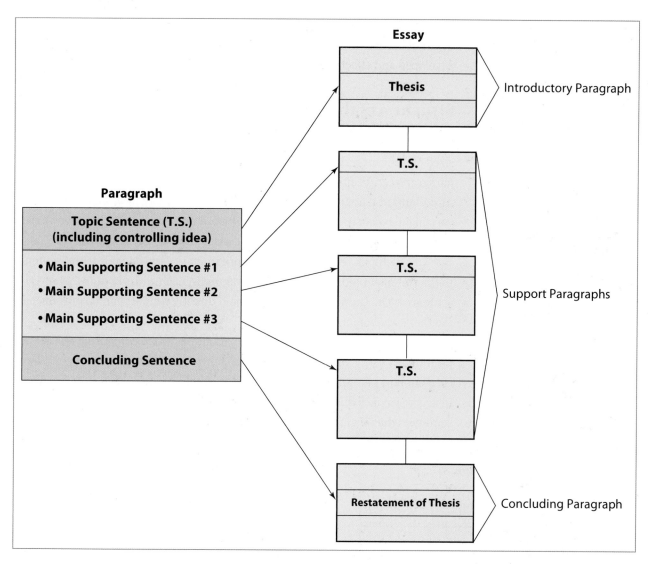

Figure 20.3: Moving from the Paragraph to the Essay

As the figure above shows, once the basic structure of a paragraph (left) has been transferred to the corresponding structure of an essay (right), it is just a matter of adding detail, especially in the area of examples, to make the essay complete. (For more about examples, see pp. 208–210 in Chapter 19: "The Paragraph.") The most important work—the identification of the topic, of the controlling idea, and of the main points (in the form of main supporting sentences in the paragraph) has already been done. The main supporting sentences in the paragraph translate into topic sentences in the essay. In fact, the wording of a main supporting sentence in a paragraph and of the corresponding topic sentence in an essay can be exactly the same.

A Third Format: The Preliminary Essay

Although not nearly as traditional as either the paragraph or the essay, a third format, the preliminary essay, is used by some instructors to fill the gap between the two more traditional formats. Learning to write preliminary essays allows you to progress from writing paragraphs to writing essays more gradually so the task does not become unmanageable. The resulting products are more likely to be well developed and effective.

Structure of the Preliminary Essay

Chapter 19, on the paragraph, introduced two types of paragraphs: the regular-sized and the extended. This chapter introduces the standard essay as a five-paragraph composition starting with an introductory paragraph, continuing with three support paragraphs, and ending with a concluding paragraph. Logically, you might expect the structural size of the preliminary essay to be somewhere in between those of the paragraph and the essay. You would be correct.

This textbook recommends that a preliminary essay include a one-sentence thesis statement plus three support paragraphs, each with about five to seven sentences. The support paragraphs should directly support and be introduced by the thesis statement.

To properly introduce the support paragraphs when composing a preliminary essay, one can write a three-point thesis statement (one point for each support paragraph). Some instructors might require this. But unless your instructor makes this a requirement, it is not necessary as long as the topic sentences that begin your support paragraphs are effectively written.

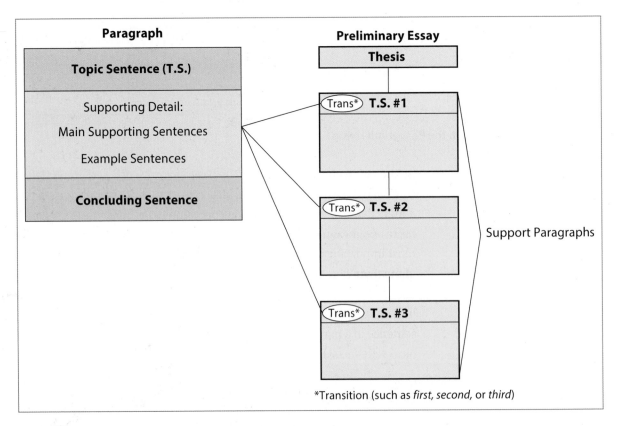

Figure 20.4: Structure of the Preliminary Essay

This figure shows how the components of a paragraph can be carried over to the preliminary essay. Note, in particular, that the main supporting sentences in a paragraph can now become the topic sentences in a preliminary essay, complete with the same transitions.

Question: If students want higher grades, what can they do?

Model Preliminary Essay: Good Habits

Thesis (one-sentence direct answer to the above question):
If students want higher grades, they can develop three good habits.

First, taking good notes in class can help in a variety of ways, all leading to better grades. For example, no one can remember everything that was said and done in two or three hours. But notes help students remember more. There is no need to take down everything, just what they think is useful to their learning. If they think, for example, that learning an extra rule about commas might help their writing, that rule should be taken down in the form of notes. The new rule might then become easier to apply the next time they do some writing, and the writing is improved as a result.

Second, assigned readings and any other assigned homework should be done for each class, whether it's worth marks or not. Even if the homework is not evaluated that day, completing it goes a long way toward better marks when the marked assignments do arrive. Not everything that a student reads will be understood. But the more a student reads, the more of what the professor says in class will make sense—and the better the student will do in the next assignment.

Finally, students should approach the professor, a tutor, or someone else who can help when something is difficult to understand. One of the limitations of the classroom is that the professor must reach as many students as possible in a very short time. He or she cannot always tell if something is not being understood. There's only so much he or she can do. This is where students are expected to take some initiative. If they need help, they should ask for it. But if things not understood do not get dealt with, the course might just get harder instead of easier as time goes on.

Questions for Analysis

1. Does the thesis answer the question?
2. What are the main transitions in this preliminary essay? What is their function?
3. How many sentences are in each paragraph?
4. Is the thesis written in third person (if required)? Does the thesis contain an opinion or controlling idea?
5. What are the topic sentences? What are their jobs?
6. Is this an effective piece? Why or why not? Be specific.

Exercise 1 **Writing a Preliminary Essay**

Look at the picture of Naheed Nenshi, mayor of Calgary, Alberta. Do some research on him, and then proceed to write a preliminary essay in response to one of the following topics:

1. Why is Mayor Nenshi so popular with Calgarians?
2. Why would Mayor Nenshi make a great prime minister one day?

Naheed Nenshi

Features of the Essay

Before you begin the process of writing your own essays, this chapter will prepare you to understand and work with these special essay features:

- Thesis statement
- Introductory paragraph
- Transitions between body paragraphs
- Concluding paragraph

What Is a Thesis Statement?

DEFINITION

The **thesis** of an essay is a statement of the main idea of that essay. It usually contains an element of opinion or argument. It is sometimes described as the claim that the evidence in the rest of the essay is expected to support.

The thesis states what you are going to explain, defend, or prove about your topic. It is usually placed in the middle or at the end of the introductory paragraph.

Plan of Development, or POD

DEFINITION

A **plan of development,** or **POD,** is an introduction to the main points that are intended to support the thesis statement. The best place for this POD is in the introductory paragraph, immediately after the thesis statement.

Some books on writing say that a thesis statement itself should contain the three points that you will discuss throughout the supporting paragraphs of your essay. For the purposes of this book, a three-point thesis is not necessary for either a preliminary essay or an essay. In fact, it is recommended here that in an essay you instead introduce these points after the thesis statement by using a plan of development or POD (see Figure 20.2, "Components of the Essay"). Separating the thesis from the points that will be used to support it allows you more freedom to write a forceful and effective thesis statement. That said, if you do come up with a thesis that introduces your three support points and is still clear, brief, and strong, feel free to go with it.

How to Recognize a Thesis Statement

1. **The thesis statement is a complete sentence.** Students sometimes confuse a thesis statement with an essay's title. Remember that titles are usually phrases rather than complete sentences.

   Title: The Advantages of All-Day Kindergarten
   Thesis: Schools should offer parents the option of an all-day kindergarten program for their children, not only for the benefit of mothers who work outside the home, but also for the sake of the children.

2. **The thesis statement presents a viewpoint about the topic that will be defended or shown in the essay.** It may be based on facts, but it is not itself a fact.

   Fact: Nearly all kindergartens in Canada offer a half-day of instruction.
   Thesis: Parents know there is more than one reason why most five-year-old children should be in school for only half a day.

 Practice 1 **Recognizing the Thesis Statement**

In the space provided, identify each of the following as (1) a title, (2) a thesis, or (3) a fact that could be used to support a thesis. Check your answers against those in the Answer Key on page 466.

_____ 1. The personal interview is the most important step in the employment process.

_____ 2. Looking for a job

_____ 3. Sixty percent of all jobs are obtained through newspaper advertisements.

_____ 4. The best time to begin learning a foreign language is in grade school.

_____ 5. The importance of learning a foreign language

_____ 6. By the year 2015, the number of students studying foreign languages was dramatically lower than what it had been two decades earlier.

_____ 7. Most Canadians doing business with Japan do not know a word of Japanese.

Writing an Effective Thesis Statement

An effective thesis statement has two or three parts:

1. **It contains a topic that is not too broad.** Broad topics must be narrowed down in scope. You can do this by *limiting the topic* (changing the term to cover a smaller part of a broad topic) or *qualifying the topic* (adding phrases or words to the general term that will narrow down the topic).

> **Broad topic:** Swimming
>
> **Limited topic:** Learning to float (Floating is a kind of swimming, more specialized than the term *swimming*.)
>
> **Qualified topic:** Swimming for health two hours a week (The use of the phrase *for health two hours a week* narrows the topic down considerably. Now the time spent swimming and the reason for swimming are parts of the topic.)

There are a number of ways to narrow a topic to make it fit into a proper essay length, as well as make it fit your experience and knowledge.

2. **It contains a controlling idea that you can defend.** The controlling idea is what you want to show or prove about your topic; it is your attitude about that topic. The controlling idea is often an adjective, such as *beneficial, difficult,* or *maddening.*

> Learning to float at the age of 20 was a *terrifying* experience. Swimming two hours a week brought about a *dramatic* change in my health.

3. **Optional: It indicates what strategy for development is to be used.** To indicate the strategy, you can use words such as *description, steps, stages, comparison, contrast, causes, effects, reasons, advantages, disadvantages, definition, analysis, persuasion, classification.*

Although not all writers include the strategy in the thesis statement, they must always have in mind what major strategy they plan to use to prove their thesis. Professional writers often use more than one strategy in a text. However, in this book, you are asked to develop your essays by using one major strategy at a time. By working in this way, you can concentrate on understanding and developing the skills needed for each specific strategy.

Study the following thesis statement:

> Although a date with the right person is marvellous, going out with a group can have many advantages.

Now look back and check the parts found within it.

General topic: Going out
Qualified topic: Going out in a group
Controlling idea: To give the advantages
Strategy for development: Contrast between the couple date and the group date

 Exercise 2 Writing the Thesis Statement

Below are three topics. For each one, develop a thesis statement by (1) limiting or qualifying the general topic, (2) choosing a controlling idea (what you want to explain or prove about the topic), and (3) selecting a strategy you could use to develop that topic. (Possible strategies include narration, description, process, comparison or contrast, definition, classification, and cause and effect.) An example has been done for you.

General topic: Senior citizens

a. Limited or qualified topic:
   Community services available to the senior citizens in my town
b. Controlling idea:
   To show the great variety of programs
c. Strategy for development:
   Classify the services into major groups.

Thesis statement: The senior citizens of New Glasgow, Nova Scotia, are fortunate to have programs available to help them deal with health, housing, and leisure time.

1. Winnipeg (or another city with which you are familiar)
   a. Limited or qualified topic:

   _____

   b. Controlling idea:

   _____

   c. Strategy for development:

   _____

   Thesis statement:

   _____

   _____

2. Shopping
   a. Limited or qualified topic:

      _____

   b. Controlling idea:

      _____

   c. Strategy for development:

      _____

   Thesis statement:

   _____

   _____

3. Canadians
   a. Limited or qualified topic:

      _____

   b. Controlling idea:

      _____

   c. Strategy for development:

      _____

   Thesis statement:

   _____

   _____

The Introductory Paragraph

DEFINITION

An **introduction** has a purpose that is twofold: to grab your readers' attention so that they will keep reading and to establish the thesis (or your main idea).

There is no one way to write an introduction. However, since many good introductions follow a few common patterns, you will find it helpful to look at a few examples of these patterns as you learn to write your own introductions. In the following examples, the thesis statement is usually at the end.

1. **Begin with a general subject that can be narrowed down to the specific topic of your essay.** Here is an introductory paragraph on astronomy from *Universe,* by W.J. Kaufmann:

   Speculation about the nature of the universe is one of the most characteristic human endeavours. The study of the stars transcends all boundaries of culture, geography, and politics. The modern science of astronomy carries an ancient tradition of observation and speculation, using the newest tools of technology and mathematics. In the most literal sense, astronomy is a universal subject—its subject is, indeed, the universe.

2. **Begin with specifics (a brief anecdote, a specific example or fact) that will broaden into the more general topic of your essay.** Here is the introduction to Miriam Waddington's "The Hallowe'en Party," an essay about a family of Russian Jews settling on a prairie farm just outside of Winnipeg:

> The year that I was twelve, my father came home one day and announced that he had bought a farm. My sister Helen and I could hardly wait to see the farm which, according to my father, consisted of 26 acres in St. Vital, just beyond the outskirts of Winnipeg. … My father had dreamed of such a farm all the years he was shut up in the dark greasy machine shop where he earned his living. Now as I look back, I can understand my father's deep hunger for land.

3. **Give a definition of the concept that will be discussed.** Here is the introduction to "Love Hurts," an essay by Jenny Yuen about the problem of love and sex addiction (see pp. 351–353 in Chapter 30). The actual definition is in the last sentence.

> For love and sex addicts, Valentine's Day may not be simply roses and candy, but rather a traumatic reminder that love hurts. February 14 may bring back painful memories of past breakups, or trigger the need to go out and find a "special someone" who may not turn out to be all that special. Sexual and love addiction is the continuing pattern of unwanted compulsive romantic behaviour that has a negative impact on the addict's personal, social and/or economic standing.

4. **Include a plan of development** (a brief summary of points that will support your thesis) **after your thesis statement.**

> Are you a *Law and Order* junkie? Well, if you are, you'll know that the State of New York has the death penalty. And it seems that it gets applied every now and again, if the TV show is any indication. But in Canada, the death penalty was abolished, and it's time to bring it back. One reason to do so is the money that taxpayers will save when the state no longer has to maintain the lives of hardened criminals who will never be freed anyway. Secondly, there is no redemption for criminals who are sentenced to life in prison. And lastly, the punishment should fit the crime.

5. **Start with an idea or statement that is a widely held point of view.** Then surprise the reader by stating that this idea is false or that you hold a different point of view. Here is an example from "A Planet for the Taking," by David Suzuki:

> Canadians live under the remarkable illusion that we are a technologically advanced people. Everything around us denies that assumption. We are, in many ways, a Third World country, selling our natural resources in exchange for the high technology of the industrialized world. Try going

through your home and looking at the country of origin of your clothes, electrical appliances, books, car. The rare technological product that does have Canada stamped on it is usually from a branch plant of a multinational company centred in another country.

6. **Include a familiar quotation or a paraphrase of something said by a famous person,** as Zack Goodman does in the following example from "City Life Beats the Small Town Blues." (For the whole essay, see pp. 321–322 in Chapter 27.)

Growing up in a small town has its perks. You might have fewer friends than you have in the big city, but you tend to keep them closer. The East Coast small town author Hugh MacLennan once said that writers who grow up in small towns have a greater knowledge of human intimacy even if their writing ideas stemming from this knowledge run dry before they turn 40. Well, not everybody agrees with either of those points. In fact, city life can offer just as much knowledge of intimacy if not more than small town life can. Life is better in the big city, and it all comes down to one general reason: more choice.

7. **Give a number of descriptive images that will lead to the thesis of your essay.** The descriptive images can make up the plan of development, which, in the case of the following paragraph, comes *before* the thesis statement.

The nuclear family is breaking up. Both parents are working and children are left on their own for long periods of time, or are sent to daycare centres. Youngsters are learning about life from television and from movies, although the life that they learn about is often far removed from the truth. The incidence of crime is increasing among children because they receive little guidance, and even less teaching, on the difference between right and wrong. Social, moral, and religious values are declining. These are among the reasons why the fabric of society is decaying.

What *Not* to Say in Your Introduction

1. **Avoid telling your reader that you are beginning your essay:**

    In this essay I will discuss …
    I will talk about …
    I am going to prove …

2. **Don't apologize:**

    Although I am not an expert …
    In my humble opinion …

3. **Do not refer to later parts of your essay:**

> By the end of this essay, you will agree …
> In the next paragraph, you will see …

4. **Don't use trite expressions.** Since they have been so overused, they will lack interest. Using such expressions shows that you have not taken the time to come up with your own words to express your ideas. Some examples of trite expressions include the following:

> He was busy as a bee.
> You can't tell a book by its cover.
> Haste makes waste.

Using Transitions to Move from One Idea to the Next

Successful essays help the reader follow the logic of the writer's thinking by using transitional expressions when needed. Transitions usually occur when the writer is moving from one point to the next. They are also useful whenever an idea is complicated. A writer may also use transitions when summarizing the points covered thus far, emphasizing a point already made, or repeating an important point. A transition may be a word, a phrase, a sentence, or even a paragraph.

In an essay, composition, or research paper, transitions link paragraphs and the ideas in them in the same way that they link ideas within a sentence or paragraph. Here are some examples of transitional expressions you might use to help the reader make the right connections between paragraphs. For your convenience, refer to the **chart on the inside back cover of this book.**

1. To make your points stand out clearly:

the first reason	second, secondly	finally
first of all	another example	most important
in the first place	even more important	all in all
	also, next	in conclusion
	then	to summarize

2. To present an example of what has just been said:

> for example
> for instance

3. To present the consequence of what has just been said:

> therefore
> as a result
> then

4. To make a contrasting point clear:

> on the other hand
>
> but
>
> contrary to current thinking
>
> however

5. To admit a point:

> of course
>
> granted

6. To resume your argument after admitting a point that does not support it:

> nevertheless
>
> even so
>
> nonetheless
>
> still

7. To call the reader's attention to the organizational structure of the text:

> Before attempting to answer these questions, let me …
>
> In our discussion so far, we have seen that …
>
> At this point, it is necessary to …
>
> It is beyond the scope of this paper to …

A more subtle way to link one idea to another in an essay is to repeat a word or phrase from the preceding sentence.

> I have many memories of my childhood in the Yukon. These *memories* include the aunts, uncles, grandparents, and friends I left behind when I moved to Ontario.

Sometimes, instead of the actual word, a pronoun will take the place of the word.

> Like many Northerners, I've had to learn to adapt to an urban way of life. *It* hasn't been easy, but today I almost think of myself as a Torontonian.

The Concluding Paragraph

A concluding paragraph has one main purpose: to give the reader the sense of reaching a satisfying ending to the topic discussed. Students often feel they have nothing to say at the end. A look at how professional writers frequently end their essays can ease your anxiety about writing an effective conclusion. You have more than one possibility; here are some of the most frequently used patterns for ending an essay.

1. **Come full circle—that is, return to the material in your introduction.** Finish in your conclusion what you started in your introduction. The material returned to might be "the grabber," as in the case of the following example. But remind the reader of the thesis, also. Whether

you're only returning to the thesis, which is mandatory, or reminding the reader of the initial grabber, also remember to remind the reader with different wording. To illustrate this, here are excerpts from the first and last paragraphs of the essay "The Cellphone: Tomorrow's Medical Menace?" (see pages 274–283 in Chapter 24).

First paragraph:

Cellphones are the latest craze—a modern addiction. For young people, the cellphone not only contributes to the look of "cool" in the way smoking once did and perhaps still does for some, but also offers them a degree of independence—a way to stay in touch with friends without having to check at home for messages.... Until it is known for certain whether people will develop serious diseases such as dementia or cancer directly due to cellphone use, it would be wise for cellphone users to err on the side of caution and take steps to minimize potential damage to the brain.

Last paragraph:

Someone walking down the street with a cellphone at his or her ear, for many young people, still rates high on the meter of "cool." It makes some people feel important when it looks like they are "well connected." ... For those who cannot quit using cellphones any more easily than it is for some to quit smoking, they might want to try the tips listed in this essay. ...

2. **Summarize by repeating the main points.** The following example of a concluding paragraph is from the essay "City Life Beats the Small Town Blues," by Zack Goodman, which appears in its entirety on pages 321–322.

A small town has its advantages; that's true. The cost of living is lower. The streets are probably safer at night. And it might even be easier to meet someone special. But if you're an arts lover who enjoys the company of people from all over the world, and you're interested in cultivating friends who help you to grow spiritually and not just to get drunk on a Saturday night, city life is tough to beat.

3. **Show the significance of your thesis by making predictions, giving a warning, giving advice, offering a solution, suggesting an alternative, or telling the results.** This example is from David Suzuki's essay "A Planet for the Taking," whose introductory paragraph was discussed earlier in this chapter, on pages 229–230.

But Canadians do value the spiritual importance of nature and want to see it survive for future generations. We also believe in the power of science to sustain a high quality of life. And while the current understanding of science's power is, I believe, misplaced, in fact the leading edges of physics

> and ecology may provide the insights that can get us off the current track. We need a very profound perceptual shift and soon.

4. **End with an anecdote that illustrates your thesis.** This example is from an essay, again by David Suzuki, entitled "Hidden Lessons," on the danger of unintentionally giving children the idea that the environment is disgusting.

> It's not easy to avoid giving these hidden lessons. I have struggled to cover my dismay and queasiness when Severn and Sarika come running in with a large wolf spider or when we've emerged from a ditch covered with leeches or when they have been stung accidentally by yellow jackets feeding on our leftovers. But that's nature. I believe efforts to teach children to love and respect other life forms are priceless.[*]

What *Not* to Say in Your Conclusion

1. **Do not introduce a new point:**

> Something else of importance …
> Additional information has come to light …
> A new idea …

2. **Do not apologize:**

> Unfortunately, this essay cannot end on a more positive note …
> If there were more space …
> It is impossible to be sure of every point …

3. **Do not end with a statement that is "up in the air," leaving the reader feeling unsatisfied.** This sometimes happens when the very last sentence is not strong enough:

> Maybe the problem will never be solved …
> There is no obvious solution …
> Hopefully, things will get better …

Titles

Be sure to follow the standard procedure for writing your title.

1. **Think of a short and catchy phrase** (approximately three to six words). Avoid complete sentences, even if they're short. Often writers wait until they have written a draft before working on a title. There may be a phrase from the essay that will be perfect. If you still cannot think of a clever title after you have written a draft, choose some key words from your

[*]David Suzuki, "Hidden Lessons." Reprinted by permission of the author.

Excerpt from the written work "Hidden Lessons," by David Suzuki. Reprinted with permission from the David Suzuki Foundation via Greystone Books Ltd.

thesis statement, especially that part of the thesis that suggests the point of view you have taken.

2. **Capitalize the first letter of the first word and the last word;** then capitalize the first letter of the other words except articles (*the, a, an*), prepositions (such as *in, of,* and *on*), and short conjunctions (such as *and, but,* and *so*).

3. **Do not put quotation marks around the title when it is in the title position.**

4. **Centre the title at the top of the page,** and remember to leave about 2.5 cm (1 inch) of space between the title and the beginning of the first paragraph.

Sample Outline Format

Now that you have learned the various components of an essay, it's time to put them all together. The following is a suggested format for an essay outline. It includes suggestions for length, but how long each element is depends on what your instructor's requirements are, what evidence comes to your mind when you are writing the essay, and so on. Next time you write an essay for practice, try using this sample format to help you structure your essay properly.

For a reminder of the difference between a main supporting sentence and an example, see pages 205–215 in Chapter 19: "The Paragraph."

Essay title: _____

(see "Titles" on pages 234–235)

First Paragraph (introduction):

Attention grabber: (1 sentence) _____

General statement: (2 sentences) _____

_____

Thesis: (1 sentence) _____

Plan of development: (1 sentence) _____

_____

Second Paragraph (first support paragraph):

Topic sentence: _____

Main Supporting Sentence #1: _____

Example Sentence: _____

Main Supporting Sentence #2: _____

Example sentence: _____

Continued on next page...

Third Paragraph (second support paragraph):

Topic sentence: _____

Main Supporting Sentence #1: _____

Example sentences: (2 sentences) _____

_____

Main Supporting Sentence #2: _____

Example example: (1 sentence) _____

Main Supporting Sentence #3: _____

Main Supporting Sentence #4: _____

Fourth Paragraph (third support paragraph):

Topic sentence: _____

Main Supporting Sentence #1: _____

_____

Main Supporting Sentence #2: _____

Example sentences: (2 sentences) _____

_____

Main Supporting Sentence #3: _____

Fifth Paragraph (conclusion):

Recap: (3 sentences) _____

_____

_____

Thesis restatement: _____

Question for further research: _____

Thought-provoking idea (prediction): _____

Working Together: Education Endangered?

1. The cartoon below uses a multiple-choice quiz to suggest reasons that education in North America is in trouble. As a class or in groups, discuss each of the four areas of concern raised by the cartoonist. Then write a five-paragraph essay on the subject (be sure it has an introductory paragraph, three supporting paragraphs, and a paragraph of conclusion). Use the information you have learned in this chapter to write a good introduction and conclusion. For your supporting paragraphs, choose three of the four

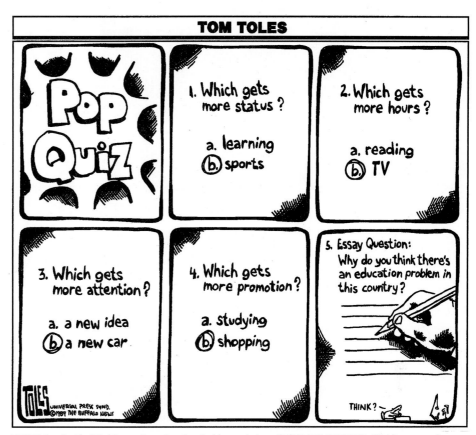

areas of concern shown in the cartoon and make each one the main idea for one of the supporting paragraphs. Be sure to make use of the ideas generated during the class discussion.

2. Join one of three groups in the class. In your group, study the introductory and concluding paragraphs in any essay in the Major Readings section of this book (Unit V). Analyze each introduction and conclusion to decide if the author has chosen one of the patterns suggested in this chapter. Which sentence, if any, is the author's thesis statement?

Stephen Coburn/shutterstock.com

Chapter 21 **Style**

Beyond Sentence Skills

Sentence skills (also known as grammar) are important. That goes without saying. Editing your writing begins with correcting your grammar, spelling, etc. But what about when you're satisfied that your grammar is correct? There are no more misspellings, no more fragments, no more run-ons, no more pronoun errors, and no more punctuation problems. And you have checked the accuracy of your content. You have answered the question on the assignment properly. You have complied with the rules of essay structure. But is that enough? Well, the answer probably depends on how much time you have left. If you still have a bit of time before the assignment is due, then there is one thing you *can* do: work on style.

What Is Style?

Style is how something is written beyond sentence skills. Can a sentence be written more effectively even though the grammar is already perfect? Chances are yes, it can.

First, let's distinguish it from grammar. Grammar includes any sentence-level writing problem for which there is usually a right or wrong answer. Style, on the other hand, relates to a sentence-level issue that is a matter of preference. Preference may be personal, but it is often based on a person's subject area. For example, a fragment is incorrect from an academic perspective; however, in journalism, a fragment is often permitted and even preferred if effect is the objective.

Second, style is an important consideration when it comes to achieving more effective writing. For example, look at the following two short sentences:

The dog chased the cat.
The cat was chased by the dog.

Which sentence is more effective? Most would say the first sentence is stronger. First of all, both sentences say the same thing. But the first is shorter. That's one thing that makes it stronger. Second, the first is in active voice, while the second is in passive voice. In a sentence in the active voice, the subject (the dog) is the doer of the action. In the second sentence, the subject (the cat) is not the doer of the action. (It gets chased; it does not do the chasing.) This is another reason the first sentence is stronger: the subject is the doer of the action. This is a matter of style since both sentences are grammatically correct.

Not everyone will agree on what is the best style. Over time, especially if writing is something you do a great deal, you will cultivate a style that works best for you. And the more time you have at your disposal, the more you will able to rework the style of your writing, making it more and more effective. After all, getting what you want in your job will very often be a result of how effective your communication skills are. And this will depend not only on your command of grammar, or sentence skills, but also on your use of style.

The following are several points of style that the authors of this textbook believe will strengthen anyone's writing. It is certainly not a complete list, but it should give you an idea of the difference between sentence skills (grammar) and style.

1. Clarity vs. Big Words and Long Sentences

The Preface of this textbook mentions that the first casualty of bad writing is clarity. This lack of clarity can be a result of a natural fear of losing face when embarking on a postsecondary education. When students first leave high school, they often think that they have to adjust their writing because they are now communicating with college professors; one thing they might change is to increase their word length and sentence length when they write. They think they have to be more sophisticated now. This is probably not a good idea, since their clarity is often sacrificed.

The problem is one of control. It can be compared to learning how to drive a car. You get behind the wheel for the first time, and you see the other cars on the road going at a certain speed. You want to be like the other drivers even though they have been on the road for years. So as not to stand out, you risk driving at a speed you're really not accustomed to. You would rather risk losing control than feel like a "loser" who's slower than everyone else. Self-image is everything, even if, in the case of the car, you risk putting your own and other lives in danger.

Unlike driving too fast, writing longer sentences is not a life-threatening act. However, it can make a difference between earning good grades and not. It can make a difference between arguing effectively or not. If you are not being understood as a result of long sentences, write shorter ones, at least until your clarity has been improved. Similarly, once you acquire more driving experience, you can begin to maintain more control of a car at a higher speed.

2. Word Economy (Absence of Wordiness)

This is very much related to the point above. Have you ever heard the saying "Less is more"? Think of it as a principle of good writing. Very often, especially when we speak, we add words not only ineffectively, but also incorrectly. For example, how many times have you heard someone say something like this:

> The reason why I was sick is because I lost too much sleep over exam week.

Look closely at the words *reason*, *why*, and *because*. What is the difference between them in terms of meaning? There is none. Not only did the writer repeat him- or herself, but the writer repeated the meaning twice.

Now look at the same sentence with all three words (with the same meaning) highlighted:

> The reason why I was sick is because I lost too much sleep over exam week.

If the writer insists on starting the sentence with "The reason," then the sentence should read this way:

> The reason I was sick is I lost too much sleep over exam week.

With the deletion of two words, the sentence is noticeably shorter.

We often use words unnecessarily without a good reason. We often weaken our arguments in doing so, which is worse. Look at an alternative sentence:

> I was sick because I lost too much sleep over exam week.

One could argue that this is better still for at least two reasons. One, it's even shorter than the last sentence that starts with "The reason." Secondly, the sentence starts with a human subject, "I," rather than "the reason." If you have a choice between using an animate subject (such as a human being) or an inanimate subject (such as a reason), use the animate because it usually makes the sentence stronger.

3. Formal Language

More and more colleges and universities, in fulfilling their mandate to help prepare students for the workplace, realize that this includes teaching them to write and speak more formally because the workplace usually requires this much more often than, for example, the home or social environments. This, of course, does not mean that formal language will be required all the time, but knowing *when* to apply formal language and when it's not so necessary is just as important as knowing *what* formal language is when it's necessary.

a. Avoid Slang

A student once pointed out to me that the term *a lot* (aside from the fact that it's often spelled wrong—*alot*—is slang. I always learn from my students, but because I used "a lot" a great deal in speech and in writing, I had to look it up to make sure. I discovered that my student was absolutely right, and since then, I have made a conscious effort not to use it either in speech or in writing, especially in the classroom, where I try my best to set an example and to practise what I teach.

Gary Lipschutz, lead author of *The Canadian Writer's Workplace*

When you look up a word or phrase in the dictionary, you might find the term *informal* or *inf.* or even *slang* after it. Other terms referring to the same thing include *conversational, casual,* and *colloquial* (or *colloq.*). When a term is discovered to be colloquial, or slang, there is always a proper way to say it instead. It might be difficult to come up with at first, but for the purpose of formal language, it's best to make the effort.

> The two students decided to hang out after class.
> The two students decided to spend some time together after class.

The first sentence contains an example of slang (*hang out*). Unless the two students are monkeys, their intentions are probably not to "hang out" anywhere.

b. Use Third Person (and Avoid Commands)

If an alien came to Earth and signed up for an English course, he, she, or it might ask, "What is easier to use to refer to people or things: first, second, or third person?" The answer of course would be third. After all, the alien can choose literally thousands of words for third person, but there are huge limitations on first and second (you could count these rather quickly, since they are all pronouns). This is a great irony of the English language. Most nouns are potential third-person references —*dog, man, alien, he, she, her, love, jacket,* etc. Despite this fact, the alien would be shocked to hear just how often people use pronouns that are in the first or second person. This is simply because we are used to speaking in the first and second person. It's what we do most comfortably when we speak. And we speak much more often than we write. When we write, most of the time we aren't doing so in a formal setting (e.g., texting), so formal language (including the use of third person) goes out the window.

Also note that a command (or order or imperative) implies the use of second person (the word *you* before the verb):

> Study for your test now!
> Give me the book.
> Go to your room.

These are all examples of commands. For the first and third examples, the word *your* already suggests second person. But all of them imply the word *you* as the subject of the commands. It would sound even more rude (impolite, and therefore informal) than it already does already if the *you* were added. See the following:

> You, study for your test now!
> You, give me the book.
> You, go to your room.

In the interest of sounding a little less rude and abrupt, we drop the *you*. But it's still in second person and, therefore, informal. This is why eliminating commands is part of the third-person reference rule when it comes to formal language.

c. Avoid Contractions

This rule of formal language is extremely difficult to master in speech unless one is reading a speech, for example. Some people maintain that contractions are permissible even in formal language. This textbook maintains that the rule of avoiding contractions should be applied to formal language. (This textbook, however, has adopted a semiformal approach: slang is avoided, but first- and second-person reference and contractions are not. This is to establish a more conversational style in the hopes that reading will be easier and more enjoyable and that student learning will be maximized.)

So next time you write a formal document, such as a research paper or a letter to a client, eliminate all contractions for the purpose of formal language. Say "do not" instead of "don't" and "There is a great deal of bad weather on the way" as opposed to "There's a lot of bad weather on the way." Notice the use of contraction AND slang in the last sentence.

Summary of the Three Rules of Formal Language
a. Avoid slang (e.g., *hang out, a lot*)
b. Use third person (and avoid commands)
c. Avoid contractions (e.g., *should've, can't*)

4. Active vs. Passive Voice

As mentioned in the introduction to this chapter, good writers most often prefer the active over the passive voice. A sentence in which the doer of the action is the subject is more likely to sound stronger.

> The student recited the poem confidently in front of the entire student body.
> The poem was recited confidently by the student in front of the entire student body.

The student is the doer and the subject of the action at the same time in the first sentence. The poem is the subject and, obviously, not the doer in the second sentence. This makes the first sentence stronger, as it is in the active voice, while the second sentence is in the passive voice.

There are some situations in which writing in the passive voice is preferable, such as when the person responsible for a decision is not as important as the decision itself. But that's usually a situation found in the workplace. (Read more on active vs. passive voice in Chapter 3: "Solving Verb Problems.")

5. Word Order

The principle of word order is simple: put all insignificant words in the middle of the sentence where possible. For example, you wouldn't put *but* at the end of the sentence. Similarly, avoid putting *however*, which means the same thing, at the end of a sentence. For instance, don't say,

> He was sick; he still came to school, however.

Instead, you would say,

> He was sick; however, he still came to school.

Emphasis, when someone reads, is often placed on the beginning and at the end of a sentence. If you don't want to put emphasis on the word *however*, for example, don't put it either at the beginning or at the end.

This stylistic principle also applies to prepositions (*to, on, at*, etc.). Although usage sometimes prevails over style and even grammar, it's still a good idea to avoid placing a preposition at the end of a sentence. "Which car did you have your eyes on?" could be replaced with "Which car did you prefer?" You don't have to choose to put the preposition elsewhere, even if it is grammatically correct: "On which car did you have your eyes?" Although this is correct, it is awkward mainly because of modern usage. You simply wouldn't hear people say this today, correct or not. CP (Canadian Press) style—to which most newspapers in Canada adhere—says that this rule should be broken when putting the preposition at the end of the sentence sounds much more natural and less awkward than the "correct" way.

Take these two examples:

> What school are you going to?
> To what school are you going?

CP style would prefer the first sentence, even if, grammatically speaking, the second sentence is more proper. The whole problem, however, might be avoided with better wording altogether:

> What school are you attending?

6. Sentence Variety

No one likes a speaker who is "monotone," which means speaking in one tone without variation. Similarly, a writer should vary his or her sentences where possible. Length is one way to apply variation; sentence type is another. A simple sentence has one subject and one verb. (The cat walked.) A compound sentence has two subjects and two verbs. (The cat walked, and the dog watched.) A complex sentence includes a dependent clause and an independent clause. (While the cat walked, the dog watched.) Vary your sentence type as well as length.

7. Breaking the Rules

As mentioned earlier, journalists sometimes break the rules of grammar. So do novelists, since the realism of characters in the novel trumps proper grammar any day. But before you will be forgiven for breaking the rules, your reader has to get the sense that you know what the rules are. Then there is a greater likelihood that you've broken the rules intentionally and for effect. If you break the rules without knowing what they are, the reader might think that you don't know how to write. And this is often unforgiveable.

8. Breaking Up the Text

There is often a need to break up the text, whether the format is a magazine page or even a formal research paper. The first thing that helps to break up the text so that it is easier to read is the proper application of paragraphing. If a paragraph is too long (say, more than twelve sentences), then it should be broken up into at least two shorter paragraphs. Don't break it up just anywhere. Find a logical spot where a second idea begins. You might have to make some minor adjustments to improve the logic and the flow.

Another way to break up the text for easier reading is to use quotations. (See Chapters 16 and 23 for more on quotations.) Just using quotation marks, in the case of a shorter quotation, can help in this regard. Or a longer quotation (more than two lines) that must be indented without the use of quotation marks might be more appropriate.

If you're writing a report rather than an academic essay, it might be appropriate to add another subtitle, again as a way to further break up the text. In the same way that you would turn a longer paragraph into two shorter ones, make sure that the content corresponds to the new subtitle, and if the transition isn't smooth, make the necessary adjustments.

9. Repetition of Words

There's a time to repeat and a time not to repeat. In fact, the preceding sentence itself is reminiscent of a line in Shakespeare's *Hamlet*: "To be or not to be, that is the question." The intended repetition of "to be" has been famous for more than 400 years and will continue to be so. Most of the time, however, people repeat words or ideas without awareness and certainly without positive effect. Most repetition weakens one's language and sometimes renders it ineffective. Editing can help to reduce the harmful effect of repetition.

10. Audience and Tone

Always consider your intended audience when you're writing. Who do you expect will read your paper? Your primary audience is, no doubt, your professor. But whom do you have in mind when you're writing your composition? If you're writing a children's story, chances are you're neither going to be discussing the topic of venereal disease nor using five-syllable words. If you're writing a formal essay, you're not going to begin by saying, "I thought I'd spill a few thoughts down on some papyrus." The identity of your intended audience, aside from the professor who will be marking your assignment, determines not only what you write, but also how you write it.

Your intended audience, for example, determines the level of formality of your writing (see "Formal Language" on p. 240). If you're writing a formal research paper, use a formal tone. Don't, for example, use contractions (*he's, she'd,* etc.). Stay in the third person (don't use *I* or *you* or commands).

Tone is a matter of attitude. You might recall one of your parents saying to you at some point, "Don't use that tone with me, young lady (or man)!" The same kind of consideration applies to your writing. Choose the appropriate attitude, such as formal or humorous, or both, based on intended audience, and then keep it consistent throughout your composition.

11. Purpose

The main reason for writing a composition at this stage in your life is probably to get a passing grade so that you can move on to the next level of English and eventually graduate in your program. The better your compositions are, the more likely you are to pass your English course. In the interest of producing a high-quality composition, be as mindful as you can of the specific reason for writing your particular piece.

This purpose should be crystal clear to you from the beginning. If it's not, it probably won't be clear to the reader either. First of all, is your purpose to inform, to persuade, or to entertain? Now that you've determined who your intended audience is, it's time to decide what you want that audience to think, do, and/or feel. Are you trying to inspire your readers to do something specific? Or do you simply want them to understand your particular point of view toward a controversial topic? Regardless, the clearer you are on the purpose of your composition, the more effective the result will be.

Make sure the reader knows exactly why you're writing. Depending on the document you're preparing or the format required, the purpose of your writing should be made clear in a certain way that has been specifically prescribed. If you're writing an essay, your thesis must be in the first paragraph, somewhere between the middle and the end. If you're writing a letter with bad news that isn't major, you might want to impart the bad news right away in the first sentence. But regardless, the purpose must be clear. If it's not, you might be better off not creating the document at all. Clarity is essential.

12. Consistency

Consistency is a principle of good writing. It's also a principle of good art, according to Greek philosopher Aristotle. But in writing, consistency needs to be applied to every sentence of every composition, no matter how short or how long, and it applies to style as much as it applies to grammar.

In grammar, for example, there's a rule regarding subject-verb agreement (even the term *agreement* in the title of this point of grammar implies the need for consistency). Another point of grammar is called pronoun-antecedent agreement. Another is person agreement (keeping sentences in the same person—first, second, or third). Consistency, when it comes to style, can be applied to tone (e.g, if the piece starts off sarcastically, it should continue in this way), or voice (narrative point of view), or level of formality (if a piece starts conversationally or casually, it should, again, continue in this way).

Consistency can usually be cleaned up at the editing stage. But if you're conscious of the need to apply it from the start, you will not need to make as many changes when you start editing.

13. Choice of Punctuation

> When the final test or exam approaches, I make a suggestion to my students: "If by now you are not 100 percent sure how to use the semicolon correctly, then try to avoid it altogether." On the other hand, if you *do* know how to use it correctly, by all means do so because it often separates the good writers from the mediocre ones.
>
> Gary Lipschutz, lead author of *The Canadian Writer's Workplace*

The precise use of punctuation can be a very effective communication tool, and it often demonstrates an impressive use of the English language. It proves, along with many other aspects of language and usage, how well a writer pays attention to detail. The writer of a piece in *Forbes* magazine once said that he, as an employer, wouldn't hire a graduate who doesn't know how to apply proper use of the comma to his or her writing since this is a huge indicator of whether or not a job candidate generally pays attention to detail.

14. Avoidance of Abstract Terms

"Abstract" means to exist in thought rather than matter; not concrete; intangible. Look at this sentence:

> The use of the vehicle was regular.

Questions arise. What kind of vehicle was it? Who used it? How was it used? What does "regular" mean exactly? The sentence is very vague because the terms used are vague. The grammar is perfect. But the style is weak because the reader still doesn't know very much.

The 16-year-old drove her new green VW to school every day.

Ah, now we have answers to every question.

Be specific. Use concrete examples as much as possible. Conjure up a picture of what you're talking about in the mind of the reader.

15. Avoidance of Jargon

Jargon (for example, legal jargon) is the special words or expressions used by a particular profession or group and is difficult for others outside of that group to understand. Always consider your audience when making a decision about jargon. If you're writing a work manual for everyone in your automotive group, then you might not have to explain automotive terms. But if you're writing to a general audience, remember to add explanations where necessary, and try to avoid jargon as much as possible.

 Exercise 1   Improving Style

Find a copy of your student newspaper. Pick a short piece and rewrite it, correcting any grammar mistakes you find, but also changing the style of any sentence that you think could be written more effectively. Identify what you've done based on any of the points from this chapter.

 Working Together: The Changing Style of *Hockey Night in Canada*

Alberto E. Rodriguez/Getty Images Entertainment

George Stromboulopoulos

Get together in a group of four or five. Discuss with your group the arrival of George Stroumboulopoulos as the new anchor of *Hockey Night in Canada* since Rogers took over this program from the CBC.

1. What is the impact of this move on hockey broadcasting in Canada? In particular, how do you think it has changed the *style* of hockey broadcasting?
2. Compare and/or contrast George Stroumboulopoulos and Ron MacLean, the former hockey anchor on CBC.
3. What do you think was Rogers' intention in replacing the former anchor?
4. Discuss the impact of this change in style on the viewing audience.
5. Compare and contrast the impact this stylistic change in hockey broadcasting is likely to have on its audience and the impact a change in linguistic style can have on its readers.

Chapter 22 **Revising and Editing**

The Final Stage

Too many writers finish a first draft and then immediately start rereading to catch mistakes. Their idea is to get the editing process over with as soon as possible. If the writer misses a few little mistakes, who's going to notice? But revising and editing involve much more than a quick rereading, hoping any mistakes will jump out. This stage involves a well-planned approach to making improvements, finding mistakes, and discovering better ways of writing.

Revising and editing are essential components of the writing process. Of course, you'll need to proofread your final copy for typos and other mistakes you may have made, but the revising and editing steps must come before proofreading.

What Is the Difference between Revising and Editing?

Revising and editing are often thought of as one and the same thing. They are not. Specifically, revising is rereading your first draft very carefully and making major improvements. You might replace an entire paragraph with a new one, for example. You might cut the length of a large anecdote in half and add a different, smaller one. Editing, on the other hand, usually means making smaller, but still important, changes. Revising often refers to changing the content, whereas editing often refers to improving the organization of the composition and the style of the writing. Too many people do not spend enough time on these parts of the writing process. However, it's better to make improvements yourself at this stage than to have your professor point out the need for them later.

Proofreading

After the revising and editing are finished, proofreading begins. Proofreading refers, mostly, to correcting mistakes at a more "micro" level; for example, grammar or spelling errors. Minor factual errors in content might also be caught at this stage.

Tips for Proofreading Essays

by Linda White

In a bid to master the skill of texting faster than they can talk, countless students rely on short forms that would make their English teachers cringe. But when it comes to proofreading essays, students are urged to slow down and take the time to read and reread their draft.

"For starters, it's important for students to understand something about themselves as writers," says John Hannah, assistant director of student learning support and manager of the writing centre at Toronto's Ryerson University.

"Based on the feedback they've gotten over the years from various instructors, they can start to recognize patterns of error. It may not be that they're making a hundred different mistakes; it may be that they're making the same kinds of mistakes over and over again." One of the most common mistakes is the sentence fragment—a group of words that seem to act like a sentence but don't form a complete thought.

A visit to your campus writing centre can provide valuable feedback that can give you a more targeted approach to proofreading.

Don't get too hung up on proofreading in the early stages of drafting your essay, when you should be free to explore ideas. Understand your limitations as a proofreader. Too many students believe reading over their paper a couple of times will suffice, but it rarely does due to "error blindness."

"Especially when you review it immediately after writing, you may be too familiar with it to see errors," says Hannah. He recommends a systematic approach to proofreading that includes the following tips:

- Take time between writing and proofreading your final draft.
- Each time you proofread your essay, have a target in mind: The first time, for example, look for sentence fragments; the next time, look for spelling errors.
- Change the font size or colour (it offers a different perspective).
- Proofread a printed copy of your draft; you're more likely to catch mistakes you'd overlook on the computer screen.
- Read your paper out loud, listening for errors.
- Ask a friend to proof your paper and read it to you aloud.
- Read your paper backwards if spelling is one of your recurring errors.
- Ensure your essay follows assignment guidelines and properly reference secondary sources using the appropriate reference guide (such as Modern Language Association [MLA] or American Psychological Association [APA]) for your discipline.

"Correctness matters," Hannah says. "You undermine your own authority and credibility each time a mistake is made. Worse than that, your essay may just end up being incoherent or unreadable."

totallyPIC.com/Shutterstock

Source: Linda White, "Tips for Proofreading Essays," 24 Hours Toronto e-edition (15 April 2013).

The Right Conditions for the Tasks

When you've finished the first draft of your work, set it aside for a day or two if you can. Then read through the whole thing, making notes, corrections, or additions based on the checklists that start below, which are adapted from *The Reluctant Writer,* by Roger Mann and John Roberts. Many instructors recommend that you read your essay out loud. Some say that writers can catch up to 70 percent of their own errors this way. At the final stage, it is important to print a hard copy of your final draft in order to proofread your work. You will have a better chance of spotting errors this way than if you do your final read-through onscreen, since the eyes read better with reflected light (off paper) than with emitted light (from a computer screen).

What you need first is a quiet place and a block of time that will allow you to complete the task in one sitting. When you have completed your own revising and editing, you might also ask someone else to read your material and offer a second opinion on the quality of your work and suggestions for improvement. Finally, keep in mind that your computer's spell check and grammar check programs are not infallible. As the writer, you are ultimately responsible for your own work; that includes the revising, the editing, and the proofreading.

Master Checklist for Revising and Editing

1. Check the macrocomposition: the content and the overall arrangement of ideas. (See "Macrocomposition Checklist," below.)
2. Check the microcomposition: the flow of thought, the sentence structure, and the wording, grammar, and usage. (See "Microcomposition Checklist" on the next page.)
3. Check the spelling.
4. Check the punctuation.
5. Check the manuscript form.

Macrocomposition Checklist

1. Have you provided enough background explanation at the outset for the reader to:
    a. recognize the context?
    b. understand what follows?
    c. want to read further?
2. Do the ideas introduced in the beginning connect logically to a continuous line of thought that moves sensibly from introduction to discussion and ends in a conclusion? Are appropriate connecting words used?
3. Are the thoughts packaged in small chunks of information that the audience is capable of following? Will the sequence of ideas convince and enlighten the reader?
4. Is the information sufficient to do the job it is intended to do? Are there any gaps? Is all of the discussion relevant to the subject and the purpose?
5. Is the point of view consistent throughout the text?
6. Are the time sequences logical and consistent? Are all the verbs in the correct tense and mood?
7. Is the wording concise, and are physical references precise and concrete? If you are dealing with ideas and concepts, are they adequately explained and illustrated? Is the wording geared to the presumed reading level of the reader?

(continued on next page)

(continued from previous page)

8. Is the tone appropriate to the situation, the purpose, and the reader? Is it consistent throughout the text?
9. Does the conclusion fulfill the intended purpose? At the end, will the reader understand the message, agree with what you have said, and be motivated to act?

Microcomposition Checklist

Check your sentences for *grammar:*

1. Is every sentence grammatically complete, with no sentence fragments?
2. In sentences with two or more independent clauses, are the clauses grammatically parallel, and either connected by coordinating conjunctions or separated by semicolons, with no run-ons?
3. Are subordinate clauses and verb phrases clearly related to the words they modify, with no dangling or misplaced modifiers?
4. Are the elements of each sentence consistent in grammar and in thought?
   - Do subjects agree with verbs?
   - Do pronouns agree with their antecedents and with each other in person and in number?
   - Is it clear which nouns the pronouns stand in for?
   - Are the verb tenses consistent?
   - If you have used lists, are the elements of each list grammatically parallel?
   - Is the word order appropriate and easy to follow?

Check your sentences for *style:*

1. Are the beginnings of your sentences varied—do some start with the subject, some with introductory phrases or clauses, and a select few with reversed word order?
2. Have you varied the clause structure of your sentences—some simple, some compound, and some complex?
3. Have you mixed your sentence lengths effectively—long sentences to convey information and establish a rhythm, short sentences to get important points across?

Check your *wording* and *usage:*

1. Have you used vocabulary suitable to the reader and the situation?
2. Are your nouns concrete, tangible, and specific?
3. Are your verbs active or passive, as is appropriate to the context?
4. Have you used adjectives and adverbs selectively and sparingly? Can you replace any adjective-noun or adverb-verb combinations with carefully selected single nouns or verbs?
5. Could you explain the reason for your choice of every word and its placement in the sentence?
6. Have you used any words that you are not entirely sure about—the spelling, the meaning, or the way the words should be used?
7. Have you used any clichés? If so, can you justify using them? If not, can you think of original expressions to replace them?
8. Have you used any idiomatic expressions? If so, are you sure you have used them correctly and appropriately?
9. Have you used jargon, such as technical terms or acronyms? Are you sure the reader will understand these terms?

(continued on next page)

(continued from previous page)

Check your *punctuation:*

1. Have you used periods at the ends of sentences and after abbreviations?
2. Do question marks indicate the ends of interrogative sentences?
3. Have you used exclamation marks to emphasize especially important points or statements? (Do not overuse this device!)
4. Have you used quotation marks properly—for all direct speech, direct quotations from sources, and titles of short works?
5. Have you used, but not overused, commas to pace the reader's understanding of the text, to separate internal parts of your sentences, and to clarify potentially ambiguous word combinations?
6. Have you used semicolons to separate parts of a sentence that are grammatically distinct, or to separate items in a complex list?
7. Have you used dashes and colons correctly?

Check your *spelling, capitalization,* and *apostrophes*:

1. Have you checked the words you traditionally have trouble with?
2. Have you checked *ie* combinations, spelling changes caused by suffixes, and consonants that must be doubled or not?
3. Have you used capital letters properly—for titles, names, places, months, countries, etc.?
4. Have you used apostrophes correctly—for possessive nouns and indefinite pronouns, or for contractions?

Check your *manuscript form*:

1. Has all your source material been suitably acknowledged and documented? (See Chapter 24: "Documentation.")
2. Have you used the proper format conventions for the form you are writing—memo, letter, report, essay?

Now that the theory behind this stage of the composition process has been discussed, it's time to apply it to an actual sample of a student essay. Of course, just as no two chefs, carpenters, or painters approach their work in quite the same way, so do no two writers. Yet most successful writers go through a surprisingly similar series of steps to reach a polished finished product.

Here is a summary of the steps in the final stage of the writing process.

Stage Four (Postwriting: Revising, Editing, and Proofreading)

1. Revise and edit the rough draft (some writers revise their work through many, many drafts before they are satisfied).
2. Write the second draft.
3. Proofread (check grammar, spelling, style, etc.).
4. Type or word-process the essay if necessary and print.
5. Check the final copy for errors (especially typos).

A Sample Student Essay in Its Fourth Stage

Some instructors have no problem with their students writing essays in the first person (using the word *I,* for example). However, the following student essay is written in a more formal tone, using the third person (without the pronouns *I* or *you*). For model essays written in a formal tone, see Chapter 24: "Documentation," Chapter 25: "Argumentation," Chapter 29: "Description," Chapter 30: "Definition," and Chapter 31: "Classification."

Sample Student Essay: Revising and Editing the Rough Draft

What follows is a rough draft that a student has written. In the margin are comments that have been added by the student's writing instructor to aid in revision. At this stage, the student is focusing on organization and content rather than punctuation and grammar. The student may correct some of the grammatical errors—for example, upon rewriting, deleting, or adding material.

A more creative title? One that does more to reflect the thesis? Add an attention grabber: what is a parent's worst fear in dropping a child off at day care?

Day Care

As any parent knows, not all day care centres are created equal, and as a result, parents need to spend a great deal of time and attention selecting the day care centre their child will attend. Few consumer decisions parents make can have a greater impact on their child's life than this one. Luckily, parents should be able to recognize a good day care centre by examining its facilities, programs, and staff.

Switch this paragraph with the next one so that points are discussed in the order they are introduced—see last sentence of first paragraph. Add a transition.

Give an example of a program or programs.

A good day care centre will offer a variety of programs designed to stimulate a child's physical, social, and intellectual development. Children should be given the opportunity to learn and interact with groups as well as the opportunity to learn through individual activities. A good centre will offer a balance between structured and unstructured learning environments. In addition to these programs, a good centre will provide nutritious meals and snacks, as well as a quiet rest period after lunch. Parents should have the opportunity to meet with their child's caregiver regularly and should receive regular feedback on their child's behaviour and progress.

Add a transition.

The facilities should be well maintained, safe, and attractive. On the outside, there should be a fenced and shaded play area with a locked gate so that strangers cannot wander into the playground. Equipment should be safe and stimulating, and in order to protect young knees and elbows, the playground should be surfaced with something other than cement. The play area should also offer a variety of play experiences. On the inside, the entire facility should be in good repair, organized and clean.

Add examples in support of this point.

Add transitions that help the reader to recognize the main supporting sentences.

The most important component of a good day care centre is the people who work there. The centre should have performed background checks on all staff members to ensure that no one with a criminal record has contact with children. The staff should be professional; they should have degrees or training in child development and first aid. There should be enough staff to adequately supervise children, no more than a one-to-five ratio for infants and a one-to-ten ratio for older children. The attitude and personality of the staff are also important. Caregivers should be warm, friendly, and, above all, patient with children. Nothing is worse than a staff member who loses patience and yells at a child.

Add a positive note to end this paragraph.

A good day care centre will help that child develop into a responsible and well-adjusted adult. Once parents find a good day care centre, they can rest a little easier knowing that their child is receiving day care as good, if not better, than they themselves would be able to provide.

Preparing the Final Copy

If you have worked hard in revising and editing the rough draft, you will feel proud of the improvements you've made as you write the final copy.

At this stage of the writing process, it is time to proofread and to use the "Checklist for the Final Copy," which can be found on page 197 in Chapter 18: "The Four Stages of Writing for a Paragraph or an Essay."

In the revised version of the essay that follows, the revisions made in response to the instructor's comments and suggestions—in the left-hand margin alongside the rough draft above—are underlined.

A Student Essay in Progress: The Revised Version

<u>Choosing a Good</u> Day Care <u>Centre</u>

<u>Nothing is harder for working parents than dropping their child or children off at a day care centre before going to work or school. At worst, visions of all the horror stories they've heard on TV about abused, mistreated, or molested children swim through their heads as they drive away.</u>

<u>At best, parents worry that their children are not getting adequate stimulation, attention, or affection.</u> As any parent knows, not all day care centres are created equal, and as a result, parents need to spend a great deal of time and attention selecting the day care centre their child will attend. Few consumer decisions parents make can have a greater impact on their child's life than this one. Luckily, parents should be able to recognize a good day care centre by examining its facilities, programs, and staff.

<u>To begin,</u> the facilities, both exterior and interior, should be well maintained, safe, and attractive. On the outside, there should be a fenced and shaded play area with a locked gate so that strangers cannot wander into the playground. Equipment should be safe and stimulating, and in order to protect young knees and elbows, the playground should be surfaced with something other than cement. The play area should also offer a variety of play experiences. On the inside, the entire facility should be in good repair, organized and clean. <u>There should be individual cubbies for each child's coat and backpack, cots or mats for naps, and child-sized tables, chairs, sinks, and toilets. Also, walls and bulletin boards should be decorated with colourful, stimulating displays, preferably of the children's artwork.</u>

<u>In addition to offering excellent facilities,</u> a good day care centre will offer a variety of programs designed to stimulate a child's physical, social,

and intellectual development. Programs such as art, music, and dance stimulate all three skills at once. Children should be given the opportunity to learn and interact with groups as well as the opportunity to learn through individual activities. A good centre will offer a balance between structured and unstructured learning environments. In addition to these programs, a good centre will provide nutritious meals and snacks, as well as a quiet rest period after lunch. Parents should have the opportunity to meet with their child's caregiver regularly and should receive regular feedback on their child's behaviour and progress.

The most important component of a good day care centre is the people who work there. <u>First</u>, the centre should have performed background checks on all staff members to ensure that no one with a criminal record has contact with children. <u>Second</u>, the staff should be professional; they should have degrees or training in child development and first aid. <u>Next,</u> there should be enough staff to adequately supervise children, no more than a one-to-five ratio for infants and a one-to-ten ratio for older children. <u>More important than training, however,</u> is the attitude and personality of the staff. Caregivers should be warm, friendly, and, above all, patient with children. Nothing is worse than a staff member who loses patience and yells at a child, <u>and nothing could be better than a caregiver who greets each child with a warm smile and makes each feel valued and special.</u>

<u>Parents should choose the centre their child attends based not on cost or convenience but on the quality of the centre's facilities, programs, and staff.</u> A good day care centre will provide a safe, supportive, and stimulating environment for a child and, and as a result, will help that child develop into a responsible and well-adjusted adult. Once parents find a good day care centre, they can rest a little easier knowing that their child is receiving day care as good, if not better, than they themselves would be able to provide.

The transitions *first, second, next,* and *more important than training, however* have been added to begin the main supporting sentences in this paragraph for better organization of the supporting detail and better flow of the paragraph in general.

A positive example of attitude has been added in response to the instructor's suggestion. It strongly suggests that a good day care facility is not just one with the absence of negative attitudes, but with the presence of positive ones.

A recap of the three main points in this essay has been added at the beginning of the concluding paragraph.

 Exercise 1 Making Revisions

Read the following paragraph. Based on the instructional material in Chapter 19: "The Paragraph," add suggestions for improvements in the left-hand margin. Then proceed to carry out these suggestions by writing the paragraph in a revised form.

It's the last time I allow my younger sister to entertain without a chaperone of my choosing. My apartment was an absolute mess. I came home to find beer bottles everywhere. I found potato chips and peanuts under the sofa. Upon closer examination, I could see cake icing on the wall, hard to see at first because the icing was a very similar colour to that of the wall paint. The enamel of the bathroom sink had been cracked. The superintendent called the next day to inform me that the police had been called because of noise complaints from several neighbours and that this would go on my record since the lease was in my name. It wasn't until I got ready to take a shower that I discovered a male teenager still passed out in the bathtub.

Exercise 2 Making Revisions

Read both the first draft of the essay about day care above and the final product. Taking into consideration the instructions in the left-hand margin of the draft essay and instructional material on supporting detail of the paragraph in Chapter 19 and the essay in general in Chapter 20, what different or further improvements could be made to the final essay? Rewrite a new version of the final essay underlining improvements that you have made.

Working Together: Revising and Editing Activity

Write two to three paragraphs in answer to the following question:

> Should volunteer work be a required component of a postsecondary (college or university) education?

Take twenty minutes to write a first draft. Then exchange it with someone else in class. Based on the content of this chapter, revise and edit the draft you've been given; then discuss what you have done with the student who wrote the draft. What have you learned from this revising and editing process?

Chapter 23 **The Research Paper**

The Research Paper

With a research paper, you are given the opportunity to showcase your work. You finally have a chance to "sink your teeth" into something you've been curious about. You can devote more time to thinking about, reading for, and writing on a subject that interests you. Because a research paper generally requires a fair amount of independent reading, you should start it early—as soon as the project is assigned. You'll maximize your potential not only for a higher grade, but also for major insights. Indeed, a research paper enables you to go on a journey of intellectual discovery.

DEFINITION

A **research paper** is a paper that presents research in support of a thesis. All ideas that are not the writer's own are expected to be fully documented according to a specific academic style such as Modern Language Association (MLA) or American Psychological Association (APA). For more on documentation, see Chapter 24. A good research paper should be well researched, well documented, and, most of all, insightful.

Standard Essay Structure

Often a research paper is assigned in a course other than an English course. If this is the case, it might be referred to by the instructor as a *report* or a *review*, rather than an essay. Your instructor might, therefore, require a number of specific subheadings and charts and/or graphs as part of the supporting detail in your paper. However, if the paper is required to be, specifically, a research *essay*, the question becomes, "What is the required format?"

Unless your instructor gives you specific direction in this regard, it can be assumed that the research essay generally should follow the structure and format of a standard essay. Usually, you will be given a word count requirement that is longer for a research essay than for a standard five-paragraph essay that might be scheduled to be written in class during, for instance, a two-hour period. A five-paragraph essay could be anywhere from 400 to 700 words, whereas a research essay might be 800 to 1200 words or longer if it's a paper for university. Therefore, expect that a research essay will have more than five paragraphs. Keep in mind that no paragraph in academic writing, whether it be in the form of a standard essay or a research essay, should be more than twelve or fewer than five sentences long.

Often, even students who apply the rules of standard essay structure to in-class essay assignments in an English course will forget to apply the same rules to a take-home research essay—not just rules about paragraph length, but also those regarding other aspects of essay structure and format, such as including a one-sentence thesis in the first paragraph, writing topic sentences at the beginning of the support paragraphs, inserting specific examples in each support paragraph, etc. (For a reminder of these rules, review Chapter 20: "The Essay.")

Responsible Research

Once you have your topic and some idea of the direction you want to take, it's time to start your research. Don't worry about a thesis until after you've done some serious reading. And once you've decided what your thesis is and what points you want to make in support of it, make sure you can find at least two pieces of evidence for every point you want to make. If you're finding this difficult to do, change your point, or even your thesis, if necessary. When students report having trouble finding sources, it's often because they've set off in a certain direction (with a particular thesis in mind) far too early in their research process. As you do more reading on your subject, the direction your paper should take will become more and more clear. Knowing too quickly what you want to say and trying to force your research to support your ideas can cause you to waste a great deal of time, not to mention frustrate you very early in the process. Allow yourself to learn. Find what exists, not what you want to see.

Books, Periodicals, and the Internet

If your topic is current, such as the topic of the sample research essay in the next chapter (cellphones and their effects on our health), you may find that most of your sources will have to come from periodicals (materials published on a regular basis, such as newspapers, magazines, and academic journals) and the Internet. But if your topic is a well established one, a good place to start is the library's catalogue for a search of relevant books. Ask the librarian for help. Every library is different. Until you are well acquainted with your library's resources, the librarian can give you some excellent advice to start you on your way.

The Literary Research Essay

Primary vs. Secondary Sources

If your instructor has assigned a research paper on literature, you may have to research both primary and secondary sources. **Primary sources** are the works of literature themselves. For example, if you are writing about Margaret Atwood, you might look up some of the novels she has written: *Cat's Eye, The Handmaid's Tale*, and so on. These are primary sources. But your instructor may want you to also include works by critics about her writing; these works are considered **secondary sources**.

The General Topic Research Essay

Primary vs. Secondary Research

For a general topic research paper, your instructor might require that you conduct primary as well as secondary research. The first can be more time-consuming than the latter. **Secondary research** is done upon a trip to the library or by research on the Internet; **primary research**, however, might consist of an interview with an expert on the subject; an experiment that you have designed and conducted, including detailed observations; a survey that you have circulated among certain people who qualify, and so on. You can always control the amount of time you spend in a library. But when it comes to primary research, the process tends to get more unpredictable and the plans you make don't always work out. Just setting up an interview, for example, can take more time than expected. Because the interview involves another human being, his or her schedule might not coincide with your own. The more time you give yourself to work on all of these things, the better.

Internet vs. Library Research

Nowadays, more and more students have computers with access to the Internet at home. As a result, whenever a research paper is assigned, the Internet is, for reasons of convenience, the first step in the research process. Whenever you do Internet research, it is important to determine the legitimacy of the online sources you consult (more on this later in the chapter, pages 262–263). Too often, unfortunately, students do not go beyond the Internet. Your instructor, however, may require you to do so. You may, for example, be instructed to go to a library to do the kinds of research that are not possible via the Internet. If so, ask a librarian for help.

Internet Research

If you already have a very specific topic in mind, start with search engines. Put in a string of keywords that are critical to your search and see what "hits" you get. The best way to determine which search engine is most appropriate is to try various ones yourself. The best one for you might depend on the project you are engaged in, as well as on your personal preferences. Here are some suggestions:

Search Engines

Google (www.google.ca) is the most popular search engine on the Internet. The same company has also introduced "Google Scholar" (https://scholar.google.ca), which is academically oriented, pointing the researcher toward technical reports, academic papers, books, and so on.

Other excellent search engines include the following:

- Bing (www.bing.com)
- Yahoo! (https://ca.yahoo.com)
- Ask (www.ask.com)

Academic Directories

The majority of websites are commercial and therefore profit-oriented. Their domains end with .com, so domains that end differently are often more useful for academic purposes: .ca, .org, .edu, .net, or .gov. You can find these domains by doing an advanced search using Google: go to the box labelled "Search within a site or domain," then type in the desired suffix (such as .org).

General directories aim to accommodate the general public. They do not meet the needs of academic research. Here is a list of academic directories designed to help researchers in specific areas:

- The Internet Public Library (www.ipl.org), organized by librarians, has links to thousands of articles, theses, magazines, newspapers, and books from around the world.
- The Virtual Learning Resources Center (www.virtuallrc.com) indexes thousands of academic information sites, selected by teachers and library professionals worldwide.
- www.Virtual Library (www.vlib.org) is a multidisciplinary academic directory.
- www.infotrac-college.com (a free four-month membership comes with this book) provides articles from *The New York Times*.
- iSeekEducation (education.iseek.com) is a targeted search engine for students, teachers, and administrators where you can search trusted resources from universities, government, and established noncommercial providers.

TIP

Be specific in the choice of words that define your topic.

If your subject search turns up too many hits to begin with, narrow your search by adding another term or by making the terms you've already entered more specific.

The use of quotation marks in your subject search can help you reduce the number of useless hits. It is particularly useful for names. For example, if you want to look up London, Ontario, but avoid all hits for London, England, type in "London Ontario."

By adding the word *AND* to your subject search, you narrow your search by requiring that one subject be associated with the other in your hits.

By adding *OR* to your subject search, you broaden your search.

By adding *NOT* to your subject search, you can exclude a term you don't want to find, therefore narrowing your search.

Exercise 1   Using a Search Engine

Pick one of the following subjects and see what you can find using more than one search engine. List three sources dealing with the subject of your choice.

1. Effects of global warming

_____

_____

_____

2. Justin Trudeau's record as Prime Minister

_____

_____

_____

3. Canadian soldiers in the Middle East

_____

_____

_____

4. Medical uses for marijuana

_____

_____

_____

Analyzing the Legitimacy of Online Sources

A great deal of excellent material can be found on the Internet, much of it for free. But not everything online is legitimate. In fact, because the electronic medium is so difficult for governmental bodies to regulate, much illegitimate and even illegal material, such as hate literature, goes unchecked and its producers avoid prosecution. However, there are guidelines you can follow to make sure you are using only proper sources. (Much of the following advice can also be used to assess the legitimacy of regular print sources.)

1. Look for the name of the writer. If you find one, do an independent online search of the name to see what, if anything, anyone else says about this person and what associations this person has. Are the associations with reputable organizations? If the source is not attributed to an actual name of a person, make sure that, at the very least, a reputable organization claims responsibility for the material. Do an independent online search of the organization. See what other organizations say about it, and, ultimately, based on the information you have gathered, use your common sense.

2. Is the writer of the source biased toward a particular point of view because of a connection to an organization with a specific agenda? Be aware of the

one-sided approach of such writers. Does he or she give the other side fair play in his or her writing? Is there a demonstrated respect for the other side of the argument? Try to discern between a point of view and an attack on an individual or identifiable group. (See the section "Common Fallacies" in Chapter 25: "Argumentation.") There are countless organizations, especially on the World Wide Web, whose only purpose, it seems, is to spew hatred at a particular group or groups of people. Avoid these attacks altogether. The writers who have the most credibility and develop the best arguments on a topic are, without question, those with no obvious agenda and no particular stake in the matter. Pieces written by such objective analysts, therefore, often make the best sources for your research paper.

3. Is the writing well edited and relatively free of errors? Is the site well designed and professionally presented? Has the site been revised recently, or does it seem to have been abandoned after being established a long time ago? In other words, how well is the site being maintained?

4. Are there links on the website? If so, where do they lead? Do they lead to other academic materials? Or do they lead to commercial or entertainment sites?

The answers to any of these questions may not provide you with conclusive evidence of anything. But with more information at your disposal, you'll be better equipped to assess the legitimacy of the sources you have found.

 Exercise 2 **Evaluating Online Sources**

Revisit the three sources you found as a result of doing the previous exercise on using search engines (pp. 261–262). Assess the legitimacy of these sources using the above criteria.

Using Quotations

By the word *quotation*, this textbook means the exact words used by an author or speaker. Therefore, the most important thing when it comes to quotations is that you must be careful to use the precise word-for-word text of the author (or the person who was quoted within the source you are using). Some quoting is good because it breaks up text and generally makes an essay more interesting to read. However, try to keep your quoting to a minimum. Quote only those things that you cannot say better yourself. And remember, whenever you include a quotation, you are expected to explain to the reader why the quotation appears in your essay and how it connects to your thesis. You might also be expected to interpret the quotation if its meaning is not straightforward enough already.

How you incorporate a quotation into your essay depends on how long the quotation is. Short quotations are embedded within your regular paragraphs. Longer quotations are indented and set apart from your regular paragraphs. For more about using quotations, see Chapter 16: "Quoting."

Working Together: Finding Appropriate Sources

Read the sample research paper entitled "The Cellphone: Tomorrow's Medical Menace?" on pages 274–283 of Chapter 24: "Documentation." Find *five* sources on the Internet that seem to oppose the point of view taken in the paper. Then answer the questions below and discuss your answers with others in your group or class.

1. How do you know if the sources you have located are legitimate?
2. What were the subject headings (or search terms) you used?
3. Which other tips or information from the chapter did you use to help you find appropriate sources?
4. Answer the following questions based on the information in this chapter and your reading of the full text of some of the sources that you've found:
   a. What observations have you made about these sources?
   b. What observations have you made about the overall issue of the possible health effects of cellphone usage?

Stephen Coburn/shutterstock.com

Chapter 24 **Documentation**

Documentation

When your instructor assigns a research paper, ask what kind of documentation is required. Is a particular academic style (such as American Psychological Association [APA] or Modern Language Association [MLA]) required? Are internal and end references expected? How accurate must the punctuation for references be before marks are deducted? This part of the research paper is considered unimportant by many and is, therefore, often neglected. Instructors frequently complain, in fact, that students end up losing more marks in this area than they should. So be sure to ask what is required of you before you submit your final paper.

DEFINITION

Documentation is the formal acknowledgment of sources in a research paper. Correct documentation makes sure credit is given for others' work and protects a writer against charges of plagiarism (theft of ideas). It involves a combination of citations (internal documentation) and a listing of sources (end documentation). The citations are inserted within the text of the research paper, while the listing of sources is always at the end, on a separate page (or pages). A particular academic style, such as MLA or APA, must be applied consistently to both the citations and the list of sources.

For more on plagiarism, see pages 172–173 in Chapter 15: Paraphrasing and Summarizing.

Two Academic Styles of Documentation: APA and MLA

Although there are several academic styles of documentation, APA and MLA are the two of the most common. APA stands for American Psychological Association. MLA stands for Modern Language Association. These are universal styles in that they are known and used in research throughout the world. Which one is used depends on the subject matter. Generally speaking, APA is commonly used for the physical and social sciences: physics, medicine, psychology, sociology, and so on. MLA, on the other hand, is used for subjects in the humanities, such as literature, philosophy, religion, and the arts. In business, APA has, in most cases, replaced MLA. If the program in which you are enrolled requires that you use one of these two styles in your research, it would be wise to continue to apply the same style to English papers as long as your English professor does not object. If it does not matter to your instructors which style you choose, you might want to briefly examine the differences between the two styles outlined below and choose the one that you think most suits your needs. Regardless of which one you end up choosing, you must apply it correctly and consistently to both the internal and the end documentation of a research paper.

Two Mandatory Parts of Documentation: Internal and End

Both of the major academic styles involve two kinds of documentation in a research paper:

- Internal documentation (sets of parentheses incorporated throughout the essay)
- End documentation (a list of sources at the end)

Connection between Internal and End Documentation

Often, students do not see the reason that both forms of documentation must be provided in a research paper. They do not understand that the two are interdependent: each one needs the other to be valid. A citation in the form of parentheses surrounding information (usually author and page number) is used to show exactly where an author's idea has been used in your paper, either in the form of a direct quotation or a paraphrased or summarized idea. (See page 165 in Chapter 15: "Paraphrasing and Summarizing.") Using the limited information between the parentheses, the reader can then go to the list of sources at the end of the paper and find out exactly what publication or website the idea was taken from. He or she could then locate the source if necessary for fact checking, further research, and so on.

Citations Not Just after Direct Quotations

Many students believe that citations are required only after direct quotations. They believe that if they put someone else's idea into their own words, then documentation is not required. This is not true. If an idea from another author has been paraphrased or summarized and is not considered common knowledge, its source must also be acknowledged in the form of both a citation and a listing at the end of the paper. If you are not sure whether or not the idea you're thinking of paraphrasing is common knowledge, check with your professor. It's better, after all, to be safe than sorry.

American Psychological Association (APA)

APA Format

Follow these guidelines for formatting your APA paper.

- **Title page:** APA requires a separate page, including the title (double spaced if more than one line) and identifying information (name and school). Most instructors require your name, the course code, the professor's name, and the date of submission. Check with your instructor to be sure you understand his or her requirements. Double space everything on the title page, and centre everything, left to right and top to bottom. Do not italicize, underline, or place quotation marks around your title. Capitalize key words (see Rule 5 on page 144 in Chapter 12: "Capitalization"). See the title page of the sample essay toward the end of this chapter (p. 275).
- **Running head:** On every page, place a shortened version of the title (no more than 50 characters, including spaces), in all capital letters, at the top left margin. Put the page number at the top right margin. You can do this using the "Header" option, found under the "View" or "Insert" menu in most word-processing programs.
- **Abstract (if your instructor requires it):** On a separate page following the title page, include an abstract, which is a block-paragraph (no indentation) summary of your paper. The title (Abstract) should appear centred, 1 inch (2.5 cm) from the top of the page. Start your abstract one double line space after the title. The length of your abstract should be between 150 and 250 words.

Internal Documentation: Print Sources (APA)

Internal documentation in APA is referred to as **reference citations.** What they include (between parentheses) depends on what is already included in your text leading up to the citation. A typical reference citation immediately following a quotation includes the author's name, the year of publication, and the page number. See the following example.

When You Do Not Name the Author in Your Text

"The battlefield is symbolic of the field of life, where every creature lives on the death of another" (Campbell, 1973, p. 238).

See how the above reference citation corresponds to the APA bibliographic entry starting with Campbell on page 269, under "Entry (from a References list)".

On the other hand, if the author is already named in your text, it is common practice to put the year in parentheses immediately after the author's name when it is mentioned. After the quotation, the only citation necessary is the page number. See the example below.

When You Do Name the Author in Your Text

In *The Hero with a Thousand Faces,* Joseph Campbell (1973) wrote, "The battlefield is symbolic of the field of life, where every creature lives on the death of another" (p. 238).

When You Paraphrase or Summarize

When developing citations for paraphrased or summarized ideas rather than quotations, there is no need for the page numbers; see the following example.

War is like life, in which some people have to die so that others can live (Campbell, 1973).

Or

Campbell (1973) says that war is like life, in which some people have to die so that others can live.

Or if two or more books by Campbell with the same publication date have been used in the research:

Campbell (1973a) says that war is like life, in which some people have to die so that others can live.

(Order such references alphabetically by title in the References list. Then add *a, b,* etc. to the publication year.)

Internal Documentation: Electronic Sources (APA)

Electronic sources include the same information as other sources, though most of the time, for an electronic source, there will be no page number. In this case, if there is a paragraph number, use this number after the abbreviation "para." instead of "p." If there is no paragraph number, the author's last name and year of publication will suffice:

(Jones, 2002)

If there is no author, use part of the title:

("Cell Phones Not Linked," 2005)

> **TIP**
>
> Remember to put article titles (or parts of article titles) in quotation marks, but to italicize titles of major works such as books, journals, and newspapers.

End Documentation: Print Sources (APA)

The list of sources in APA style at the end of your essay is referred to as **References.** This is the word that should appear as the title of this list. The list of entries under this title must be alphabetized according to the first word (usually the author's last name) of each entry. If two entries begin with the same name, go to the year after the name and put the entry with the earlier year first, and so on.

Entry (from a References list)

The first name of the author is abbreviated with the initial(s) only.

The year of publication comes in parentheses immediately after the author's name. The period immediately follows the parentheses.

The book title is in italics. For titles of books and articles, capitalize only the first word of the title and of the subtitle, if any, and any proper nouns. However, don't forget to use the capitalization rule for titles (see p. 144) when using these titles in the text of your essay.

Campbell, J. (1973). *The hero with a thousand faces.* New York, NY: Princeton University Press.

The second line (and any subsequent ones) of a References list in APA style must be indented. If there were a third line, it would align with the second line.

End Documentation: Electronic Sources (APA)

The general principle with electronic sources is that you should include as much information as you can so that someone else can find your source. Make sure the URL (website address) is copied with complete accuracy. The slightest incorrect detail (a hyphen, for example) can invalidate the entire URL. Include URLs without hyperlinks. To eliminate a hyperlink, right-click on the hyperlink, select "Remove Hyperlink" from the box of choices that appears, and left-click on this.

The following model is commonly used for citing electronic sources in APA style.

Article in a Periodical

The author's last name is followed by only an initial, not the full first name.

Because the source is a newspaper, the date includes the day and month as well as the year.

The title of the periodical is in italics. Because it is a major publication title, the regular capitalization rules for titles apply (see p. 144).

McLean, C. (2006, July 27). Wireless overtakes local service. *Globe and Mail Update.* Retrieved from http://www.theglobeandmail.com

If you consult an online academic journal, you may find that the articles each have a digital object identifier (DOI). This is a code designed to help researchers identify and locate the article on the web, even if it is moved to a different part of a website. For example, the article found at http://jama.ama-assn.org/content/305/8/808 has the DOI 10.1001/jama.2011.186. If an item you used in your research has a DOI, provide the DOI in your References list instead of the URL. (Again, be sure to copy it accurately.)

Exercise 1 **Formatting APA Entries for a References List**

Use the sources you have found as a result of the search engine exercise toward the end of the last chapter (pp. 261–262). Formulate their entries for a References list (end documentation) according to APA style. Remember to list them alphabetically according to the first word of the entry.

Modern Language Association (MLA)

MLA MLA format

Follow these guidelines for formatting a paper using the MLA style of documentation. (The *MLA Handbook*, Eighth Edition, does not include formatting guidelines. Formatting guidelines are unchanged from the seventh edition and are provided at the MLA's online Style Center at style.mla.org/.)

- **Title page:** For MLA style, a separate title page is not required unless your instructor requires one. If none is required, type the following information flush left and double spaced, starting 2.5 cm (1 inch) from the top of your first page: your name, your professor's name, your course code, and the date the paper is submitted:
  - Johann Hilton
  - Professor Einstein
  - COMM 301
  - 23 April 2015
- If your instructor does require a separate title page, centre your title (which should be not underlined, not in quotation marks, and not in italics). Apply capitalization rules for titles (see page 235 in Chapter 20: "The Essay"). Centre the information listed above underneath the title. Double space this information here, also.
- **Headers:** Create a header with your last name and the page number (e.g., Hilton 1) for the top right corner of all pages, beginning with the first page of your paper (whether this is a separate title page or not). You will find the "Header" option under the "View" or "Insert" menu in most word-processing programs. This header also appears on the page containing the Works Cited list (see "End Documentation (MLA)" on page 272.)

Internal Documentation: Print Sources (MLA)

Internal documentation in MLA style is referred to as **in-text citation** or **parenthetical documentation.** As in any citation style, an in-text citation must appear after you refer to a source within your essay whether this reference is a direct quotation or paraphrased idea.

The in-text citation usually consists of parentheses containing the author's last name and the page number from which you have taken the quotation or idea.

When You Do Not Include the Author's Name in Your Text

"The battlefield is symbolic of the field of life, where every creature lives on the death of another" (Campbell 238).

Notice that there is no period before the end quotation mark. The period that ends the sentence comes after the reference in parentheses. Also notice that there is no comma between the author's last name and the page number inside the in-text citation.

When you include the author's name in the body of your text leading up to the quotation or paraphrased idea, there is no need to include the name of the author within the in-text citation. The page number is enough.

When You Include the Author's Name in Your Text

Campbell states, "The battlefield is symbolic of the field of life, where every creature lives on the death of another" (238).

Notice there is still no period before the second (end) quotation mark. The period still comes after the parentheses.

When the Source Has Two Authors

"Perhaps the Canadian experience can serve as a paradigm, since Canadian writers also searched for a voice through much of the twentieth century" (Sullivan and Levene 9).

When the Same Author Has Written At Least Two Sources in Your Works Cited List

"The battlefield is symbolic of the field of life, where every creature lives on the death of another" (Campbell, *Hero* 238).

Notice that you need to mention the title in the in-text citation if the author is responsible for two different sources in your paper, so readers can tell which work is being referred to. But the title of the book need not be complete (the full title in the example above is *The Hero with a Thousand Faces*). Ideally, use the first noun and any adjectives that come before it. Leave out any definite or indefinite articles (such as *the* or *a*). Any title (or part title) of a book must be italicized (or underlined); the in-text citation is no exception.

Internal Documentation: Sources without Page Numbers (MLA)

Some sources—usually electronic ones—don't always provide page numbers, and some numbering systems that track your location in a work may vary from device to device. For this reason, you should only use stable locators, such as chapter or paragraph numbers (make sure you identify the type of locator you are using). If neither a page number nor a paragraph number is provided, use the author's last name only.

(Statistics Canada, par. 28)
(Rogers)

End Documentation (MLA)

As already discussed, documentation would not be complete without an alphabetized **Works Cited list** in which all your sources are listed. This list starts on a new page. When a reader sees an in-text citation such as (Campbell 238), he or she may look right away at the Works Cited list to see more information on the book to which you have referred. In the Works Cited list, the first thing the reader looks for is the name Campbell, since it is the first thing in the in-text citation. The reader might find a Works Cited entry like the one below.

Sample Works Cited Entry 1

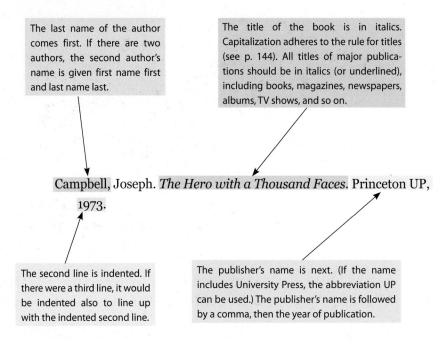

The last name of the author comes first. If there are two authors, the second author's name is given first name first and last name last.

The title of the book is in italics. Capitalization adheres to the rule for titles (see p. 144). All titles of major publications should be in italics (or underlined), including books, magazines, newspapers, albums, TV shows, and so on.

Campbell, Joseph. *The Hero with a Thousand Faces*. Princeton UP, 1973.

The second line is indented. If there were a third line, it would be indented also to line up with the indented second line.

The publisher's name is next. (If the name includes University Press, the abbreviation UP can be used.) The publisher's name is followed by a comma, then the year of publication.

For each entry—whatever the format of the source—you should include what the *MLA Handbook*, Eighth Edition, calls "core elements." The core elements of a citation are the name of the author; the title of the source you are quoting; the title of the "container" (more on this in a moment); the names of any other contributors, such as editors or translators; the version you are using; the number of the source; the publisher of the source; the date the source was published; and the location within the source of the piece you are quoting (for example, the page or the paragraph number).

Most of these elements are self-explanatory, but the "container" needs a few words of clarification. When a source you are using forms part of a larger whole, you should think of the larger whole as the container. For example, if you are quoting one essay from a series collected in a book, the book is the container. If you're quoting a journal article, the journal is the container. If you're quoting an article from a website, the site itself is the container—and so forth.

Sample Works Cited Entry 2

The author's full name (if provided) appears, last name first, then the first name, followed by a period.

The title and subtitle (if provided) of the web page or article appear in the quotation marks with a period typed inside the end quotation mark.

Manuel-Logan, Ruth. "20 Facts about Maya Angelou that You May Not Know." *The Sacramento Observer*, vol. 51, no. 26, 5 June–11 June 2014, p. F4. *ProQuest* 1540933764.

The title of the "container" of information (such as a journal or website name) appears in italics, with the version or volume number (if any), followed by the publication date. For online sources, if no date is provided, use the date when the website was either established or last revised.)

The newspaper article was accessed through *ProQuest*—so *ProQuest* must be listed as the second "container," and the article ID must be included.

- Both the title of a print source and the title of a website or other "container" are italicized. Titles of articles appear in quotation marks.
- Use the publication date that is most relevant to your research. The original date of publication or accessed date for a website may be included to provide context.
- If other contributors, such as editors or translators, were involved in the production of the source, include their names (first name, last name) after the title and the period. Their names are preceded by "Edited by," "Translated by," and so on.
- Web sources do not include http:// or https:// (see style.mla.org/whats-new/).

Article in a Periodical (With Author's Name)

McLean, Catherine. "Wireless Overtakes Local Service." *The Globe and Mail,* 17 Mar. 2009, www.theglobeandmail.com/report-on-business/wireless-overtakes-local-service/article18168819/.

Article in a Periodical (Without Author's Name)

"Cellphone Radiation." *CBC News,* 3 June 2004, www.cbc.ca/news2/background/cellphones/radiation.html.

Article from a Database:

Hardell, Lennart, et al. "Mobile Phone Use and Risk of Glioma in Adults." *The BMJ*, vol. 332, no. 7548, 2006, pp. 1035–1036. *JSTOR*, www.jstor.org. ezproxy.library.yorku.ca/stable/25456794.

 Exercise 2   Formatting MLA Entries for a Works Cited List

Use the sources you have found as a result of the exercise on search engines on pages 261–262. Formulate their entries for a Works Cited page according to MLA style. Remember to list them alphabetically according to the first word of the entry.

Sample Research Paper

An example of a formal research paper is presented below. The paper uses the APA style of documentation. At the end, one paragraph from it and the end documentation is repeated using the MLA style. The topic is cellphones and their possible effects on the human brain. (You may also wish to read the related readings "Smartphones and Lousy Friends," starting on page 295 in Chapter 25, and "Face to Face," starting on page 430 in Unit V.)

APA   APA Sample Essay Using APA Style Documentation

It was always important for a tobacco company to portray someone who smoked as "cool."

Sychugina/Shutterstock.com

Some scientists say cellphone usage is the modern version of smoking. It might seem "cool" to some, but like smoking, it might prove to be addictive and dangerous. In the sample research essay that follows, the striking similarities between these two addictions are further discussed.

milanrajce/thinkstock.com

Note: The format of *cellphone* has evolved from two words to one. Sometimes the term will appear as two words (in article titles, for instance) because of research that has been collected before the change. The old format cannot be updated in these cases due to copyright law.

The Cellphone: Tomorrow's Medical Menace?

Leila Sayeed

Sheridan College

Please note: This sample title page does not include the course code, the instructor's name, and the date, because these are not APA requirements. Ask your instructor whether you should include this information on your title page.

Note: This sample research paper demonstrates the correct usage of the APA style of documentation. The format is typeset according to the textbook's design. For word-processed documents, APA recommends that your essay be typed, double spaced, on 8.5" x 11" paper, with 1" margins on all sides. You should use a clear font that is highly readable. APA recommends using 12 pt. Times New Roman. Consult with your instructor for more information on formatting to be sure you understand his or her requirements.

Cellphones are the latest craze—a modern addiction. For young people, the cellphone not only contributes to the look of "cool" in the way smoking once did and perhaps still does for some, but also offers them a degree of independence—a way to stay in touch with friends without having to check at home for messages. Like smoking, however, not everything about the cellphone is positive. The cellphone, for example, is being blamed for an increasing number of car accidents. And some claim that the cellphone, like the computer and the television, is just another piece of technology that people use—unconsciously, perhaps—to avoid real intimacy. But what might be the worst consequence of all is the one that users seem to be ignoring the most. Startling evidence from scientists around the world has shown that the cellphone does, in fact, interfere with DNA and the human brain. The trouble is, no one is absolutely sure of the long-term effects because the technology is simply not old enough. Until it is known for certain whether people will develop serious diseases such as dementia or cancer directly due to cellphone use, it would be wise for cellphone users to err on the side of caution and take steps to minimize potential damage to the brain.

The cellphone is a microwave transmitter. It uses electromagnetic energy to transmit signals from fixed base stations. The growth rate of cellphone technology has been massive and rapid. The number of cellphone users reached 2 billion around the world at the end of 2005 (Reuters, 2005). In Canada, the number of cellphone users increased by 13 percent in 2005 to 17 million (McLean, 2006) and in 2015 to 22 million (Canadian Wireless Telecommunications Association, 2015). Despite the enormity of the industry's expansion, the technology (the cellphone in its present form) has only been around since the 1980s. And those researchers who believe cellphones will cause cancer also say cancer takes decades to develop. It may be years, if not decades, therefore, before we start to hear about cases of direct linkage between cellphones and brain cancer, making it easy for cellphone companies to insist in the meantime that their product is safe. This is ominously reminiscent of the decades during which tobacco companies had insisted smoking could not be linked to lung cancer.

Several studies of cancer and its possible link to cellphone use have been conducted in the United States and Europe between 1993 and the present day. One such study was sparked by a lawsuit that a Florida man filed in 1993. He claimed his wife's brain tumour had been caused by her cellphone. In response to this lawsuit, the Cellular Telecommunications Industry Association (CTIA) formed Wireless Technology Research (WTR) and granted it more than $25 million to study possible health risks of cellphone use. After six years, George Carlo, public health scientist and WTR's chairman, announced an alarming conclusion:

We found evidence of genetic damage in human blood. We have suggestions of excessive mortality from brain cancers among wireless phone users, and we have very clear evidence of a statistically significant higher risk of neuroepithelial tumors. We now have more data suggesting problems with wireless phones than the FDA (U.S. Food and Drug Administration) had when it banned silicone breast implants. (Bass, 1999, p. 62)

The CTIA, which funded the study, is, in turn, funded by huge companies that produce mobile phones and communications infrastructure. It is not surprising, therefore, that these results were not widely publicized. Cellphone companies, like tobacco companies before them, are in the habit of reporting that research has shown that their products pose "no known health risk" (Bass, 1999, p. 62).

In the book *Cell Phones: Invisible Hazards in the Wireless Age*, Dr. Carlo and syndicated columnist Martin Schram (2001) write how Carlo, after running the cellphone industry's research program for six years, quit due to a conscience he could no longer ignore. He could not say what the industry wanted him to—that all was well. "The big picture is becoming disturbingly clear: There is a definite risk that the radiation plume that emanates from a cell phone antenna can cause cancer and other health problems" (p. 248).

Links between microwave radiation and DNA damage in rat brains have been established by several scientists in the United States alone. In 1997, U.S. neurosurgeons Henry Lai and N.P. Singh of the University of Washington in Seattle reported damage to the brain cells of rats exposed to microwave radiation, according to U.S. magazine *Business Insurance*. The two neurosurgeons claim a "hot spot may develop in the brain, causing cell damage which could lead to neurodegenerative diseases [such as Alzheimer's] and cancer" (Aldred, 1997, p. 25). Although human brains are not rat brains, "We have similar physiology, and our brain cells work basically in similar ways to theirs," says Sheila Rogers DeMare (2003), founder and director of the international nonprofit organization Association for Comprehensive NeuroTherapy. Ross Adey is a professor of biochemistry at the University of California at Riverside. He found a link between low-intensity microwaves and DNA damage in rat brain cells. Even if cellphone microwaves do not damage human DNA, their interference alone may impede the ability of DNA to repair itself when damaged by other causes (Bass, 1999).

In Europe, one of the most alarming major research studies was conducted in Sweden in 2006. Researchers at the Swedish National Institute for Working Life looked at 2200 cancer patients and compared them with an equal number of healthy control cases. Of the cancer patients, 905 had a malignant brain tumour, and a tenth of these were heavy users of cellphones (usage of at least one hour a day for at least ten years). There was also a high incidence of the tumour appearing on the side of the head that the phone was generally used. Researchers in this study concluded that long-term mobile phone use raises the risk of brain tumours, especially in people who start using by the age of 20 (Reuters, 2005). And if anyone thinks cordless phones are safer, they should think again. Cordless phones (marked 900 megahertz or 2.4 gigahertz) give off the same microwave radiation as cellphones do (Worthington, 1998).

Not all of the research has resulted in negative findings. The National Cancer Institute (U.S.) supported an earlier study of approximately 1600 people in the year 2000. It found that cellphone users are "no more likely than anyone else to develop benign tumors or malignant brain cancers" (Kolata, 2000, p. A1). The American Health Foundation, a private non-profit research organization in Valhalla, New York, conducted a smaller study in the same year. It found similar results after examining 1000 people. The latter study was funded by the U.S. government and the cellphone industry (Kolata, 2000).

More recently, in 2010, the International Agency for Research on Cancer (IARC) identified radio frequency fields (including those from cellphones) as a "possible cause of cancer." It concluded that a small number of studies do show links between cellphones and cancer, but that most research does not. IARC conducted a large international project called INTERPHONE to look into the question of whether cellphones cause cancer. Data were collected from thirteen countries, Canada among them. The result of the study showed no increased risk of brain cancer in adults within ten years of cellphone usage (Canadian Cancer Society, n.d.). However, the INTERPHONE Study Group (2010) reported, "The possible effects of long-term heavy use of mobile phones require further investigation" (p. 675).

According to the Children's Health Expert Panel, a five-person American panel (including two medical doctors) representing citizens concerned about the proliferation of wireless technologies and their impact on health, as of 2013, nine types of cancer—including brain cancer, eye cancer, testicular cancer, leukemia, and breast cancer—were linked to cellphone use (Mercola, 2013).

The Canadian Cancer Society (n.d.) mentions on its website that there is not much research on cellphone usage by children, whose bodies are still developing, and long-term health effects. According to the Children's Health Expert Panel, however, the results are more alarming:

> The latency period between cell phone use and brain cancer is thought to be 20 to 30 years. Brain cancer rates are double for people who've been using cell phones for 10 years or more, appearing on the side of the head where they hold their phones, and risks are

5x greater for children using cell phones under the age of 20 than those over the age of 50. (Mercola, 2013)

It is extremely unlikely that an essay like this will convince anyone to get rid of his or her cellphone. But at the very least, people could use some tips gathered from *CBC News* ("Cellphone radiation," 2004) and *CTV News* ("Cellphones not linked," 2005):

- Use a headset whenever possible, especially in a location where the signal to the phone is weak, such as in a basement. Headsets and cellphones with speakerphone capability are highly recommended. Both allow the phone to be positioned safely away from the user's brain.
- Try to text instead of talk, or use the cellphone only for emergency purposes, not for long conversations. When and where possible, use a landline or phone booth. The British government currently advises cellphone users to keep their calls short.
- Using the phone in a moving car is particularly dangerous, so minimize this usage as much as possible. Not only can it cause accidents, but a cellphone works particularly hard to receive a signal when the car is moving, so the electromagnetic field is stronger, putting one's brain further at risk.
- If you are not using a headset, do not put the cellphone to your head until after the call is established. Until the signal is established, the phone is working harder to find the signal, therefore increasing the electromagnetic field.
- Try as much as possible to use the cellphone only when it is fully charged or when the signal it receives is at its strongest (check the signal bars). Again, the harder the cellphone has to work to receive a signal, the harder it is on your brain.
- A person under the age of 16 should only use a cellphone for essential calls, since his or her head and nervous system might still be developing. Children under the age of 10 should not use cellphones at all.

Someone walking down the street with a cellphone at his or her ear, for many young people, still rates high on the meter of "cool." It makes some people feel important when it looks like they are "well connected." It can appear to take the loneliness out of being alone. But today's craze might be tomorrow's tragedy. Smoking has already proven to be a major medical menace of today. What seems like a new addiction (especially among youth) may prove to be the medical menace of tomorrow. For those who cannot quit using cellphones any more easily than some could quit smoking, they might want to try the tips listed in this essay. But if others are more serious about self-improvement, the best solution is obvious: they should go back to using a landline. They might be saving some money. They might also be saving their lives.

References

magazine article

Aldred, C. (1997, January 6). Cell phone dangers require further study. *Business Insurance, 31*(1), 25.

magazine article

Bass, G. (1999, December). Radar: Is your cell phone killing you? *PC/ Computing,* 62.

website article

Canadian Cancer Society. (n.d.). Cell phones and radiofrequency fields. Retrieved from http://www.cancer.ca/en/cancer-information/cancer-101/what-is-a-risk-factor/environmental-risks/radiation/cell-phones/?region=bc#ixzz3WpRt63zq

website article

Canadian Wireless Telecommunications Association. (2015). Facts and figures. Retrieved from http://www.cwta.ca/facts-figures

book with two authors

Carlo, G., & Schram, M. (2001). *Cell phones: Invisible hazards in the wireless age.* New York, NY: Carroll & Graf.

online newspaper article

Cell phones not linked to brain cancer: Study. (2005, August 31). *CTV News, Shows and Sports.* Retrieved from http://www.ctv.ca

online newspaper article

Cellphone radiation. (2004, June 3). *CBC News.* Retrieved from http://www.cbc.ca/news/background/cellphones/radiation.html

online journal article with DOI

INTERPHONE Study Group. (2010). Brain tumour risk in relation to mobile telephone use: Results of the INTERPHONE international case-control study. *International Journal of Epidemiology, 39,* 675–694. doi:10.1093/lje/dyq079

newspaper article

Kolata, G. (2000, December 20). Two studies report no links to cancer in cell phones' use. *The New York Times,* p. A1.

online newspaper article

McLean, C. (2006, July 27). Wireless overtakes local service. *Globe and Mail.* Retrieved from http://www.theglobeandmail.com

blog post

Mercola, J. (2013, October 3). Cell phones and wi-fi—Are children, fetuses and fertility at risk? [Web log post]. Retrieved from http://www.marioninstitute.org/blog/2013/10/cell-phones-wi-fi%E2%80%95are-children-fetuses-and-fertility-risk

online news service

Reuters. (2005, January 18). Two billion cell phone users and counting. Retrieved from http://www.msnbc.msn.com

posting to a web forum

Rogers DeMare, S. (2003, January 31). Electromagnetic radiation: New study on mobile phones and brain [Online forum message]. Retrieved from ACN Forum: http://www.latitudes.org

online magazine article

Worthington, A. (1998). Cellphones shrink brain cells. *Health, Wealth & Happiness.* Retrieved from http://www.relfe.com/wp/children/cell-phones-shrink-brain-cells/

A portion of the previous essay is being repeated here to demonstrate how the same text would look using MLA in-text citations (parenthetical references). A full Works Cited list in MLA style (the equivalent of the APA References list) is also provided.

Sayeed 3

Links between microwave radiation and DNA damage in rat brains have been established by several scientists in the United States alone. In 1997, U.S. neurosurgeons Henry Lai and N.P. Singh of the University of Washington in Seattle reported damage to the brain cells of rats exposed to microwave radiation, according to U.S. magazine *Business Insurance*. The two neurosurgeons claim a "hot spot may develop in the brain, causing cell damage which could lead to Alzheimer's disease and cancer" (Aldred 25). Although human brains are not rat brains, "We have similar physiology, and our brain cells work basically in similar ways to theirs," says Sheila Rogers DeMare, founder and director of the international nonprofit organization Association for Comprehensive NeuroTherapy (Rogers DeMare). Ross Adey is a professor of biochemistry at the University of California at Riverside. He found a link between low-intensity microwaves and DNA damage in rat brain cells. Even if cellphone microwaves do not damage human DNA, their interference alone may impede the ability of DNA to repair itself when damaged by other causes (Bass 62).

Works Cited

magazine article

Aldred, Carolyn. "Cell Phone Dangers Require Further Study." *Business Insurance*, 6 Jan. 1997, 25.

magazine article

Bass, Gordon. "Radar: Is Your Cell Phone Killing You?" *PC/Computing*, Dec. 1999, 62.

book with two authors

Carlo, George, and Martin Schram. *Cell Phones: Invisible Hazards in the Wireless Age*. Carroll & Graf, 2001.

website article

"Cell Phones and Radiofrequency Fields." *Prevention and Screening*, Canadian Cancer Society, www.cancer.ca/en/prevention-and-screening/be-aware/harmful-substances-and-environmental-risks/cell-phones/?region=on. Accessed 11 Apr. 2015.

online newspaper article

"Cell Phones Not Linked to Brain Cancer: Study." *CTV News, Shows and Sports*, 31 Aug. 2005, www.ctv.ca.

online newspaper article

"Cellphone Radiation." *CBC News*, 3 June 2004, www.cbc.ca/news2/background/cellphones/radiation.html.

website article

"Facts and Figures." *CWTA/ACTS*, Canadian Wireless Telecommunications Association, www.cwta.ca/facts-figures.

online journal article with DOI

INTERPHONE Study Group. "Brain Tumour Risk in Relation to Mobile Telephone Use: Results of the INTERPHONE International Case-Control Study." *International Journal of Epidemiology*, vol. 39, no. 3, June 2010, pp. 675-694, doi:10.1093/lje/dyq079.

newspaper article

Kolata, Gina. "Two Studies Report No Links to Cancer in Cell Phones' Use." *The New York Times*, 20 Dec. 2000, p. A1.

online newspaper article

McLean, Catherine. "Wireless Overtakes Local Service." *The Globe and Mail,* 17 Mar. 2009, www.theglobeandmail.com/report-on-business/wireless-overtakes-local-service/article18168819/.

blog post

Mercola, Joseph. "Cell Phones and Wi-Fi—Are Children, Fetuses and Fertility at Risk?" *Marion Institute*, 3 Oct. 2013, www.marioninstitute.org/blog/2013/10/cell-phones-wi-fi%E2%80%95are-children-fetuses-and-fertility-risk.

posting to a web forum

Rogers DeMare, Sheila. Comment on "Electromagnetic Radiation: New Study on Mobile Phones and Brain." *ACN Lattitudes*, 31 Jan. 2003, latitudes.org/forums/index.php?s=817bef853b9c28153626e7ba707e9f67&showforum=260.

online news service

"Two Billion Cell Phone Users and Counting." *MSNBC*, 18 Jan. 2005, www.msnbc.com.

online magazine article

Worthington, Amy. "Cellphones Shrink Brain Cells." *Health, Wealth & Happiness,* 1998, www.relfe.com/wp/children/cell-phones-shrink-brain-cells/.

Questions for Analysis

1. What, in your own words, in one sentence, is the thesis of this research essay?
2. Which sentence in particular presents the author's thesis?
3. What is the evidence that supports the thesis?
4. Does the author provide evidence that contradicts her thesis? If so, what is it?
5. If you answered yes to question 4, do you think this evidence helps or hinders the author's argument?
6. Is the author's argument effective? Why or why not?
7. Who is the intended audience?
8. What does the author want her audience to think or do as a result of reading this essay?
9. Do the sources seem legitimate? Why or why not?
10. Consider the sentence toward the top of page 4 of the essay: "Researchers in this study concluded that long-term mobile phone use raises the risk of brain tumours, especially in people who start using by the age of 20." What do the last few words, "who start using…" suggest? Does this suggestion correspond to anything else in the essay? Discuss.

 Working Together: Documenting Sources

For this activity, which is competition-based, the class will need to be equipped with computers, or everyone will need a laptop with Internet access. Form groups of at least three people. If you haven't already done so, read the sample research essay ("The Cellphone: Tomorrow's Medical Menace?"). Pretend that your group is planning to do more research on the issue of the possible long-term health effects of cellphone usage. Find as many sources as possible, and create a list of sources of which half seem to support the point of view taken in the essay and the other half seem to refute it. Be sure your list follows either MLA or APA style correctly (you must use one or the other consistently for the whole list). After one hour, the group with the longest list of correctly documented end sources wins.

Unit IV Writing Strategies for the Paragraph and Essay

anucha maneechote/shutterstock.com

Chapter 25 **Argumentation**

All of the chapters in this unit apply to both the paragraph and the essay. If you wish, you can move immediately to the essay portion of any chapter (found roughly in the middle of the chapter). Even if you do this, however, you might also want to scan the first half of the chapter to see if you can pick up anything that could be of value to your writing experience. After all, where writing strategies are concerned, a great deal of what applies to the paragraph applies to the essay as well. Most suggested topics for paragraphs, for example, can also be used for essays and vice versa.

What Is Argumentation?

Your purpose in many writing assignments might be to describe, narrate, or explain by using various writing strategies for development. Still another purpose in writing is to argue. In fact, **argumentation** is "arguably" the most important strategy of all because it is the one we use most often to get what we want.

> **DEFINITION**
>
> **Argumentation** is an attempt to change the reader's present viewpoint, or at least to convince her or him that your viewpoint is a valid one.

Every time you write a paper for a course, you are trying to persuade your professor that what you are presenting is a reasonable view of the subject matter. You might want to show, for example, that Canadian airlines are among the safest in the world, or that the crime novel is becoming Canada's favourite form of fiction. As you approach these types of assignments, you need to be aware of each part of the argumentative process so that you will be able to both analyze other people's arguments more effectively and write better ones of your own.

Argumentation vs. Persuasion

You could view most writing as persuasive, since one of the writer's main goals is to get the reader to see, think, and believe in a certain way. Although "persuasiveness" is a quality of *all* paragraph and essay writing strategies (narration, classification, etc.), formal argumentation is considered a separate writing strategy altogether, one that follows certain guidelines. If you have ever been a member of a debating team, you have spent a good deal of time studying this special form. How to use techniques of argument in your own writing is the main subject of this chapter.

Persuasive Appeals That Are Not Logical

Logic is always at the root of a good argument. However, effective persuasive techniques can also include an appeal to emotion, aesthetic appeal (appeal to one's sense of beauty or appearance), and the restatement of a common point of view. These techniques are not necessarily wrong in themselves, but overuse or exclusive use of them can prove counterproductive.

- **Appeal to emotion:** Causing the reader to have a strong feeling can be an extremely effective persuasive technique. The writer makes the reader extremely sad, for example, by discussing the homelessness of a child. We can't help but identify with the child in some way, perhaps because of his or her innocence.
- **Appeal to aesthetics:** Everyone has a sense of what is beautiful, even if this sense changes slightly from one individual to another. Advertisements on TV (and, it can be argued, most TV programs and films) use this type of appeal to sell products and services and to boost ratings.
- **Appeal to common points of view:** Writers sometimes take advantage of what they know are common beliefs, such as cultural values, to get their point across, even if these views are illogical. It's a safe bet that many readers will be on their side because of the popular appeal of the belief.

Other Strategies for Argumentation

Some of the strategies you will read about in this text also fall under the umbrella of argumentation. Cause and effect, for example, is argumentative most of the time, even where science is concerned. For example, the sample research essay on cellphones and their possible effects on our long-term health (pp. 274–283 in Chapter 24) argues that there is a very good chance that cellphone usage and brain damage are connected. Despite the current sophistication of science, the results of this research are far from conclusive. So while this paper has its basis in science, it is, most definitely, an essay of argumentation. In fact, responsible scientists know that their findings are subject to further analysis.

Critical Thinking and Analysis

Students sometimes wrongly offer paraphrasing and summarizing (see Chapter 15) where argumentation is expected. Many instructors at the postsecondary level, in fact, agree that it is the original use of critical thinking and analysis that usually sets an "A" paper apart from others. Thinking critically and analyzing arguments are vital components in the argumentation process.

What Is Critical Thinking?

> **DEFINITION**
>
> **Critical thinking** is evaluating an argument. This skill is used to determine how convincing someone else's argument is for the purpose of making a decision or of helping you establish a credible argument of your own.

Critical Thinking in Everyday Life

Critical thinking is something you should practise every day, not just when forming an argument but also when considering the arguments of others. When you listen to a TV commercial, you should be asking, "Does this make sense?" Of course, an advertisement can still be effective even without a good argument; for example, it might carry with it an emotional or aesthetic appeal, as discussed earlier.

Most of the time, however, it is important that things do make sense. What you choose to eat, for instance, is probably not based only on what tastes good; you have to consider nutrition and other factors. How you vote in the next election likely does not just depend on how the candidates look on TV, but also on how much sense they make in their answers to questions. You are always making decisions, and much of the time, though surely not all of the time, you are making those decisions based on some aspect of critical thinking.

More Tools and Components of Argumentation

As mentioned earlier, the more familiar you become with the different parts of the argumentation process, the more likely you will be able to develop more effective arguments of your own.

> **DEFINITION**
>
> **Analysis** is the process of breaking down an argument made by someone else in order to assess its validity for the purpose of either supporting it or criticizing it and, perhaps, of suggesting a better argument.

Original analysis is often what sets apart a superior student paper from others, especially those that do not engage in analysis at all but merely quote, paraphrase, or summarize material from research conducted.

DEFINITION

A **claim** is a position taken by a writer; it must be supported in order to establish credibility in the minds of readers. A claim may also be called the **conclusion** of an argument. Where an essay is concerned, it may be the **thesis statement;** in a paragraph, it may be the **topic sentence.**

DEFINITION

Evidence is a collection of facts or **premises** provided to support a claim made by the writer in order to establish the credibility of that claim. In a paragraph or an essay, the evidence is often referred to as **supporting detail** or just **support.**

DEFINITION

An **argument** is the combination of a claim and the evidence used to support that claim. If an essay contains an argument, the essay is referred to as an **essay of argumentation.**

	Claim	Capital punishment should be brought back to Canada.*
+	**Evidence**	1. It costs too much to keep a murderer in jail.
		2. A serial killer is not likely to be rehabilitated.
		3. The punishment should fit the crime.
	An Argument**	The combination of both components (*claim* and *evidence*) above

* Note that the words *I believe* are not used in the claim.

** Note that "An" suggests this is only one person's argument that can be supported or refuted by someone else.

Figure 25.1: Components of an Argument

When you make a claim or write a topic sentence or thesis, there is no need to actually say "I believe" or "I think" because these words are, in fact, implied. It is generally agreed upon that the use of the word *I*, in particular, makes the argument seem less effective. The word *I* is usually avoided when writing in a formal tone, such as in a research paper.

Underlying Assumptions

When an argument is made, a claim and its supporting detail are often clearly expressed. What is often not apparent is an assumption underlying the argument. **An underlying assumption is a belief that someone holds about oneself, others, or the world that he or she considers indisputably true.** An entire argument can fail if a faulty underlying assumption is detected, identified, and discredited.

Example: Peter would be a great choice of a marriage partner. (claim)

Peter is rich. (evidence)

Anyone who is rich is a great choice of a marriage partner. (underlying assumption)

Why Are Underlying Assumptions Not Expressed?

There are two basic reasons that writers fail to express underlying assumptions: (1) they are unaware of their own assumptions, or (2) they don't want to draw attention to the underlying assumptions of the argument because, at some level, they know these assumptions are logically indefensible or, at the very least, unacceptable to many readers. Underlying assumptions may be the result of a writer's upbringing, religion, community values, etc. For example, racist sentiment or religious intolerance is an underlying assumption of many so-called arguments, even though you won't hear many people actually saying, "People outside of my race or religion are inferior." Arguments built on top of such underlying assumptions must be constantly questioned and critically assessed.

Analyzing the Intention of Argument: The Importance of Virtue

Good writing should not only depend on effectiveness, but also on good intentions. Consider the actions of the characters in the movie *In the Company of Men* (dir. Neil Labute, 1997), in which two men decide to target a young deaf woman who works at the same company they do. As part of a betting game, they both try to get her to fall in love with them, and one succeeds. In the end, she is emotionally crushed when she finds out that the man she has fallen in love with has no intention of being with her. The other man, who, in the meantime, does actually fall in love with her, asks the first man why he has hurt her so. The man replies, "Because I could."

Communication, like behaviour, cannot be independent of morality. More important than a writer's ability to convince ought to be his or her intention. For example, does the writer appear to be interested only in benefiting himself or herself, or his or her own? Or is there a more honourable attempt to achieve a greater good? Richard L. Epstein and Carolyn Kernberger, in the preface to their book *The Pocket Guide to Critical Thinking,* wrote, "Because your reasoning can be sharpened, you can understand more and you can avoid being duped. You can reason well with those you need to convince.... But whether you will do so depends not just on method, not just on the tools of reasoning, but on your goals, your ends. And those depend on virtue."

We Become What We Communicate

So whether you are formulating an argument of your own or responding to the argument of someone else, an analysis of the arguer's intention and underlying assumptions, which are often not obvious, is an essential part of critical thinking and our communication. Ultimately, the way we think and the way we communicate influence what we do and what we become. The method of arguing well is critical, but so is the reason behind the argument itself.

Argumentative Techniques

1. **State a clear topic sentence (for a paragraph) or thesis (for an essay).** Take an obvious stand or position. You might want to use words such as *must, ought,* and *should,* although they are, of course, not necessary (see the third thesis below). For example:

   > Canada's military should be better funded.
   > Canada must reform its prison system.
   > Romantic love and marriage are inevitably incompatible.
   > All information on the Internet should be free.

2. **Use examples.** Well-chosen examples are the heart of any paragraph or essay. Without them, the writing is flat, lifeless, and unconvincing. Providing a good example for each of your main points helps make a much stronger argument. Examples help your reader *see* what you are talking about.

3. **Use opinions from recognized authorities to support your points.** One of the oldest methods of supporting an argument is to cite one or more authorities that lend weight to your position. People usually believe what well-known experts claim. You should choose your experts carefully to help make your position on the topic more persuasive; be sure that your authority is someone who is respected in the area you are discussing. For example, if you are arguing that we must end the nuclear arms race, your argument will be stronger if you quote a respected scientist who can accurately predict the consequences of a nuclear war. Quoting a famous movie star saying the same thing might be more glamorous and get more attention, but would not be as convincing, as the star would not be as great an authority as the scientist.

4. **Answer your critics in advance.** When you point out beforehand what your opposition is likely to say in answer to your argument, you are writing from a position of strength. You are letting your reader know that you are aware that there is another side to the argument you are making. By pointing out this other side and then answering its objections in advance, you are strengthening your own position.

5. **Point out the results.** Help your reader see what will happen if your argument is (or is not) believed or acted upon as you think it should be. You should be specific and rational when you point out results, making sure that you avoid exaggeration of any kind. For example, if you argue against the possession of handguns, it would be an exaggeration to say that everyone is going to be murdered if the opposition's point of view is listened to instead of yours.

6. **Define certain terms that are central to the argument.** Often there seems to be disagreement where there should not be any, simply because the people who appear to be arguing have not defined their terms. For example, the term *religion* is potentially quite controversial in itself. Does it mean an organized system of beliefs that might be political as well as spiritual? Or does it refer to a narrower definition: the expression of a belief in the

divine? Or perhaps its meaning refers to its Latin root, which translates literally as "to bind back." If it's the third definition that both parties agree upon, what does it mean to bind back to—old ways of living and traditions, or one's spiritual instead of material values? Or is religion an individual's way to bring about reconciliation with the paradoxes of human life? Clearly, before arguing what the benefits or harm of religion are, it is critical that a writer first define the term. The same is true, of course, of countless other terms and concepts.

7. **Avoid common fallacies (errors) in your argument.** And use critical skills in analyzing the fallacies of others. Several common fallacies are outlined in the next section.

Common Fallacies

Common fallacies help us identify bad arguments because they are based on faulty reasoning. It is impossible to present a definitive or complete list of all possible fallacies an argument might contain, but the following are some of the most common ones. Try to learn to recognize these fallacies whether you can name them or not—that way you can criticize them in someone else's bad argument and prevent employing them in your own.

1. *Ad hominem* **attack:** In this fallacy, the person making the argument expresses a personal attack against an opponent—literally, an attack "on the man"—rather than addressing the actual issue. Often, when someone resorts to the *ad hominem* attack, it is in desperation, because she or he cannot find actual evidence to support a claim that makes someone else look bad.

   For example, Kim Campbell, the first and only female prime minister of Canada, ran for election against Jean Chrétien of the Liberal Party in 1993. The following was an argument made by the Liberals during the campaign, a campaign infamous for personal attacks made by both parties:

   > Kim Campbell is a divorcee. If Kim Campbell couldn't manage her marriage, how could she possibly manage the country?

   This is clearly an *ad hominem* attack on Kim Campbell. First of all, a divorce in itself is not necessarily the result of the inability to "manage a marriage." And secondly, it cannot automatically be argued that her divorce has anything to do with whether or not she is capable of serving as prime minister.

   During the same campaign, the Conservatives were also guilty of an *ad hominem* attack. A photograph in which Chrétien's partial facial paralysis was prominent was used in a Conservative ad until it was pulled amid a huge public outcry.

   Prime Minister Justin Trudeau, son of the late Pierre Trudeau, another former prime minister of Canada, gave a eulogy at his father's funeral in 2000. He said that as a child, with the aim of gaining his father's approval, he insulted a man whom he knew was his father's political rival. His father, with a stern look on his face, told Justin that it was fine to criticize someone's point of view, but that this ought to be done without attacking the individual on a personal level. Everyone, after all, deserves to live with dignity and respect. No one has the right to take those away. An *ad hominem* attack, unfortunately, aims to do just that.

2. **Practical (common) point of view or belief (also known as the democratic fallacy):** The person making an argument takes advantage of a common point of view to persuade the reader of another point of view. The danger here is the assumption that the will of the majority determines what is right and what is wrong. Mahatma Gandhi of India, on the other hand, once said that history will judge a country on the basis not of how it treats its majority, but of how it treats its minorities. This statement speaks volumes.

   > *Example:* The teacher asks the students, "Is it okay to lie?" One student responds, "Lying is okay because everyone does it."

   First of all, there is a dangerous assumption here. The student assumes that everyone lies. She may have evidence that her parents have lied on occasion. Her friends might lie even more often. She sees evidence in the news of heads of state lying. And so the student's conclusion is that everyone lies. But these examples of evidence do not support the idea that everyone lies. Unless the student has evidence that actually shows all people lie (evidence that would be impossible to obtain), such a broad statement should never be made. Secondly, even if it could be proven that everyone does lie, does that make it fine for the student to lie? Is it not possible that everyone is doing something that is wrong?

3. **Straw man ("Putting words into someone's mouth"):** This fallacy consists of an attack on an argument that is similar to, but not exactly the same as, the one your opponent holds. For example, former U.S. president Bill Clinton vehemently told his country that he did not have sexual relations with former White House intern Monica Lewinsky. He meant what he said very technically, in that he did not have intercourse with her, when in fact he knew he was being accused of an improper relationship with her in general. He was guilty of employing a "straw man" to dispute a claim he knew to be true.

4. **False analogy:** This fallacy occurs when an argument involves an unfair comparison. When two things are so different they cannot be compared, but someone tries anyway, he or she is making a false analogy.

   > *Example:* Guns don't kill people. People kill people. Guns are like cars. Therefore, it should be just as easy to get a gun as it is to get a car.

   The fact is, guns are not like cars. A car is a vehicle. A gun is a weapon.

Writing the Paragraph of Argumentation

In all of the chapters in this unit, more emphasis is placed on the development of the paragraph than on the essay. This chapter takes the opposite approach. The most effective arguments are those supported by several points that are treated thoroughly. For this reason, an essay of argumentation is usually a more effective piece of writing than a single paragraph of argumentation, so long as the points are thoughtful, well expressed, and directly supportive of the writer's overall assertion or claim. However, that is not to say that a good paragraph of argumentation cannot be written. Of course it can. If you do attempt to write such a paragraph, just remember to establish your claim in the form of a topic sentence that is clear and strong, and to make sure your supporting details include the strongest evidence in support of your claim that you can find. (See page 199 in Chapter 19: "The Paragraph.")

Developing Paragraphs: Argumentation

The following argumentative paragraph was written in response to one of the questions (#5 on p. 373) that follows the narrative essay "Transparent Silhouette" (pp. 372–373).

> **Question:** Did the writer foreshadow the ending of the essay? (In other words, are there several clues throughout the essay that enable the reader to predict the eventual death of the writer's friend?)

Model Paragraph: Clues of an Unhappy Ending

Many clues exist in the story by Akis Stylianou that his friend will end up dead. First, there is the title of the essay itself: "Transparent Silhouette." It might conjure up the mental picture of the outline of a ghost. Second, there is the third line in the first paragraph of the story, in which Stylianou uses the words "the woman I knew"; "knew," after all, is in the past tense, not the present. Third, the last line in the first paragraph includes the words "where I can delay my misery." If Stylianou is miserable because of his friend, whatever has happened to her cannot be good. Fourth, the second paragraph describes her sad childhood, full of abuse and the loneliness that results. A traumatic childhood is often, though not always, an omen of bad things to follow in life. And, finally, the events Stylianou describes throughout the story seem to get more and more dangerous, starting with getting mixed up with the "wrong" crowd, becoming an exotic dancer, and finally becoming a porn star. All in all, the abundance of clues throughout the story strongly suggest that the writer's friend will end up in a very bad state, as she does.

Questions for Analysis

1. How can you tell from the form of this text that it is one paragraph, and not two or three?

2. Is the paragraph a proper length, according to what Chapter 19 says about paragraph structure?
3. What is the topic sentence? Does it directly answer the question?
4. Are there transitions in the paragraph? What are some examples?
5. Is there sufficient support of the topic sentence? Discuss.
6. Is the difference between the main supporting details and specific examples or explanations that support them apparent?
7. Is there a concluding sentence in this paragraph? If so, what is it?
8. Is the transition "finally" used for the last supporting detail of the paragraph or for the concluding sentence?

Developing Essays: Argumentation

The following piece by Zosia Bielski (published in the *Globe and Mail* on July 17, 2014) is about the relationship between smartphones and friendship. As you read the article, look for the major parts of an effective argument: strong thesis, carefully chosen examples, quotations from authorities, answers to the opposition, and predictions. Can you find any weaknesses or fallacies in the argument?

Model Essay: Smartphones and Lousy Friends

by Zosia Bielski

Hi, I'm up here.

The mere presence of a cell or smartphone on the table can disengage people during in-person conversations and hinder their empathy, according to a new Virginia Tech study that finds your attention is divided even if you're not actively looking at your phone.

The study, "The iPhone Effect: The Quality of In-Person Social Interactions in the Presence of Mobile Devices," examines how "distracting digital stimuli" undermine the character and depth of our face-to-face interactions. Networked technologies, write the authors, let us manage several loyalties—work, family, friends—at once. But they also breed "a persistent state of 'absent presence' ... a technologically mediated world of elsewhere."

For many, digital distraction involves the "constant urge to seek out information, check for communication and direct their thoughts to other people and worlds," the authors write. The phone becomes "representative of people's wider social network and a portal to an immense compendium of information." (A previous study by two of these researchers found that people checked their phones every three to five minutes, regardless of whether it rang or buzzed.)

The current study involved 200 people, paired off and placed in two groups at coffee shops. They were instructed to discuss either a serious topic (the most meaningful events of that year) or a trivial one ("plastic holiday trees") over the course of 10 minutes. A lab assistant observed unobtrusively nearby, watching the respondents' non-verbal behaviour. The assistants noted whether the pairs put a mobile device on the table or held it in their hands (29 did, 71 didn't). After the conversation, participants answered questions that are designed to measure "empathic concern" and "feelings of interpersonal connectedness." (Sample: "To what extent did your conversation partner make an effort to understand your thoughts and feelings?")

Whether the talk was heavy or light, researchers found that "the quality of the conversation was rated to be less fulfilling" when either of the two had a phone in their hands or on the table. Empathy also dropped, particularly among people who knew each other. Those clutching their phones, even if not using them, "were less friendly with each other."

"Individuals are more likely to miss subtle cues, facial expressions, and changes in the tone of their conversation partner's voice, and have less eye contact," the researchers write in the study, published in the journal *Environment and Behavior* this month.

The research comes on the heels of Parents on Phones, a Tumblr feed that shames inattentive, iPhone-consumed mothers and fathers. Pundits seem split on whether the behaviours depicted—a mom tapping away as her daughter sits by, her leg in a cast—are bad parenting or necessary modern tool.

"Smart technologies offer the possibility of instantaneous and continuous global communities where knowledge is shared, opinions are contributed, relationships are rekindled, expressions of support are enhanced and social movements are spawned," the current study's lead author, Shalini Misra, an assistant professor of urban affairs and planning at Virginia Tech, said in an interview by e-mail.

"But these new global communities deserve closer examination, for as this study finds, they may emerge at the cost of face-to-face interpersonal relationships."

So resist the digital pull, be it Buzzfeed quiz or cat-related Facebook update, and look up.

Questions for Analysis

1. In your own words, what is Bielski's thesis statement? Which sentence, in particular, is *her* thesis statement?
2. What is her strongest supporting detail? Why? What is her weakest supporting detail? Why?
3. What does she want her readers to do?
4. Is her argument reasonable? Why or why not?

Assignment **Paragraph or Essay of Argumentation**

Choose a topic (see the suggestions below), and write either an extended paragraph or an essay of at least five paragraphs. Argue for or against the topic of your choice. Use the following techniques of argumentation, discussed earlier in this chapter, as a guide for your writing.

1. Write a strong thesis statement.
2. Provide examples for each of your reasons.
3. Use at least one authority to support your thesis.
4. Admit that others have a different point of view.
5. Indicate the results or your predictions in the conclusion.
6. Define certain terms that are central to your argument.

Suggested Topics

1. Capital punishment
2. Censorship of Internet hate literature
3. Same-sex marriages
4. Gun control
5. Prayer in public schools
6. Ban on junk food in schools
7. Control of pornography

Many, many more topics for paragraphs or essays of argumentation can be found in Unit V under the heading "Writing Ideas" at the end of the questions immediately following each major reading. Some of the questions under the heading "Questions for Discussion" (also after each major reading) might also be deemed suitable writing topics for argumentation.

While developing your paragraph or essay, you may want to review Chapter 18: "The Four Stages of Writing for a Paragraph or an Essay," in particular the following sections:

"Brainstorming"

"Choosing the Topic and the Controlling Idea"

"Outlining"

"The Rough Draft"

"Revising and Editing the Rough Draft"

"Proofreading"

"Checklist for the Final Copy"

For help in connecting your sentences and paragraphs smoothly and clearly, you may wish to consult the list of transitional words and phrases, categorized by their function, found on the inside back cover of this book.

Working Together: Identifying Good and Bad Arguments

Form small groups of four or five. Look at several recent newspapers and choose an editorial about a subject of interest to everyone in the group. Read it and comment on the argument in terms of what you now know about good and bad arguments. Answer the questions below. You may want to assign a different question to each person in the group.

1. Are there any common fallacies in the writer's argument? Explain.
2. Does the writer employ the techniques of argumentation listed in this chapter? Explain.
3. What is the writer's overall claim?
4. Is the evidence used to support the claim generally good or bad? Discuss.

anuchamanecchote/shutterstock.com

Chapter 26 **Cause and Effect**

What Is Cause and Effect?

People have always looked at the world and asked the questions "Why did this happen?" and "What are the likely results of that event?" Ancient societies created beautiful myths and legends to explain the origin of the universe and our place in it, while modern civilization has emphasized scientific methods of observation to find the cause of a disease or to determine why the planet Mars appears to be covered by canals. When we examine the spiritual or physical mysteries of our world, we are trying to discover the connections, or links, between events. In this chapter, we will refer to connections between events as **causal relationships**.

> **DEFINITION**
>
> **Cause and effect** is an examination of either the causes of a particular effect (why something happened) or the effects of a particular cause (what is likely to happen as a result of a particular event). In either case, the establishment of causal relationships must be based on a sense of logic.

Causal relationships are part of our daily lives and provide a way of understanding the cause, result, or consequence of a particular event. The search for a cause or effect is a bit like detective work. Probing an event is a way of searching for clues to discover what caused an event or what result it will have in the future.

For example, we might ask the question "Why did the car break down just after it came back from the garage?" as a way of searching for the cause of the car's new problem. Or we might ask, "What will be the side effects of a certain medicine?" to determine what effect a particular medicine will have on the body. This search for connections can be complex. Often the logical analysis of a problem reveals more than one possible explanation. Sometimes the best one can do is find *possible* causes or *probable* effects.

Two Types of Cause and Effect Paragraph or Essay

There are two types of cause and effect paragraph or essay. In the first type, the *cause* is identified in the topic sentence (for a paragraph) or thesis statement (for an essay), and the emphasis is placed on the effects; the supporting detail, therefore, is made up of several *effects*. In the second type, the *effect* is identified in the topic sentence or thesis statement, but the emphasis is placed on the causes; as a result, the supporting detail, this time, is made up of several *causes*.

> **TIP**
>
> Do not try to deal with *both* the causes *and* effects of an event in the supporting detail of a single cause and effect paragraph or essay.

Developing Paragraphs: Cause and Effect

The Topic Sentence of a Cause and Effect Paragraph

The **topic sentence** of a cause and effect paragraph should reveal whether the paragraph will focus on causes or effects. For example, the following topic sentence uses the word *factors* to indicate that causes are about to follow:

> Several factors contributed to my decision to lose weight.

Losing weight is the effect; the causes will be discussed in the remainder of the paragraph.

On the other hand, this next topic sentence begins with the cause and states that a number of *effects* are about to follow:

> Losing weight had a number of positive effects on my life.

Supporting Detail of a Cause and Effect Paragraph

Again, the supporting detail in this type of paragraph should contain *either* causes or effects, but not *both*.

Importance of Logic

In a good cause and effect paragraph, a cause must *lead to* an effect, not just come before it. That's why writing a cause and effect paragraph requires analysis to determine that a logical connection exists between events. For example, the fact that a person walked under a ladder just before he got hit by a car does not prove cause and effect. The walking under a ladder merely preceded the car accident. To suggest that walking under a ladder caused the accident is to use **faulty logic**. (See "Common Fallacies" on pp. 292–293 in Chapter 25: "Argumentation.") It is the writer's responsibility to ensure that the relationship between a cause and its effects is clear.

> ### Avoid These Common Errors in Logic
> 1. Do not confuse coincidence or chronological sequence with evidence.
> 2. Look for underlying causes beneath the obvious ones and for far-reaching effects beyond the ones that first come to mind. Often what appears to be a single cause or a single effect is a much more complex situation.

Here is an example of a possible error in logic:

> Every time I try to write an essay in the evening, I have trouble getting to sleep. Therefore, writing must prevent me from sleeping.

In this case, writing may indeed be a stimulant that makes it difficult to sleep. However, if the writer is serious about finding the cause of the insomnia, he or she must observe whether any other factors may be to blame. For instance, if the person is drinking several cups of coffee while writing each evening, caffeine is a more likely cause of the wakefulness.

The following is an example of a good cause and effect paragraph.

Notice how the topic sentence makes clear whether the emphasis in the paragraph will be on causes or effects.

Model Paragraph: Recipe for Disaster

A number of factors caused my car accident on Deerfoot Trail last week. First, the weather was horrible that night. It was dark, and the rain made it even harder to see where I was going. The rain also made the roads very slippery, which meant that controlling my car was more difficult than usual. There was another factor that made my car difficult to control that night. I was returning home with a very heavy concrete birdbath for our backyard. When I slammed on my brakes and turned the steering wheel to avoid getting hit, the weight in my trunk shifted and caused the back end of my small car to swing around. Perhaps the most important factor was negligence. The driver of a black sports car was speeding and driving erratically. Rather than slow down when I changed into his lane ahead of him, he sped up, swerved, and cut directly in front of me. I had to slam on my brakes and turn my steering wheel sharply to avoid hitting him. As a result, my car spun around in a complete circle in the middle of the highway. I wound up in a ditch on the side of the road, a little shaken, but realizing things could have ended much worse.

 Practice 1 **Looking for the Causal Relationship**

Study each of the following situations. In each case, if the sequence of events is merely coincidental or chronological, put a *T* (for "time") in the space provided. If the relationship is most likely causal, write a *C*. Be prepared to explain your answers in class. Check your answers against those in the Answer Key on page 466.

_____ 1. Every time I carry my umbrella, it doesn't rain. I am carrying my umbrella today; therefore, it won't rain.

_____ 2. We put fertilizer on the grass. A week later, the grass grew 5 cm and turned a deeper green.

_____ 3. On Tuesday morning, I walked under a ladder. On Wednesday morning, I walked into my office and was told I had lost my job.

_____ 4. The child was born with a serious kidney condition. Seven days later, the child died.

_____ 5. Tar and nicotine from cigarettes damage the lungs. People who smoke cigarettes increase their chances of dying from lung cancer.

_____ 6. A political scandal was exposed in the city on Friday. On Saturday night, only twenty-four hours later, a power blackout occurred in the city.

_____ 7. Very few tourists came to the island last year. The economy of the island declined last year.

Practice 2 Separating the Cause from the Effect

In the following practice exercise, there is an action or event above a group of related sentences. Put a *C* next to sentences that describe causes and an *E* next to sentences that describe effects. Check your answers against those in the Answer Key on page 466.

1. I quit smoking.

_____ a. Smoking costs a lot of money.

_____ b. There are fewer public places that allow smoking now.

_____ c. My terrible cough is gone.

_____ d. I have gained 5 kg.

_____ e. It bothered my friends and family.

_____ f. I have found that my food tastes better.

2. I recently bought a new car.

_____ a. I got a great deal on financing.

_____ b. My old car was unreliable.

_____ c. I have less money every month because I have to pay more for insurance and gas.

_____ d. My popularity at school has increased.

_____ e. I was tired of having to take the train whenever I wanted to visit my family.

_____ f. I was embarrassed to drive my rusted old car.

Exercise 1 Separating the Cause from the Effect

In each sentence, separate the cause, problem, or reason from the effect, solution, or result. Remember, the cause is not necessarily given first.

1. More than half of mothers with children under one year of age work outside the home, which has resulted in an unprecedented need for daycare in this country.

   Cause: _____

   _____

   Effect: _____

   _____

2. By 2000, two-thirds of all preschool children and four-fifths of school-age children had working mothers, facts that led to increased strain on our system of daycare.

   Cause: _____

   _____

   Effect: _____

   _____

3. In one national survey, over half the working mothers reported that they had either changed jobs or cut back on their hours in order to be more available to their children.

   Cause: _____

   _____

   Effect: _____

   _____

4. Many mothers who work do so only when their children are in school, while other mothers work only occasionally during the school year because they feel their children need the supervision of a parent.

   Cause: _____

   _____

   Effect: _____

   _____

5. Many mothers experience deep emotional crises as a result of their struggle to meet both the financial obligations of their home and their own emotional needs as parents.

   Cause: _____

   _____

   Effect: _____

   _____

Writing the Cause or Effect Paragraph Step by Step

To learn a skill that has so many different aspects, it is best to follow a step-by-step approach, so that one aspect can be worked on at a time. This approach will ensure that you are not missing a crucial point or misunderstanding a part of the whole. There are other ways to go about writing an effective paragraph, but here is one logical method you can use to achieve results.

Steps for Writing the Cause or Effect Paragraph

1. After you have chosen your topic, plan your topic sentence.
2. Brainstorm by jotting down all possible causes or effects. Ask others for their thoughts. Research if necessary. Consider long-range effects or underlying causes.
3. Cross out any points that are illogical, merely coincidental, or the result of only time sequence. Then choose the three or four best points from what remains on your list.
4. Decide on the best order for these points. (From least important to most important is one way to organize them.)
5. Write at least one complete sentence for each of the causes or effects you have chosen from your list.
6. Write a concluding statement.
7. Finally, put your sentences into standard paragraph form.

 Exercise 2 **Writing the Effect Paragraph Step by Step**

Starting with the suggested topic below, follow the seven steps outlined in the box above to work through the writing process for a cause or effect paragraph. (These steps are similar to those used for the narrative paragraph in Chapter 32; refer to pp. 367–369 for a step-by-step example and a completed sample paragraph.)

Topic: What are the effects when students have part-time jobs after classes?

On Your Own: Writing Cause and Effect Paragraphs from Model Paragraphs

The Causes of Disaster

The following model paragraph looks at the causes for the loss of life in the sinking of a supposedly unsinkable ship on its maiden voyage more than a century ago.

Model Paragraph: Titanic Blunders

One of the most tragic events of the twentieth century was the sinking of the British ship *Titanic* in the Atlantic Ocean on April 15, 1912, with the loss of over 1500 lives. The immediate cause of this terrible loss of life was a large iceberg that tore a ninety-metre gash in the side of the ship, flooding five of its watertight compartments. Some believe that the tragedy took place because the crew members did not see the iceberg in time, but others see a chain of different events that contributed to the tragedy. First was the fact that the ship was not carrying enough lifeboats for all of its passengers: it had enough boats for only about half of the people on board. Furthermore, the ship's crew showed a clear lack of concern for the third-class, or "steerage," passengers, who were left in their cramped quarters below decks with little or no help as the ship went down. It has often been said that this social attitude of helping the wealthy and neglecting the poor was one of the real causes of the loss of life that night. Indeed, some of the lifeboats that were used were not filled to capacity when the rescue ships eventually found them. Finally, the tragedy of the *Titanic* was magnified by the fact that some ships nearby did not have a radio crew on duty and therefore missed the distress signals sent by the *Titanic*. Out of all this, the need to reform safety regulations on passenger ships became obvious.

 Assignment **Cause and Effect Paragraph (Effects)**

Select a community or regional disaster that you have personally experienced or heard about. This could include a severe climatic condition or a manufactured disaster. Instead of writing a paragraph about the disaster's *causes* as in the above paragraph, point out the *effects* it had on you or the people involved.

Suggested Topics

(For more suggested topics, see the list given for the essay "Assignment" on pp. 307–308.)

1. The effects of an earthquake
2. The effects of a power blackout on a major city or town
3. The effects of a flood or other extensive water damage on a home or community
4. The effects of a chemical spill on land or offshore
5. The effects of a transit strike on a community
6. The effects of a major fire on a downtown block

Developing the Cause and Effect Essay

Like the cause and effect paragraph, the essay of the same type should focus on either causes or effects, but not both. And it should be self-evident from the thesis statement of the essay which one will be discussed.

As in other kinds of essays, the thesis appears somewhere between the middle and the end of the first paragraph. Each support paragraph deals with one cause or one effect.

Bear in mind that all the causes or all the effects included in the essay should directly support your thesis, whatever it is. If not, you must make some adjustments: either change your thesis or change your support paragraphs. Which option you take is up to you. In some cases, only one support paragraph needs to be reworked. If you're writing the essay in class and have a rigid time limit, you may decide to make whatever changes require the least amount of time.

For a review of the essay form and its standard format (which applies to all the writing strategies in this unit), see Chapter 20: "The Essay." For a review of the writing process that can be applied to both the paragraph and the essay, see Chapter 18: "The Four Stages of Writing for a Paragraph or an Essay."

Two model essays that demonstrate the strategy of cause and effect are found on the next few pages. The first, by Donald Pianissimo, is very informal and personal (notice the use of the word *I*). The second, which forms part of the exercise "Working Together: Identifying Causes" that concludes the chapter, is called "The Zen of Zzzzzz." Written by Antonia Zerbisias, it contains more formal research that is used to support the author's claim.

Model Essay I: Whose Choice Is It, Anyway?

by Donald Pianissimo

It is so easy to think that the decisions you make are your own choices. But when you consider the events leading up to those decisions, it may not be so easy to claim the decisions as your own. My decision to go into journalism was, I thought, something I had chosen completely on my own without external influence. But when I think of three particular events in my life before leaving high school, I begin to think my say in the matter was minimal at best. I begin to think I was simply following a path that had already been laid out for me.

My mom used to be a nurse, and she confided in me long after I'd dropped chemistry in high school that she always wanted me to be a doctor. My dad, although a writer, never called himself a journalist; journalism was not the kind of writing he preferred to do. But perhaps I underestimated his influence on my choice to enter a writing career. In fact, it was he who encouraged me to publish an article in a local magazine when I was only nine years old. I still remember his editing my work. I also remember the thrill of my anticipation of seeing my name in print. It was the first taste of being published I would get, and it wouldn't be the last.

A second incident is as vivid in my memory as the first. In Grade 8, the first English teacher who would truly inspire me with his passion for teaching announced to the class one day that there were three essays he had marked that were worthy of recognition. He asked three students to read their essays out loud in front of the entire class, and I was one of them. He made me feel I had a gift, a gift worth sharing.

And finally, by the time I'd gotten to high school, a classmate and I were asked by a teacher to co-edit the school newspaper. I never thought I would have so much fun. Better still, the paper was a hit with the other students.

Our high school hadn't seen so successful a student newspaper in years. I couldn't help but love the popularity that came with it, too.

I envied those students who knew they wanted to be doctors, or lawyers, or engineers since the time they could talk. I just figured I wasn't so blessed with such an ardent and focused career desire. By the time I'd graduated from high school, I chose to enter a field of study for my postsecondary education based on one of my most enjoyable pastimes: writing for an audience. Journalism seemed the logical choice. What didn't occur to me until much later was that my choice seemed the logical conclusion of a number of monumental events in my young life. Were they random events, or were they meant to lead me in a certain direction? Your guess is as good as mine.

Questions for Analysis

1. Of the two types of cause and effect essay discussed in this chapter, which type of essay is this?
2. Does the writer support the idea of free will or the idea of fate?
3. What evidence in this essay suggests his support for one or the other?
4. How much does the author attribute his choices to the influence of parents and teachers?
5. What, in your own words, is the author's thesis? Which sentence states the actual thesis? Based on just this thesis, what would a reader think the support is going to be about? Why?
6. Is the thesis adequately supported? Explain.

Exploring the Topic

1. How did you decide to enter your current field of study? Was it free will or fate? Discuss.
2. Does reading this essay make you think twice about whether you made the choice to enter your field of study totally independently of outside influence? Explain.

 Assignment Cause and Effect Essay

Choose a topic from the list below (or, if you prefer, from the list given for the paragraph "Assignment" on p. 305), or come up with one of your own. Write a cause and effect essay of at least five paragraphs to develop this topic.

Suggested Topics

1. The causes of war
2. The causes of failing a course
3. The causes of breaking up with a boyfriend/girlfriend
4. The causes of addiction (alcohol, drugs, sex, relationship, etc.)
5. The causes of lying
6. The effects of lying
7. The effects of parents who don't show their children affection
8. The effects of poverty in the home
9. The effects of fame
10. The effects of dating a real "hottie"

> While developing your essay, you may want to review Chapter 18: "The Four Stages of Writing for a Paragraph or an Essay," in particular the following sections:
>
> "Brainstorming"
>
> "Choosing the Topic and the Controlling Idea"
>
> "Outlining"
>
> "The Rough Draft"
>
> "Revising and Editing the Rough Draft"
>
> "Proofreading"
>
> "Checklist for the Final Copy"
>
> For help in connecting your sentences and paragraphs smoothly and clearly, you may wish to consult the list of transitional words and phrases, categorized by their function, found on the inside back cover of this book. In particular, you may find the first section, "Transitions for Cause and Effect," useful for work in this chapter.

 Working Together: Identifying Causes

1. Read the following article by Antonia Zerbisias, entitled "The Zen of Zzzzzz." Write either an extended paragraph or an essay in response to one of the following topics. Make sure the ideas you include are from the article by Zerbisias, and that you acknowledge the author in your composition. (For more on paraphrasing, summarizing, and acknowledging the author, see Chapter 15.)

    a. The causes of sleep deprivation

    b. The effects of sleep deprivation

Model Essay II: The Zen of Zzzzzz*

by Antonia Zerbisias

Sometime in my early 20s, in the early morning, something—a short circuit maybe—tripped Montreal's Cold War-era, the-Russians-are-coming air raid sirens.

While the entire city was ducking and covering under their beds, I remained blissfully unawake and unaware under the covers.

I am not joking when I say I could sleep through a nuclear war.

This is not to say I've haven't had my share of tossing and turning. An unfortunate encounter with bedbugs. Jet lag. The Sunday night blues. Noisy old hotels on busy European city streets. The now-gone monthly wakefulness that nature must have endowed women with so that we could be aware of predators following the scent of blood.

So I know what it is to stare at the clock, pound the pillows, kick out the sheets ... But I have never experienced that yawning "hole in the night" that has plagued Patricia Morrisroe for just about every one of her 59 years.

She is not alone in the dark. Sleeplessness haunts one in seven Canadians over the age of 15, Statistics Canada reports, and some 40 million Americans.

Which is why the self-described "fourth generation insomniac" and former New York magazine contributor went on a quest to examine and understand sleep, one that resulted in her new book, *Wide Awake: A Memoir of Insomnia*.

Part autobiography and part magical mattress tour, *Wide Awake* begins with her childhood in the "House of Punk Sleep" where her family tiptoed around her mother and, via drugstores, sleep labs, yoga, dream therapy, cognitive behavioural therapy, brain music therapy, and even an ice bed in Iceland, ends with illumination just two blocks away from her Manhattan home.

"Sleep seems to be a very, very hot topic these days; it's replaced depression," she says on the phone. "It's like people said, 'What more could be said about depression?' So we kind of needed to move on to sleep."

The New York Times recently introduced *All-Nighters*, a blog about insomnia, with musings from artists, scientists and opinionators.

Earlier this year, Arianna Huffington and *Glamour* magazine launched their joint "Feminist Sleep Challenge" because, although sleep deprivation is epidemic across the gender divide, working women are most affected.

"A nation of sleepy women is even less capable of greatness," wrote Huffington and *Glamour* editor-in-chief Cindi Leive in January.

Sleep, says Morrisroe, is a $24 billion business, if you factor in the herbal remedies, the hypnotherapy, the white noise machines, the ear plugs, the blackout drapes, the cushy new beds built so high a girl needs a step stool to climb in and all the desperate measures the sleep-disordered take in order to get some Zzzz.

How did we get to this?

"There are some people who just don't know when to turn off the computer and they just think that they can get by. Those are certain lifestyle choices. There are other people who just may not be able to sleep because they can't fall asleep; they have sleep maintenance insomnia when they wake up in the middle of the night; they may just have very fractured sleep; or they may not be getting enough deep sleep.

"I really knew nothing about sleep when I went into this. I just knew that I wasn't a great sleeper. And it was astounding to me the number of sleep disorders there are out there.

"There are people who will take their car, who will be sleep driving and not aware that they are doing that. There was somebody who went on ABC News and talked about trying to strangle and stab his wife repeatedly over a 30-year marriage, which is REM behaviour disorder. Another reason is sleep apnea, which affects more men than women."

Except, of course, when affected men snore so loudly they keep their partners awake.

Morrisroe believes two factors in particular have made sleep "The New Depression"—aging Baby Boomers and Big Pharma.

"Sleep does fall off as you age. It's not as robust as it used to be," she says. "People need to accept that. But the Baby Boomer generation expect to be perfect in all things, that if they have problems with their knees, they'll just go get knee replacement surgery, hip replacement surgery."

Meanwhile, drug companies looking for conditions to medicalize and new markets to target have roused a dormant monster.

"Sleep used to be the backwaters of medicine," she explains, referring to when insomnia was seen as a symptom of something else: anxiety, depression, chronic pain, any one of a number of different problems. "I went back and looked at a lot of the articles and I could pinpoint exactly when we suddenly realized that we weren't sleeping.

"It was in the early 1990s, when Searle introduced Ambien," Morrisroe continues. "They got together with the National Sleep Foundation which is a non-profit organization—they do get a lot of money from drug companies— and started this 'sleep in America' poll and, all of a sudden, it was how are we sleeping, how much are we sleeping. Not that pills, which include the much-advertised Lunesta, help much," insists Morrisroe: "When I started to look at the clinical trials, and when I really started to look at the amount of time of sleep you get on things like Lunesta and Ambien, it's really only 11.4 minutes over a placebo. It's very very small.

"And they can cause you to have a form of amnesia so that you don't remember how badly you have been sleeping. They can also leave you with some cognitive impairment the next day which can make you feel like you haven't slept."

It's no secret that staring at a computer or TV screen late into the night is not exactly restful. Teens texting late into the night stumble into class, where teachers think they suffer from attention deficit disorders. The economy has been keeping millions awake. Some of the most sleep-deprived people anywhere are those with the longest commutes—and, as a study of 19 major cities published last month revealed, Torontonians have the worst commutes in North America, which might explain road rage.

And, if that doesn't keep you awake at night, how about this? Sleep deprivation messes with hormones—and could lead to overeating and obesity.

To counteract the effects of sleepiness, a whole new industry has sprung up.

"The new area is wake," notes Morrisroe. "A lot of students are taking modofinil and that's being used as a smart drug, to stay up.

"And then you have all those energy drinks, packed with caffeine. There's now caffeine-infused food, like caffeine-infused oatmeal. The idea that you have caffeine-infused food and even caffeine-infused drinks for children, that's not helping people sleep at all."

In fact, it's the stuff of nightmares.

But is insomnia a modern problem? Are we sleeping less than we used to? Did people in prehistoric and ancient times really crash with the sunset and sleep till the cocks crowed? Is the prescribed eight hours a construct to suit industrial times?

In his 2005 ground-breaking book *At Day's Close: Night in Times Past*, American historian Roger Ekirch documented how humans slept through the ages—but not necessarily through the night.

"He said that people slept in segmented sleep," says Morrisroe. "They'd fall asleep for a couple of hours. They'd get up. They might talk. They might have sex with their bedfellows, as there were often multiple people in beds because they often had communal beds. They'd pray. They would analyze their dreams. Maybe some would go out and steal livestock. Then they would go back to sleep.

"So this concept of segmented sleep may be very natural to us."

And how is she sleeping since she completed her quest?

"I sleep much better—but right now I am sleeping much less because of all the press and this book coming out."

Jack Layton, the late leader of the national NDP, celebrates the party's historic results in the federal election of 2011.

REUTERS/Fred Greenslade

2. Form groups of three or four. Look at the picture above of Jack Layton, former national leader of the New Democratic Party (NDP) of Canada, who in the spring of 2011 became the Leader of the Opposition in Parliament. Although he held the post for only a few months before succumbing to cancer in August 2011, Mr. Layton was the first NDP leader to achieve this status in the history of this country. This photo shows him just after the election, raising his cane (which he needed as a result of hip surgery) in an expression of spiritual triumph. Since Layton's monumental achievement for the national NDP, Rachel Notley of Alberta became that province's first NDP premier, upsetting a forty-four-year Progressive Conservative streak. Working collaboratively with your group, write a paragraph or essay on what you think are the causes behind the NDP's historic achievement in the federal election of 2011 or the possible effects of the same party's historic achievement in Alberta in 2015.

Chapter 27   **Comparison and/or Contrast**

What Are Comparison and Contrast?

Comparison and contrast are two related methods of explaining topics.

> **DEFINITION**
>
> **Comparison** emphasizes the similarities between two topics. **Contrast** emphasizes the differences. An essay or paragraph may deal with either similarities or differences, or with both.

We sometimes use the word *comparison* to refer to both similarities and differences between people or things, but it is more precise to use *comparison* for similarities and *contrast* for differences. For example, if you were to write about twin sisters you know, describing how close they are in appearance and personality, the similarities you noted would make up a comparison. On the other hand, if you wanted to emphasize some important differences between the two sisters, the result would be a contrast.

We use comparison and contrast in a variety of ways every day: we talk about what a boyfriend and girlfriend have in common; we put similar products side by side in the store before we decide to buy one of them; we listen to two politicians on television and think about the differences between their positions before we vote for one of them; and we read college and university catalogues and talk to our friends before we decide which school to attend.

Developing Paragraphs: Comparison and/or Contrast

Working with Comparison and/or Contrast: Choosing the Two-Part Topic

The most common problem most students face when it comes to writing a good comparison and/or contrast paragraph is finding an appropriate two-part topic. While you must be careful to choose subjects that have enough in common to make them comparable, you must avoid choosing two things that have so much in common that you cannot possibly handle all the comparable points in one paragraph or even in ten paragraphs. For example, a student trying to compare the French word *chaise* with the English word *chair* might be able to come up with only two sentences of material. With only a dictionary to consult, the student is unlikely to find enough material for several points of comparison. On the other hand, contrasting Canada with Europe would present such an endless supply of points to compare that the student would have room, in a typical essay, to give only general facts that most readers probably already know. When the subject is too broad, the writing is often too general. A better two-part topic might be to compare travelling by train in Europe with travelling by train in Canada.

A good comparison and/or contrast paragraph should devote an equal (or nearly equal) amount of space to each of the topic's two parts. If a writer is interested in only one of the topics, the paragraph may end up being very one-sided.

Formulating an Evaluative Topic Sentence

When writing a topic sentence for a comparison and/or contrast paragraph, keep in mind two things:

1. It should clearly identify the two items you've chosen to compare and/or contrast (the topic).
2. It should be **evaluative**—that is, it should tell the reader essentially what your feeling is with respect to the two things being compared and/or contrasted (the controlling idea). For example, it should indicate which one is better than the other (ideally using more specific language than the word *better*).

Here is an example of an evaluative topic sentence (the model paragraph that begins with this sentence can be found on p. 316). The evaluative portion, in particular, is highlighted:

> Now, of course, I knew that it was going to be as difficult making an income as a freelance editor as it was as an editor on staff at the magazine, but the benefits of freelancing seemed to far outweigh the disadvantages.

There are several things one can assume about the rest of the paragraph based on this topic sentence:

1. There will be a contrast. There might be some comparison, but, for sure, the paragraph will not entirely be a comparison.
2. The two things being compared and/or contrasted are being a freelance editor and working as an editor on staff at the magazine.
3. In the end, after all the comparing and contrasting are finished, one will get the distinct impression that the writer prefers freelancing.

Now, with respect to the balance of content within the paragraph, here's an example of a one-sided contrast within a sentence:

> While Canadian trains go to only a few towns, are infrequent, and are often shabby and uncomfortable, European trains are much nicer.

The following example is a more balanced contrast that gives more of an equal amount of attention to both topics:

> While Canadian trains go to only a few large cities, run very infrequently, and are often shabby and uncomfortable, European trains go to virtually every small town, are always dependable, and are clean and attractive.

 Practice 1 Evaluating the Two-Part Topic

Study the following topics and decide which are too broad for a paragraph and which are suitable as topics for a paragraph of comparison and/or contrast. Mark your choice in the appropriate space to the right of each topic. The first two have been done for you. Check your answers against those in the Answer Key on page 466.

Topic	Too Broad	Suitable
1. Australia and England	√	
2. Indian elephants and African elephants		√
3. Canadian wine and French wine		
4. Wooden furniture and plastic furniture		
5. Wood and plastic		
6. Photography and oil painting		

Two Methods: Point-by-Point and Block

The first method for ordering material in a paragraph or an essay of comparison and/or contrast is known as the **point-by-point method.**

> **DEFINITION**
>
> The **point-by-point method** is one way to order the material in a comparison and/or contrast paragraph or essay. In this method, you compare and/or contrast a particular point as it relates to one topic with the same point as it relates to the other topic before going on to the next point.

What follows is a paragraph in which the writer uses the point-by-point method to compare the difficulties of being a freelance editor with those of working as an editor on staff at a magazine.

Model Paragraph: The Freedom of Freelancing (I)

Now, of course, I knew that it was going to be as difficult making an income as a freelance editor as it was as an editor on staff at the magazine, if not more so, but the benefits of freelancing seemed to far outweigh the disadvantages. I would be at home hustling editing contracts via telephone while everyone else spent their mornings at the office gabbing over endless cups of coffee. I sometimes resented having to work so hard to make a living while my old colleagues on staff sat in meetings, went to conferences, and attended company luncheons. But I never envied them on their way to work on cold, dark winter mornings. And I wondered how many of them would have gladly switched places with me as I worked outside on my patio in the summer while they looked longingly out their office windows.

Notice how, after the opening topic sentence, the writer uses half of each sentence to describe a freelance editor's experience and the other half of the same sentence to describe the experience of an editor who works for a magazine. This technique is effective in such a paragraph, and it is most often used in longer pieces of writing that include many points of comparison. This method helps the reader keep the comparison and/or contrast carefully in mind at each point.

Looking at this paragraph in outline form will help you see the shape of its development.

Point-by-Point Method

Topic sentence: Now, of course, I knew that it was going to be as difficult making an income as a freelance editor as it was as an editor on staff at the magazine, if not more so, but the benefits of freelancing seemed to far outweigh the disadvantages.

Point one

First topic: I would be at home hustling editing contracts via telephone . . .

Second topic: . . . while everyone else spent their mornings at the office gabbing over endless cups of coffee.

Point two

First topic: I sometimes resented having to work so hard to earn a living . . .

Second topic: . . . while my old colleagues on staff sat in meetings, went to conferences, and attended company luncheons.

Point three

First topic: But I never envied them on their way to work on cold, dark winter mornings.

Second topic: And I wondered how many of them would have gladly switched places with me as I worked outside on my patio while they looked longingly out their office windows.

What follows is another version of the same model paragraph, written using the **block method.**

Model Paragraph: The Freedom of Freelancing (II)

Now, of course, I knew that it was going to be as difficult making an income as a freelance editor as it was as an editor on staff at the magazine, if not more so, but the benefits of freelancing seemed to far outweigh the disadvantages. I spent my mornings hustling editing contracts on the telephone, and I sometimes resented having to work so hard to earn a living. On the other hand, I didn't envy my old colleagues on their way to work on cold, dark winter mornings. They could spend as much time as they wanted to gabbing over endless cups of coffee and going to meetings, conferences, and company luncheons; but I wonder how many of them would have gladly switched places with me as I worked outside on my patio in the summer.

In this version, the first half of the paragraph presents almost all of the details about being a freelance editor, while the second half presents all of the information about being an editor on staff. This method is often used in shorter pieces of writing, where it is possible for the reader to keep in mind a block of information on one topic while reading about the other.

Here is this version of the paragraph in outline form.

Block Method

Topic sentence: Now, of course, I knew that it was going to be as difficult making an income as a freelance editor as it was as an editor on staff at the magazine, if not more so, but the benefits of freelancing seemed to far outweigh the disadvantages.

First topic (points one, two, and three): I spent my mornings hustling editing contracts on the telephone, and I sometimes resented having to work so hard to earn a living. On the other hand, I didn't envy my old colleagues on their way to work on cold, dark winter mornings.

Second topic (points one, two, and three): They could spend as much time as they wanted to gabbing over endless cups of coffee and going to meetings, conferences, and company luncheons; but I wonder how many of them would have gladly switched places with me as I worked outside on my patio in the summer.

You will want to choose one of these methods before you write a comparison and/or contrast assignment. The block method is most often used for writing shorter pieces such as paragraphs; however, you will have the opportunity to practise both the block method and the point-by-point method.

Each of the following passages is an example of comparison and/or contrast. Read each paragraph carefully and decide whether the writer has used the point-by-point method or the block method. Indicate your choice in the spaces provided after each example. Also indicate whether the piece emphasizes similarities or differences. Check your answers against those in the Answer Key on page 467.

1. Female infants speak sooner, have larger vocabularies, and rarely demonstrate speech defects. (Stuttering, for instance, occurs almost exclusively in boys.) Girls exceed boys in language abilities, and this early linguistic bias often prevails throughout life. Girls read sooner, learn foreign languages more easily, and, as a result, are more likely to enter occupations involving language mastery. Boys, in contrast, show an early visual superiority. They are also clumsier, performing poorly at tasks such as arranging a row of beads, but excel at activities calling for total body coordination. Their attentional mechanisms are also different. A boy will react to an inanimate object as quickly as he will to a person. A male baby will often ignore the mother and babble at a blinking light, fixate on a geometric figure, and, at a later point, manipulate it and attempt to take it apart.

   _____ Point-by-point   _____ Block

   _____ Similarities   _____ Differences

2. It is hard to decide who are the better inventors, Canadians or Martians. Canadians have invented wonderful devices that have made a significant contribution to their civilization, but then so have the Martians. Canadians invented the chainsaw, the paint roller, the power mower, and the zipper. But Martians are no slouches, having come up with the intergalactic spaceship, the long-range power blaster, and the moon-dust mobile home. Of course, not all Canadian inventions have been stellar successes; consider, for example, the cast-iron airship, the reverse cooking stove, and the patent medicine carrot cure-all. But neither have Martians hit a winner every time: who can forget the ill-fated interplanetary bicycle, the invisible mirror, or the boomerang rocket? In the ingenuity department, you'd have to say it's a tie.

   _____ Point-by-point   _____ Block

   _____ Similarities   _____ Differences

Exercise 1 **Using the Point-by-Point and Block Methods**

Choose one of the paragraphs from the above Practice and rewrite it using the opposite method for comparison and/or contrast. For instance, if a paragraph uses the point-by-point method, rewrite it using the block method.

Tips on Transitions: *Like* vs. *As*

Be careful to use transition words correctly when comparing and/or contrasting. In particular, watch out for *like* and *as*, which have different functions. Therefore, they cannot be used in place of each other.

TIP

Like is a preposition and is used within a prepositional phrase with a noun.

My sister is just *like* me.

TIP

As is a subordinate conjunction and is used in a clause below with a subject and a verb.

My sister sews every evening, *as* does her oldest daughter.

For additional common transitions, see the chart on the inside back cover of this book.

Writing the Comparison and/or Contrast Paragraph Step by Step

To learn a skill with some degree of ease, it is best to follow a step-by-step approach so that various skills can be worked on one at a time. This approach will ensure that you are not missing a crucial point or misunderstanding a part of the whole. There are other ways to go about writing an effective paragraph, but here is one logical method you can use to achieve results.

Steps for Writing the Comparison and/or Contrast Paragraph
1. Study the given topic, and then plan your topic sentence, especially the dominant impression.
2. List all your ideas for points that could be compared and/or contrasted.
3. Choose the three or four most important points from your list, and put them in order.
4. Decide whether you want to use the point-by-point method or the block method of organizing your paragraph.
5. Write at least one complete sentence for each of the points you have chosen from your list.
6. Write a concluding statement that summarizes the main points, makes a judgment, or emphasizes what you believe is the most important point.
7. Finally, copy your sentences into standard paragraph form.

 Exercise 2 **Writing the Comparison and/or Contrast Paragraph Step by Step**

Starting with the suggested topic below, follow the seven steps outlined in the box above to work through the writing process for a comparison and/or contrast paragraph. (These steps are similar to those used for the narrative paragraph in Chapter 32; refer to pp. 368–369 for a step-by-step example and a completed sample paragraph.)

> **Topic:** Compare and/or contrast going to work with going to college immediately after high school.

 Assignment **Comparison and/or Contrast Paragraph**

Write a paragraph in which you compare and/or contrast two places you know, either from personal experience or from your reading.

Suggested Topics

(For more suggested topics, see the list given for the essay "Assignment" on p. 322.)

1. Two neighbourhoods
2. Two towns or cities
3. Two vacation spots
4. Two provinces
5. Two countries
6. Two streets
7. Two colleges or universities

The Comparison and/or Contrast Essay

In a comparison and/or contrast essay, the thesis statement, like the topic sentence in a paragraph, identifies what is being compared and/or contrasted (the topic) and what the author's overall feeling toward the comparison and/or contrast is (the controlling idea). For example, here is a possible thesis statement for an essay on the contrast between two cars:

The Honda Civic beats the Toyota Corolla in many respects.

If you're using the block method, the second paragraph of the essay might be used for everything you want to say about the Honda, and the third paragraph for everything you want to say about the Toyota (contrasting it with what you've said in the previous paragraph about the Honda). The fourth paragraph could then be a conclusion that contains a restatement of your thesis but in different words (for more on concluding paragraphs, see Chapter 20: "The Essay"). A four-paragraph essay would therefore be appropriate if you are using the block method for your comparison and/or contrast essay.

If, on the other hand, you're using the point-by-point method, the second paragraph of the essay would compare and/or contrast both the Honda and the Toyota based on the first point you have chosen. The third paragraph of the essay would deal with both cars in terms of your second point, and so on. Ideally, you will discuss your findings on the basis of three points, which would produce a standard five-paragraph essay: an introduction, three support paragraphs (one for each of your three points), and a conclusion.

> For a review of the essay form and its standard format (which applies to all the writing strategies in this unit), see Chapter 20: "The Essay." For a review of the writing process that can be applied to both the paragraph and the essay, see Chapter 18: "The Four Stages of Writing for a Paragraph or Essay."

The sample essay below explores the differences between living in a small town and living in a big city. Although the opinion of its author, Zack Goodman, is pretty clear from the outset, someone else could just as easily argue for the opposite point of view. What's important in an essay is that the thesis is clear and that there is evidence supporting it. Determine if Zack achieves these goals.

Model Essay: City Life Beats the Small Town Blues

by Zack Goodman

Growing up in a small town has its perks. You might have fewer friends than you have in the big city, but you tend to keep them closer. The East Coast small town author Hugh MacLennan once said that writers who grow up in a small towns have a greater knowledge of human intimacy even if their writing ideas stemming from this knowledge dry up before they turn 40. Well, not everybody agrees with either of those points. In fact, city life can offer just as much knowledge of human intimacy if not more than small town life can. Life is better in the big city, and it all comes down to one general reason: more choice.

One of the areas in which having choice can be extremely valuable is that of friends. Like leaving home to seek greater knowledge of yourself, picking your own friends from a greater number of people can aid in your journey to seek self-knowledge. After all, if you go out with the same group of small town friends all the time, not because you necessarily like them all that much, but because they're the only ones available, this can prove quite limiting when it comes to your growth as an individual. The big city, on the other hand, offers an endless number of opportunities to meet people of like interests. You're much more likely to cultivate relationships with people who help you to grow.

If you're the type of person who enjoys learning about other cultures and meeting people of many different ethnicities, you're much more likely to do both of these things in a big city. People from all over the world prefer the big city, to which to emigrate because they might already have relatives there, or at least some sort of community similar to the one they've left in their country of origin. They might not have to learn English right away to get along because there are enough people with whom they can speak in their native tongue, and in general, the big city can afford more resources to make them more comfortable. In a small town, you might have to get used to a group of people of one origin, maybe even a community in which there is only one religion. If this is what you want, there's no problem. But if you consider yourself a citizen of the world, a one-ethnicity town might be pretty boring after a while.

And finally, if you're a person who enjoys the arts, the small town probably won't be able to hold a candle to the arts community of a big city. A small town might have one cinema that shows maybe three different movies at any one time. A big city can have more than 100 theatres showing at least a hundred different movies, and not all mainstream film, but independent film, B-movies, foreign film (do Canadian movies qualify as foreign films in Canada?) and second-run movies for those who missed them the first time around. But movies are only one form of entertainment in the big city on any given night. There's the Broadway-style musical, the independent stage theatre, ballet, modern dance, cabaret, poetry reading, cafés and nightclubs with live music including jazz, house, Latin, retro, hip-hop (you ask for it; the big city's got it), street festivals in the summer, outdoor skating and indoor tennis in the winter, and so on and so on. A small town may have some of this some of the time, but a big city is more likely to have most of it most of the time.

A small town has its advantages; that's true. The cost of living is lower. The streets are probably safer at night. And it might even be easier to meet someone special. But if you're an arts lover who enjoys the company of people from all over the world, and you're interested in cultivating friends who help you to grow spiritually and not just to get drunk on a Saturday night, city life is tough to beat.

Questions for Analysis

1. An essay of comparison points out the similarities between two subjects, while an essay of contrast examines the differences. With this in mind, is the essay you have just read an essay of comparison, of contrast, or of both? What is your evidence for your answer?

2. Does the writer use the point-by-point method or the block method in writing this essay?

3. Does the writer provide an equal number of details that relate to the small town and the big city?

4. Specifically, how does the writer demonstrate what he thinks is the superior nature of the big city?

 Assignment **Comparison and/or Contrast Essay**

Choose a topic from the list below (or, if you prefer, from the list given for the paragraph "Assignment" on p. 320) and write a comparison and/or contrast essay of at least five paragraphs to develop that topic.

Suggested Topics

Compare and/or contrast:

1. High school classes with college classes
2. Life in a city with life in a rural area
3. Two movies (the acting, the cinematography, the quality of the story)
4. A friend from your childhood with a present friend
5. Two similar items you have owned (e.g., cars, bicycles, radios)
6. Seeing a play with seeing a movie
7. Two vacation spots
8. Two apartments or houses where you have lived
9. Researching in a library with researching on the Internet
10. Cooking dinner at home with eating out

While developing your essay, you may want to review Chapter 18: "The Four Stages of Writing for a Paragraph or an Essay," in particular the following sections:

"Brainstorming"

"Choosing the Topic and the Controlling Idea"

"Outlining"

"The Rough Draft"

"Revising and Editing the Rough Draft"

"Proofreading"

"Checklist for the Final Copy"

For help in connecting your sentences and paragraphs smoothly and clearly, you may wish to consult the list of transitional words and phrases, categorized by their function, found on the inside back cover of this book.

 Working Together: Reaching Consensus

In a group of three to five students, decide among yourselves which two movies, fashion items, concerts, or advertisements you'd like to compare and/or contrast. Make sure that everyone in your group has seen both items. Then try to reach a consensus about your overall conclusion before you begin to compare and/or contrast the items on the basis of at least three points. Discuss your results with the rest of the class. Was it easy to reach consensus on everything? What did you learn by the process? Did most groups end up comparing, contrasting, or both?

amucha maneechote/shutterstock.com

Chapter 28 **Process**

What Is Process?

DEFINITION

Process is the explanation of how to do something or the demonstration of how something works. There are two kinds of process writing: **directional** and **informational.**

A **directional process** actually *shows* you, step by step, how to do something. For example, if you wanted to show someone how to brew a perfect cup of coffee, you would take the person through each step of the process, from selecting and grinding the coffee beans to pouring the finished product. Instructions on a test, directions for getting to a wedding reception, recipes for spaghetti sauce—these are a few examples of the kinds of process writing you see and use regularly. You can find examples of directional process writing everywhere you look: in newspapers, magazines, and books, as well as on the containers and packages of products you use every day.

An **informational process** *tells* you how something is (or was) done, for the purpose of informing you about it. For example, in a history course, it might be important to understand how Upper and Lower Canada were joined by the process of Confederation. Of course, you would not use this process yourself; its purpose would be to give you information.

Developing Paragraphs: Process

The following paragraph, from Mary Finlay's *Communication at Work,* is an example of directional process writing that describes some preliminary steps to follow when preparing an oral presentation.

Model Paragraph: Planning Your Presentation

Ascertain how long your presentation is expected to take. Normally, a speech is delivered at about 150 words a minute. Make sure that your material is adequate for the time allotted. Of course, this does not mean that a ten-minute oral report will be as dense as a 1500-word essay. Rehashing points you have already made in order to fill up your time is a sure-fire way to annoy and frustrate your listeners. Leave time for questions and feedback. If there is none, don't fill in the time by answering the questions nobody asked. This suggests that you are having second thoughts about the organization and planning of your report.

The following paragraph provides an example of informational process writing, giving an overview of the process leading up to Canadian Confederation:

Model Paragraph: Years in the Making

Confederation, the political union of British North America, didn't happen overnight. Starting as a topic of discussion among politicians before the 1860s, it began to take shape after 1864 with a conference in Charlottetown to discuss the possibility of a union, followed by a second conference at Quebec the same year. The details were hammered out at yet another conference in London, England, in 1866, leading to the passage of the *British North America Act* in March of 1867 and resulting in the formation of the Dominion of Canada on July 1, 1867.

Working with Process: Don't Overlook Any of the Steps

The writer of the process essay is almost always more of an authority on the subject than the person reading the essay. When giving directions or information on how something is (or was) done, it is possible to leave out a step that you think is so obvious that it is not worth mentioning. The reader, on the other hand, may not necessarily fill in the missing step as you did. An important part of process writing, therefore, is understanding your reader's level of ability. All of us have been given directions that, at first, seemed very clear, only to find that, when we actually tried to carry out the process, something went wrong. A step in the process was misunderstood or missing. The giver of the information either assumed we knew more than we did about certain parts of the process, or didn't stop to think through the process completely. To avoid causing this kind of difficulty for your reader, make sure the directions in your process writing are complete and accurate. Here is one further consideration: if special equipment is required to perform the process, be sure that the directions include a clear description of the necessary tools.

 Exercise 1 Is the Process Complete?

In the following process, try to determine what important step or steps have been omitted. Imagine yourself going through the process using only the information provided.

How to Prepare for an Essay Exam

1. Read the relevant chapters as they are assigned, well in advance of the test.
2. Take notes in class.
3. If the teacher has not described the test, ask her or him what format the test will take.
4. Get a good night's sleep the night before.
5. Bring any pens or pencils that you might need.
6. Arrive at the classroom a few minutes early to get yourself settled and to keep yourself calm.

Missing step or steps: _____

_____

_____

Coherence in Process: Order in Logical Sequence

When you are writing about a process, it is important to make sure not only that the steps in the process are complete, but also that they are given in the right sequence. For example, if you are describing the process of cleaning a mixer, it is important to point out that you must first unplug the appliance before you remove the blades. The importance of this step is clear when you realize that neglecting it could cost someone a finger. Improperly written instructions could cause serious injuries or even death.

 Practice 1 Coherence: Order in Logical Sequence

The following steps describe the process of setting up an effective filing system. Number the steps in their proper sequence in the blanks to the left. Check your answers against those in the Answer Key on page 467.

_____ When your mind begins to blur, stop filing for that day.

_____ Now label a file folder and slip the piece of paper in.

_____ Gather together all materials to be filed so that they are all in one location.

_____ Alphabetize your file folders and put them away in your file drawer, and you are finished for that session.

_____ Add to these materials a recycling container, folders, labels, and a pen.

_____ Pick up the next piece of paper and go through the same procedure, but ask yourself whether this new piece of paper might fit into an existing file rather than one with a new heading.

_____ Pick up an item from the top of the pile and decide whether this item has value for you. If it does not, recycle it. If it does, go on to the next step.

_____ Finally, to maintain your file once it is established, riffle through each file folder you consult, picking out and recycling the deadwood.

_____ If the piece of paper is worth saving, ask yourself the question "What is this paper about?"

Use transitional words and phrases to make a paragraph flow smoothly and coherently—see the section "Using Transitions to Move from One Idea to the Next" in Chapter 20 (pp. 231–232), and the discussions of using spatial order and time sequence to order paragraphs in Chapters 29 (pp. 338–340) and 32 (pp. 366–367), respectively.

 Exercise 2 **Using Transitions to Go from a List to a Paragraph**

Refer back to the process "How to Prepare for an Essay Exam" outlined in the first exercise in this chapter (pp. 325–326). Using words listed under the heading "For Process" in the chart of common transitional words and phrases on the inside back cover of this text, change the list of steps from the exercise into a process paragraph that is coherent and flowing.

Writing the Process Paragraph Step by Step

To learn a skill with some degree of ease, it is best to follow a step-by-step approach so that you can work on the steps one at a time. This will ensure that you are not missing a crucial point or misunderstanding a part of the whole. There are other ways to go about writing an effective paragraph, but here is one logical method you can use to achieve results, which in itself is a process.

Steps for Writing the Process Paragraph

1. Write a topic sentence.
2. List as many steps or stages in the process as you can.
3. Eliminate any irrelevant points; add references to any equipment needed or special circumstances of the process.
4. Put your final list in order.
5. Write at least one complete sentence for each of the steps you have chosen from your list.
6. Write a concluding statement that says something about the results of completing the process.
7. Finally, copy your sentences into standard paragraph form.

 Exercise 3 **Writing the Process Paragraph Step by Step**

Starting with the suggested topic below, follow the seven steps outlined in the box above to work through the writing process for a process paragraph. (These steps are similar to those used for the narrative paragraph in Chapter 32; refer to pp. 368–369 for a step-by-step example and a completed sample paragraph.)

Topic: How to burglar-proof your home

The incidence of break-and-enter crimes increases yearly, and many people are concerned about their homes when they are away on vacation. Give advice to a homeowner on how to protect a house against burglary.

On Your Own: Writing Process Paragraphs from Model Paragraphs

Directional Process: How to Care for Your Health

Concern for health and physical fitness is enjoying great popularity, bringing in big profits to health-related magazines, health clubs, health food producers, and sports equipment manufacturers. The following paragraph tells us how to get a good night's sleep.

Model Paragraph: Road to Restfulness

The process of getting a good night's sleep depends on several factors. First, the conditions in your bedroom must be correct. Be sure the room temperature is around 18°C and the room is as quiet as possible. Next, pay attention to your bed and how it is furnished. For example, a firm mattress is best, and wool blankets are better than blankets made of synthetic material. Similarly, a firm pillow is best; after all, one that is too soft can cause a stiff neck and lead to a night of poor sleep. Also, keep in mind that what and how you eat are part of the process of preparing for bed. For example, do not go to bed hungry, but do not overeat, either. And avoid candy bars or cookies; the sugar they contain acts as a stimulant. Finally, do not go to bed until you are sleepy. Do something relaxing until you are tired. In conclusion, everything you do can have an effect on how well you sleep.

 Assignment **Process Paragraph**

Write a paragraph in which you give the major steps in some area of caring for your physical or mental health.

Suggested Topics

1. How to plan a daily exercise program
2. How to choose a sport that is suitable for you
3. How to live to be 100
4. How to pick a doctor
5. How to make exercise and dieting fun
6. How to stop smoking
7. How to deal with depression

Informational Process: How to Accomplish a Task

Note that the topics presented above are all examples of directional process writing. Read the following model paragraph for an example of informational process writing, describing how an insect builds a nest.

> ### Model Paragraph: Waspy Ways
>
> The insect known as the hunter wasp goes through a regular procedure when it builds a nest. First, it digs a small tunnel into the earth. Then it goes in search of a cicada, a large insect that resembles a cricket. After stinging and paralyzing the cicada, the hunter wasp brings it to the tunnel, lays an egg on the helpless insect, and seals the tunnel. The hunter wasp then leaves. When the egg hatches, the larva uses the cicada as a source of food.

Assignment   **Process Paragraph**

Write a paragraph in which you show how a task is accomplished. The task may be something that is frequently done by humans or that occurs in the world of nature.

Suggested Topics

(For more suggested topics, see the list given for the essay "Assignment" on p. 332.)

1. How cheese is made
2. How to burn a CD
3. How people obtain a divorce
4. How to get a driver's licence
5. How yeast causes bread to rise
6. How a bill becomes a law
7. How planets are formed

Writing the Process Essay

Any process paragraph can easily be turned into a process essay by simply increasing the amount of detail in all of the steps. Follow the essay format and structure as described in Chapter 20: "The Essay," and devote each support paragraph to a single step in the process.

Exercise 4   **When Process Goes Wrong**

It is your sister's birthday. You have bought her a gift that you must first put together. Carefully following the instructions, you try to assemble the item, but something is wrong. It does not work. Either you have not followed the instructions properly, or the instructions themselves are not clear. All of us have found ourselves in this situation at one time or another. It reminds us that it takes careful thought to write about a process, and that the writer should not assume the reader knows more than he or she is likely to know.

Answer the following questions in further exploration of this topic.

1. Think of a time when you had to put something together but were not given adequate directions. What did you do?
2. When people write instructions or give directions, what do they usually neglect to keep in mind?
3. Recall a time when you had to explain a process to someone. Perhaps you were showing someone how to get somewhere or writing a detailed description of how to do a science experiment. What was the process? Was it hard to explain? Why or why not?
4. What was your worst experience with trying to follow a process? You could have been trying to work something out yourself or follow someone else's directions. How did you overcome your difficulty?

For a review of the essay form and its standard format (which applies to all the writing strategies in this unit), see Chapter 20: "The Essay." For a review of the writing process that can be applied to both the paragraph and the essay, see Chapter 18: "The Four Stages of Writing for a Paragraph or an Essay."

Much of the instruction in this book is process writing. This very chapter, for instance, outlines the process of writing a process paragraph or essay. Some processes are familiar to most of us, such as assembling furniture from printed instructions. The sample essay below describes a process that everyone has heard about, but not everyone has actually done: changing a flat tire. Cara had never changed a flat tire until she accidentally came upon a brochure on how to do it. Until she read what the steps were, she assumed it was actually a difficult process. The power of words made her realize her fears were unfounded. So the next time her tire went flat, she proudly put her new skills to work. She hopes that her essay can serve the same purpose for others.

Model Essay: Replacing a Tire

by Cara Watters

What happens when you get a flat tire? Do you immediately call Roadside Assistance or the CAA (Canadian Automobile Association)? Or do you consider a flat tire the equivalent of your window washer fluid running out? If you wouldn't call the CAA to replace the fluid, why would you call someone to help you replace a tire, right? Well, that choice is yours. But if you haven't replaced a tire yet, and would like to know how to do it if you ever experience the need, read on. Maybe the sense of accomplishment in itself is worth forgoing the call for help. To replace a flat tire, you need to follow a few easy steps.

The first thing to do is ensure safety. As soon as you know your tire has "bitten the dust," drive the car, if you can, onto the shoulder of the road (where it is as level as possible) so that both you and the car are out of harm's way. Put the transmission into park and apply the parking brake. If you are driving a stick shift, place the shift into gear. Turn the engine off and turn on your hazard lights. With more and more drivers on their cellphones these days, you want to make sure you're as visible as possible. For this reason, it might also be a good idea to open your hood until you're ready to drive away.

Secondly, prepare the car for the tire change. You can start to pretend you're a doctor who's prepping for surgery. If you're not perfectly level, place a wheel chock (or large rock) either behind (if on an incline) or in front of (if on a decline) the wheel that is diagonally opposed to the one that needs changing. Get out the spare tire, a lug wrench (tire iron), and the car jack.

Thirdly, the actual changing of the tire, or surgery, so to speak, begins. Remove the hubcap, if necessary. Turning the lug wrench counterclockwise, loosen the lug nuts before jacking up the car. Loosen the lugs in star formation: this means first loosen one lug, then the one opposite, then another and so on until each lug has been loosened a few times. Carefully jack up the car. And never go under your car when only a jack is holding it up. Jack up the car a little higher than it is necessary to remove the old tire so that there is room to put the spare on. Remove the lug nuts all the way and put them in a place that is safe and where you know they will not roll away. Then remove the flat tire and put it aside. Put the spare on the threaded studs, making sure the air valve is facing out.

Now it's time to finish the job. Close up your patient by first replacing the lug nuts. Tighten them the same way you loosened them, by the star formation: tighten one a little, then tighten the one opposite a little. Go to the next lug, and so on. Every lug should be tightened a few times. Slowly lower the jack, and remove it. Give all the lug nuts a final tightening until you can't tighten any more. Replace the hubcap. Make sure everything you've put down is picked up, and you're ready to go.

Of course, once you've changed a tire the first time, it will automatically get easier the second time (if there is a second time). With these steps, the surgery promises to be quite painless. Before that first time, however, it's always a good idea to remember a few tips: for example, have a strong, hollow pipe (about two feet [60 cm] in length) in your car that can help you with leverage when you're using the lug wrench. Have some penetrating oil on hand that you can squirt on the lug nuts if they stick. (After you squirt some, wait a moment, and then try again.) Use gloves when removing a flat tire. If the tire is bald, after all, there may be steel strands sticking out that can cut you. And check your spare tire before any of this happens to make sure it is inflated properly. Apparently, many spare tires are flat because people don't check on this. Imagine going as far as taking your flat tire off only to find out your spare is flat too! You'd have to call for help after all.

Questions for Analysis

1. Is this process essay more directional or informational?
2. What method did the writer use for the introduction? (See pp. 228–231.)
3. What method did the writer use for the conclusion? (See pp. 232–234.)
4. How many main steps are there to the process as the writer described it?
5. Identify all the parts of the passage where the writer gives specific examples to make a step clear.
6. Identify some of the transitions used by the writer.

 Assignment Process Essay

Choose a topic from the list below (or, if you prefer, from the list given for the paragraph "Assignment 2" on p. 329) and write a process essay of at least five paragraphs to develop that topic.

Suggested Topics

1. How to give a speech
2. How to do well in a job interview
3. How to plan a backpacking trip
4. How to buy a used computer
5. How to study for a test
6. How to choose the right college
7. How to redecorate a room
8. How to buy clothes on a limited budget
9. How to learn to sing
10. How to make new friends

Writing the Process Essay: How to …

Thousands of books and articles have been written that promise to help us accomplish some goal in life: how to start a business, how to cook, how to lose weight, how to install a shower, how to assemble a bicycle. In the essay you are about to write, you have the opportunity to describe how you once went through a process to achieve a goal of some kind.

While developing your essay, you may want to review Chapter 18: "The Four Stages of Writing for a Paragraph or an Essay," in particular the following sections:

"Brainstorming"

"Choosing the Topic and the Controlling Idea"

"Outlining"

"The Rough Draft"

"Revising and Editing the Rough Draft"

"Proofreading"

"Checklist for the Final Copy"

For help in connecting your sentences and paragraphs smoothly and clearly, you may wish to consult the list of transitional words and phrases, categorized by their function, found on the inside back cover of this book.

 Working Together: Campus Woes

1. As a class, discuss and list some of the problems on your particular campus today. Then form groups of three or four. As a group, choose one of the problems from the list and discuss it for a few minutes, then draw up a list of steps that need to be taken to improve the situation.

2. Use the list to create sentences that will go into a letter to be sent to the appropriate college or university official suggesting the process that could be followed to solve the problem. Add an introductory paragraph that presents the problem and a conclusion that thanks the official for his or her attention. Write the finished letter.

3. Imagine you're an advice columnist who has received the letter shown here (to the right). Read the letter and answer the following question:

> What would you tell this person to do? Explain the process she should follow to solve her problem.

> **DEAR ABBY,**
>
> I am doing my co-op placement at a cable television company as a computer operator. Lately, every morning when I sign in on my computer, I find suggestive messages from the man I relieve from the night shift.
>
> I am a single mother. I am also dating another man and have no interest in this co-worker. Should I report him to my supervisor? Someone in my office suggested that I file a sexual harassment charge.
>
> —Harassed

In a small group, consider the following questions:

a. Should the letter writer confront the man who is harassing her?

b. Should she go to her supervisor? Should she tell her co-workers about the problem?

c. Should she share her problem with the man she is dating?

d. Should she avoid the problem and quit her job?

e. How important is evidence for a person in this situation? How and when should she gather documentation for a possible formal action?

f. Does she need a lawyer? Does she need to consider the consequences of a formal action?

Chapter 29 **Description**

What Is Description?

> **DEFINITION**
>
> **Description** is the use of words to help the reader understand how people, places, or things are perceived. How a particular food tastes, looks, and smells, for example, might be the subject of a descriptive paragraph or essay.

Description is one of the basic building blocks of good writing. When you are able to write an effective description of a person, an object, a place, or even an idea, you are in control of your writing. Good description also makes you able to control what your reader sees and does not see.

The key to writing a good description is the choice of the **specific details** you will use. Specific details make your descriptions real and help your reader remember what you have written. A careful writer always pays special attention to specific details in any piece of writing.

A second important aspect of good description is the use of **sensory images.**

> **DEFINITION**
>
> **Sensory images** are details that relate to your sense of sight, smell, touch, taste, or hearing.
> **Example:** The deafening screams and relentless yelling of the children on the school bus drove the driver mad.

When you appeal to at least some of the five senses in your descriptive writing, your reader will be able to relate directly to what you are saying. Sensory images also help your reader remember what you have written.

A third important aspect of good description is the **order** in which you place the details you have chosen. The combination of specific details, sensory images, and a well-chosen order in which you present these details and impressions will help your reader form a **dominant impression** of what you are describing.

Some descriptive writing is more objective than subjective (e.g., a police report). If your descriptive piece is more objective, give the readers enough facts to allow them to come up with their own dominant impressions. If your descriptive piece is subjective instead, your dominant impression should be suggested from the outset, even if it's not completely obvious. Establishing a dominant impression is the job of the topic sentence of a paragraph or the thesis statement of an essay.

Developing Paragraphs: Description

The following example of a descriptive paragraph includes all the elements of a good description. As you read this description of a typical neighbourhood delicatessen, note the specific details and the sensory images the writer uses. After you have read the description, ask yourself whether the writer has provided a dominant impression. If so, state that dominant impression in your own words. What is your evidence for this conclusion? Does the paragraph feature subjective or objective description?

Model Paragraph: Delicatessen Decor

The delicatessen was a wide store with high ceilings that were a dark brown colour from many years of not being painted. The rough wooden shelves on both sides of the store were filled from floor to ceiling with cans of fruits and vegetables, jars of pickles and olives, and special imported canned fish. A large refrigerator case against one wall was always humming loudly from the effort of keeping milk, cream, and several cases of pop and juice cool at all times. At the end of the store was the main counter with its gleaming white metal scale on top and its cold cuts and freshly made salads inside. Stacked on top of the counter beside the scale today were baskets of fresh rolls and breads that gave off an aroma that contained a mixture of onion, caraway seed, and pumpernickel. Behind the scale was the friendly face of Mr. Rubino, who was in his store seven days a week, fourteen hours or more each day. He was always ready with a smile or a friendly comment, or even a sample piece of cheese or smoked meat as a friendly gesture for his "growing customers," as he referred to us kids in the neighbourhood.

Working with Description: Selecting the Dominant Impression

When you use a number of specific sensory images as you write a description, you should do more than simply write a series of sentences on a particular topic. You should also create a dominant impression in your reader's mind. Each individual sentence that you write is part of a picture that becomes clear when the reader finishes the paragraph.

For example, when you describe a place, the dominant impression you create might be of a place that is warm, or friendly, or comfortable; or it could be a place that is formal, or elegant, or artistic. When you write a description of a person, your reader could receive the dominant impression of a positive, efficient person who is outgoing and creative, or of a person who appears to be cold, distant, or hostile. All the sentences should support the dominant impression you have chosen.

Here is a list of descriptive words for you to use as a guide as you work through this chapter. (Not surprisingly, all these words are adjectives, since adjectives are words that *describe* persons, places, and things.) Picking a dominant impression is essential in writing the descriptive college paragraph.

Selecting the Dominant Impression

Possible Dominant Impressions for Descriptions of Places

crowded	cozy	inviting	cheerful	dazzling
romantic	restful	dreary	drab	uncomfortable
cluttered	ugly	tasteless	unfriendly	gaudy
stuffy	eerie	depressing	spacious	sunny

Possible Dominant Impressions for Descriptions of People

creative	angry	independent	proud	withdrawn
tense	shy	aggressive	generous	sullen
silent	witty	pessimistic	responsible	efficient
snobbish	placid	bumbling	Bitter	easygoing

 Exercise 1   Selecting the Dominant Impression

Each of the following places could be the topic for a descriptive paragraph. First, the writer must decide on a dominant impression. Fill in each blank to the right of the topic with an appropriate dominant impression. Use the list above if you need help. The first one is done for you.

Topic	**Dominant Impression**
1. The college pub on pub night	_____loud_____
2. A park at dusk	_____
3. The room where you are now sitting	_____
4. The variety store nearest you	_____
5. The college bookstore in September	_____
6. An overcrowded waiting room	_____
7. The kitchen in the morning	_____

Revising Vague Dominant Impressions

Certain words in the English language have become so overused that they no longer have any specific meaning for a reader. Careful writers avoid these words because they are almost useless in descriptive writing. Here is a list of the most common overused words:

- good, bad
- nice, fine, okay
- normal, typical
- interesting
- beautiful

The following paragraph is an example of the kind of writing that results from the continued use of vague words:

> ### Model Paragraph: A Day in the Life ... (I)
>
> I had a typical day. The weather was nice and my job was interesting. The food for lunch was okay; supper was really good. After supper, I saw my girlfriend, who is really beautiful. That's when my day really became fun.

Notice that all of the details in the paragraph are vague. The writer has told us what happened, but we cannot really see any of the details that are mentioned. This is because the writer has made the mistake of using words that have lost much of their meaning. Replacing the vague words in the paragraph will create an entirely different impression:

> ### Model Paragraph: A Day in the Life ... (II)
>
> I had an event-filled day that was typical of the kind of day I've been enjoying lately. The weather on this summer day was perfect for late June, and the challenge of my job in the healthcare field made me feel that this warm and sunny day was made just for me. I had a delicious lunch in a tiny Italian restaurant, and a supper to excite the taste buds at a cozy Greek restaurant that just oozed atmosphere. After supper, I met my girlfriend, who has a warm sense of humour and who is a partner in a major law firm down the street from where I work.

The following exercise will give you practice in recognizing and eliminating overused words.

 Exercise 2   **Revising Vague Dominant Impression**

In each of the spaces provided, change the underlined word to give a more specific dominant impression. An example has been done for you.

> **_Vague:_** The tablecloth was beautiful.
> **_Revised:_** The tablecloth was <u>of white linen with delicate blue embroidery</u>.

1. The sunset was <u>beautiful</u>. _____
2. The water felt <u>nice</u>. _____
3. Horseback riding was <u>fun</u>. _____
4. The traffic was <u>bad</u>. _____
5. The hotel lobby was <u>typical</u>. _____
6. The main street is <u>interesting</u>. _____
7. The dessert tasted <u>good</u>. _____

Working with Description: Sensory Images

One of the basic ways all good writers communicate experiences to their readers is by using sensory impressions. We respond to writing that makes us see an object, hear a sound, touch a surface, smell an odour, or taste a flavour. When a writer uses one or more of these sensory images in a piece of writing, we tend to pay more attention to what she or he is saying, and we tend to remember the details of what we have read.

For example, if you come across the word *door* in a sentence, you may or may not pay attention to it. However, if the writer tells you it was a *brown wooden* door that was *rough to the touch* and *creaked loudly* when it opened, you would hardly be able to forget it. The door would stay in your mind because the writer used sensory images to make you aware of it.

The following sentences are taken from the description of Mr. Rubino's delicatessen on page 335. Notice how in each sentence the writer uses at least one sensory image to make the details of that sentence remain in our minds. The physical sense the writer is appealing to is indicated for each sentence.

1. A large refrigerator case against one wall was always humming loudly from the effort of keeping milk, cream, and several cases of pop and juice cool at all times.

    Physical sense: hearing

2. Stacked on top of the counter … were baskets of fresh rolls and breads that gave off an aroma that contained a mixture of onion, caraway seed, and pumpernickel.

    Physical sense: smell

3. He was always ready with … a sample piece of cheese or smoked meat as a friendly gesture …

    Physical sense: taste

When you use sensory images in your own writing, you will stimulate your readers' interest and create images in their minds that they will remember.

Coherence in Description: Putting Details in Spatial Order

In descriptive paragraphs, the writer often chooses to arrange supporting details according to their location in space. With this method, you place yourself at the scene and then use a logical order such as moving from nearby to farther away, right to left, or top to bottom. Often you move in such a way that you save the most important detail until last in order to achieve the greatest effect.

In the paragraph about the delicatessen on page 335, the writer first describes the ceilings and walls of the store, then proceeds to the shelves and large refrigerator, and ends by describing the main counter of the deli with its owner, Mr. Rubino, standing behind it. The details are thus presented starting with the outer limits of the room and moving inward to the man who is central to the point of this paragraph. A description of a clothes closet might order the details differently—perhaps the writer would go from the ground up, beginning with the shoes standing on the floor and finishing with the hats and gloves arranged on the top shelf.

Here is a paragraph from Thierry Mallet's *Glimpses of the Barren Lands,* a description of his travels through the Canadian Arctic:

> Our camp had been pitched at the foot of a great, bleak, ragged hill, a few feet from the swirling waters of the Kazan River. The two small green tents, pegged down tight with heavy rocks, shivered and rippled under the faint touch of the northern breeze. A thin wisp of smoke rose from the embers of the fire.

Notice that the writer begins with a description of the landscape, then gives a description of the camp, and ends with a picture of the small fire. In spite of the shortness of the paragraph, we are able to follow the writer through the description because there is a logical plan. No matter what method of spatial order you choose to organize the details in a descriptive paragraph, be sure the results allow your reader to see the scene in a logical order.

 Practice 1 **Coherence: Putting Details in Spatial Order**

Each of the following topic sentences is followed by descriptive sentences that are out of order. Put these descriptive sentences in order by placing the appropriate number in the space provided. Check your answers against those in the Answer Key on page 467.

1. The young woman was a teen of the twenty-first century.
   (*Order the material from top to bottom.*)

   _____ She wore hip-hugging, low-rise faded jeans.

   _____ Her nose was pierced with a subtle gold stud.

   _____ She displayed a tasteful tattoo of a single red rose on her left shoulder blade above her tight-fitting tube top.

   _____ Her brown hair was cut unevenly and streaked with blond.

   _____ Her wedge sandals looked cute and comfortable at the same time.

2. The locker room was in chaos.
   (*Order the material from near to far.*)

   _____ Immediately to my right, I saw Pat and Chris slapping each other with towels.

   _____ Behind the pair, a row of locker doors banged open and shut.

_____ I squeezed past a noisy group crowding the doorway.

_____ At the back, the rest of the team was hugging and congratulating our hero in celebration of her winning goal.

Writing the Descriptive Paragraph Step by Step

To learn a skill with some degree of ease, it is best to follow a step-by-step approach so that you can work on the steps one at a time. This will ensure that you are not missing a crucial point or misunderstanding a part of the whole. There are other ways to go about writing an effective paragraph, but what follows is one logical method you can use to achieve results.

Steps for Writing the Descriptive Paragraph
1. Study the given topic, then plan your topic sentence, especially the dominant impression.
2. List at least ten details that come to mind when you think about the topic.
3. Choose the five or six most important details from your list. Be sure these details support the dominant impression.
4. Put your final list in a logical order.
5. Write at least one complete sentence for each of the details you have chosen from your list.
6. Write a concluding statement that offers some reason for describing this topic.
7. Finally, copy your sentences into standard paragraph form.

 Exercise 3 **Writing the Descriptive Paragraph Step by Step**

Starting with the suggested topic below, follow the seven steps outlined in the box above to work through the writing process for a descriptive paragraph. (These steps are similar to those used for the narrative paragraph in Chapter 32; refer to pp. 368–369 for a step-by-step example and a completed sample paragraph.)

Topic: A person you admire

On Your Own: Writing Descriptive Paragraphs from Model Paragraphs

Description of a Person

In the following model paragraph, from Alistair MacLeod's story "The Lost Salt Gift of Blood," the author describes his mother in Nova Scotia.

> **Model Paragraph: Mother Fortress**
>
> My mother ran her house as her brothers ran their boats. Everything was clean and spotless and in order. She was tall and dark and powerfully energetic. In later years, she reminded me of the women of Thomas Hardy, particularly Eustacia Vye, in a physical way. She fed and clothed a family of seven children, making all of the meals and most of the clothes. She grew miraculous gardens and magnificent flowers and raised broods of hens and ducks. She would walk miles on berry-picking expeditions and hoist her skirts to dig for clams when the tide was low. She was fourteen years younger

than my father, whom she had married when she was 26, and had been a local beauty for a period of ten years. My mother was of the sea as were all of her people, and her horizons were the very literal ones she scanned with her dark and fearless eyes.

 Assignment   Descriptive Paragraph

Describe a person—preferably one you have observed more than once. If you have seen this person only once, indicate the details that made him or her stay in your mind. If you choose to describe a person with whom you are familiar, select the most outstanding details that will help give your reader a single, dominant impression.

Suggested Topics

(For more suggested topics, see the list given for the essay "Assignment" on p. 344.)

1. A loyal friend
2. A local musician
3. A cab driver
4. A fashion model
5. A gossipy neighbour
6. A police officer
7. An aerobics instructor

Writing the Descriptive Essay

Like the topic sentence of a descriptive paragraph, the thesis of a descriptive essay identifies what is being described and includes the overall impression the author has of the topic. Each support paragraph might deal with one component of whatever is being described. The following is a brief outline of a descriptive essay:

Thesis:	The 100-year-old house was definitely haunted.
Topic sentence for paragraph #1:	First of all, every time people entered any room in the house, somethingseemed to be out of place, contrary to the owner's insistence that she never changes a thing.
Topic sentence for paragraph #2:	Second, visitors constantly scurry out of the house in a fright, claiming later they've sighted at least one ghost.
Topic sentence for paragraph #3:	Scariest of all are the stories about visitors to the house constantly hearing what seems like moaning coming from all around, as if the walls are filled with sick people struggling to break free.

For a review of the essay form and its standard format (which applies to all the writing strategies in this unit), see Chapter 20: "The Essay." For a review of the writing process that can be applied to both the paragraph and the essay, see Chapter 18: "The Four Stages of Writing for a Paragraph or an Essay."

The following descriptive essay was written by an unnamed tourist to Ottawa. This writer claims to have been to our nation's capital many times. But he was shocked to see one thing, not only because he hadn't seen it before and wondered when it got there, but also because of the impact it made on him.

Model Essay: A Monumental Experience

Strolling along in the area of Elgin and Laurier Streets of Ottawa, one can't help but see several impressive national landmarks: the House of Commons, of course, the National Art Gallery, the historic Rideau River Locks, and the War Memorial and Tomb of the Unknown Soldier, which reminds us all of the tragic shooting of Corporal Nathan Cirillo on October 22, 2014. But out of nowhere, a single monument demands one's attention with a pull that is mysterious and deeply spiritual. It's the National Aboriginal Veterans Monument in Confederation Park, designed in 2001 by artist Noel Lloyd Pinay of the Peepeekisis First Nation in Saskatchewan. Made of bronze and granite, the six-metre-high structure pays tribute to Native Canadian soldiers who fought and died for this country in the First, Second and Korean Wars, even when they were deprived of the right to vote. One can't help but examine it from all sides just to see what else is there. At a glance, it's difficult to figure out what everything means, but there's an overwhelming sense that

Marbury/Shutterstock.com

it's all extremely important. Tourists, locals and students stare at it for a long time as if it casts a spell.

Most prominent of the structure is the central figures, those of four Native people, sitting back to back facing four directions, looking serene and proud, soldier-like, ready for battle. Two hold weapons, and the other two hold spiritual items. The spiritual items two of the Native people hold are the eagle's feather fan and a peace pipe. The combination of the weapons and spiritual items conveys a sense of balance suggesting that even in the midst of war lies the hope for peace. One look at the overall structure yields a sense of honour, duty, resilience, balance and harmony with the environment.

Soaring above the heads of the First Nations people is the spread-winged eagle, majestic and powerful, known as the Thunderbird, symbol of the Creator. The eagle encompasses everything spiritual about the Native peoples and life itself. To cultures throughout the world, the eagle both unites and guides those below. It carries prayers to the Creator. It represents great power and balance, dignity and grace. With its ability to rise above the material world to see the spiritual, it represents both intuition and higher truth.

The four animals that surround the statue include the grizzly, the wolf, the buffalo and the elk. They are the spirit guides, each with a specific attribute. The huge grizzly symbolizes healing powers. The wolf represents family values, the buffalo, tenacity and the elk, wariness. The grizzly and the wolf are depicted as howling as if they are in conference with the cosmos. The presence of these beautiful creatures suggests a spiritual connection between the Native peoples and the animals and the environment.

The nation's capital is a must see with its historic sites, the Ottawa River separating Ontario from Quebec, the beautiful bike paths, including the ones along the Rideau Canal for bike enthusiasts or even tourists who want a more natural scenic tour of the city while getting some exercise. The National Aboriginal Veterans Monument in Confederation Park, however, is uniquely awe-inspiring. It drives home the truth that all life must be respected: all people, animals and the environment. It grabs your mind and spirit. A tribute to First Nations people, it's not just about First Nations people. It envelops you regardless of your background and your experience. You eventually leave the monument feeling a little more connected to everything and everyone than you were before.

Questions for Analysis

1. What part of speech enriches the descriptive value of this piece more than any other?
2. Give some examples from this piece of this particular part of speech.

3. What is the object of the description in this essay? Could it be argued there are several? Why or why not?

4. What is different between the first paragraph and the last paragraph?

5. Why do you think the author chooses to remain anonymous?

 Assignment **Descriptive Essay**

Choose a topic from the list below (or, if you prefer, from the list given for the paragraph "Assignment" on p. 341) and write a descriptive essay of at least five paragraphs to develop that topic.

Suggested Topics

1. The best job I ever had
2. The career of my dreams
3. My favourite aunt or uncle
4. My pet _____
5. My first car
6. The ideal mate
7. The most embarrassing date
8. The best dance club
9. My best friend
10. The best meal I ever had
11. The worst restaurant I've ever eaten in
12. My favourite music
13. My tattoos and/or piercings
14. The worst hospital I've ever been in
15. The best float in the _____ parade

While developing your essay, you may want to review Chapter 18: "The Four Stages of Writing for a Paragraph or an Essay," in particular the following sections:

"Brainstorming"

"Choosing the Topic and the Controlling Idea"

"Outlining"

"The Rough Draft"

"Revising and Editing the Rough Draft"

"Proofreading"

"Checklist for the Final Copy"

For help in connecting your sentences and paragraphs smoothly and clearly, you may wish to consult the list of transitional words and phrases, categorized by their function, found on the inside back cover of this book.

Working Together: The Hunt for a Roommate

The following personal advertisement appeared in a local newspaper:

> Young man seeks neat, responsible roommate to share off-campus apartment for next academic year. Person must be a nonsmoker and respect a vegetarian who cooks at home. Furniture not needed, but CD player would be welcome!

Finding the right roommate in a college or university residence, the right person with whom to share an apartment, or the right long-term companion can be difficult. People's personal habits have a way of causing friction in everyday life. Divide into groups for a brief discussion of the kinds of problems one finds in sharing the same space with another person.

1. Imagine that an agency that matches people up with roommates has asked you to write a paragraph or two in which you provide a character description of yourself. As you write, be sure you include information about your hobbies, habits, attitudes, and any other personal characteristics that could make a difference in the kind of person the agency will select for you.
2. Imagine that the agency has asked you to write a paragraph or two in which you provide a character sketch of the roommate you would like the agency to find for you.

Chapter 30 **Definition**

What Is Definition?

Definition is one of the most useful forms of writing. The ability to provide accurate definitions is crucial to ensuring that your audience understands your words and ideas. Most of the essays you will write in college or university will require you to define terms.

Writing a definition means explaining what a word, phrase, or concept means. You will often need to define terms in your writing when they are likely to be unfamiliar to your reader. For example, the writer of a health sciences report for the general public who uses the word *contusion* may want to explain that it is another word for a bruise. In fact, defining a term or concept is often an effective way to begin an essay. Thus, the writer of an essay on discrimination may first want to provide a definition of the term before describing examples of discrimination.

More Personal Meaning

There may also be situations where you want to give a more personal meaning to a common term. For instance, you may think that you have a clear idea of what the word *success* means. But if you talk with your classmates about their definitions of success, you will probably find that everyone has a different mental picture of what success looks like. For some, a successful person might be one who has a great deal of money. For others, success might mean achieving a personal goal, such as competing in the Olympics. Still others might think of success as having a happy family life. Personal definitions are useful in writing because they cast new light on ordinary terms and make us question our preconceptions about our day-to-day lives.

DEFINITION

A **definition** is an explanation of the meaning or significance of a term or concept. The starting point for a good definition is to group the term into a larger category or class. (See page 355 in Chapter 31: "Classification.")

For example, a trout is a kind of fish, a doll is a kind of toy, and a shirt is an article of clothing. Here is a dictionary entry for the word *myth* (from the *Webster's New World College Dictionary, Fifth Edition*):

myth (mith) ***n.*** [LL. *mythos* < Gr. *mythos*, a word, speech, story, legend] **1.** a traditional story of unknown authorship, ostensibly with a historical basis, but serving usually to explain some phenomenon of nature, the origin of man, or the customs, institutions, religious rites, etc. of a people: myths usually involve the exploits of gods and heroes: cf. LEGEND **2.** such stories collectively; mythology **3.** any fictitious story, or unscientific account, theory, belief, etc. **4.** any imaginary person or thing spoken of as though existing.

To what larger category does the word *myth* belong? According to the first meaning above, it is a kind of story, or narrative.

DEFINITION

Once a word has been put into a larger class, its definition gives the **identifying characteristics** that make the word different from other members in the class.

Stating what class or category a word belongs to is typically the first step in defining it, but more is usually required. What makes a *trout* different from a *bass*, a *doll* different from a *puppet*, a *shirt* different from a *sweater*, a *myth* different from a *parable*? Once again, the dictionary can offer some assistance. From the first dictionary definition of *myth* above, we learn that a myth is a specific kind of story that offers an explanation of the behaviour of individual human beings or the religious practices of a people, often involving the adventures of gods and heroes.

When you write a paragraph or an essay that uses definition, the dictionary entry is only the beginning. It is not the function of a dictionary to go into great depth. It can provide only the basic meanings and synonyms. For your reader to understand a difficult term or idea, you will need to expand these basics into what is called **extended definition**.

DEFINITION

An **extended definition** seeks to analyze a concept in order to give the reader a more complete understanding.

For instance, you might include a historical perspective of a word or term. When or how did the concept begin? How did the term change or evolve over the years? How have different cultures understood the term? You will become involved in the connotations of the word (not just what it means, but what it implies). Extended definition uses more than one method to arrive at an understanding of a term.

Developing Paragraphs: Definition

Religion scholar Karen Armstrong is the author of *A Short History of Myth*. In the following passage, the author's starting point resembles the first two meanings from the dictionary definition of *myth*, but she goes on to shed light on the other two dictionary meanings as well. First, here is a reminder of the dictionary definition of the word:

myth (mith) *n.* [LL. *mythos* < Gr. *mythos*, a word, speech, story, legend] **1.** a traditional story of unknown authorship, ostensibly with a historical basis, but serving usually to explain some phenomenon of nature, the origin of man, or the customs, institutions, religious rites, etc. of a people: myths usually involve the exploits of gods and heroes: cf. LEGEND **2.** such stories collectively; mythology **3.** any fictitious story, or unscientific account, theory, belief, etc. **4.** any imaginary person or thing spoken of as though existing.

> ## Model Paragraph: The Meaning of Myth
>
> ## by Karen Armstrong
>
> Myths are universal and timeless stories that reflect and shape our lives—they mirror our desires, our fears, our longings, and provide narratives that attempt to help us make sense of the world.... Today the word "myth" is often used to describe something that is simply not true.... When we hear of gods walking the earth, of dead men striding out of tombs, or of seas miraculously parting to let a favoured people escape from their enemies, we dismiss these stories as incredible and demonstrably untrue.... A myth is essentially a guide; it tells us what we must do in order to live more richly. If we do not apply it to our own situation and make the myth a reality in our own lives, it will remain as incomprehensible and remote as the rules of a board game, which often seem confusing and boring until we start to play.

The author, like the dictionary, puts the term into a larger class: myths are stories. She also identifies the characteristics of these stories that are different from other stories: they are universal and timeless. They reflect and shape our lives. She also goes on to explain the relationship between one dictionary meaning and another that seems at first to be very different: a story that is about gods who walk the earth seems incredible and untrue; therefore, a myth comes to be known as a falsehood. She argues that it is important for humanity to reclaim the real meaning of the term *myth*.

 Exercise 1   **Working with Definition: Class**

Define each of the following terms by placing it in a larger class. Keep in mind that when you define something by class, you are placing it in a larger category so that the reader can see where it belongs. Use the dictionary if you need help. The first example has been done for you.

Chemistry is <u>one of the branches of science</u> that deals with a close study of the natural world.

1. A *motorcycle* is _____

2. *Poetry* is _____

3. *Democracy* is _____

4. *Sugar* is _____

5. A *viola* is _____

Exercise 2 **Working with Definition: Distinguishing Characteristics**

Using the same terms as in Exercise 1, give one or two identifying characteristics that differentiate each term from other terms in the same class. An example has been done for you.

Chemistry is concerned with the structure, properties, and reactions of matter.

1. A motorcycle _____

   _____

   _____

2. Poetry _____

   _____

   _____

3. Democracy _____

   _____

   _____

4. Sugar _____

   _____

   _____

5. A viola _____

   _____

   _____

Writing the Definition Paragraph Step by Step

To learn a skill with some degree of ease, it is best to follow a step-by-step approach so that the various aspects of the skill can be worked on one step at a time. This approach will ensure that you are not missing a crucial point or misunderstanding a part of the whole. There are other ways to go about writing an effective paragraph, but the following is one logical method you can use to achieve results.

> **Steps for Writing the Definition Paragraph**
> 1. Write a topic sentence that identifies what you are going to define.
> 2. List all the possible concepts for your extended definition.
> 3. Review the list and eliminate inappropriate concepts.
> 4. Put your final list in order.
> 5. Write at least one complete sentence for each of the concepts on your final list.
> 6. Write a concluding statement that summarizes the most important parts of your definition.
> 7. Finally, copy your sentences into standard paragraph form.

 Exercise 3 **Writing the Definition Paragraph Step by Step**

Starting with the suggested topic below, follow the seven steps outlined in the box above to work through the writing process for a definition paragraph. (These steps are similar to those used for the narrative paragraph in Chapter 32; refer to pp. 368–369 for a step-by-step example and a completed sample paragraph.)

Topic: Intelligence

To help you get started on a topic sentence below, read the following:

> We often equate intelligence with being "smart" or with having above-average ability in some area. Yet we likely all know some rather intelligent people who don't act very smart, or who are very absent-minded. We could also have a pet that is "intelligent." What is intelligence as you understand it?

 Assignment **Paragraph of Definition**

Some of us are dreamers and some of us are realists; we all have distinguishing characteristics within the larger class of human being. Using one of the following suggested topics, write a paragraph of definition of who or what you are.

Suggested Topics

(For other suggested topics, see the list given for the essay "Assignment" on p. 353.)

1. Happy-go-lucky
2. Creative
3. A friend to all
4. A comedian
5. Reserved

Developing an Essay of Definition

The thesis in this type of essay, of course, identifies what is being defined. It also should provide a good, but general, definition. Then each support paragraph explains a different component or aspect of what has been defined in the first paragraph.

For an example, see the essay on the next page by Jenny Yuen on sexual addiction, entitled "Love Hurts." The first support paragraph (the second paragraph of the essay) deals with the question of how common the addiction is. The third support paragraph (fourth essay paragraph) deals with a particular example. The fifth support paragraph (sixth essay paragraph) deals with the notion that attending twelve-step program meetings may not be enough to control this addiction.

No one support paragraph should deal with more than one component or aspect of whatever is being defined. But once the support paragraph has identified the component to be discussed in its first sentence (the topic sentence of that paragraph), the author, of course, can go ahead and add various supporting details (including examples) to support the topic sentence.

For a review of the essay form and its standard format (which applies to all the writing strategies in this unit), see Chapter 20: "The Essay." For a review of the writing process that can be applied to both the paragraph and the essay, see Chapter 18: "The Four Stages of Writing for a Paragraph or an Essay."

When Jenny wrote the following piece, she was a student in a journalism program. The piece was originally written for publication in a newspaper, which is why much of the writing seems journalistic in nature. The paragraphs are longer than typical newspaper paragraphs, however, because the story was adapted to suit a more academic style of essay for the purpose of this chapter.

Model Essay: Love Hurts[*]

by Jenny Yuen

For love and sex addicts, Valentine's Day may not be simply roses and candy, but rather a traumatic reminder that love hurts. February 14 may bring back painful memories of past breakups, or trigger the need to go out and find a "special someone" who may not turn out to be all that special. Sexual and love addiction is the continuing pattern of unwanted compulsive romantic behaviour that has a negative impact on the addict's personal, social and/or economic standing.

Sex and love addiction are more common than you might imagine, says Rob Hawkings, a psychotherapist at Bellwood Health Services in North York (part of Toronto), Ontario. These addictions are also very complex disorders in which the victims may not realize that their behaviour falls into the "addict" category. How can you tell whether you have "normal" relationship problems or that you're in love with love and sex? (See questionnaire at the end.) The answer is another question: Are you in control? But having self-control is much easier said than done. "We look for a pattern of out-of-control behaviour, whether that's with pornographic material or flirting or continually getting into romantic involvements in a serial kind of way

[*]Jenny Yuen, "Love Hurts." Reprinted by permission of Jenny Yuen.

or giving into simultaneous multiple [relationships]," says 51-year-old Hawkings, a recovering alcoholic and sex addict, himself, who has been working in the field for a decade.

Although the demographic of addicts varies, most of the people who attend the 12-step meetings are males in their late 20s to late 50s. Still, there are no definite statistics of how much of the Canadian population is affected by sexual and love addiction, although Hawkings says more patients would be checking into Bellwood for therapy if they realized it is a problem.

Judy, 37, tormented herself with obsessive sexual fantasies for four years. She had constant fantasies about extra-marital relationships, and suffered from sexual anorexia, trying to avoid her problems so she wouldn't have to deal with them. "I was in a marriage, and I started thinking about men outside my marriage so much that it was affecting my work life. I hate to use the word obsession … but I found myself powerless over my thoughts."

While Bellwood is new at the sex addiction game, SLAA (or Sex and Love Addicts Anonymous), also known as The Augustine Fellowship, has been working worldwide with addicts for more than 30 years. SLAA champions the Alcoholics Anonymous 12-step program as an efficient treatment program for sufferers of sex and love addiction. Currently, SLAA has more than 1200 meeting locations throughout the world, open to all who believe they may have a problem. People who believe they may suffer from love and sexual addiction may come in anonymously and tell their stories and listen to others.

Although Bellwood avidly encourages its sex addiction patients to attend these meetings, Hawkings says 12-step programs are not enough. Bellwood's program includes life-skills coaching to help addicts deal with communication and feelings. In some special cases, Bellwood prescribes medication for sex addicts. "There are situations where there are some people who need a carefully prescribed anti-depressant," says Hawkings, who is careful not to recommend addictive medication such as Valium. "We sometimes get people coming in who have real psychiatric problems as well as addictions going on."

The question still remains: Can the love and sex addict be cured? "The classic stereotype is AA, where people are recovering for the rest of their lives, but for the rest of their lives need not forget they're alcoholics," Hawkings says. By and large, that is the case with sexual addiction. People are always going to be susceptible to using the sexual-addictive fix that they might have used in the past when they were under stress. "One thing we work very hard on in recovery is managing the stress in their lives."

Judy was fortunate enough to alter her sexual behaviours into healthier ones because of the SLAA program. "I felt freedom right away. I was really fortunate," Judy says. "You don't graduate from [a 12-step program]. They call it being 'restored to sanity,' but a better way to put it is we now have a choice over our decisions."

***

The following is a questionnaire to help determine if you are a sex and/or love addict. If you answer yes to most of these questions, you may be.

- Do you still see someone, even though you know the relationship has a destructive effect on you?
- Do you feel like you *have* to have sex?
- Do you have sex regardless of the consequences?
- Do you feel you lack dignity and wholeness?
- Is your life unmanageable because of your sexual or romantic behaviour?

Contact Information:

- SLAA Toronto message line: (416) 486-8201 or email: info@slaa-ontario .org (website: www.slaa-ontario.org)
- Bellwood Health Services (Toronto): toll free 1-866-475-3254
- Dr. Patrick Carnes' website: www.sexhelp.com
- Pia Mellody's website: www.piamellody.com

Questions for Analysis

1. What is the central thing being defined in this essay?
2. In what ways is sexual addiction like alcoholism? In what ways is it different?
3. What surprises you the most in this piece by Jenny Yuen?
4. What do you think is the main purpose of this essay? Why?
5. Why do you think more men go to meetings for sex and love addiction than do women?
6. Do you think sex and/or love addiction can be as destructive as alcohol or substance abuse? Why or why not?

 Assignment **Essay of Definition**

Choose one of the topics below, or come up with one of your own. Write an essay of definition to develop that topic. The essay should be at least five paragraphs long.

Suggested Topics

1. Definition of your favourite martial art
2. Definition of a particular disease or medical condition
3. Definition of love
4. Definition of a term in your particular field of study
5. Definition of Impressionism or other kind of painting theory

While developing your essay, you may want to review Chapter 18: "The Four Stages of Writing for a Paragraph or an Essay," in particular the following sections:

"Brainstorming"

"Choosing the Topic and the Controlling Idea"

"Outlining"

"The Rough Draft"

"Revising and Editing the Rough Draft"

"Proofreading"

"Checklist for the Final Copy"

For help in connecting your sentences and paragraphs smoothly and clearly, you may wish to consult the list of transitional words and phrases, categorized by their function, found on the inside back cover of this book.

 Working Together: What Does the Cover Mean to You?

One could argue that to interpret a picture is to define it. Look at the cover of this book and come to a one-sentence conclusion as to what it means to you. Then use this one-sentence conclusion as the topic sentence or thesis statement for a paragraph or essay of definition. Look at the various components of the picture and pick the three that make the biggest impression on you. Write one or more sentences about each of these three parts as points that support your one-sentence interpretation.

Then exchange papers with someone else. Determine whether the three supporting points actually back up the topic sentence or thesis statement. Discuss your observations with a small group or as a class. Are there several interpretations of the book cover? Are there certain universal points that everybody has made? Do any or all of the interpretations relate to the study of writing?

Chapter 31 **Classification**

What Is Classification?

> **DEFINITION**
>
> **Classification** is the placing of items into separate categories for the purpose of helping us think about these items more clearly. This approach can be extremely useful and even necessary when large numbers of items are being considered.

To classify things properly, you must first establish a **basis for classification.** For example, if you are writing about computers, you could decide to classify them according to where they are made. Then put the items into **distinct categories,** making sure that each item belongs in only one category. For example, your categories might be Canadian-made computers, U.S.-made computers, and computers made overseas. However, if you made your categories imported computers, Canadian-made computers, and used computers, this would not be an effective use of classification; the category of used computers does not conform to the basis for classification you established (where the computers are made), and an imported computer or a Canadian-made computer could also be a used computer, so the categories are not distinct.

A classification should also be **complete.** For example, if you were to classify computers into the two categories of new and used, your classification would be complete because any item must be either new or used. But if you tried to classify computers into desktop and portable computers, there would be many computers that would not fit either category (what about large mainframes?).

Developing Paragraphs: Classification

In the following paragraph, the writer describes different classes of neighbours.

Model Paragraph: Nice and Neighbourly?

To me, there are only two kinds of neighbours: those who are friendly and those who are not. The friendly neighbours always greet me with a smile regardless of the situation. They are the ones whose names I usually know, and they are always either asking me to come over, or they're interested in talking about what's going on in their lives or asking me about mine. The unfriendly neighbours, on the other hand, could be mistaken for complete strangers no matter how long they've lived in the neighbourhood. I don't know their names. They pass me on the street as if they've never seen me before. It's those neighbours who make me think that if I dared to try to strike up a conversation with them, they'd scowl, or, in some way, they'd make me feel sorry for ever trying. I just hope that if one day my house is on fire, my friendly neighbours are at home so that I can run up to *them* for help.

In this paragraph, the writer presents two distinct types of neighbours: friendly ones and unfriendly ones. These are the only types that have any significance for the writer. The writer's classification is complete because it covers the entire range of neighbours—there are, in the writer's opinion, no kinds other than these two. Since most of us have neighbours, we might be able to identify with the writer to some extent even if we don't think the writer's classification system is complete enough.

 Exercise 1 **Working with Classification: Deciding on a Basis for a Classification**

For each of the following topics, pick three different ways this topic could be classified. You may find the following example helpful.

Topic: ways to choose a vacation spot

Basis for classification: by price, by its special attraction, by the accommodations

1. **Topic:** Cellulphones

Basis for classification: _____

_____

2. **Topic:** Relatives

Basis for classification: _____

_____

3. **Topic:** Snack foods

Basis for classification: _____

_____

4. **Topic:** News sources

Basis for classification: _____

_____

5. **Topic:** Medicines

   Basis for classification: _____

   _____

Making Distinct Categories

Once you have established your basis for classification, you're ready to come up with distinct categories. These are ways in which you have chosen to divide each basis for classification. In other words, they are examples of your basis for classification.

Topic	Basis for Classification	Distinct Categories
ways to choose a vacation spot	price	first class
		medium price
		economy
	special attraction	the beach
		the mountains
		the desert
	accommodation	hotel
		motel
		cabin

 Exercise 2 **Working with Classification: Making Distinct Categories**

First, pick a basis for classifying each of the following topics. Then use that basis to create distinct categories. You can list as many categories as you think the basis for classification requires—you don't have to stick with three.

Remember to choose your categories in a way that each item you classify will belong to only one category. For example, if you were to classify cars, you would not want to make sports cars and international cars two of your categories because several kinds of sports cars are also international cars. You may find the following example helpful.

Topic: wine
Basis for classification: colour
Distinct categories: red, white, rosé

or

Basis for classification: national origin
Distinct categories: French, Australian, Italian, Canadian, Chilean, etc.

1. Clothing stores

   Basis for classification: _____

   Distinct categories: _____

   _____

2. Television commercials

   Basis for classification: _____

   Distinct categories: _____

   _____

3. Olympic sports

   Basis for classification: _____

   Distinct categories: _____

   _____

4. Mail

   Basis for classification: _____

   Distinct categories: _____

   _____

5. Art forms

   Basis for classification: _____

   Distinct categories: _____

   _____

Writing the Classification Paragraph Step by Step

To learn a skill with some degree of ease, it is best to follow a step-by-step approach so that various aspects of the skill can be worked on one at a time. This approach will ensure that you are not missing a crucial point or misunderstanding a part of the whole. There are other ways to go about writing an effective paragraph, but here is one logical method you can use to achieve results.

Steps for Writing the Classification Paragraph

1. Write a topic sentence, stating the basis of the classification.
2. List all the possible distinct categories in your classification.
3. Review your list and eliminate any inappropriate distinct categories.
4. Put your final list in order.
5. Write at least one complete sentence for each of the distinct categories you have chosen from your list.
6. Write a concluding sentence that emphasizes the basis of the classification.
7. Finally, copy your sentences into standard paragraph form.

 Exercise 3   Writing the Classification Paragraph Step by Step

Starting with the suggested topic below, follow the seven steps outlined in the box above to work through the writing process for a classification paragraph. (These steps are similar to those used for the narrative paragraph in Chapter 32; refer to pages 368–369 for a step-by-step example and a completed sample paragraph.)

Topic: Games

We play games as children. Some of these we continue to play as adults, and we play different types of games. We are even accused of "playing games"—mind games—from time to time. There are board games, mind games, and electronic games. How many other categories of games can you think of?

 Assignment **Classification Paragraph**

Pick a topic from the list below, and write a paragraph in which you classify relationships.

Suggested Topics

(For more suggested topics, see the list given for the essay "Assignment" on p. 362.)

1. Friends
2. Classmates or colleagues at work
3. Girlfriends/boyfriends
4. Pets
5. Teachers
6. Bosses
7. Casual acquaintances

Developing an Essay of Classification

The thesis statement of a classification essay, like the topic sentence of the classification paragraph, identifies what is being classified. In the essay, it's important to devote each support paragraph to a distinct category of the items you are discussing. For example, in the model essay below, Margo Fine classifies people into four groups according to what psychiatrist M. Scott Peck considers an evolution of spirituality. The first support paragraph (the second paragraph of the essay) deals only with the least spiritually evolved group (the first group); each subsequent support paragraph discusses one of the other groups. Because four groups are being classified, Margo found it appropriate to write a six-paragraph essay as opposed to the standard five that many professors insist upon, or at least strongly recommend, especially when students are required to complete the essay in a two-hour period or less.

> For a review of the essay form and its standard format (which applies to all the writing strategies in this unit), see Chapter 20: "The Essay." For a review of the writing process that can be applied to both the paragraph and the essay, see Chapter 18: "The Four Stages of Writing for a Paragraph or an Essay."

Model Essay: The Evolution of Spirituality

by Margo Fine

Psychiatrist and prolific author M. Scott Peck is probably most famous for his book *The Road Less Traveled,* which has appeared on the *New York Times* Best Seller's List for more than 25 years. Peck entitled a sequel to this book *Further Along the Road Less Traveled*—a title that is appropriate if unoriginal. It is in this book, however, that Peck discusses a model of spiritual evolution into which, he says, every single person can be fit according to a particular classification system. Peck classifies people into four groups according to the extent to which they have spiritually evolved: the first group being the least evolved and the fourth being the most.

The first group is made up of people who are governed by their emotions. These are the quintessential charmers of the model. How nice they are, and therefore, how well they treat others, depends on whether they want something at that particular time. As soon as they get what they want, they're gone, or they're not so nice anymore: narcissism and greed are most apparent in this group. Their responses to people are generally unpredictable as these responses depend solely on these people's emotions. There is little or no self-examination or self-evaluation here.

The second group up from the bottom can quite aptly be called the "organizational clingers." These people are aware of the fact that left to their own devices, they would be completely governed by their own emotions like those in the first group. People in the second group inherently know this would prove disastrous. To avoid such a consequence, they opt to cling to an organization of some sort, one that promises to take care of them, one that offers a sense of protection and belonging, but also discipline by means of a strict code of conduct. This organization prevents them from depending on their emotions for answers to their important questions. Organized religion is often the structure to which people in this group cling. In fact, Peck would put most religious fundamentalists (of any religion) in this category.

The third group up from the bottom (and therefore, the second from the top) is the group that seems to react quite vehemently to the second group (especially to religious fundamentalists). These are the secularists. These people are often very well educated in the sciences or the arts, and they are often politically active or motivated. People in this group often pride themselves on being free thinkers, especially when they compare themselves to people in the second group. However, they, themselves, depend on a structure, however, less rigid than those in the second group, for answers to their important questions. After all, the sciences, especially, are dependent upon laws and knowledge of the natural world—the world people can only perceive with any or all of their five senses, the part of existence that we can see and hear, etc. Despite their self-declaration of being the free thinkers of the world, it is often they who dismiss the idea that there is an order to the universe that is not explainable by science or that cannot be proven by anything empirical.

It is the fourth group that is most spiritually evolved, says Peck. These people, like their counterparts in the third group, are often very well educated. And although they probably call themselves secularists, they can probably be better described by the word "seekers," or perhaps "mystics." Like Albert Einstein, they may be highly regarded for their achievements in the secular world, but at the same time, they know there is more to life than that which we can see and hear or perceive with any of our five senses. People in the fourth group are very much aware of the importance of intuition, or an inner voice and the idea that something else is at work in the universe that cannot be explained by science that makes a great deal of sense whether we can understand it or not. They are not necessarily quick to call it God or Allah or a cosmic consciousness, but whatever it is, it is definitely in the realm of the supernatural. But unlike those in the second group, people in the fourth group are not satisfied with any one set of holy books or especially any one set of interpretations that a single religion can offer in its explanation of a higher power.

It's difficult to avoid value judgments (especially in the case of the first group) in this classification system of spiritual evolution, but Peck notes that the system is only a model. Most people are, most often, a combination of two or more of these groups, but he says every individual is usually more strongly associated with one group as opposed to any other. To which group does each of your friends/family belong? With which group do *you* identify? Life is constantly changing, and our spiritual evolution is no exception, says Peck. If you don't think you're in the fourth group, don't despair: self-awareness and self-examination are already indicators of upward movement.

Questions for Analysis

1. What are the topic, basis for classification, and distinct categories in this essay of classification?
2. Do you agree with Peck's classification system? Why or why not?
3. How do you think, based on the above essay, Peck would define "spirituality"?
4. Does the author of the above essay agree with Peck's classification system? What evidence is there to suggest the author does agree? Is there evidence to the contrary?
5. Do you know people who would clearly fit into one of these categories? Discuss.

6. Do you think it is possible to go backwards on this scale of evolution? Discuss.

7. If you agree with Peck, at least in principle, what do you think it usually takes for a person to progress (or regress?) from one category to another?

8. What role does education seem to play in Peck's classification? Could an educated person be found in the least spiritual group? Explain.

 Assignment **Essay of Classification**

Choose a topic from the list below (or, if you prefer, from the list given for the paragraph "Assignment" on p. 359) and write a classification essay of at least five paragraphs to develop that topic.

Suggested Topics

1. Different kinds of beer or wine
2. Different types of music
3. Different models of Honda (or any other make of car)
4. Different types of teachers/professors
5. Different types of fashion
6. Different kinds of first dates (blind, set-up, Internet, etc.)
7. Pick a typical classification system within your field of study

While developing your essay, you may want to review Chapter 18: "The Four Stages of Writing for a Paragraph or an Essay," in particular the following sections:

"Brainstorming"

"Choosing the Topic and the Controlling Idea"

"Outlining"

"The Rough Draft"

"Revising and Editing the Rough Draft"

"Proofreading"

"Checklist for the Final Copy"

For help in connecting your sentences and paragraphs smoothly and clearly, you may wish to consult the list of transitional words and phrases, categorized by their function, found on the inside back cover of this book.

 Working Together: Brainstorming for Classification

Brainstorming can be wonderfully helpful when several people put their heads together. As a class, select a classification topic. Divide into groups and brainstorm on one of the classification topics given below. After the members of each group have thought of everything they can, come together as a class and put your classifications on the board. Compare and contrast them. What makes one group's classification more successful than another? Can you use each other's material?

Suggested Topics for Brainstorming

1. Fads

   What is a fad? Classify as many different types of fads as you can.

2. Friendship

   What is friendship? Classify as many different types of friendships as you can.

3. Causes of car accidents

   What causes car accidents? Classify as many different types of causes as you can.

4. Sports events

   What are the different kinds of sports events? Classify as many different types of sports events as you can.

5. Alcoholic beverages

   What are the different kinds of alcoholic beverages? Classify as many different types of alcoholic beverages as you can.

Your professor might now ask you to write your own individual paragraph or essay using this material.

Chapter 32 **Narration**

What Is Narration?

> **DEFINITION**
>
> **Narration** is the oldest and best-known form of verbal communication. It is, quite simply, the telling of a story.

Every culture in the world, past and present, has used narration to provide both entertainment and information for the people of that culture. Since everyone likes a good story, various forms of narration, such as novels, short stories, soap operas, and full-length movies, are always popular.

Developing Paragraphs: Narration

The following narrative paragraph, taken from an essay by Al Purdy titled "The Iron Road," tells the story of Purdy's trip westward in 1937, at the height of the Great Depression, when he was looking for work. In this passage, Purdy has been caught illegally riding a freight train by the railway police, and he is imprisoned in a caboose.

> ### Model Paragraph: Prison-on-Wheels
>
> When returned to my prison-on-wheels, I felt panic-stricken. I was only seventeen, and this was the first time I'd ventured far away from home. I examined the caboose-prison closely, thinking: two years. Why, I'd be nineteen when I got out, an old man! And of course it was hopeless to think of escape. Other prisoners had tried without success, and windows were broken where they'd tried to wrench out the bars. And the door: it was wood, locked on the outside with a padlock, opening inward. It was a very springy door, though. I could squeeze my fingertips between sill and door, one hand at the top and the other a foot below. That gave me hope, blessed hope, for the first time. My six-foot-three body was suspended in air by my hands,

> doubled up like a coiled spring, and I pulled. The door bent inward until I could see a couple of daylight inches between door and sill. Then Snap! and screws fell out of the steel hasp outside. I fell flat on my back.*

Working with Narration: Using Narration to Make a Point

At one time or another, you have met a person who loves to talk on and on without making any real point. This person is likely to tell you everything that happened in one day, including every cough and sideways glance. Your reaction to the seemingly needless and endless supply of details is probably one of fatigue and hope for a quick getaway. This is not narration at its best! A good story is almost always told to make a point: it can make us laugh, it can make us understand, or it can change our attitudes.

When Al Purdy tells the story of his escape from the caboose, he is careful to use only those details that are relevant to his story. For example, the way the door is constructed is important. Had it not been wooden and springy, he might never have been able to get his fingertips in and force an opening. He might have had to spend two years in prison. Then Purdy would have had a different story to tell.

What is Purdy's point in this paragraph? The excerpt is part of an essay about Purdy's experiences during the Depression; this part is specifically about the dangers of travelling illegally by train during that time, which many thousands of people had to do, illegal and dangerous as it was. On its surface, then, the story is merely about a trip, although an unusual one. Being imprisoned in the caboose, however, can also be seen as a metaphor: the caboose in which Purdy was imprisoned might represent the life of hopeless despair caused by unemployment that he and thousands of others were trapped in, and Purdy's escape could be a symbol of the escape from despair toward the hope that a trip to the West could bring, with its opportunities for a better life.

 Exercise 1 **Using Narration to Make a Point**

Each of the following examples is the beginning of a topic sentence for a narrative paragraph. Complete each sentence by providing a controlling idea that could be the point for the story.

1. During my trip to the East Coast, I was surprised by _____
   _____

2. When I couldn't get a job, I realized _____
   _____

3. After going to the movies every Saturday for many years, I discovered _____
   _____

* Al Purdy, "The Iron Road," *Starting from Ameliasburgh: The Collected Prose of Al Purdy*, edited by Sam Solecki, 1995, Harbour Publishing, www.harbourpublishing.com.

4. When I arrived at the room where my business class was to meet, I found _____

_____

5. When my best friend got married, I began to see that _____

_____

Coherence in Narration: Placing Details in Order of Time Sequence

Ordering details in a paragraph of narration usually follows a time sequence. That is, you tell what happened first, then next, then after that, until finally you get to the end of the story. An event could take place in a matter of minutes or over a period of many years.

In the following paragraph, the story takes place in a single day. The six events that made the day a disaster are given in the order in which they happened. Although some stories flash back to the past or forward to the future, most use the natural chronological order of the events.

Model Paragraph: A Day to Forget

My day was a disaster. First, it had snowed during the night, which meant I had to shovel before I could leave for work. I was mad that I hadn't gotten up earlier. Then I had trouble starting my car, and to make matters worse, my daughter wasn't feeling well and said she didn't think she should go to school. When I eventually did arrive at the school where I teach, I was twenty minutes late. Soon I found out the secretary had forgotten to type the exam I was supposed to give my class that day. I quickly had to make another plan. By three o'clock, I was looking forward to getting my paycheque. Foolish woman! When I went to pick it up, the woman in the office told me that something had gone wrong with the computers. I would not be able to get my cheque until Tuesday. Disappointed, I walked down the hill to the parking lot. There I met my final defeat. In my hurry to park the car in the morning, I had left my parking lights on. Now my battery was dead. Even an optimist like me had the right to be discouraged!

 Practice 1 Coherence: Placing Details in Order of Time Sequence

Each of the topics below is followed by six supporting details. These supporting details are listed in random order. Order the events according to time sequence by placing the appropriate number in the space provided. The first one has been done for you. Check your answers against those in the Answer Key on page 467.

1. The driving test

_____2_____ She had her last lesson with Mr. Panakos on Saturday morning.

_____5_____ As she ate breakfast Monday morning, Daniela read the driver's manual one more time because she knew it was her last chance to review.

1	Daniela's driving test was scheduled for Monday morning.
3	On Sunday afternoon her father gave her some advice on what to be careful of when she took her road test.
6	As her mother drove her to the motor vehicle bureau, Daniela tried to relax and not think about the test.
4	The night before her test, Daniela had phone calls from two friends who wished her good luck.

2. Making up my mind

_____	By the time I saw the dean for final approval of the change, I knew I had made the right decision.
_____	When I registered for my new courses for the next semester, I knew that I was doing what I should have done all along.
_____	I spent the summer of my second year thinking about the career I really wanted to follow.
_____	I suppose the experience taught me that you should always make a change in your life after you have thought it through completely.
_____	When I finally did decide to change majors, my friends acted as though I had decided to change my citizenship.
_____	When I told my favourite professor about my change of mind, he was very supportive, even though I had begun my major with him.

Writing the Narrative Paragraph Step by Step

To learn a skill with some degree of ease, it is best to follow a step-by-step approach so that various steps can be worked on one at a time. This approach will ensure that you are not missing a crucial point or misunderstanding a part of the whole. There are other ways to go about writing an effective paragraph, but here is one logical method you can use to achieve results.

Steps for Writing the Narrative Paragraph

1. Study the given topic, and then plan your topic sentence with its controlling idea.
2. List the events that come to mind when you think about the topic you have chosen.
3. Choose the five or six most important events from your list.
4. Put your final list in order.
5. Write at least one complete sentence for each of the events you have chosen from your list.
6. Write a concluding statement that gives some point to the events of the story.
7. Finally, copy your sentences into standard paragraph form.

Step-by-Step Example of Writing a Narrative Paragraph

The following example starts with a suggested topic and then uses the seven steps above to work through the writing process.

> **Topic:** At one time or another, many people decide to buy or lease a car. Often it's not the type of car chosen that leads to a story, but the process of acquiring it. Write a narrative paragraph about buying or leasing a car (or some other expensive process, such as renting an apartment).

1. Write a topic sentence.

   > Because my classes were at different campuses, and because I lived quite a distance from the college, I decided to buy a car.

2. Make a list of events.
   a. Tired of waiting for the bus
   b. Budget—gas, insurance, licence, repairs, financing
   c. Car loan
   d. Discussed with Dad
   e. Newspaper ads—dealerships
   f. Classified ads
   g. Asked friends for advice
   h. Comparison shopping

3. Choose the five or six events you believe are the most important for the point of the story.

   > a, b, c, e, h

4. Make sure the order of your final choices makes sense. Reorder if necessary.

   > In this case, the original order (a, b, c, e, h) makes sense.

5. Using your final list, write at least one sentence for each event you have chosen.
   a. I was tired of waiting for the bus on cold and rainy days, and being late for class when the bus was late didn't impress my professors.
   b. My budget didn't allow me to purchase a new car, especially when I calculated the price of gasoline, insurance, repairs, licensing, and finance charges.
   c. My bank manager was very helpful when it came to arranging a car loan, but even though the payments were spread out over a long period of time, it was still an expensive proposition.
   e. I looked in the newspaper for ads from car dealerships, trying to decide whether I'd be better off buying from a dealer, with at least a minimal warranty on the car, or from a private seller.
   h. Comparison shopping was a long and tedious, but necessary, process.

6. Write a concluding statement.

> I finally bought a car, although it wasn't what I really wanted because of my financial situation. At least I don't have to wait for the bus anymore.

7. Put your sentences into standard paragraph form on a separate piece of paper or in a word-processing file.

> Because my classes were at different campuses, and because I lived quite a distance from the college, I decided to buy a car. I was tired of waiting for the bus on cold and rainy days, and being late for class when the bus was late didn't impress my professors. My budget didn't allow me to purchase a new car, especially when I calculated the price of gasoline, insurance, repairs, licensing, and finance charges. My bank manager was very helpful when it came to arranging a car loan, but even though the payments were spread out over a long period of time, it was still an expensive proposition. I looked in the newspaper for ads from car dealerships, trying to decide whether I'd be better off buying from a dealer, with at least a minimal warranty on the car, or from a private seller. Comparison shopping was a long and tedious, but necessary, process. I finally bought a car, although it wasn't really what I wanted. At least I don't have to wait for the bus anymore.

 Exercise 2 **Writing the Narrative Paragraph Step by Step**

The following exercise will guide you through the construction of a narrative paragraph. Start with the suggested topic. Use the seven steps (repeated below) and the example on pages 368–369 to help you work through each stage of the writing process. Refer to the section above for a completed sample.

> **Topic:** Recount the plot of a book you have read recently or a movie you have seen within the last few weeks.

1. Write a topic sentence.
2. Make a list of events.
3. Choose the five or six events you believe are the most important for the point of the story.
4. Make sure the order of your final choices makes sense. Reorder if necessary.
5. Using your final list, write at least one sentence for each event you have chosen.
6. Write a concluding statement.
7. Put your sentences into standard paragraph form.

On Your Own: Writing Narrative Paragraphs from Model Paragraphs

Model Paragraph: Better Early Than Late

I hate to be late. So when I began my new job, I was determined to be on time for my first day. I awoke early, had a leisurely breakfast, and gave myself lots of time to get through the traffic. I entered my new office building and sat down at my new desk a good fifteen minutes before starting time. My boss noticed me, smiled, and came over to my desk. "I'm glad you're early," she said. "In fact, you're a week early. You start *next* Monday."

 Assignment **Narrative Paragraph**

Write a paragraph telling the story of a day or part of a day in which you faced an important challenge of some kind. It could be a challenge you faced in school, at home, or on the job. The paragraph above gives an example.

Suggested Topics

(For more suggested topics, see the list given for the essay "Assignment" on page 374.)

1. The day I started a new job
2. Becoming a member of a sports team
3. The morning of my big job interview
4. Facing a large debt
5. Sharing the telephone
6. The day I started driving lessons
7. Losing

Writing the Narrative Essay

Like the narrative paragraph, the narrative essay also tells a story. The essay, however, gives you the opportunity to write a longer story with more detail. Although the narrative is the most informal type of essay, you still need to organize it. Make sure there is some logic to the paragraphing—there should be some sort of shift with each new paragraph. You might, for example, devote each support paragraph to a single event or to a different character or idea in your story. Don't fall into the trap of starting a new paragraph simply because the old one is getting too long.

For a review of the essay form and its standard format (which applies to all the writing strategies in this unit), see Chapter 20: "The Essay." For a review of the writing process that can be applied to both the paragraph and the essay, see Chapter 18: "The Four Stages of Writing for a Paragraph or an Essay."

In the following piece, written in 2014, the Toronto-born author reminisces about her days as a youngster when, through innocent teasing by her elders, she was given some information that she would never forget. In fact, the few details she remembers would lead her, later in life, to ask some very important questions about the nature of history in Canada, not to mention questions that challenge the very way we think about ghosts.

Model Essay I: Childhood Whispers

by Karen Naidoo

I remember being told when I was a little girl that my newly developed home, located in the area of Bishop Tutu and Lakeshore Boulevards, was built on top of a graveyard. I thought that I was told this tale as a scare tactic. How could the dead exist underneath my feet?

I remember lying on the floor and thought that if I was perfectly quiet, I would be able to hear the whispers of the dead. I thought maybe they would tell me their stories. Instead, I told them mine. I told them my dolly's tales and prayed that my parents would not yell too loudly, in fear of "waking the dead." I remember telling my uncle my secret about the dead that lived beneath our feet. He would haunt me every time I played with my dinner, threatening to "call the dead," as if the ghosts were meant to be feared and not to build relationships.

The dead were real! In fact, there were whole communities that existed with deep histories long before my community was built. I did a bit of research and found out that Fort York Boulevard was once considered protected land, belonging to the French, only that it did not really belong to the French. It was First Nations peoples' land. After the arrival of the French, it became land that was the heart of the fur trade, of which the British later claimed ownership. According to official Canadian documents, Fort York Lakeshore was a part of the "1787 Surrender."

Was the land "surrendered" or "stolen"? Who would write a story about stolen land? No official document would ever publish such nonsense that would state, "1787, Stolen." Stolen from whom? The story that I was once told, included such constructions as "recent," "occupied," "imperial," "developed," "surrendered," but never "stolen." Many immigrant families, like mine, are always told that they are needed to fill the abundance of land that Canada has to offer. They are never told how or why the land was in such abundance.

I wish I could go back to when I was a little girl, wishing that the dead underneath my floorboards could hear me. I would ask more questions, questions that focused on healing and telling of their own stories. I would ask, "How could we better work together?" or "Is it possible to have healing?" and "How can the ancestors from the earth teach us?" I would lie in silence and try to listen more carefully. And I would never be fearful of "waking the dead," as their stories are a part of mine.

Questions for Analysis

1. Who is telling the story?
2. What is the tone of the story?

3. Why does the author make these decisions (answers to the questions above)?
4. Do these decisions contribute to the quality of the piece?
5. What can be presumed about the author's cultural background?
6. What is the relationship between the storyteller and the story?
7. How can the narrative be used to teach history?
8. Who usually writes the history books that are studied in school? Who are the books' heroes? Who are the villains? Why are the stories of the "villains" silenced?
9. Who is likely to identify very quickly with the author?
10. How does the author present her own history that is intertwined with the history that is foreign to hers?
11. Who is likely to object to the author's tone?
12. In paragraph 1, the little girl says she's scared that her parents will yell too loudly, therefore waking the dead. What might this represent, if this is a metaphor? In other words, what else might the author be suggesting here about people's fears?
13. In paragraph 2, the author draws attention to the difference between the words *surrendered* and *stolen* in referring to land of the First Nations peoples. Does it matter which word is used? What does this suggest about the use of language?
14. Most people who believe in ghosts think they are scary. If we replace ghosts with our own ancestors, how might this affect the way we regard ghosts? Discuss the author's approach to this understanding of ghosts.

The following narrative essay was written by a former Centennial College student in 2001. As you read, see how Akis follows a logical sequence of events while keeping the reader in suspense.

Model Essay II: Transparent Silhouette*

by Akis Stylianou

On many lonely nights when I am too far from home to remember where home is and too beat to care where I lay my head, I have often heard an echo or seen a reflection that reminded me of a woman I knew. A silhouette through the window reflects the image of a petite yet shapely figure with long strands of silken hair falling over her shoulders. The wind whistling through the trees calls her name, taking me to another place where I can delay my misery.

*Akis Stylianou, "Transparent Silhouette." Reprinted by permission of the author.

We met early in life as classmates in elementary school. She used to stand alone in the schoolyard, surrounding herself with the walls she had built. It was a few years later before I could find the strength to enter those walls and discover her world. She told me she came from a broken home with an alcoholic mother and an abusive father. Being the only child, she was often the target of their frustration and rage, though she constantly dreamt of escaping her parents. By the time we reached our teens, she was running out of ways to numb her pain, and, soon after, she left home to live on the streets. Caring as much as I did, it tore me apart knowing there was nothing I could do to help.

She met the wrong kind of people and got involved with their crowds. She did many things she would come to regret, but, if the price was fitting, she was willing to sacrifice herself. My role as her friend was never to judge the path she had chosen; thus, friendship was never compromised. Most people considered her character unethical and immoral. However, she could smile with relief because she had finally escaped from the chains that weighed her down in the past.

One night, she was working as a dancer in a sleazy downtown bar when one of her customers began boasting about his position as an adult film producer. He told her that she had the look he was interested in. Soon after, she started acting, and her status as an adult film star rocketed. Before her twenty-fifth birthday, she had a brand-new sports car, a beautiful apartment in the heart of the city, and a bank account holding her six-figure salary. On one occasion, we met at a restaurant for dinner. As she entered the room, all eyes were on her, as if they were in a hypnotic state. The men wanted to be with her, and the women were jealous of her graceful presence. Behind all her jewellery, fur coat and expensive clothing, I could still see the frightened, bruised little girl I cared about. She pretended it didn't bother her, but beneath her polished exterior, I could see inside she wanted to explode.

That was the last chance I had to see her before her body was found lying lifeless in an empty apartment. The police said it was a burglary that went wrong and resulted in a homicide. She taught me to accept the good with the bad. After the rain falls, I walk the streets where she once lived, and the dried-up puddles remind me of her permanent tears.

Questions for Analysis

1. What, in your own words, do you think is the writer's thesis?
2. What is the writer's tone?
3. What is the meaning of the essay's title?
4. How do you think the writer feels about his friend?

5. Did the writer foreshadow the ending of the essay? (In other words, are there several clues throughout the essay that enable the reader to predict the eventual death of the writer's friend?)

6. If your answer to question 5 was yes, why did the writer foreshadow the ending? If your answer was no, why not?

7. Identify the transitions in the writer's essay.

8. Speculate on what might have caused the writer's friend's demise, in spite of what the police reported.

A model paragraph that answers question 5 above can be found on page 294 in Chapter 25: "Argumentation."

 Assignment **Rewrite the Conclusion**

Rewrite the last paragraph of Akis's essay using your own ideas. Try to stay faithful to the rest of the narrative essay so that you don't end up contradicting anything that comes before.

 Assignment **Narrative Essay**

Choose a topic from the list below (or, if you prefer, from the list given for the paragraph "Assignment" on page 370) and write a narrative essay of at least five paragraphs to develop that topic.

Suggested Topics

1. My worst classroom experience
2. A parent who would not listen
3. My first _____
4. When I tried to convince someone to hire me for a job
5. My experience with an aggressive salesperson
6. A day when nothing went right
7. A misunderstanding with a friend
8. Trouble at the workplace
9. A day that changed my life
10. A major disappointment
11. How my nervousness made matters worse
12. A perfect evening
13. The best summer of my life
14. An embarrassing experience
15. Learning something surprising about myself

While developing your essay, you may want to review Chapter 18: "The Four Stages of Writing for a Paragraph or an Essay," in particular the following sections:

"Brainstorming"

"Choosing the Topic and the Controlling Idea"

"Outlining"

"The Rough Draft"

"Revising and Editing the Rough Draft"

"Proofreading"

"Checklist for the Final Copy"

For help in connecting your sentences and paragraphs smoothly and clearly, you may wish to consult the list of transitional words and phrases, categorized by their function, found on the inside back cover of this book.

 Working Together: Spontaneous Creativity or Combustion?

1. As a class or in smaller groups, try the old but still-amusing parlour game of telling a story by creating it on the spot. One person begins with a sentence that sets the scene. Then the story is continued, sentence by sentence, as each person takes a turn. (Elect one student to put the sentences on the board.) Continue for perhaps twenty minutes; then discuss the outcome. In what ways is the narrative a success? What are its weaknesses?

2. In an Assignment (p. 374) for this chapter, you were asked to write a narrative essay. Divide into groups and share your essay with the other members of your group. Attach a sheet of paper to each essay you read and use it to critique the essay by answering the following two questions:

    a. In your opinion, what is one aspect of the essay that you believe is very strong? Explain.

    b. In your opinion, what is one aspect of the essay that still needs improvement? Explain.

Unit V Major Readings

OJO_Images/istockphoto.com

Note on Unit V:

Many schools subscribe to the philosophy that reading and writing are inseparable components in the process of improving one's writing skills. The readings that follow include works of nonfiction, fiction, and poetry, all Canadian, and all written by seasoned writers. Many of these do not represent specific essay models as described earlier in this book, but as is often the case, a single essay written by a professional writer can contain a mixture of different modes and styles. These readings have been selected in the hope that they will inspire meaningful discussion and well-written student responses.

Excuses, Excuses

Adrian Lee

Student excuses are getting more sophisticated, but so are the investigative tactics of teachers. Adrian Lee is the digital editor of *Maclean's* magazine; he also prides himself on being its resident hip hop expert. In this article, Lee explores the world of the excuses used today and the proof students might need to back them up.

1   It was his first month teaching at Northern Illinois University, and the last thing Christopher Schneider expected to see in his classroom was a topless student.

2   A young woman had missed a class and, afterward, in front of a line of people waiting to talk to him, pulled out a picture, which showed one healthy breast and one covered with a bloody bandage. "She says, 'I had a lump removed,'" recalls the sociology professor, who now teaches at the University of British Columbia (UBC). "I put my hands up over the image. I say, 'This is entirely not necessary; a doctor's note would have been just fine.'"

3   It's a cringe-inducing tale, but it's evidence of a **truism**: Student excuses are evolving. And if you miss a class, need an extension on a paper or have to rewrite an exam, you'd better have a good one. And some proof.

4   The days of "the dog ate my homework" are well behind us and, as tuition fees skyrocket and the job market tightens, the stakes have never been higher for busy students desperate to juggle looming deadlines. The digital age both gives and takes away: One website boasts it was "voted the Internet's most reliable (source of) fake doctors' excuse notes," while instructors trying to ensure academic honesty are verifying car accidents and crimes, not to mention searching death notices and obituaries. It's class warfare—and the professors appear to be winning.

5   "It's a terrible era [in which] to lie to your professor, because so much of it can be double-checked," said Marina Adshade, a professor of economics at UBC. One of her students wanted to skip an exam because his father was in the hospital. "So

Adrian Lee, "How Student Excuses are Evolving," *Maclean's*, 7 February 2014. Reproduced by permission of *Maclean's* Magazine.

"Some hacker from an obscure university in China ate my homework."

I said, 'That's fine, all you need to do is take a photograph of your father's hospital bracelet, email it to me, and I'll make the adjustments necessary for you.' And, of course, I never hear from the student again."

6   The death of a loved one has become such a **facile** excuse that the "dead-grandmother syndrome" is an inside joke for many instructors. In 1990, a satirical essay in the *Connecticut Review* suggested that exams were causing so many grandmothers to die that it was **presaging** downfall of American society," and suggested the solution was for universities to accept only orphans. A 2002 follow-up from Rutgers University said its solution—the threat of a difficult makeup essay—"saved the lives of four out of every five grandmothers who would typically die during the week leading up to a major exam."

7   McGill political science professor Rex Brynen has taught an estimated 17,000 students in his career, and no one has ever complained about being asked for a death notice. The documentation policy helps sift the **scofflaws** from the sufferers: Brynen remembers asking for proof a grandparent had died in the Middle East, but the student said his culture did not employ death notices. Unfortunately for the student, it happened to be a culture that Brynen has spent plenty of time studying and writing about. "I told him, 'Not only do you have death notices, but you have really big death notices,'" he says. "He backed off the excuse and there was no further attempt. That relative never appeared again."

8   While wariness is key, so, too, is empathy. Serious issues such as sexual assault and mental illness can cause students to clam up or be vague in their explanations, which can come across as deception. Brynen's advice—to be a good and willing listener—is especially urgent. A 2013 survey of 30,000 students by the Canadian Organization of University and College Health found that, in the January to April semester, nearly 90 per cent of students reported feeling overwhelmed by their workloads. More than nine per cent had seriously considered suicide in the past year. "For every lame excuse I find, there are two

or three actually really good excuses that we have to remain sensitive to," said Brynen.

9   Frances Woolley, an economics professor at Carleton University, recently explored the so-called "dead-grandmother syndrome" and found that demographics could explain it.

10   According to Statistics Canada, an 80-year-old grandmother would have a 4.7 per cent chance of dying in any given year. But, Woolley noted, a class of 100 students can have as many as 400 grandparents. "The odds of all of the grandparents making it through are actually fairly low." She also points out that students are more likely to report a loss when something is on the line. "People will typically only report what's going on in their personal lives on a need-to-know basis."

11   But changing demographics mean the dead-grandparent syndrome is **morphing** into the dead-parent syndrome, says UBC's Adshade. When four students missed time last year because of their parents' failing health, she looked at Statscan's 2011 General Social Survey, which monitors changes in the living conditions and well-being of Canadians. It showed that 25 per cent of fathers and 12 per cent of mothers in Canada would be in their 60s by the time their children completed their undergraduate education, an increase from 16 and 6.5 per cent, respectively, last time the survey was done in 1990.

12   "That whole generation grew up, they postponed getting married, they postponed having children, they focused on their own education and their own careers," she said. "Their kids are now dealing with older parents at earlier stages in their lives." And parents are a much bigger responsibility than grandparents. "Let's say your grandfather is having an operation; you wouldn't expect all the grandchildren to turn up and sit at his bedside. But when it's a parent, you do."

13   Honesty is still always the best policy. In fact, extra time doesn't often produce a significantly better result, Adshade says. But if you are going to sneak one by the prof? Well, even they will admit they're only human.

14   "I'm a dog lover, and I know that, if something happened to my little guy, I'd be very cut up," said Woolley. "That's a hard one, whether or not it's a legitimate one, because it does hurt. I'm a bit of a **schmuck** for it."

Glossary

truism: self-evident or indisputable truth

facile: easily obtained, but not so highly valued

presaging: warning that something unpleasant is about to happen

scofflaws: people who do not comply with laws that are difficult to enforce

morphing: transforming

schmuck: (slang) objectionable or contemptible person

Comprehension Questions

1.   Who appears to be winning the war when it comes to student excuses, according to Adrian Lee, and why?

2.   How did Rutgers University solve the problem of the dead-grandmother syndrome?

3. Why is the expectation of documentation a good antidote to lame excuses? Give an example of how it worked for McGill political science professor Rex Brynen.

4. What is the thing that Brynen says professors should remember in spite of all the lame excuses?

Questions about Form

1. Why does Lee start the reading with an anecdote?

2. Why did he use the anecdote about the young woman in particular?

3. Besides the anecdotes, what other evidence is used in this essay? Why?

Questions for Discussion

1. A CBC documentary on cheating suggested that students care less about academic honesty these days and more about "getting the grade," no matter what it takes. Do you agree that this is the trend? What is your evidence for your answer? What would the implications of such a trend be?

2. Some students argue that doctors' notes are expensive. Is this a valid complaint? Discuss.

3. Many faculty report that, along with more imaginative student excuses for missed assignments, there are also more "sketchy" doctors' notes. These notes might be real in that they are really issued by doctors; on the other hand, there are more and more notes on which doctors write content such as, "This patient visited my office today and should miss school for a few days." Discuss.

Writing Ideas

1. In a paragraph or an essay, explain why students might use a false excuse for missing an assignment. Use examples in support of your points.

2. In a paragraph or an essay, explain why honesty might be better than using a false excuse for missing an assignment.

3. In a paragraph or an essay, state whether you think it is ethical for doctors to write and charge for notes in which they basically say what the students (their patients) want them to.

✦ ✦ ✦

How to Get Happily Married

Julia McKinnell

With the divorce rate in Canada at 40 per cent, young people may wonder what it takes to increase the chances of marital success. Julia McKinnell of *Maclean's* magazine may have the answer. In this piece, published on June 7, 2010,

Julia McKinnell, "How to Get Happily Married." Reprinted by permission of the author.

she refers to a newly published book authored by an experienced marriage counsellor and divorce lawyer.

1   If you want a long happy marriage, "your twenties shouldn't be spent finding a man; your twenties should be spent finding yourself." That's the advice in a new book for young single women called *Last One Down the Aisle Wins: 10 Keys to a Fabulous Single Life Now and an Even Better Marriage Later*.

2   The book's co-authors are Shannon Fox, a marriage psychotherapist, and her best friend Celeste Liversidge, a divorce lawyer. They married at 29 and 30, and write that "for the past 16 years, we have been working with women in crisis, trying to save their troubled marriages. We listened to women pour their hearts out and share their stories of disappointment, regret, disillusionment and guilt. We'd often **commiserate** about how frustrating it was to enter our clients' lives after the damage to their marriages was already done."

3   They wondered what could be done to better people's chances of having a successful marriage. "Here's the key," they concluded. "Don't marry young. In fact, don't get married until you're 30." Forget notions of marrying at 25 and pregnant at 28, they write. "Marrying young, before you know yourself and have a solid handle on your life, is a bad idea."

4   Spend your twenties investing in new friendships with women, they suggest. "You're finally moving past the unavoidable high school and college drama into a place of maturity, where you can develop true, solid friendships. Take it from us, you're going to need your girls!" Don't think your husband will be your best friend, they say. "Like it or not, your husband is not going to be able to tend to each and every one of your emotional needs. It will be disastrous for you to expect him to do so."

5   In your twenties, "you have ample time to spend in long, late night conversations with girlfriends." Do this, because "it is these friends who will remind you of who you used to be when you find yourself knee-deep in diapers and Disney character lunch boxes."

6   Before you marry, improve your relationship with money, they also advise. "Your husband is more likely to lose respect for you if you are a damsel in financial distress," they write. "Some women believe the rubbish that they are not as good at math as men and therefore inherently unable to understand money.

monkeybusinessimages/thinkstock.com

What a load of crap! You are not hopeless in matters of money. You are probably just inexperienced and fearful."

7   They cite the statistic that money is one of the top two causes of divorce, second only to **infidelity**. "If you fail to take practical steps to take charge of your finances, you will remain financially blind and put your future marriage at risk." Also, if you're still getting money from your parents, it's time for that to end, they write.

8   If you have eating issues, sort them out before you marry. The book cites a recent study in which 80 per cent of women said their negative body image was ruining their sex life; 67 per cent of men said their wife's poor body image was a significant source of frustration for them, and had a negative impact on the happiness of their relationship. One husband said, "When Michelle and I first started dating, she seemed super-confident. But just before we got married, I started to see how critical she was about her appearance. Over the past seven years, I've come to understand that Michelle truly thinks of herself as fat, ugly and unworthy—which is so far from the truth it's just plain ridiculous." He went on, "I'm starting to lose respect for her as a mature adult. She's acting like a teenager, always worried about how she looks." The authors write, "Your twenties and early thirties is the right time to right this **adversarial** relationship with your body."

9   The book promises, "If you spend your twenties learning how to be a fabulous, stable, independent, fulfilled single woman, it will naturally follow that you will choose a guy to marry who possesses these same wonderful qualities."

10   "You will lose your taste for the long-on-**charisma** and short-on-character guys whom you found yourself drawn to like a moth to a flame. And you will have what it takes to be a great wife and partner in a lasting and loving marriage."

Glossary

commiserate: express or feel pity

infidelity: unfaithfulness

adversarial: involving opposition or conflict

charisma: great charm or personal power that can attract and/or influence others

Comprehension Questions

1.   What often happens when a woman marries in her twenties, according to the authors?

2.   Instead of looking for a man to marry, what should women in their twenties do to find friendship? Why?

3.   The author mentions that money is one of the two top reasons for divorce, after unfaithfulness. What should a woman do with respect to the finances in anticipation of this very possible prospect?

4.   Why should eating issues be sorted out before a woman gets married, according to the authors?

5.   What is the evidence used in the book to back up some of its claims?

Questions about Form

1. In the last paragraph, the author uses a quotation from the book by Shannon Fox and Celeste Liversidge. The first sentence includes the phrase "like a moth to a flame." What does this mean, and why is it used in the quotation?

2. What is the key word in the title of this essay? Why is it so important?

Questions for Discussion

1. Many religious organizations encourage young people to get married much younger than the authors cited in this reading do. Speculate as to why.

2. What might the advantages be of getting married in your twenties, despite what the authors say?

3. Find out what the current divorce rate is in Canada. Then find out at what age most of those who are getting divorced got married. Before you look anything up, what do you think you will find? Do your findings support or refute those of the authors?

Writing Ideas

1. What is the best age at which to get married and why? Discuss your reasons in a paragraph or an essay. Add examples in support of your points.

2. What might the reasons be for not getting married at all? Discuss these reasons in a paragraph or essay. Add examples in support of your points.

3. In a paragraph or essay, explain some good reasons for getting married. Add examples in support of your points.

◆ ◆ ◆

Canada, My Canada*

Tomson Highway

Celebrated novelist and award-winning playwright Tomson Highway is a Cree from Brochet, in northern Manitoba. He holds three honorary degrees and is a member of the Order of Canada. This piece by Highway, first published in 2000, is quite flattering of our nation. How would you expect a member of an Aboriginal group to view Canada today? When you finish reading the following piece by Highway, compare or contrast your answer to this question with your observation of Highway's article.

1   Three summers back, a friend and I were being hurtled by bus through the heart of Australia, the desert flashing pink and red before our disbelieving eyes. It seemed never to end, this desert, so flat, so dry. The landscape was very unlike ours—scrub growth with some exotic cacti, no lakes, no river, just sand and rock forever. Beautiful, haunting even—*what the surface of the moon must look like,* I thought as I sat in the dusk in that almost empty bus.

2   I turned to look out the front of the bus and was suddenly taken completely by surprise. Screaming out at me in great black lettering were the words CANADA NO. 1 COUNTRY IN THE WORLD. My eyes lit up, my heart gave a heave, and I felt a **pang** of homesickness so **acute** I actually almost hurt. It was all I could do to keep myself from leaping out of my seat and grabbing the newspaper from its owner.

3   As I learned within minutes (I did indeed beg to borrow the paper), this pronouncement was based on information collected by the United Nations from studies comparing standards of living for 174 nations of the world. Some people may have doubted the finding, but I didn't, not for an instant.

4   Where else in the world can you travel by bus, automobile or train (and the odd ferry) for ten, 12 or 14 days straight and see a landscape that changes so spectacularly: the Newfoundland coast with its white foam and roar; the red sand beaches of Prince Edward Island; the graceful curves and slopes of Cape Breton's Cabot Trail; the rolling dairy land of south-shore Quebec; the maple-bordered lakes of Ontario, the haunting north shore of Lake Superior; the wheat fields of Manitoba and Saskatchewan; the ranch land of Alberta; the mountain ranges and lush rain forests of the West Coast. The list could go on for pages and still cover only the southern section of the country, a sliver of land compared with the North, the immensity of which is almost unimaginable.

5   For six years in a row now the United Nations has designated Canada the No. 1 country in which to live.

6   We are so fortunate. We are water wealthy and forest rich. Minerals, fertile land, wild animals, plant life, the rhythm of four distinct, undeniable seasons—we have it all.

7   Of course, Canada has its problems. We'd like to lower the crime rate, but ours is a relatively safe country. We struggle with our health-care system, trying to find a balance between **universality** and affordability, but no person in this country is denied medical care for lack of money. Yes, we have our concerns, but in the global scheme of things we are well off.

8   Think of our history. For the greater part, the pain and violence, tragedy, horror and evil that have scarred forever the history of too many countries are

© momentimages/Jupiter Images

largely absent from our past. There's no denying we've had our trials, but they pale by comparison with events that have shaped many other nations.

9   Our cities are gems. Take Toronto, where I have chosen to live. My adopted city never fails to thrill me with its racial, linguistic and cultural diversity. On any ordinary day on the city's streets and subway, in stores and restaurants, I can hear the muted ebb and flow of 20 different tongues. I can feast on food from different continents, from Greek souvlaki to Thai mango salad, from Italian **prosciutto** to Jamaican jerk chicken, from Indian lamb curry to Chinese lobster.

10   And do all these people get along? Well, they all enjoy a life of relative harmony, co-operation and peace. They certainly aren't terrorizing, torturing and massacring one another. They're not igniting pubs, cars and schools with explosives that blind, cripple and maim. And they're not killing children with machetes, cleavers and axes. Dislike—**rancour,** even—may exist here and there, but not, I believe, hatred of the blistering intensity we see elsewhere.

11   Is Canada a successful experiment in racial harmony and peaceful **coexistence?** Yes, I would say so—and proudly.

12   When I, as an Aboriginal citizen of this country, find myself thinking about all the people we've received into this beautiful homeland of mine, when I think of the millions to whom we've given safe haven, following agony, terror, hunger and great sadness in their own home countries, well, my little Cree heart just puffs up with pride. And I walk the streets of Canada, the streets of my home, feeling tall as a maple.

Glossary

pang: sudden and brief pain, physical or emotional

acute: severe and sharp

universality: the quality of not being restricted to a privileged few

prosciutto: spicy Italian ham, served in thin slices

rancour: continuing and bitter hatred

coexistence: living side by side

Comprehension Questions

1. What in the newspaper sparked Highway's interest? What was the basis for the findings in the newspaper story?

2. What does Highway say is the most important thing about Canada that makes it great?

3. What problems in Canada does Highway admit to, and how does he defend Canada in spite of them?

Questions about Form

1. In paragraph 1, Highway uses italics for the words "what the surface of the moon must look like." Why do you think he uses italics here? What is his tone? What effect is he looking for? Does he achieve this effect?

2. If this is a piece about Canada, why does Highway start out by talking about Australia?

Questions for Discussion

1. In paragraph 8, Highway refers to the history of Canada as being quite tame when compared to that of other countries. Compare or contrast this comment to the message Rita Joe is sending in her poem "I Lost My Talk," on pages 387–388. What do you make of the fact that both of these writers are members of First Nations?

2. Do you agree with Highway when he says Canada is a "successful experiment in racial harmony and peaceful coexistence"? Why or why not?

3. At any time throughout this piece, do you expect Highway to mention the fact that Canada has not always been kind to Aboriginal peoples, or that the governments of the past have even committed genocide against his people? Why do you think he doesn't? Does it help to be told this piece appeared before in a journal called the *Imperial Oil Review?* Why or why not?

4. In paragraphs 9 and 10, Highway refers to the multicultural mix of Toronto in particular and of Canada in general. Compare or contrast his attitude to that of Neil Bissoondath in "Selling Illusions," which begins on page 414.

5. Paragraph 10 uses some rather harsh language. What countries do you think Highway might be referring to by the examples he uses?

6. Look up poems by the American poet Walt Whitman. Is there a poem whose title is similar to Highway's title of this piece? Account for the similarity.

Writing Ideas

1. In a paragraph or essay, compare or contrast Canada with any other country in the world with which you are very familiar.

2. Is Canada one of the best places in the world to live? In a paragraph or essay, explain why or why not.

✦ ✦ ✦

I Lost My Talk*

Rita Joe

The writings of Rita Joe, a Mi'kmaq, are about First Nations people. She was born on a reservation in Whycocomagh, on Cape Breton Island in Nova Scotia. At the age of 12, after both her parents had died, she requested that she be placed in an Indian residential school in Shubenacadie, Nova Scotia. An acclaimed poet, Rita Joe published several collections, including *Lnu and Indians We're Called* (1991). She became a member of the Order of Canada in 1990 and was active in Aboriginal issues until her death in 2007. This poem was written in 1989.

1   I lost my talk
The talk you took away.
When I was a little girl
At **Shubenacadie** school.

*Rita Joe, "I Lost My Talk." From SONG OF ESKASONI. Reprinted with permission.

2 You snatched it away:
I speak like you
I think like you
I create like you
The scrambled **ballad,** about my word.

3 Two ways I talk
Both ways I say,
Your way is more powerful.

4 So gently I offer my hand and ask,
Let me find my talk
So I can teach you about me.

Glossary

Shubenacadie: a town in Nova Scotia

ballad: a popular song, generally of a personal or political nature

Comprehension Questions

1. What do you think Rita Joe is saying in the first stanza of her poem?

2. What does "scrambled ballad" mean? Might it have more than one meaning? If so, explain what they are.

3. What does the author mean by the word *word* at the end of the second stanza (verse)?

Questions about Form

1. What is the difference in tone between the first line of the poem and the very last line? How might this contribute to an interpretation of the poem's theme?

2. What might be the reason for the repetition in the second stanza?

3. How would you describe the type of language being used here? Does it contribute to an overall deliberate effect? Why or why not?

Questions for Discussion

1. What do you know of Canadian history that relates to this poem? What might have been the reasons the school authorities did what they did?

2. Does the knowledge that Rita Joe placed herself in the school at Shubenacadie affect your interpretation of her poem? Why or why not?

Writing Ideas

1. Do some research on what Canadian school authorities did to assimilate Aboriginal Canadians, and take a position either for or against this action in a paragraph or essay.

2. In a cause and effect paragraph or essay, discuss the repercussions of a person's voice being denied. You may want to talk more specifically of a child whose voice is not taken seriously, or of women whose voice is silenced in certain cultures, or of North American Blacks who have been marginalized and/or discriminated against ever since the days of slavery, and so on.

3. Besides the obvious difference between this work by Rita Joe and the piece by Tomson Highway that begins on page 384, which is that they are two different genres, are there any other differences? In a paragraph or essay, compare or contrast the two works.

◆ ◆ ◆

A Matter of Postal Codes

Ken MacQueen

In the futuristic movie *Gattaca*, starring Uma Thurman and Ethan Hawke, the likelihood of an individual's success was determined by genetic engineering rather than education or experience. This sounds scary and far-fetched. But how far-fetched is it? Some doctors in Canada already predict a person's lifespan, not as determined by genetic engineering, but by the neighbourhood the individual lives in. In this piece, published on March 3, 2013, Ken MacQueen of *Maclean's* magazine takes a look at this scary scenario, not of the future, but of right now.

1   What if you could see the future? What if you could see a young pregnant woman walking down Barton Street in Hamilton's depressed north end and know her unborn child had already lost life's lottery; that his or her fate was predetermined by Mom's postal code?

2   You would know that this mother—in this neighbourhood, and in the bottom 20 per cent of the city's income earners—is six times less likely than the wealthiest Hamiltonian to seek first-**trimester** prenatal care, and more than six times as likely to be a teenager or to have dropped out of school. You'd know the chances of her baby being born underweight and needing weeks in **neonatal** intensive care would also be higher.

Ken MacQueen, "Where You Live May Decide How Soon You Die," *Maclean's*, 3 March 2013. Reproduced by permission of *Maclean's* Magazine.

3   And the child's life would get no easier thereafter. If its parents lived an average life in this neighbourhood, they would die an average Third World death—at 65.5 years of age. If they lived five or six kilometres away, say, on Rice Avenue in the city's leafy suburbs, they would live beyond 86 years.

4   What if you knew one of the world's most advanced **acute**-care health facilities was here in Hamilton, yet was powerless to change the fate of this mother-to-be? What would you do?

5   What's to be done is the challenge facing Hamilton and communities across Canada. The statistics are among the findings of *Code Red*, a groundbreaking analysis of life and death in 135 Hamilton neighbourhoods and census tracts. The multi-part series was written by *Hamilton Spectator* investigative reporter Steve Buist in collaboration with Neil Johnston, an **epidemiologist** and faculty member in McMaster University's department of medicine.

6   The social **determinants** of health—income, housing, education, employment, early childhood development and race—divide us as certainly as any **caste** system. Where you sit on the income **gradient** sets your life course, determining how well you live and how soon you die. Divide Hamilton into income quintiles, and the average age of death for the wealthiest 20 per cent is 81.4 years. Death comes years earlier with each step down the income ladder. By the bottom rung, the poorest 20 per cent of Hamiltonians die at 69—12 years sooner.

7   Working on *Code Red* left Johnston feeling outraged at the waste of human potential, he said in a recent online presentation. He recalled how today's hardest-hit inner-city neighbourhoods were thriving communities 40 years ago until the city was gutted by the decline of well-paying industrial, steel and manufacturing jobs, and by an **exodus** to the suburbs. "The chasm between neighbourhoods in the downtown core and the suburbs in determinants of health and health-service use is perhaps the single most important reason why Hamilton may never again be able to regain the relative prosperity it enjoyed 40 years ago," he said.

8   The phenomenon isn't unique to Hamilton. The district health unit in Sudbury, Ont., is a strong advocate for redefining what makes us healthy, and has compared the "most deprived" and "least deprived" areas of that city. Among the most deprived: births to teenage mothers were 205 per cent higher; infant mortality, 139 per cent higher; and premature death, 86 per cent higher. The health region in Saskatoon also looked at health disparities in their city. In six low-income neighbourhoods, rates of infant mortality were 448 per cent higher; teen births, 1,549 per cent higher; and suicide attempts, 1,458 higher. "Moral reasons aside, it is in our collective interest to reduce social disparity," the health region concluded.

9   Focusing on non-medical social problems is a priority for the Canadian Medical Association (CMA), which advocates for a sustainable, equitable and more effective health care system. Health is more affected by socio-economic factors than by doctors, drugs and hospitals, CMA president Anna Reid, an emergency room doctor in Yellowknife, said in an interview. "We feel we have a responsibility—a duty, actually—to start advocating for policies that change people's life circumstances."

10   If society must be fixed in order to heal the individual, where does one begin? Reid concedes doctors don't have the answers. "We're not the experts on how to fix the housing crisis, [although] we certainly are the experts on seeing the downstream effects of people who have no housing," she said. "We don't know how to fix the education system, but we know that if you don't have an education, this is what it's going to do to your health."

11   Studies find the problem is a lack of accountability and inadequate budgeting for such necessities as housing, education, social services, child care, policing and other non-health determinants, which rest with different levels of government, each responsible for one puzzle piece that rarely fits into a complete picture. Experts say it's a jurisdictional nightmare and an excuse for inaction.

12   Dennis Raphael, a professor of health policy at Toronto's York University, has written extensively on Canada's missed opportunities and the false economy of neglecting the web of social determinants. Canadians are among the world's leading researchers on issues such as the health effects of poverty on early childhood development, but the results are more likely to be implemented in Scandinavia and European countries like France and Germany, where the concept of a welfare state is not dismissed out of hand, Raphael says.

13   While Canada spends heavily on a health care system designed to fix the sick, it's a middling performer among fellow wealthy nations in health outcomes and in value for money spent, according to a much-ignored 2009 Senate report, *A Healthy, Productive Canada: A Determinant of Health Approach*. Fully 75 per cent of factors influencing health rest outside the health care system, it found. "Passively waiting for illness and disease to occur and then trying to cope with it through the health care delivery system is simply not an option."

14   Sudbury's is among the health units working to shift government priorities. It produced a short video, *Let's Start a Conversation about Health . . . and Not Talk about Health Care*, which has been picked up and modified by health authorities across Canada, says the unit's Stephanie Lefebvre. As manager of health equity, one of Lefebvre's roles is to bridge the divide among a range of services and to ensure that the potential health impacts of local initiatives are considered in advance.

15   In Hamilton, *Code Red* has inspired changes including implementation of a nurse-family partnership program to guide high-risk mothers, and incorporation of the implications of social determinants into McMaster University curriculums for health professionals. It influenced McMaster's decision to build its new $86-million health campus in the inner city, where it will provide primary care to an underserved population and give medical students an understanding of the challenges residents face.

16   Mark Chamberlain, a successful Hamilton businessman and a member of the city's roundtable on poverty reduction, knows many people who live in the city's blighted neighbourhoods. "They're fantastic people, but their health outcomes aren't determined by how fantastic they are and how much they volunteer," he says. "Once they know where a baby is born from a postal code perspective— based on not changing our scenarios in how we invest—they can pretty much

predict the outcome of that child, when and how they're going to die." It's a glimpse of a future he can't accept, and one he'd like to think there is growing determination to change.

Glossary

trimester: period of three months

neonatal: pertaining to children immediately after birth

acute: pertaining to diseases of a short duration, but typical severity

epidemiologist: a person who studies the incidence, distribution and possible control of diseases

determinants: factors that decisively affect the nature or outcome of something

caste: system of Hindu classes in which the members of one class have no contact with the members of another

gradient: degree of inclination or the rate of ascent or descent

exodus: mass departure of people

Comprehension Questions

1. In one sentence, and in your own words, what is the thesis that the author is arguing in the reading?

2. Explain the reasons for differences in life expectancy between the richest and poorest people in Hamilton.

3. What do studies demonstrate is the cause of the health problems?

4. What are some of the initiatives or programs in place that are beginning to solve the health problems?

Questions about Form

1. What does the author use to get your attention? Is this method effective? Why or why not?

2. Read paragraph 3, on the prediction of life expectancy. Is this paragraph effective? Why or why not?

Questions for Discussion

1. Canada has a worldwide reputation for universal health care. Would the author of this piece agree that this reputation is well deserved? Why or why not?

2. Based on this reading, do you think Canada's good reputation for healthcare is well deserved?

Writing Ideas

1. Why is there a big difference in life expectancy between the people who live in different Canadian neighbourhoods? In an essay or a paragraph, refer to the reading and your own experience in support of your answer.

2. Choose one "rich" neighbourhood and one "poor" neighbourhood in a particular town or city. Then write a paragraph or an essay that explains why

it would be obvious that there would be a difference in the health condition of residents.

3. In a paragraph or an essay, explain what steps you think governments should take to help people who are most at risk of having health issues.

✦ ✦ ✦

A Tough Approach That Might Work*

James C. Morton

A lawyer, legal educator, and author, James C. Morton has written more than twenty-five legal texts as well as numerous papers and articles. He is past president of the Ontario Bar Association and a long-time human rights and community activist. He's served as a governor for the Canadian International Peace Project, counsel for the Canadian Somali Congress, and legal counsel (pro bono) for Artists Against Racism, a registered charity fighting racial and religious prejudice. In this piece, published in the *Ottawa Citizen* on October 13, 2008, Morton argues that tough punishment is not the solution to the common problem of chronic offences in the area of petty theft.

1   In a season of tough talk on crime, I would like to propose a challenge to our political leaders. In this country, one group of criminals commits a disproportionate number of crimes that we could easily reduce with more coercive sentencing. However, our usual form of **coercion**—imprisonment— doesn't work for them. They need a different kind of sentence. But to make that happen—and to significantly reduce the number of crimes they commit—would require a degree of will and wisdom that our legislators can't seem to muster.

© iQoncept/Shutterstock

*Source: James Morton, "A Tough Approach That Might Work," *The Ottawa Citizen* (October 13, 2008). Reprinted by permission of the author.

2   The legal system refers to these men—they are almost all men—as **chronic** offenders. What everyone knows—but the justice system doesn't acknowledge—is that they are also drug addicts, hooked on heroin or crack cocaine. They steal not for gain but to support their addiction, to pay for their next fix.

3   This has nothing to do with getting high. For an addict, the point is to avoid the effects of withdrawal—in the case of heroin, including cramps and muscle spasms, fever, cold sweats and goose bumps (hence the phrase "cold turkey"), insomnia, vomiting, diarrhea and a condition called "itchy blood," which can cause compulsive scratching so severe that it leads to open sores. For addicts, drug use is not a lifestyle choice that's easy to change. Many have been addicted for their entire adult lives, and as a result have spent half their lives behind bars, serving dozens of sentences for minor crimes. These are the "revolving door" criminals that some critics point to—arrested, tried, sentenced to a few weeks or months, then dumped back out on the street, only to be arrested, tried and convicted again a few weeks later.

4   Canada has hundreds of criminals like that, mainly in the larger cities. Vancouver alone recently identified 379. According to a report by the Vancouver Police Department, the vast majority were addicted to drugs or alcohol. Many also suffer from a mental disorder, generally untreated. In the five years between 2001 and 2006, Vancouver's few hundred chronic offenders, as a group, were responsible for 26,755 police contacts—more than 5,000 contacts per year, 14 a day. The costs are staggering. Arrests, prosecutions and incarcerations end up costing some $20,000 per criminal per month—per month! There has to be a better way.

5   Punishment alone is not it, though, for a couple of reasons. For one, the idea of punishing criminals is based at least partly on the concept of specific **deterrence**. You steal, we lock you up. Applied most strongly to property crimes—which is what these offenders mainly commit—specific deterrence assumes that the criminal is a rational actor who will consider: Is it worth it? And in fact, specific deterrence often works; many offenders really do stop committing crimes after fairly short jail sentences. But not addicts.

6   The problem is the presumption of a rational actor. That is exactly what we do not have with drug addicts, who do not—usually cannot—stop to consider the likely punishment for a crime they are about to commit. They see only the escape from the more immediate and dire punishments of drug **deprivation**. By comparison, the threat of being caught and thrown in jail is nothing.

7   As well, because chronic offenders tend to commit minor crimes and draw short sentences—say, 30 to 90 days for theft—their lives shift constantly between jail and the streets.

8   We could use longer sentences to "warehouse" chronic offenders—the American "three strikes and you're out" approach. But long-term imprisonment would be a very high-cost way to deal with what is really a public health issue.

9   And there's the **crux** of the problem. The criminal justice system is not designed to treat addicts. While prisons do provide some drug treatment, it is almost always short-term and underfunded. And these offenders, with their short sentences, rarely get even that. The voluntary drug treatment programs

offered by the public health system seldom work for them either, because kicking an addiction is extremely unpleasant and requires willpower and usually some money, neither of which street addicts have.

10   Clearly, Canadians need more protection from chronic offenders than we are now getting. While their crimes may be petty, their victims number in the thousands. And those victims are left not only with a monetary loss, but also with a lingering fear that affects their sense of personal safety and their trust in the criminal justice system. But blaming that system, as many do, misses the point—which is our failure as a society to deal with severe drug and alcohol addiction.

11   With chronic offenders, the first step is to recognize that what we have is an issue of both criminal law and public health. The next step is to require addicted offenders to undergo serious, long-term drug treatment.

12   Canada's experience with mandatory drug treatment is quite limited. In the late 1970s, British Columbia passed legislation under which heroin addicts could be compelled to take part in an intensive government-funded treatment program. The Supreme Court of Canada upheld the statute but the provincial legislature ultimately repealed it, concerned about civil liberties. (This was the time of *One Flew Over the Cuckoo's Nest*.)

13   These days, Vancouver's Downtown Community Court tackles street crime by taking guilty pleas and moving the accused into treatment as part of their sentencing, but only with their consent, which misses the point.

14   We're less constrained with juvenile offenders. Since 1996, Alberta law has required minors with an apparent alcohol or drug addiction to participate, with or without their consent, in an assessment and treatment program. Saskatchewan and Manitoba have similar legislation and even allow parents of drug-addicted children to ask a court to require treatment, whether or not the child is in trouble with the law.

15   Although the research is scant, mandatory treatment does appear to have about the same success rate as voluntary treatment. A 1970s American study looked at the effectiveness of methadone maintenance treatment for those who entered the program under high, moderate or no coercion and found no significant difference in outcomes for the three groups.

16   Given the costs of incarceration—not counting the costs to future victims— paying for mandatory drug treatment for them hardly seems an issue, even if it only works some of the time. As for whether mandatory treatment is somehow inhumane, how humane is it to sentence these addicts to punishments we know don't work and then dump them back on the street no better than before?

17   More than costs or moral qualms, though, the main obstacle to mandatory drug treatment for addicted offenders is probably institutional. Both the justice system and the health system have entrenched groups with turf to protect: prisons, parole boards, hospitals. Collaboration would mean breaching walls; even with good intentions, a mandatory treatment program would raise irksome issues such as which ministry pays, health or justice, and which is responsible. But don't we elect our leaders to solve such problems?

18   The question is not whether we will be soft on crime but whether we can be smart about crime. Crime in the real world is not an exciting TV show. Crime has real costs and victims. Politics aside, Canadians generally—and victims of crime specifically—deserve evidence-based criminal justice policies that actually reduce crime. Our challenge is to make the tough choices that move beyond "tough on crime" **rhetoric** and produce real change.

Glossary

coercion: the act of persuading or restraining a person by force

chronic: persisting for a long time

deterrence: discouragement of someone from doing something

deprivation: the denial of something considered to be a necessity

crux: the decisive or most important point at issue

rhetoric: language designed to persuade or impress (often with an implication of insincerity or exaggeration)

Comprehension Questions

1. In your own words, and in one sentence, what is the author's main opinion in this article?

2. Describe thoroughly what Morton refers to as the "revolving door" criminal discussed in the article.

3. What, specifically, is the cost of dealing with the type of criminal discussed in this article?

4. What does Morton mean by the "rational actor" when it comes to offenders? How does this contrast with the "chronic" offender?

5. What does the author mean by "regular punishment," and why does it not work for the type of criminal discussed in this article?

6. What does the author suggest as a solution for dealing with the particular offender discussed in his article?

7. What practical steps, according to the author, need to be taken in order to implement his suggested solution?

Questions about Form

1. Morton uses first-person references (*I*, *we* and *our*) throughout his article. Is this an effective strategy or not? Explain.

2. In the first sentence of the last paragraph, Morton juxtaposes the cliché "soft on crime" with his term "smart about crime." How effective is this juxtaposition? Explain.

Questions for Discussion

1. Mental health problems have often been stigmatized within society. Do you think that if the judicial system begins to focus more on mental health, we will see a reduction of petty crime, as the author suggests?

2. In the last paragraph, Morton writes, "Our challenge is to make the tough choices that move beyond 'tough on crime' rhetoric and produce real change." What do you think the author means by this? Do you agree or disagree? Explain.

3. Morton describes the general challenges to the solution he suggests as relating to lack of public funding and to logistical complications given the short sentences usually served by this class of offenders. In your opinion, are these challenges insurmountable? Explain.

Writing Ideas

1. If it is true that most thefts are committed by drug addicts who are avoiding withdrawal, why do you think society is so slow to first discover, and then effectively deal with, the problem? Write a paragraph or an essay outlining your reasons.

2. Considering the author's argument as to what the problem is, write a paragraph or an essay in which you point out other solutions (or parts of the solution) that the author has not discussed.

3. To what extent does the problem of addiction relate to crimes committed across the country other than the kind of petty theft described here for which police are constantly arresting offenders? Would the same solution that Morton suggests be relevant to those crimes? Explain in a paragraph or an essay.

✦ ✦ ✦

Grammar and Your Salary

Peter Harris

It's no secret that few students look forward to learning grammar. But what many might not want to hear is the close relationship some say exists between one's grammar and his or her career success. Peter Harris is the editor-in-chief of Workopolis.com. What he says in this piece, published on March 19, 2013, might cause students to want to pay more attention to their language skills.

1   Want to get ahead at work? Take a little extra time to formulate grammatically correct sentences and carefully proofread everything you write. How important are the minor details of word usage and punctuation? A report put out by **Grammarly** earlier this month shows that people who use proper grammar advance further and faster in their careers.

2   For this study, they analysed the LinkedIn profiles of native English speaking professionals, and compared their language skills with their career trajectories over a ten-year period. Their findings are telling. People with poor grammar skills don't rise to the top. Those who had not reached a director-level position in the first ten years of their working lives made 2.5 times as many grammatical mistakes as people who earned director-level titles or higher. The professionals who made fewer grammatical mistakes were promoted more often and changed jobs more frequently than did their more error-prone **contemporaries**.

Peter Harris, "How Your Grammar Skills Affect Your Salary." Reprinted by permission of Workopolis.

3   Beyond just getting promoted and moving up the ladder, using proper grammar can be critical to getting hired at all. One of the easiest ways to sink your **candidacy** for a position is to have typos or spelling mistakes in your resume. Hiring managers interpret such errors as signs of carelessness, laziness, or a lack of language skills on the job seeker's part. If you can't take the time to produce an error-free document when you're trying to get hired in the first place, how will you perform on the job?

4   Kyle Wiens, CEO of iFixit, recently wrote in the *Harvard Business Review* that he flat out won't hire someone who uses poor grammar—even for a programming role that doesn't require writing for the public. He explains, "On the face of it, my zero tolerance approach to grammar errors might seem a little unfair. After all, grammar has nothing to do with job performance, or creativity, or intelligence, right? Wrong. If it takes someone more than twenty years to notice how to properly use 'it's,' then that's not a learning curve I'm comfortable with."

5   There are some fairly obvious reasons why the proper use of grammar would be associated with greater career success. First off, taking the time to formulate proper sentences and carefully proofread your work shows an attention to detail. People who care about producing quality, error-free work generally get promoted above people who don't. Having proper grammar skills can often be an indication that someone has a greater level of education, which in many fields still **coincides** with higher positions.

6   When I mentioned that I was writing about this, my coworker Christina, a professional editor, became quite passionate about the proper use of "your" (belonging to you) and "you're "(you are.) Apparently she is "driven batty" when her friends who are native English speakers get this one wrong. With style guides, dictionaries and numerous grammar-related websites readily available online, there's really no excuse anymore for some of the classic grammatical errors. If you don't know whether to use "affect" or "effect," "who" or "whom," or "fewer" or "less," just look it up.

Glossary

Grammarly: a company that sells online products that help people with their grammar

contemporaries: people who live at the same time

candidacy: position or status as a candidate (for a job position, as in the case of this reading)

coincides: occurs at the same time

Comprehension Questions

1. What evidence is used in this reading to support the claims made by the author?

2. According to the author, what does a poorly written resumé suggest about future performance?

3. What does Kyle Wiens, CEO of iFixit, say is the typical argument against the proper use of grammar? What is his response to this argument?

4. Why is the ability to pay attention to detail important? What is the relationship between this quality and grammar?

5. What are some "common goofs" that the author says make people look silly?

Questions about Form

1. Why does the author begin with a question? Why does he begin with the question that he does?

2. Why is the use of LinkedIn profiles mentioned so early (paragraph 2) in the reading?

3. Is the title of the reading a good one? Why or why not?

4. The source for many of the facts in this reading is *Forbes* magazine. How might knowing this affect the targeted readership of *Canadian Writer's Workplace*?

5. Is including examples of "grammar goofs" at the end of this reading effective? Why or why not?

Questions for Discussion

1. Most students seem less than enthusiastic about having to learn grammar. Why is this the case, considering the paramount role it plays, according to the reading, in anyone's career success?

2. Many students who come through the same school system have very different skill sets when it comes to grammar. What accounts for some of those differences?

3. How effective are online resources when it comes to applying grammar rules to one's writing?

Writing Ideas

1. What is the best way to learn better grammar outside of the classroom? In a paragraph or an essay, answer this question and make at least one reference to the reading.

2. In a paragraph or an essay, explain how you might change the mind of someone whose grammar is poor, but who thinks it doesn't matter since English is his only language and he or she speaks and writes it well enough to "get by."

3. Write a paragraph or an essay about what any English department could and should do to encourage students to do more work on their language skills outside of class.

4. What are the causes of poor grammar among young people today? Make at least one reference to the reading in a paragraph or essay.

♦ ♦ ♦

The Economic Cost of Depression

Gary Lamphier

In spite of the usual stigma and taboos, depression is becoming more and more a topic of discussion now that there's a huge price tag attached to it. It's still a difficult illness to diagnose, and probably more difficult to cure. But what's certain is that it's costing Canadian taxpayers heaps and heaps of money. Gary Lamphier of the *Edmonton Journal* examines this issue in this article published on August 14, 2014.

1 The shocking suicide of Robin Williams brought a tragic end to the life of one of Hollywood's most gifted and beloved comic actors.

2 With his passing, we can only hope Williams's death will help shine a spotlight on a topic that is anything but funny, and all too often swept under society's rug: depression.

3 Depression is a very big deal in Canada, and in many other nations around the globe. The World Health Organization (WHO) says some 350 million people suffer from depression worldwide. That's roughly 10 times the entire population of Canada.

4 The Conference Board of Canada estimates that 16 per cent of women and 11 per cent of men in this country will suffer a major depression at some point in their lives.

5 In the workplace, roughly four per cent of adults are **clinically** depressed at any given time. So if your organization employs 500 people, odds are that 20 of them are seriously depressed and in need of medical help as you read this column.

6 Anyone who has suffered through major depressions—as Williams apparently did throughout his life—or who knows someone who has, realizes just how crippling and socially isolating "the black dog" can be.

7 It afflicts politicians and wealthy **tycoons**, artists and academics, scientists and pop stars, athletes and war heroes, as well as your neighbours and family members.

8 Winston Churchill, Eric Clapton, Woody Allen and Ray Charles all suffered from depression. So did Ingmar Bergman, Ernest Hemingway, Isaac Newton and Abraham Lincoln.

9 Contrary to popular belief, a person who is depressed can't simply "snap out of it" or "pull up his socks" to escape its ill effects, any more than a cancer patient can wish his disease away. Nor is depression a sign of personal weakness.

10 Depression may be triggered by some external event—such as job loss, retirement, or the death of a spouse—or it may stem from a chemical imbalance in the brain.

11 Whatever the cause, it happens between one's ears, so it's invisible to the naked eye. Unlike a broken leg or a sprained ankle, it doesn't immediately evoke sympathy from friends or colleagues. Often, it provokes the opposite response: **indifference**.

12 And unlike a tumour, a doctor can't perform a **biopsy** on a patient's brain tissue to see if he or she is depressed. Although depression can be and often is treated successfully with medication, that, too, can involve lots of trial and error, including multiple medications and dosages before an effective remedy is found.

13   Those who suffer from depression endure a hailstorm of body-slamming symptoms, from loss of sleep and appetite to **lethargy**, an inability to focus and even recurring feelings of guilt or obsessive thoughts of suicide.

14   For the Canadian economy, the cost of depression is staggering in terms of worker absenteeism, loss of productivity, drug prescription costs and a phenomenon known as "presenteeism," which refers to depressed employees who are still at work, but functioning at a reduced level.

15   "The Conference Board did an analysis of the six most important mental health issues in Canada, and the top two are depression and chronic depression," says Louise Chenier, the 'board's manager, workplace health and wellness research. "The cost to the economy is estimated to be $20.7 billion per year and it's expected to increase to $29.1 billion annually by 2030, so it's a huge number."

16   Even that lofty figure **understates** the magnitude of the problem, however. If one includes the costs associated with "presenteeism" in the calculation, Chenier says the price tag would actually be several times larger.

17   The good news? Just as it's important to encourage employees to be physically active and healthy, organizations are slowly coming around to the view that mental health is also vitally important, not only in terms of workplace culture but to the bottom line.

18   As a result, an increasing number of organizations are providing programs and support services to help employees stay mentally healthy, and to get proper treatment if they need it, Chenier says.

Christine Glade/istockphoto.com

19   That said, depression and other mental health issues still carry a stigma, and many companies are uncomfortable addressing it in the workplace. The "'just suck it up" attitude remains all too pervasive, and destructive.

20   "For some reason mental health issues are still less often discussed, and I think it's because it's more invisible, and people don't know how to react when colleagues have experienced a mental health issue," says Chenier.

21   "They don't know what to say, and often people are very uncomfortable talking about emotions, so they don't know how to broach the subject. So it leads to situations where a colleague who has had to take a leave of absence for depression and returns to work, they almost feel ignored. Meanwhile someone who comes back after breaking his leg gets all this empathy. It's simply because people are uncomfortable. So the more we learn to talk about it the better it will be for everyone."

Glossary

clinically: in terms of observed symptoms

tycoons: wealthy and influential business people

indifference: lack of interest or attention

biopsy: removal and examination of living tissue to determine the extent of a disease

lethargy: lack of energy or enthusiasm

understates: expresses in restrained terms

Comprehension Questions

1. How widespread in the world is the problem of depression, according to the reading?

2. Why, according to the reading, does depression not evoke sympathy from someone in the same way a broken leg might?

3. Why is depression difficult to treat, according to the reading?

4. What are the costs of depression to the economy?

5. How are organizations beginning to respond to the reality of depression?

Questions about Form

1. Why does the reading open with such a major reference to Robin Williams?

2. Why is the example of Robin Williams so ironic?

3. Why are statistics included so early in the reading?

4. What is the purpose of the last paragraph in this reading?

Questions for Discussion

1. The reading by Lamphier keeps mentioning the notion of the stigma around depression. Besides the fact that depression is an "invisible" condition, what else do you think contributes to the stigma? Why are people so uncomfortable sympathizing with people who have it?

2. Why do some people expect those with depression to just "snap out of it"?

Writing Ideas

1. The last paragraph mentions how much someone who returns to work after a leave of absence due to depression might be ignored. What can someone do to comfort the person returning?

2. What, in your opinion, can organizations do to accommodate employees with depression that perhaps they are not already doing?

✦ ✦ ✦

The Other Family*

Himani Bannerji

Himani Bannerji teaches in the Department of Sociology at York University in Toronto. She has an active teaching connection with India, especially West Bengal, through the School of Women's Studies, Jadavpur University, Kolkata. She has taught and published extensively in the areas of Marxist theory, anti-racist feminism, and nationalism. In the following story about a little girl and her mother, first published in 2009, Bannerji gives us a glimpse into the home of an immigrant family caught between the desire to fit into a new community and the fear of losing its identity.

© Photos India/Photolibrary

*Himani Bannerji, "The Other Family." Reprinted by permission of Himani Bannerji.

1   When the little girl came home it was already getting dark. The winter twilight had transformed the sheer blue sky of the day into the colour of steel, on which were etched a few stars, the bare winter trees and the dark wedges of the housetops. A few lit windows cast a faint glow on the snow outside. The mother stood at her window and watched the little hooded figure walking toward the house. The child looked like a shadow, her blue coat blended into the shadows of the evening. This child, her own, how small and **insubstantial** she seemed, and how alone, walking home through a pavement covered with ice and snow! It felt unreal. So different was this childhood from her own, so far away from the sun, the trees and the peopled streets of her own country! What did I do, she thought, I took her away from her own people and her own language, and now here she comes walking alone, through an alien street in a country named Canada.

2   As she **contemplated** the solitary, moving figure, her own solitude rushed over her like a tide. She had drifted away from a world that she had lived in and understood, and now she stood here at the same distance from her home as from the homes which she glimpsed while walking past the sparkling clean windows of the sandblasted houses. And now the doorbell rang, and here was her daughter scraping the snow off her boots on the doormat.

3   Dinner time was a good time. A time of warmth, of putting hot, steaming food onto the table. A time to chat about the important things of the day, a time to show each other what they had acquired. Sometimes, however, her mother would be absentminded, worried perhaps about work, unsettled perhaps by letters that had arrived from home, scraping her feelings into a state of rawness. This was such an evening. She had served herself and her child, started a conversation about their two cats and fallen into a silence after a few minutes.

4   "You aren't listening to me, Mother."

5   The complaining voice got through to her, and she looked at the indignant face demanding attention from the other side of the table. She gathered herself together.

6   "So what did he do, when you gave him dried food?"

7   "Oh, I don't quite remember, I think he scratched the ground near his bowl and left."

8   The child laughed.

9   "That was smart of him! So why don't we buy tinned food for them?"

10   "Maybe we should," she said, and tried to change the topic.

11   "So what did you do in your school today?"

12   "Oh, we drew pictures like we do every day. We never study anything—not like you said you did in your school. We drew a family—our family. Want to see it?"

13   "Sure, and let's go to the living room, OK? This is messy." Scraping of chairs and the lighting of the lamps in the other room. They both made a rush for the most comfortable chair, both reached it at the same time and made a compromise.

14   "How about you sit in my lap? No? OK, sit next to me then and we will squeeze in somehow."

15   There was a remarkable resemblance between the two faces, except that the face of the child had a greater intensity, given by the wide open eyes. She was fine

boned, and had black hair framing her face. Right now she was struggling with the contents of her satchel, apparently trying to feel her way to the paintings.

16   "Here it is," she said, producing a piece of paper. "Here's the family!"

17   The mother looked at the picture for a long time. She was very still. Her face had set into an expression of anger and sadness. She was trying very hard not to cry. She didn't want to frighten the child, and yet what she saw made her feel distant from her daughter, as though she was looking at her through the reverse end of a telescope. She couldn't speak at all. The little girl too sat very still, a little recoiled from the body of her mother, as though expecting a blow. Her hands were clenched into fists, but finally it was she who broke the silence.

18   "What happened?" she said. "Don't you like it?"

19   "Listen," said the mother, "this is not your family. I, you and your father are dark-skinned, dark-haired. I don't have a blond wig hidden in my closet, my eyes are black, not blue, and your father's beard is black, not red, and you, do you have a white skin, a button nose with freckles, blue eyes and blond hair tied into a ponytail? You said you drew our family. This is not it, is it?"

20   The child was now feeling distinctly cornered. At first she was startled and frightened by her mother's response, but now she was prepared to be defiant. She had the greatest authority behind her, and she now summoned it to her help.

21   "I drew it from a book," she said, "all our books have this same picture of the family. You can go and see it for yourself. And everyone else drew it too. You can ask our teacher tomorrow. She liked it, so there!"

22   The little girl was clutching at her last straw.

23   "But you? Where are you in this picture?" demanded her mother, by now thoroughly aroused. "Where are we? Is this the family you would like to have? Don't you want us anymore? You want to be a *mem-sahib,* a white girl?"

24   But even as she lashed out these questions, the mother regretted them. She could see that she made no sense to the child. She could feel the unfairness of it all. She was sorry that she was putting such a heavy burden on such young shoulders.

25   "First I bring her here," she thought, "and then I try to make her feel guilty for wanting to be the same as the others." But something had taken hold of her this evening. Panic at the thought of losing her child, despair and guilt galvanized her into speech she regretted, and she looked with anger at her only child, who it seemed wanted to be white, who had rejected her dark mother. Someday this child would be ashamed of her, she thought; someday she would move out into the world of those others. Someday they would be enemies. Confusing thoughts ran through her head like images on an uncontrollable television screen, in the chaos of which she heard her **ultimate** justification flung at her by her daughter—they wanted me to draw the family, didn't they? "They" wanted "her" to draw "the family." The way her daughter pronounced the words "they" or "the family" indicated that she knew what she was talking about. The simple pronoun "they" definitely stood for authority, for that uncontrollable yet organized world immediately outside, of which the school was the ultimate expression. It surrounded their own private space. "They" had power, "they" could crush

little people like her anytime "they" wanted to, and in "their" world that was the picture of the family. Whether her mother liked it or not, whether she looked like the little girl in it or not, made not one jot of difference. That was, yes, that was the right picture. As these thoughts passed through her mind, her anger ebbed away. Abandoning her fury and distance, the mother bowed her head at the image of this family and burst into sobs.

26   "What will happen to you?" she said. "What did I do to you?"

27   She cried a great deal and said many **incoherent** things. The little girl was patient, quietly absorbing her mother's change of mood. She had a thoughtful look on her face, and bit her nails from time to time. She did not protest any more, but nor did she cry. After a while her mother took her to bed and tucked her in, and sat in the kitchen with the fearful vision of her daughter always outside of the window of the blond family, never the centre of her own life, always rejecting herself, and her life transformed into a gigantic peep show. She wept very bitterly because she had caused this destruction, and because she had hated her child in her own fear of rejection, and because she had sowed guilt into her mind.

28   When her mother went to bed and closed the door, the child, who had been waiting for a long time, left the bed. She crossed the corridor on her tiptoes, past the row of shoes, the silent gathering of the overcoats and the mirror with the wavy surface, and went into the washroom. Behind the door was another mirror, of full length, and clear. Deliberately and slowly the child took off the top of her pajamas and surveyed herself with grave scrutiny. She saw the brownness of her skin, the wide, staring, dark eyes, the black hair now tousled from the pillows, the scar on her nose and the brownish pink of her mouth. She stood a while lost in this act of contemplation, until the sound of soft padded feet neared the door, and a whiskered face peeped in. She stooped and picked up the cat and walked back to her own room.

[. . .]

29   It was snowing again, and little elves with bright coloured coats and snow in their boots had reappeared in the classroom. When finally the coats were hung under pegs with names and boots neatly stowed away, the little girl approached her teacher. She had her painting from the day before in her hand.

30   "I have brought it back," she said.

31   "Why?" asked her teacher, "don't you like it any more?"

32   The little girl was looking around very intently.

33   "It's not finished yet," she said. "The books I looked at didn't have something. Can I finish it now?"

34   "Go ahead," said the teacher, moving on to get the colours from the cupboard.

35   The little girl was looking at the classroom. It was full of children of all colours, of all kinds of shapes of noses and of different colours of hair. She sat on the floor, placed the incomplete picture on a big piece of newspaper and started to paint. She worked long at it—and with great concentration. Finally it was finished. She went back to her teacher.

36   "It's finished now," she said, "I drew the rest."

37   The teacher reached out for the picture and spread it neatly on a desk. There they were, the blond family arranged in a semicircle with a dip in the middle, but next to them, arranged alike, stood another group—a man, a woman, and a child, but they were dark-skinned, dark-haired, the woman wore clothes from her own country, and the little girl in the middle had a scar on her nose.

38   "Do you like it?"

39   "Who are they?" asked the teacher, though she should have known. But the little girl didn't mind answering this question one bit.

40   "It's the other family," she said.

Glossary

insubstantial: not large in size or amount; weak

contemplated: looked at or considered in a calm, reflective manner

ultimate: preeminent or decisive

incoherent: unintelligible; not able to be understood

Comprehension Questions

1. Is there mutual respect between mother and daughter? Cite the evidence.

2. What was the immediate thing that upset the little girl's mother when she saw the first picture her daughter had drawn?

3. What is the mother afraid of? Where is the evidence of this fear?

4. How did the little girl resolve the issue?

Questions about Form

1. Is this an essay or a story? Explain.

2. Although this piece is told in third-person narration, is the narrator more knowledgeable about a particular character? Explain.

3. Does the author make effective use of transitions in this piece? Give three examples of transitions.

4. What are the effects of the extensive use of dialogue?

Questions for Discussion

1. Because this piece is fictional, the author's thesis is not explicit. What do you think, in your own words, is the author's message? What evidence would you cite from the piece in support of your answer?

2. How do the mother's fears relate to the idea of young people dating people of other races and religions? How do problems in this area tend to get resolved?

Writing Ideas

1. How important are pictures and words when it comes to helping people develop strong self-esteem? Write a paragraph or essay supporting your answer, and refer, in your writing, to evidence from Bannerji's piece.

2. This piece is about the conflict between the desire to fit in and the fear of losing one's identity. Write a paragraph or essay in which you discuss a personal experience that relates to these themes, and explain how your own situation was resolved.

✦ ✦ ✦

Let's Unplug the Digital Classroom

Doug Mann

More technology, more technology, more technology! That message is loud and clear, admit many faculty in colleges and universities today. But what if technology actually makes people "dumber and dumber"? Does anyone want to hear that message, even if it's true? Doug Mann is a professor in the Department of Sociology and the Faculty of Information and Media Studies at Western University, but his message is not the one echoing through the halls and meeting rooms of educational institutions. This article was published in the *Toronto Star* on October 6, 2012.

1   We are entering an age when the "digital delivery of course content can free faculty in traditional institutions to engage in direct dialogue and mentorship with students." So says the Ontario government's 2012 white paper on education, *Strengthening Ontario's Centres of Creativity, Innovation and Knowledge*. Professors muse that the classroom must "evolve or die" to become more "fun and engaging" for the modern student.

2   Such views are misinformed at best, crude propaganda for Apple and Microsoft at worst. The use of digital technology in higher education has promoted ignorance, not knowledge, and severely degraded basic reading, writing and thinking skills. It's time to hit the off button.

3   One problem with the most enthusiastic **futurists** is that too many of them haven't spent any time in the classroom in the last decade. If they had, they'd realize that digital technology is already **omnipresent** there, used by both students and professors. Almost all undergraduate students in North America are addicted to texting on their smartphones and checking their Facebook pages on an hourly basis. Almost all professors use computers, projectors, PowerPoint presentations and the Internet as part of their lectures. Calling for more digital technology in education today is like calling for more white people in the Republican party.

michaeljung/thinkstock

Doug Mann, "Let's Unplug the Digital Classroom." Reprinted by permission of the author.

4   The real question is how computers, smartphones and iPods are used, and whether these uses contribute anything to the main goal of higher education: to improve students' minds and characters by helping them to learn facts, debate ideas and understand the world better. The answer, for the most part, is no—study after study shows that digital technology has dumbed down higher education. They may make education more "fun" and "engaging." But that's only saying that they've turned education into a form of entertainment. Writing essays, reading difficult texts or figuring out complex mathematical problems have never been "fun"—and never will be.

5   On the plus side, the use of the computer as a delivery device for texts and images is largely a positive development. Gone are the nights spent in the bowels of the university library looking through card catalogues and the social science index for books and articles. It's also useful from a teacher's point of view to be able to display images and video via classroom computers when teaching things like fine art, comics and film.

6   Laptops in the classroom are much more of a problem. Yes, one student in 10 actually uses them to look up relevant facts and issues, but the other nine are using classroom Wi-Fi to check their Facebook pages, email or celebrity websites. Portable computers combine all four of the general functions of digital technology: information delivery, peer communication, entertainment and procrastination. Cellphones concentrate on the last three functions and have no **pedagogical** purpose. Anyone who has walked to the back of a university classroom and looked at what students are actually looking at on their various screens will abandon any sense that digital technology plays a positive role in the classroom. Facebook and celebrity websites dominate their screens.

7   What's especially frustrating when we hear the blind support for digital technology **bruited** in government white papers and the mass media today is the refusal to acknowledge the substantial **empirical** research over the last 15 years that questions the value of such technology. Mark Bauerlein's *The Dumbest Generation* contains literally dozens of studies that show how digital technology has helped to create a generation of proud **bibliophobes** who avoid complex knowledge like the plague.

8   Jean Twenge and Keith Campbell's *The Narcissism Epidemic* shows how celebrity culture, the web 2.0 and soft parenting have accelerated young people's sense of self-esteem beyond all reasonable boundaries of actual achievement. The mass culture tells them that everyone can be a star, facts be damned. Digital **narcissists** don't care about their inability to read and write English or their ignorance of a range of basic historical and political facts.

9   My solution? Hit the off button in as many places as we can. Turn off Wi-Fi in the classroom, restricting it to student lounges scattered across campus. Create a schoolwide policy that bans the use of cellphones during lectures and seminars. Since texting has become an addiction for many, treat cells like cigarettes: if you want to text, do it outside. Ban the use of social networking websites during class.

Stop promoting Internet-managed distance-education courses: these are cheap imitations of the real thing. Digital technologies can be great delivery devices. But what they too often deliver has nothing to do with education.

Glossary

futurists: people who are concerned with or study the future

omnipresent: existing everywhere at the same time

pedagogical: having to do with teaching methods

bruited: spread (as in a report or rumour)

empirical: verifiable either by observation or experience rather than by pure theory

bibliophobes: people who dislike or fear books

narcissists: people with excessive interests in themselves

Comprehension Questions

1. At the end of paragraph 3, the author writes, "Calling for more digital technology in education today is like calling for more white people in the Republican party." What does he mean by this?

2. What is the author's solution to the problem of too much digital technology?

Questions about Form

1. Does the author use first or third person references throughout this reading? Is this usage effective? Why or why not?

2. Why does the author begin with a quotation from the Ontario government's 2012 white paper on education? How does the author feel about the government's direction for education in Ontario?

Questions for Discussion

1. The author suggests that by making education more "engaging" through the use of technology, student learning is diminished. Do you agree or not? Explain.

2. Do you agree with the author that most students who use technology in the classroom use it for personal purposes, such as texting their friends and family and going on social media? If so, what is the point of allowing such usage? How should the school deal with this to maximize student learning?

3. If the classroom is intended to foster creativity, does the use of technology contribute to this process or stifle it? Explain.

Writing Ideas

1. In a paragraph or an essay, discuss the pros of banning technology for personal use in the classroom.

2. In a paragraph or an essay, discuss the cons of banning technology for personal use in the classroom.

3. Cellphones are more and more often being banned from the boardroom because they distract employees from the task at hand. If CEOs have made the decision to ban these devices, should this ban be extended to the classroom? Outline your position and the reasons behind it in a paragraph or an essay.

◆ ◆ ◆

Cyber Misogyny

Brett Throop

Cyberbullying, or hatred of women online? Let's call a spade a spade. The term *cyberbullying* may, in fact, be an attempt to water down or even completely conceal the truth, which is that the Internet is just another place to harass women. And too many men and boys get away with it because the law might not have caught up with the technology . . . until now anyway. Brett Throop of *CBC News* documents this in a story first posted on August 8, 2014.

1   When Canadian teen Amanda Todd committed suicide after intimate photos of her were circulated online, the media referred to the circumstances as a case of cyberbullying.

2   But according to a Vancouver-based women's advocacy group, online harassment has a "hugely disproportionate impact on women and girls" and needs to be called what it is: cyber **misogyny**.

3   "Cyberbullying has become this term that's often thrown around with little understanding of what the underlying causes of this harassment, this hate speech, these threats, actually [are]," said Kasari Govender, executive director of the Vancouver-based West Coast Legal Education and Action Fund (LEAF).

4   LEAF uses the term cyber misogyny "to reveal the underlying discriminatory attitudes," Govender said in an interview with Francine Pelletier, guest host of CBC Radio's *The Sunday Edition* this week.

5   "We think it's important to name the forces that are motivating this in order to figure out how to address it."

6   While the term cyberbullying suggests that women and men are equally victimized, it's much less common to see cyberbullying directed at men,

© Mike2focus | Dreamstime.com - Cyber Internet Computer Bullying Photo

CBC Licensing

Govender said. Online hate speech or harassment directed at men is usually racist, homophobic or transphobic in nature, she said.

7   Cyberbullying "isn't a problem that only impacts women and girls, but it is a problem that disproportionately impacts women and girls," Govender said.

"Revenge Porn," a Major Concern

8   According to LEAF, cyber misogyny differs from regular bullying in that it uses online and digital communication tools to harass women and girls solely because of their gender.

9   One of the most prevalent forms is the distribution of intimate images of someone by text message or email without their consent. Similar to this is so-called "revenge porn," in which **aggrieved** individuals publish intimate photos or videos of a former partner online with the purpose of shaming them.

10   Women are also more vulnerable than their male counterparts to cyber-stalking, which is when an individual sends "unwanted advances" online, even using spyware to monitor another person's activity online.

11   Most of this online harassment falls through the cracks of Canada's criminal code, meaning the online realm remains a **"wild west"** when it comes to civil rights, Govender said.

12   In Saskatchewan this year, a man was acquitted of theft and mischief charges in a revenge porn case after publishing nude images of his ex-girlfriend online. The judge found the accused's conduct "despicable," but could not charge him under existing laws.

13   This lack of regulation, combined with widespread misogyny online, effectively limits women's speech on the internet, Govender said.

14   When women are threatened, stalked or harassed online, it "shuts women's voices down and means that in fact they're not speaking, they're not able to participate in those same forums," Govender said.

15   In the absence of legal protections, many women and girls who are harassed online feel that their only option is to close their social media accounts and stay off the internet, Govender said.

16   That was what police told Amanda Todd's mother when she reported that her daughter was being harassed, Govender said.

17   For most young people, that is "not an option," because online social networking and texting are "so much a part of youth culture," Govender said.

18   "And it also really dismisses the potential of the internet to be a very positive place."

The Pros and Cons of Bill C-13

19   Govender and her organization are supportive of parts of the controversial legislation put forward by the federal government that would crack down on online harassment.

20   Bill C-13, also known as the Protecting Canadians from Online Crime Act, would make it illegal to distribute intimate images without consent. But other

provisions of the bill would expand police powers, including creating what some say would be an incentive for warrantless disclosure of information to police. This has raised concerns among many, including Canada's privacy commissioner.

21   LEAF wants to see the bill split in two in order to expedite the passage of the measures that directly target online harassment.

22   "My concern is that if it's passed as a whole that it will actually be held up quite significantly because there will likely be a constitutional challenge to its use," Govender said.

23   She is hoping that the legislation can be tweaked to "keep women and girls safe without engaging in [a] wholesale override of freedom of speech and privacy rights online."

24   Bill C-13 passed second reading in the House of Commons in April. A committee report on it will be considered by the House and Senate when Parliament resumes in the fall.

25   Govender said the federal government's refusal to reconsider the aspects of the bill with the potential to infringe on privacy "really takes away from its commitment to ensure that women and girls are safe."

Note from Canadian Writer's Workplace: Bill C-13 became law on Monday, March 9, 2015.

Glossary

misogyny: hatred of or contempt for women

aggrieved: having the feeling of being unfairly treated

"wild west": refers to the western region of the U.S. when it was lawless

expedite: make something go faster

Comprehension Questions

1.   What, in your own words, is the thesis of this piece by Brett Throop?

2.   What is the meaning of the title?

3.   What's wrong with the term *cyberbullying*, according to Kasari Govender?

4.   What makes it difficult to prosecute people of cyberbullying?

5.   What is controversial about Bill C-13?

Questions about Form

1.   Is the title of this piece effective? Why or why not?

2.   "Cyber Misogyny" is divided into three parts. Why is the piece split up this way? Is this division effective? Why or why not?

3.   Why does the writer start the piece by mentioning the Amanda Todd case?

Questions for Discussion

1.   Do you agree that the term *cyberbullying* is too gender-neutral for what it really depicts? Why or why not?

2. Is it fair to expect victims of online harassment to leave the social network altogether, as the police advised Amanda Todd's mother when she complained about the harassment of her daughter? Why or why not?

3. In the beginning of the movie *The Social Network,* about the birth of Facebook, founder Mark Zuckerberg was seen "cyberbullying" his girlfriend, who had just dumped him. When he realized, after his online rant, that his site had received thousands of hits in an hour, he knew he had an idea worth a great deal of money. How does this scene in the movie relate to the reading?

Writing Ideas

1. In a paragraph or essay, discuss other forms of cyberbullying besides "revenge porn."

2. In a paragraph or essay, discuss strategies that could be used to prevent young people from cyberbullying their peers.

3. In a paragraph or an essay, address the following questions: Is cyberbullying really cyber misogyny? If so, why are men more often guilty of this than women? If you think this is not the case, supply evidence in support of your answer. Also, add examples where you can.

◆ ◆ ◆

Selling Illusions*

Neil Bissoondath

Novelist, short story writer, and essayist Neil Bissoondath was born in Arima, Trinidad, in 1955, and now lives in Canada. The following piece is an excerpt from his book *Selling Illusions: The Cult of Multiculturalism in Canada*, published in 1994. In this piece, Bissoondath exhibits some strong feelings about multiculturalism in Canada and how perhaps it's not what it is purported to be. In the following piece, he relates his experience as an eighteen-year-old who has just come to Canada to attend York University.

1   If the York University campus was a safe haven from which to discover the pleasures of Canada ... it was also the place where I first encountered reasons for unease.

2   York operates on a college system. New students choose, or are assigned to, one of the various colleges on the campus. Unfamiliar with the system, ignorant of the purposes behind the individual colleges, I allowed myself to be assigned to Bethune College.

3   Familiarity with the college brought a certain dismay. Bethune College, named in honour of **Dr. Norman Bethune,** is an institution devoted to Third World studies; it had a certain reputation for left-wing radicalism. The reason for my dismay was simple: my major was to be French language and literature. The

bilingual Glendon College, my logical "home," was never mentioned. I can only assume that I was enrolled at Bethune in part because I had come from a Third World country and in part because my adviser assumed that I would be most comfortable in an environment where a high percentage of students were, like me, non-white. It was an assuredly benign assumption, one made with the best of intentions, but also with no regard to my personal beliefs or intellectual interests. My adviser, then, had looked at me through the lens of her own stereotype and guided me according to the presumed comforts of "sticking with your own."

4　　Although I was not at first aware of it, the concept of "sticking with your own" was just then in vogue at York. This became clear the moment you entered the main cafeteria at Central Square in the massive concrete bunker of the Ross Building. It was large and brashly lit, institutional in character, a place for feeding oneself rather than enjoying a meal. I remember it as a loud and busy place, brash with the sounds of trays and cutlery roughly handled, of a multitude of voices blended into a steady roar.

5　　And yet, it seemed a benign atmosphere, friendly in an impersonal way. The controlled chaos offered an anonymity that would ease the task of inserting oneself, of fitting in. Or so it seemed at first.

6　　Chaos is always subtly ordered, and it did not require a very discerning eye to decode the chaos of the Central Square cafeteria. Indeed, a map could be drawn, various sections coloured in to denote defined areas. To highlight, for instance, the table at which Chinese students congregated behind a wall of Cantonese; or the tables over in the corner protected by the raucous enthusiasm of West Indian accents; or the table more subtly framed by **yarmulkes** and Star of David pendants.

7　　To approach any of these tables was to intrude on a clannish exclusivity. It was to challenge the unofficially designated territory of tables parcelled out so that each group, whether racially, culturally or religiously defined, could enjoy its little enclave, its own little "homeland," so to speak, protected by unspoken **prerogatives**.

8　　The idea of "sticking with your own" was reinforced by various student organizations, many of which were financially assisted by the university. Controversy arose at one point when an application for membership in the Black Students' Federation was received from a student—a writer for the campus newspaper, as it turned out—whose skin colour seemed to disqualify him. Questions arose: Was being black a prerequisite for belonging to the Black Students' Federation? Or was a commitment to the issues raised by the association sufficient justification for belonging? Just how relevant was skin colour, how relevant cultural background, how relevant political belief?

9　　A hint of the complexity of the question may be discerned in a story once told to me by a friend. One afternoon, he stopped in at his favourite coffee house in Toronto's Kensington Market, a small place brightly decorated in the tropical style. It featured reggae music and the rich Blue Mountain coffee from Jamaica. As he sipped his coffee, he eavesdropped on a conversation at the table behind him, three young men, evidently musicians, discussing their next gig. My friend understood little of what was said—their thick Jamaican accents made their words **undecipherable**—but he enjoyed listening to their speech in the same way that he enjoyed the sounds of reggae. Cup empty, he rose to leave. On his way out he glanced at the men and with delight saw, as he put it, "one black guy with dreadlocks and two white guys with blond hair and blue eyes." An encounter, then, with the wickedness of history. He left the coffee house thrilled at abandoning the wreckage of a stereotype.

10   The issue at York was eventually settled by the decision to admit the white student to the Federation—not on the grounds that race was irrelevant but that, as an organization financially assisted by the university, it had to respect the university's regulations prohibiting discrimination on the grounds of race and colour. I did not belong to the Federation, but the resolution was pleasing anyway, even though there was a tincture of discomfort at the way in which it had come about: through a technicality, and not through the application of principle. None of the real questions had been grappled with, none answered.

11   Questions of segregation and **exclusivity** kept raising their heads. One day a Jewish friend invited me to join him for coffee in the Jewish Students' Federation lounge. I was reluctant—the lounge seemed to me governed by even stronger proscriptions than the table in the cafeteria—but he insisted. As he fixed us each a coffee, he said in a voice clearly intended for others in the room that I should feel free to help myself from the coffee-machine at any time. And then he added in strained tones that the lounge, provided by the university, was open to all: I was to ignore anyone who tried to stop me. It was in this way that he sought to make me part of unsuspected **internecine** tensions, while publicly declaring his own position.

12   The issues made me wary: I neither joined the Black Students' Federation nor revisited the Jewish Students' Federation lounge. I learned instead to keep my distance from the tables that would have welcomed me not as an individual but as an individual of a certain skin colour, with a certain accent, with a certain assumed cultural outlook—the tables that would have welcomed me not for who I was and for what I could do but for *what* I was and for what they presumed I represented. I had not come here, I decided, in order to join a ghetto.

13   Alone in a new land, I faced inevitable questions. Questions about my past and my present, about the land left behind and the land newly found, about the nature of this society and my place in it. At eighteen, about to embark on a new life, I felt these to be weighty issues.

14   For many people at those cafeteria tables, though, these were questions of no great importance. They were almost aggressive in dismissing any discomfort they might have experienced by flaunting the only government policy that seemed to arouse no resentment: Canada as a multicultural land. Officially. Legally. Here, they insisted, you did not have to change. Here you could—indeed, it was your duty to—remain what you were. None of this American melting-pot nonsense, none of this remaking yourself to fit your new circumstances: you did not have to adjust to the society, the society was obligated to accommodate itself to you.

15   An attractive proposal, then, a policy that excused much and required little effort. And yet I found myself not easily seduced.

16   The problem was that I had come in search of a new life and a new way of looking at the world, "to expand my horizons" (to use a cliché) from the narrow perspectives of my youth in Trinidad. I had no desire to transport here life as I had known it: this seemed to me particularly onerous baggage with which to burden one's shoulders. Beyond this, though, the very act of emigration had already changed me. I was no longer the same person who had boarded the aircraft in Trinidad bound for Toronto: I had brought with me not the attitudes of the tourist but those of someone embarking on an adventure that would forever change his life. This alone was a kind of psychological revolution.

17   Multiculturalism, as perceived by those at whom it was most explicitly aimed, left me with a certain measure of discomfort.

18   At the end of my first university year, I returned to Trinidad to visit my parents. It wasn't long before I was impatient to get back to Toronto. This had to do in part with the realization that, even after so short a time, old friends had become new strangers, and that old places had remained simply old places. More importantly, though, the desire to return had to do with me and with the life I had begun constructing in my adopted city. I relished the freedom this life offered, the liberation of the anonymity of the big city. I had made new friends—some of them from among "my own kind," some not—and had found all the books, magazines and films denied me in Trinidad. I had, for the first time in my life, found a place other than my parents' house that I wished to call home: a place where I could be myself.

19   Sharing this with those who wished me to bolster their ethnic bastion in Toronto made me distinctly unpopular. I was seen as a kind of traitor, unwilling to play the game by indulging in a life best described as "Caribbean North." If there was any **alienation,** it came not from the society at large but from those who saw themselves as the front-line practitioners of multiculturalism. By establishing cultural and racial exclusivity, they were doing their bit to preserve the multicultural character of the country, while I, seeking to go beyond the confines of my cultural heritage, was seen as acting counter to those interests.

20   To put it succinctly, they coveted the segregated tables of the cafeteria, while I sought a place at tables that would accommodate a greater variety.

Glossary

Dr. Norman Bethune: a Canadian surgeon and international humanitarian revered in China for his heroic and selfless treatment of the wounded in that country's struggle for a republic; he died of blood poisoning in 1939

yarmulkes: skullcaps often worn by male Jews, especially during prayer and religious functions

prerogatives: exclusive rights or privileges

undecipherable: unable to be understood

exclusivity: the act of shutting out

internecine: of or relating to a struggle within a nation, an organization, or a group

alienation: feeling estranged from one's social environment

Comprehension Questions

1. What does Bissoondath mean by the "homeland" in paragraph 7? Why does he not want to join the "homelands"?

2. Why does Bissoondath think he was assigned to Bethune College?

3. What was really happening, according to Bissoondath, when his Jewish friend served him a coffee in the Jewish Students' Federation lounge?

4. What is the story told to Bissoondath by his friend who visited Toronto's Kensington Market? What is the meaning of it? How does it support Bissoondath's overall thesis?

Questions about Form

1. What does Bissoondath include in this piece that helps you to identify with his concerns?

2. What is the setting of Bissoondath's essay? Does this help to make the piece more effective? Why or why not?

3. Is the last paragraph of this piece effective? Why or why not?

Questions for Discussion

1. Do "homelands," as Bissoondath would define them, exist at your school? What do you think are the reasons they exist there? Do they do more harm than good, as Bissoondath suggests?

2. Do you generally "stick" with people "of your own kind"? From your own experience, what are the advantages and disadvantages of this behaviour?

3. Are there clubs at your school that seem exclusive to people of a certain skin colour, religion, or culture? Would they refuse to accept a student who wanted to join if this student didn't seem to "belong"? Is this a violation of human rights law?

4. Judging only by this essay, what would you say is the author's attitude toward multiculturalism in this country? Do you agree with this attitude? Why or why not?

5. Do you think Canadians in general are less racist than Americans? Why or why not? What in this article by Bissoondath supports your answer?

Writing Ideas

1. In a paragraph or essay, argue whether you think multiculturalism, the way it is promoted at your school, contributes to or combats racism.

2. In a paragraph or essay, argue whether or not a club should be able to offer exclusivity to people of only one skin colour, one culture, or one religion.

3. Imagine you are creating your own college/university social club. In view of Bissoondath's concerns, what would the basic guidelines regarding membership of your new club be? Support them in a paragraph or essay.

4. Identify a social club that seems to be exclusive to a particular race, religion, or culture. Write a paragraph or essay supporting or criticizing this perception of exclusivity.

◆ ◆ ◆

What's Missing?

Gary Lipschutz

The world would have us think that the greatest source of our happiness is money. The more money we have, the more we can get what we want. Too often, according to the lead author of *The Canadian Writer's Workplace,* who also teaches English at Toronto's Centennial College, the money we work so hard to make goes toward addiction, and happiness is the last thing we find when this happens. This piece was written in 2015.

1   Michael Jackson, Whitney Houston, Amy Winehouse, Philip Seymour Hoffman—what do they all have in common? All were abundantly talented. All seemed to have everything and more. All died far too early. All died from their **addictions**. What more do people want that these talented celebrities didn't already have? What's missing?

2   Besides material wealth that never completely satisfies, people seem to be in search of something else. Maybe it's the comfort in knowing that their lives mean something. Maybe it's the experience of feeling truly alive. Maybe it's the feeling of being connected to other human beings. Psychologist Dr. Gerald May wrote a book called *Addiction and Grace.* In it, he claims that most of the patients he treats for depression are seeking God or something spiritual—something bigger than themselves, whether they realize it or not. Dr. May says that they too often look for this mysterious, spiritual, missing thing in addiction. But, ironically, he says, whatever it is we're missing actually lies on the other side of withdrawal.

3   So many people are addicted to something without even being aware of it. Addiction is the out-of-control compulsion to do something or to take something for the sole purpose of making you feel better. You can be addicted to drugs, money, power, gambling, sex, love, cellphone usage, social media, video games, alcohol, smoking, food, shopping, etc. One addiction tends to lead to another. Instead of finding what they're looking for, addicts find that their lives actually worsen because the "high" from addictions is only temporary and the long-term effect is damage to their health and/or welfare. And to keep achieving the same "high," addicts often must **amplify** the "fix," leading to enormous expense, greater health risk and/or more depression.

4   So that's the problem. Although we want to be happy, we often look for happiness in all the wrong places. But at the risk of sounding more cliché, there is a silver lining in this cloud. What's bad can actually help you find what's good. It's like registering for a college program you discover you don't like only to discover what program you really do want. The journey from addiction to happiness (or freedom or heroism) can be divided into three stages: 1. awareness of one's addiction, 2. the desert experience, and 3. the realization of one's purpose and passion.

Stage One: Awareness ("I don't want to go through this anymore.")

5   Awareness of an addiction can come by monitoring your energy supply. We only have so much energy to spend on a daily basis before it's time to sleep and re-energize. If you spend all your energy on something unproductive, such as an addiction, there's not much left for something productive, such as something for which you have enormous talent, desire and passion. If you spend every weekend getting drunk or high or several hours every day obsessing over social media or a new man or woman in your life, think of what you could be producing if you spent that time developing your photography skills or your songwriting ability or your flair for painting portraits. When you become aware of your addiction, which takes you away from your talents, you are already on your way to recovery.

6   Your choice of people with whom you spend a great deal of time is extremely important. These people, after all, have an enormous influence on your spiritual journey. First, there's the possibility that you are going to take part in the same addictions as those of your friends. Second, if you spend all your energy with people who bring you down rather than lift you up, think about how this is going to affect your self-esteem and, consequently, your other life choices. By spending time with the wrong people, you might be shaping a destructive lifestyle.

Stage Two: The Desert Experience ("How do I make my life unimaginably better?")

7   The call of the desert can come by way of a "still, small voice." A man called Abraham lived with his family in Mesopotamia (present-day Iraq). "A still, small voice" told Abraham to "Go forth." Why? He already lived in a bustling city where he enjoyed the riches of the land, his multitude of cattle and the many family members who surrounded him. Life was predictable, comfortable and relatively secure. What more could a man possibly want? But this voice was a voice he couldn't ignore. It wasn't the loud, booming, resounding voice of the God that is portrayed in many movies. It was a "the still, small voice" inside himself that Abraham heard and attributed to God. The voice not only told him to go forth, but to go forth into the desert. Why would a man of great wealth go into the desert, where he isn't even guaranteed the water he needs to survive, let alone a better life than the one to which he's already grown accustomed?

Pascal RATEAU/Shutterstock

The answer is simple: something is missing, and the answer lies somewhere in the desert, where there is little noise and less distraction, but lots of mystery, and the promise of a better place that lies ahead.

8   The desert is not exactly an inviting vacation destination. It's the toughest part of the journey from addiction to freedom. But it's also the most spiritual. We may go there willingly. If we don't, life has a habit of forcing us there. For Abraham, the desert meant departure from an old place and the promise of a better one. This takes courage and faith. For an addict, according to Dr. May, the desert symbolizes **withdrawal** (the discontinuation of something such as a drug addiction). Few drug addicts look forward to withdrawal. (Remember Amy Winehouse and her song "Rehab"? When watching the music video on YouTube, one might get the awful feeling that the video foreshadows her death.)

9   Your desert might come in the form of rehab, depression, or solitude. Any desert experience is a painful one. It's also referred to as "the dark night of the soul." It is fraught with uncertainty, danger and discomfort—all the things we pay dearly to avoid. It's in the desert that you find out that material things cannot and will not save you. It is in the desert where you will be stripped of your egotistical pride and your juvenile belief that the world owes you something or anything. But it's also in the desert where a space opens up—a space in which you become freer to find what you are truly looking for now that your addiction no longer controls or distracts you.

10   You are tested in the desert. If you accept your responsibilities that life demands of every adult and you no longer blame anyone else for your problems, you can be **transformed**, which often means a kind of spiritual conversion (you see life differently now). You discover humility and gratitude, and you realize that respect must be earned. You undergo a change that has everything to do with character and not just something cosmetic like a different name or a new tattoo. You can return from the desert a new person, free of addiction, ready to take on the world, dedicated to helping your fellow human beings with a new sense of purpose and appreciation for life. The desert is where heroes are realized and readied for the heroic tasks that lie ahead.

11   You are never alone in the desert, although it may certainly feel that way for a while. You're not expected to manage the journey by yourself. Yes, it's where you will face your demons, your temptations (continuation of the addictions) and your worst fears. But you will get help from the strangest of sources. The desert tests you on your choices, but it also tests your faith. The many twelve-step programs—based on the mother of twelve-step programs, Alcoholics Anonymous—point out to their members at every meeting that they need to surrender to a higher power, regardless of what people might call it. Let yourself be carried through the desert and allow it to show you what you need to learn.

12   After a class discussion about the "still, small voice," a student approached me and asked the question, "How do I listen to this voice?" The question I heard was "How do I enter the desert?" I responded: "Figure out how to shut out some of the noise in your life." It might be actual noise, such as the constant ringing

of your cellphone, the sitcoms on TV, or the **plethora** of parties normally scheduled for the weekend. Or it might be something that the word *noise* symbolizes, such as the misguided or bad advice of friends or family or the oodles of time spent with the people in your life who constantly "bring you down." When you effectively shut out the noise, you start to hear the still, small voice. And it tells you exactly what you need to hear.

13   Psychologist (and former student of Freud) Carl G. Jung tells a story of a patient who comes to him and says, "Doctor, I'm depressed. I just lost my job." Jung takes out a bottle of champagne. The patient is immediately confused. "What are you doing?" asks the patient. "Didn't you hear what I just said? I'm depressed. I feel like I want to die." Jung responds, "You don't understand. It's in these times that there is immense opportunity because a space has been opened. You are forced to look inward and grow—discover what you want to do next. It's time to celebrate!" A desert experience can come in many different forms and, of course, more than once. But you have to be willing to accept what it offers.

Stage Three: The Realization of One's Purpose ("What was I born to do?")

14   The return from the desert is filled with opportunity. With confidence and a brand-new attitude, one is ready to take on the world, ready to serve fellow human beings, ready to fulfill one's purpose on earth—to do what one was born to do, to help others become happier than they are. Figure out what your talents are and use them to make the world a better place. Become a part of something that takes you outside of yourself. Addiction feeds your ego. But that which gives you spiritual fulfilment nourishes you with self-respect. You feel good not from an addiction that might give you instant if temporary gratification, but from a longer-lasting feeling of joy because you know you've done something good for others.

15   In the movie *Schindler's List*, Schindler is a German businessman who wants to make as much money as possible. He owns a factory that makes shells for the German war effort in World War II. He takes advantage of the war, in which prisoners are not allowed to get paid for their work. He lets them work in his factory. This is a win-win situation; after all, while they are working for the war effort, they are not sent to their death. Schindler is not a bad man. He just likes to make money. But when he sees a little girl murdered, something changes in him. He can no longer bear to watch the acts of inhumanity without doing something. With every piece of gold he has, he buys the freedom (and saves the life) of every prisoner that he can. Most powerful is the scene in which he falls to his knees and weeps uncontrollably because he realizes he could have sold his wedding ring to save one more human life. The man found what was missing . . . his humanity.

16   Thirteenth Century theologian Meister Eckhart said that if you're holding onto your attachments, they will be like demons tearing your life away. But if you let go of your attachments, your demons turn into angels that are freeing you from the earth.

Glossary

addictions: substances or activities that people are compelled to use or do to feel good

amplify: increase the strength or volume

withdrawal: a retreat or discontinuation

transformed: changed in a major way, as in one's character

plethora: abundance

Comprehension Questions

1. What, in your own words, and in one sentence, is the author's thesis?

2. What are the three stages of the spiritual journey the author discusses?

3. What does the author mean by "the desert experience"?

4. What is the point of the story about Carl Jung and his patient?

Questions about Form

1. What is the purpose of starting the reading with the names of four celebrities?

2. How does the author choose to organize this reading? Is it effective? Why or why not?

3. How do the stories about Abraham, Carl Jung, the author's student, and Schindler affect the reading?

4. Why does the author end the reading with a reference that is 800 years old?

Questions for Discussion

1. Why are addictions so tempting and at the same time so unfulfilling?

2. Does everyone have to undergo the journey that the author discusses?

3. It can be argued that the three stages the author discusses are parallel to the three stages of the heroic journey of many characters in literature or modern movies. Come up with an example and apply the three stages to that character's journey.

Writing Ideas

1. What causes a person to become an addict? In a paragraph or an essay, discuss these causes, and include examples in support of your points.

2. What are some of the consequences of having an addiction? Discuss them in a paragraph or an essay, and add examples in support of your points.

3. What are some solutions to the problem of addiction? Discuss them in a paragraph or an essay, with examples in support of your points.

◆ ◆ ◆

What Cuba Can Teach Canada

Rachel Browne

Canada's reputation for universal healthcare is impressive. But can we still learn something from a Caribbean island with a Communist regime? Doctors cited in the following piece by Rachel Browne say that we can and we should. It may be a matter of life or death. The article was first published in *Maclean's* magazine on February 11, 2015.

1   When a group of doctors and professors from Nova Scotia took a trip to Cuba in 2006 to study how the country managed infectious diseases, they were struck by how knowledgeable the average person was about vaccines, and decided to conduct an informal experiment: Quiz random passersby on the streets of Havana about their basic knowledge of their country's vaccine safety program (the process by which vaccines are created and made safe) and their personal immunization records.

2   "Without fail, everyone knew exactly what immunizations they already had, the scientific evidence behind them, and at what ages they needed to be updated," says John Kirk, professor of Spanish and Latin American studies at Dalhousie University, whose research focuses on Cuba's health care system. The research team also asked the Cubans their opinion on anti-vaccine movements in countries such as Canada and the United States. "They were **dumbfounded**. They thought we were joking," Kirk recalls. "I guarantee you won't meet a single person there who has doubted vaccines for a moment. For Cubans, vaccines aren't only seen as a basic human right, but also as an obligation."

3   Upon their return, Kirk and his colleagues wrote an article for the *Canadian Journal of Infectious Diseases*, in which they conclude Canada can learn a great deal from the Cuban approaches to vaccinations and health care.

4   The numbers say it best. According to the WHO's 2014 global summary on vaccine-preventable diseases and academic studies, Cuba has not had a single reported case of measles since 1993, nor rubella since 1989. Five cases of mumps have been reported since 2000; the last one was in 2010. And pertussis hasn't been

Rachel Browne, "What Cuba Can Teach Canada About Vaccines," *Maclean's*, 11 February 2014. Reproduced by permission of *Maclean's* Magazine.

reported since 1994. In contrast, Canada has had 2,203 cases of measles, at least 1,529 cases of mumps, and 21,292 cases of pertussis reported since 1990.

5   At a time when new cases of preventable diseases are regularly cropping up and a loud—albeit small—contingent of "**anti-vaxxers**" keeps getting louder, it's a good time to figure out how to change those numbers.

6   Granted, Cuba's population is around one-third the size of Canada's, but Dr. Noni MacDonald, professor of paediatrics at Dalhousie University and consultant to the WHO's committee on vaccine safety, who went on the research trips with Kirk, says one of the most innovative aspects of its public health system is its emphasis on vaccine education from an early age—something that's lacking in Canada. From the time kids start school through to graduation, vaccination is consistently incorporated into courses and class discussions.

7   "Our schools need to be teaching about vaccines and immunizations and their importance to our health, starting in primary school," says MacDonald. "I don't want a course in **vaccinology**. I want the topic woven into the fabric of our curricula: into science, history and health." This might include discussing how military campaigns throughout history were brought down because of vaccine-preventable diseases or the outbreak of smallpox during the founding of Canada. She says this would be an effective way to prevent anti-vaccine ideology from makings its way into society in the future.

8   Kirk attributes Cuba's immunization successes to the higher number of doctors in the country and their deep relationships with community groups and the government. There is approximately one doctor for every 200 Cubans, compared to one doctor for every 476 Canadians. Cuba's Family Doctor and Nurse program, which started in 1984, lies at the heart of the country's health care system. Their mandate is geared toward preventive—instead of curative—medicine, as they cannot afford to treat illnesses as they come up. The program makes a point of meeting with patients twice a year and keeping meticulous immunization records. They are directly involved with education campaigns in schools, and students get a checkup every month. Kirk says this closeness with medical staff fosters trust and builds personal relationships between doctors and patients.

9   Just as important as the **primary care** providers, Cuba's community groups carry out directives from health authorities and follow up on vaccine schedules. For example, the Committees to Defend the Revolution and the Federation of Cuban Women, established in 1960 after the revolution, go into neighbourhoods on a regular basis to discuss legislation and government policies, and share news about personal and public health. Every year, the Federation of Cuban Women tracks down every baby to ensure he or she has been immunized.

10   MacDonald says it's unlikely such enforcement of immunizations would ever occur in Canada, but it shows the potential for community groups to shoulder some responsibility for public health outcomes and awareness, especially when Canada does not have a national vaccine registry. "Even if vaccines weren't mandatory, Cubans would do it anyway," she says. "Because they've been taught how to do it [and] they've been asked to participate in it, they've been asked to take pride in doing it."

11   For Eve Dubé, a medical anthropologist at Laval University studying vaccination ethics, Canada is a world leader in health services, but Health Canada could take a page from the Cubans on vaccine awareness. She is co-authoring a study on the vaccine choices of pregnant women in Canada, most of whom are choosing to vaccinate their children, but aren't fully confident in their choice—meaning they might change their minds as their children grow older. "What we see is that these mothers—whether they decide to vaccinate or not—are still unsure whether they've made the right decision," she says. "They are trusting friends, family members, even themselves, more than health care professionals." Dubé says it's not enough for parents to simply agree to get their children vaccinated; they need deeper understanding in order to prevent them from changing their minds or forgetting to keep immunizations up-to-date.

12   At home, Kirk says he has tried to get the province of Nova Scotia to consider implementing some aspects of the Cuban model, such as mandatory courses on health, but he isn't hopeful this will happen any time soon. A government minister told him the **optics** of doing so wouldn't be so great." He wondered how we, a province in a wealthy, developed country, could learn from a rinky-dinky communist country. But we need to do something soon. We've been looking at it through the wrong end of the telescope for too long and we're paying the price."

Glossary

dumbfounded: greatly shocked or astonished

anti-vaxxers: informal term used to refer to people in the anti-vaccination movement

vaccinology: the science or methodology of developing vaccines

primary care: the medical care received on first contact with the medical system (before being referred elsewhere)

optics: the way a situation looks to the general public

Comprehension Questions

1. What, in your own words, is the author's argument?

2. What are the statistical differences, according to the article, between Canada and Cuba in the area of infectious diseases?

3. How does Dr. Noni MacDonald view education on vaccination in Canada?

4. What is the difference between Canada and Cuba when it comes to prevention, and why?

5. Why does MacDonald think that Cubans would opt for immunization even if it weren't mandatory?

6. Why is Nova Scotia, and, by extension, Canada as a whole, slow to learn from Cuba despite the value of the education?

Questions about Form

1. The reading begins and ends with Nova Scotia. Why? Is this effective? Why or why not?

2. Who and what are the sources of information in this reading? What is the effect of these sources on the persuasive element of the reading? Will this effect be the same on all readers? Why or why not?

Questions for Discussion

1. What were your impressions of the Canadian healthcare system before reading this article? How have they changed, and what aspects of the article are responsible for these changes?

2. Do you agree with the author's argument? Why or why not?

3. Besides getting immunized, should Canadians be as knowledgeable as the Cubans about the details of immunization?

4. Should people be allowed to say no to immunization? Does their decision affect only them, or does it also endanger society?

Writing Ideas

1. Should vaccines be mandatory, or should they be an individual choice? Support your answer with reasons in either a paragraph or an essay.

2. Is there a strong case, as Dr. Noni MacDonald argues, for integrating teaching about vaccines and immunization into the school curriculum? Include reasons in support of your answer in a paragraph or essay.

3. Why is it important for the Canadian government to promote preventative care? Write a paragraph or essay in which you support your answer with reasons.

4. What can the Canadian government do to promote preventive care? Include in a paragraph or essay a discussion on incentives to the corporate sector for subsidized gym memberships.

✦ ✦ ✦

Banning Junk Food

Leah McLaren

Obesity is a problem in Canada—this is indisputable. But how far should the war against obesity go before it starts to cause new problems? This piece, published in the *Globe and Mail* on September 18, 2014, was written by Leah McLaren. It documents an example of the adverse effects when the war against obesity goes too far.

1   You may have heard of Keenan Shaw, the 17-year-old student at Winston Churchill High School in Lethbridge Alta., who got suspended this week for selling **contraband** soda pop on school property. This freckle-faced, glinty-eyed teenpreneur stocked his locker with a case of Pepsi, a beverage banned under the Lethbridge School District's new nutritional guidelines (only diet pop is allowed). Hawking his wares at an undisclosed markup, Shaw sold out in minutes and

Source: Leah Mclaren, "Does banning junk food make it more alluring to kids," *The Globe and Mail* (19 September 2014). Reprinted by permission of the author.

pocketed a tidy profit, only to pour it into more cases of pop, which he promptly sold the following day.

2   School administrators didn't think his enterprising scheme was so sweet. They gave Shaw a warning, and when he refused to heed it, they suspended him. "I thought it was a joke. I didn't know they could suspend me for selling pop," Shaw complained to a reporter after the fact. His mother was also indignant, saying that while she understood the need for rules, suspension seemed a bit harsh. Besides, she liked the idea of her son "being an entrepreneur."

3   Bracketing for a moment the fact that actively praising your child in public for selling banned substances probably isn't the wisest parenting strategy, let's look at what's actually going on here. For as long as I can remember, high school cafeterias were essentially the nutritional equivalent of a **red light district**—scary buffets of Tater Tots, gravy fries and quivering Jello bowls, with an obligatory platter of overripe, untouched fruit at the cash register.

4   Things are much better now, in the post-Jamie Oliver school-lunch age. For one thing, schools these days have "nutritional guidelines," and they actually pay attention to what kids are eating. With any luck, this means offering students food that might be good for them, or even culturally interesting, as opposed to providing them nothing but processed crap.

5   Look, I'm all for sustainable-fish curry and quinoa in schools (what self-respecting **bourgeois** mother wouldn't be?). But I do get unnerved when I hear about certain foods being "banned" on school property. This is because I grew up in a house where junk food was **anathema**. There was a single tin of heart-shaped spelt ginger snaps my mother kept on top of the fridge and my sister and I were allowed one each after dinner, but that was basically it. Even our peanut butter was the oily health food store kind that came from a grinder.

6   As a result, I spent most of my late childhood obsessed with sweets. I'd comb the sofa cushions for spare change and sneak off school property at lunch hour to buy candy at the corner store. Back at school, I'd lock myself in a bathroom cubicle and feast on gummy worms and Fizz Whiz until my brain tingled with a glucose rush. My friend Amy, who had a candy dish on her coffee table (always full!) and pop in her fridge, thought my obsession was weird. "Why don't you just come to my house after school and have a Sprite? We get it in club packs from Costco," she'd say. And I did. But for me, that wasn't the point. Sugar was verboten, so the pleasure was all in the sneaking.

7   (This) brings us back to the **enterprising** young Shaw and his Lethbridge soda-pop racket. Is it actually possible that Winston Churchill High is to blame for creating the market that led Shaw to his entrepreneurial heights in the first place? By banning bad food, do we make it more alluring to our children, not less?

8   Not necessarily, says my old friend Ceri Marsh, co-author of *How to Feed a Family,* a book based on the popular cooking-with-kids blog Sweet Potato Chronicles. In her view, bans on junk food in schools should be mandatory—like seatbelts and smoking laws. "It's no exaggeration to say that when it comes to the dietary health of North American youth, we are in the middle of an outright crisis," she says. "Sodas and garbage food are hugely to blame for that. Kids can get them, and they will get them. They just shouldn't be able to get them at school."

9   Part of the problem, Marsh explains, is that we live in a culture that, for half a century or more, has normalized fast food and candy as regular stuff to eat. "Instead, we should be teaching our kids to be more discerning, to actually enjoy and be interested in real food that tastes good—and to see junk as a very, very occasional treat."

10   The numbers are well-known but still startling: A third of Canada's five- to 17-year-olds are "identified as overweight or obese," according to Statscan. So proponents say schools have to be part of the solution. Dr. Yoni Freedhoff, founder of Ottawa's Bariatric Medical Institute, told the *Globe* that research, including a 2010 study published in the *New England Journal of Medicine,* showed school-based programs can reduce child obesity rates.

11   I agree in theory, but I wonder about the execution. One major problem with a junk-food ban is it's not always clear which treats should be classified as "bad" and which are okay for our kids to consume. I know plenty of parents who would much rather see their kids drink an occasional sugary drink than a diet one filled with artificial sweeteners.

12   What we should be working toward is a culture in which junk food is understood to be unhealthy, but is neither glorified nor demonized. A world in which enterprising opportunists like Keenan Shaw simply wouldn't be able to find much of a market.

Glossary

contraband: anything smuggled, imported, or exported illegally

red light district: an area containing sex workers and their clients

bourgeois: of or pertaining to the middle class and its materialistic values and conventional attitudes—often derogatory

anathema: a detested thing

enterprising: imaginative and/or energetic; resourceful

Comprehension Questions

1. What, in your own words, is the thesis of this piece?

2. Why was Keenan Shaw suspended?

3. What does the author mean in paragraph 3 by "the nutritional equivalent of a red light district"?

4. Does the author think junk food should be banned? Why or why not?

5. What story does the author tell about when she was a child?

Questions about Form

1. Why does the author start and end her article with the case of Keenan Shaw? Is this effective, and why or why not?

2. What is the function of the last paragraph in this reading? What would you suggest as an alternative?

Questions for Discussion

1. The author says in the last paragraph that what we should be striving for is "a world in which enterprising opportunists like Keenan Shaw simply wouldn't be able to find much of a market." What, specifically, would have to change for such a world to exist?

2. Some parents believe that to be good parents, they have to praise their children for everything they do, even if it's bad, such as selling banned substances. What is behind this approach to raising children? Do you support it or not? Give reasons for your answer.

3. What might have prevented the kind of extreme behaviour that the author recalls in paragraph 6?

Writing Ideas

1. In a paragraph or essay, explain how a parent should approach the whole issue of food in the house to achieve a healthy balance. Add examples in support of your points.

2. In a paragraph or essay, discuss what schools should do to create an atmosphere of a healthy balance so that students like Keenan Shaw are not encouraged to set up shop. Include examples that support your argument.

◆ ◆ ◆

Face to Face

Brian Bethune

We all love our cellphones. What would we do without them? But is it possible that they are responsible for our loss of trust in people? And when the trust is gone, what's left? Brian Bethune's piece suggests we should pause and examine our lives in light of this technology and its effects on our social interaction. His article was first published in *Maclean's* magazine on September 1, 2014.

1   Susan Pinker knows as well as anyone what's been won and what's been lost in the modern era of personal mobility and global connections. "Our digital devices are fabulous for gaining information, for scheduling our lives, for reaching the

Brian Bethune, "How Face-to-Face Contact Makes Us Happier," *Maclean's*, 1 September 2014. Reproduced by permission of *Maclean's* Magazine.

people we want and avoiding the people we detest," says the Montreal-based developmental psychologist and author of *The Village Effect: How Face-to-Face Contact Can Make Us Healthier and Happier*, in an interview. "But those digital devices have not been good for human relationships, because they cannot **engender** trust."

2   That trust is what we need, Pinker argues in her narrative-rich book. She ranges over poll results and new medical research, mostly concentrated in North America but with a detour to isolated Sardinian mountain villages, where men—who, on worldwide average, die five to seven years before women—live to 100 at a rate 10 times that of just about anywhere else. The secret to that longevity, she concludes, is the same as the cost: The old men, socially wealthy and surrounded by constant (mostly female) attention, "were impossible to meet alone," she says, "because they never were." While there were undeniable health benefits for both, the way in which lives—mostly younger and female—were dedicated to the care of the elderly is virtually **anathema** in the modern West, where fostering independence is a primary parental goal.

3   We have less of that village-level contact now than we ever did, because that's the way we want it, but also, Pinker asserts, because "we have been making trade-offs we haven't understood." Even when people begin to recognize the physical and psychological cost of increasing isolation, they are dangerously prone to thinking their new online relationships replace in-person ones. They do not: The benefits humans derive from close interaction—the empathy, the understanding, the firing of mirror neurons that cause us to **mimic** to whom we are speaking, and the trust all that creates—require "being in the same room," Pinker says. Adding to the problem, "surveys show that highly social people use their digital connections to **buttress** their live ones, while less social people—introverts and the shy—use them to avoid personal encounters." The socially rich, in other words, are getting richer and the poor poorer.

4   The situation mirrors the way we were once fitter—or, at least, leaner—when everyday life required more physical effort, in everything from shovelling coal into the furnace to running a wringer washer. Now we have to schedule physical exercise for its own sake. In the same manner, our social structures used to force more interaction with others upon us, except, Pinker believes, we don't grasp the **social deficit** the way we noticed the lack of exercise. "Everybody gets into

a funk sometimes. Does anybody wonder, 'Maybe I haven't had enough social contact?' That's the main reason I wrote the book, to ask why we aren't making a big deal of this."

5   Pinker doesn't just describe the "big deal," as she puts it; she doesn't hesitate to suggest solutions, starting with her own. "There's no way you can do this sort of research for four years without it affecting you. I joined a swim team for the collegiality, for what we **disparage**—and we shouldn't, because it's important—as water-cooler talk. Now I'm in a locker room with 25 other women gossiping, talking about their families or great new restaurants." People need to make an effort now to engage with others and, crucially, to keep refilling gaps in their networks as they age. "It's like a perennial garden; every spring, you find you've lost a few plants, and you have to fill in those spaces."

6   Like many other contemporary thinkers who are not devout themselves, Pinker is strongly interested in religion. **Secular-minded** social scientists don't think much of belief or the power of prayer, but they are impressed by the benefits of community: A seven-year study of 90,000 women from across the U.S. found that those who attended religious services at least once a week were 20 per cent more likely to have longer lifespans. Small wonder there are increasing attempts to establish atheist churches to reap the same benefits of community and comforting ritual. In 2012, British philosopher Alain de Botton published *Religion for Atheists*, to convince his fellow atheists that religions should not "be abandoned simply to those who believe in them." As much as the gathering itself, Pinker emphasizes the physical **synchrony** of religious practice, the way "praying, chanting, singing, swaying and rocking all together" is "brain-soothing," even for non-believers.

7   Church service or team swimming might not do for everyone, Pinker allows, but something will. And we need to go out and find that real social interaction, just as "every day, we eat." It's a matter of life or death.

Glossary

engender: bring about

anathema: a detested thing or person

mimic: imitate

buttress: provide with support

social deficit: an inability or unwillingness to act in accordance with one's age, physical condition, and/or intelligence

disparage: regard to be of little worth; belittle

secular-minded: believing that religion should not be involved in the organization of society or education

synchrony: simultaneous action

Comprehension Questions

1. What is the thesis, in your own words, of this piece?

2. What are the benefits of electronic communication, according to the author?

3. What does the author say is missing from electronic communication? Why is it missing?

4. At the end of paragraph 3, the author writes, "The socially rich, in other words, are getting richer and the poor poorer." What does this mean?

5. According to the author, what is the relationship between convenience and happiness? Is the answer the one you expected? If not, why is this so?

6. How does the issue of fitness relate to the issue of electronic communication, according to the author?

Questions about Form

1. In paragraph 1, "face-to-face" is hyphenated in the title of the book cited. But in the title of this reading, it is not. Why?

2. In your opinion, how effective is the title of the piece? Does the title contain a double meaning? Explain.

Questions for Discussion

1. Discuss a situation in which communication took place electronically, but could have been more effective if it had been done "face to face." What was missing?

2. If electronic communication does not "engender trust," what effect might continuous communication of this type have on society?

Writing Ideas

1. What can people do to make sure their electronic communication engender more trust? Discuss the possibilities in a paragraph or an essay. Add examples in support of your points.

2. What can an individual do to reduce the amount of electronic communication and increase the amount of face-to-face contact in his or her own life? Provide specific examples in support of your points in a paragraph or essay.

✦ ✦ ✦

Canada Must Do More

David Suzuki and Ian Hanington

You would think that by now, after years of discussions of global warming at the highest levels of government all over the world, we would be well on our way to saving the planet. Not so, say many scientists. In fact, Canada, one of the richest nations on earth, has a record that some would call globally embarrassing. David Suzuki, with contributions from senior editor of *Science Matters* Ian Hanington, based the following article on a report from Canada's Commissioner of the Environment and Sustainable Development. It was first published on October 14, 2014.

Article reprinted from "Commissioner's Report Shows Canada Must Do More for the Environment," by David Suzuki. Reprinted with permission from the David Suzuki Foundation via Greystone Books.

1　Canadians expect to have our environment protected, and to know how it's being protected. A report from Canada's Commissioner of the Environment and Sustainable Development shows we're being **short-changed.**

2　"In many key areas that we looked at, it is not clear how the government intends to address the significant environmental challenges that future growth and development will likely bring about," commissioner Julie Gelfand said of the report, which used government data, or lack thereof, to assess the government's success or failure to implement its own regulations and policies.

3　Among other things, the report concludes Canada is not on track to meet its greenhouse gas emissions targets, has delayed monitoring of **oil sands** pollutants and lacks plans to monitor the oil sands beyond next year, and has no clear guidelines regarding what projects require environmental assessments. On top of that, the government has been promising oil and gas sector emission regulations since 2006, but has yet to release them. It claims new regulatory proposals were completed a year ago, but the report finds those are based on consultation only with "one province and selected industry representatives" — all unnamed. The oil and gas industry is Canada's fastest-growing source of emissions, especially the oil sands.

4　The report also found government reporting on emissions to be misleading, especially in not giving due credit. For example, what little progress has been made in reducing Canada's **greenhouse gas** emissions comes mainly from Ontario's move to shut down its coal-powered generators. And total emissions continue to rise. "There's no overall plan, national plan, for how we're going to achieve our target," Gelfand told reporters at a news conference. "And climate change is affecting all Canadians." She also noted the federal committee responsible for the climate plan hasn't met in three years.

5　Although government has a "Northern Strategy," the commissioner found surveying and the capacity to make charts of the Arctic are inadequate and that icebreaking services have decreased, while vessel traffic has increased. Considering the profound changes from global warming in the north, this is serious.

6　Sadly, the inability of governments to deal with climate change is neither just national, nor recent. We've been saddled with government **indolence** on climate and pollution for far too long, and in far too many places around the world. But Canada has been singled out for getting in the way of progress at global climate negotiations, and we're the only country to have pulled out of the legally binding **Kyoto Protocol**. In rejecting the notion of proven methods to reduce emissions through **carbon pricing**, our prime minister said, "No matter what they say, no country is going to take actions that are going to deliberately destroy jobs and growth in their country."

7　But evidence from around the world shows numerous economic benefits from acting on climate change, while failing to act comes with massive and increasing costs, including to human health and well-being. The idea that we should base our economic progress on digging up and selling our resources — from coal to liquefied natural gas to oil sands **bitumen** — as quickly as possible is absurd.

Even if we ignore pollution and global warming, wasting these valuable resources borrows from our children and grandchildren and leaves them nothing in return.

8   Everywhere, people are demanding change. More than 300,000 attended the People's Climate March in New York in September, with many more joining scores of solidarity marches in cities around the world. A growing number of business leaders and global organizations, including the World Bank and International Monetary Fund, are calling for carbon pricing through carbon taxes or cap-and-trade systems to help address the crisis. Religious leaders, including the Pope and Desmond Tutu, have joined scientists and scientific organizations from every continent to demand action.

9   During the David Suzuki Foundation's cross-country Blue Dot Tour, I've heard from countless Canadians who are doing their part to protect the air, water, soil and biological diversity that keep us alive and healthy. They expect our elected representatives to do the same.

10   As the environment commissioner said of the government's inability to meet its own targets, "When you make a commitment, you need to keep it." That's especially true when it comes to global warming, the most serious challenge our species has faced.

Glossary

short-changed: cheated accidentally or intentionally

oil sands: deposits of loose sand saturated with highly glutinous tar (Oil recovered from tar sands is often referred to as synthetic crude.)

greenhouse gas: contributes to the greenhouse effect, which is the heating of the earth's surface and lower atmosphere

indolence: laziness

Kyoto Protocol: international treaty designed to reduce gas emissions that contribute to global warming

carbon pricing: one method for reducing global-warming emissions by charging those who emit carbon dioxide (CO_2) for their emissions

bitumen: any of various flammable mixtures of hydrocarbons and other substances found in asphalt and tar

Comprehension Questions

1.   What, in your own words, is the author's thesis?

2.   What evidence is used to support the author's claim?

3.   How did former prime minister Stephen Harper respond to the notion of carbon pricing as a strategy for reducing emissions?

4.   According to the authors, who is demanding change?

Questions about Form

1.   What are the similarities between the first and last paragraphs? What's different, and why?

2. The byline contains two names in it, so why is *I* used in the reading? To whom does it probably refer? Why?

Questions for Discussion

1. In paragraph 6, former prime minister Stephen Harper is quoted as saying, "No matter what they say, no country is going to take actions that are going to deliberately destroy jobs and growth in their country." Is this a reasonable defense against the accusation that the government is not doing enough for the environment?

2. With respect to the quotation above, did the former prime minister feel differently about jobs in the sex trade? Why did he feel one way toward the tar sands and another toward the sex trade?

3. When the government is blamed for putting the environment at risk, what effect does this have on the country's youth and their behaviour? Discuss.

4. What difference does it make when religious leaders join scientists in the fight to effect environmental change? Why is it still so difficult to get everyone on board?

Writing Ideas

1. Why are some governments more likely to take steps to protect the environment while others are not? In a paragraph or essay, answer this question and support your answer with at least one reference to the reading.

2. Using the reading and other ideas you might have, what are three things that the Government of Canada should do to help reduce global warming? Support your points in a paragraph or essay, using concrete examples where possible.

Unit VI **Appendices**

merzzie/shutterstock.com

Appendix A   Distinguishing between Words Often Confused

Words That Sound Alike

allowed (*verb*)   permitted
aloud (*adv.*)   out loud

> Examples:
> The boy was finally allowed to stay up late.
> Her question was stated aloud for all to hear.

altar (*noun*)   an elevated place or table for religious rites
alter (*verb*)   to change or adjust

> Examples:
> The altar was decorated for the church service.
> If you alter the plans, they won't work out.

a part (*noun*)   a piece of something that forms the whole of something
apart (*adverb*)   separately; into pieces

> Examples:
> They did everything to become a part of their children's lives.
> The baby ripped the box apart.

aural (*adj.*)   having to do with the ear or hearing
oral (*adj.*)   having to do with the mouth or speech

> Examples:
> I have poor aural skills because I won't listen.
> The history of the First Nations is kept alive through their oral traditions.

brake (*verb*)   to stop

       (*noun*)   a device used for slowing or stopping

break (*verb*)   to smash, crack, or come apart

       (*noun*)   a crack, severing; an interruption, change

> Examples:
> Apply the brake when you want to stop.
> You'll have to break the lock to get in.
> Give me a break!

capital (*adj.*)   chief; major; fatal

       (*noun*)   leading city; money

capitol (*noun*)   a building in which a U.S. state legislature assembles

> Examples:
> Ottawa is the capital of Canada.
> The capitol building for the New York state legislature is in Albany.

chord (*noun*)   three or more musical tones sounded together; harmony

cord (*noun*)   a small rope of twisted strands; any ropelike structure; a unit of cut fuel wood

> Examples:
> Many guitar chords are easy to play.
> A strong cord is needed to tie the bundle together.

close (*verb*)   to shut

clothes (*noun*)   garments

cloth (*noun*)   fabric; a piece of material

> Examples:
> Close the door and keep the cold out.
> T-shirts are our favourite type of summer clothes.
> His coat was made of cloth, not leather.

coarse (*adj.*)   rough; not fine; common or of inferior quality

course (*noun*)   direction or path of something moving; part of a meal; a school subject

> Examples:
> Coarse sandpaper is used to make a rough finish.
> One course I'm taking this year is English grammar.

complement (*noun*)   something that completes or makes up a whole

       (*verb*)   to complete; to supplement, enhance

compliment (*noun*)   an expression of praise

       (*verb*)   to give praise

complementary (*adj.*)   complementing, often completing a pair or group of things that go together

complimentary (*adj.*)   expressing a compliment; given free as a favour

fair (*adj.*)   unbiased; light colour; free of clouds; promising; lovely

   (*noun*)   an exhibition; regional event; market

fare (*noun*)   a charge for transportation; food

   (*verb*)   get along; do

flour (*noun*)   the powder produced by grinding a grain

flower (*noun*)   a blossom of a plant

   (*verb*)   to blossom

for (*prep.*)   directed to; in the amount of; on behalf of; to the extent of

   (*conj.*)   because

four (*noun, adj.*)   number

forty (*adj.*)   Notice that this number is spelled differently from *four, fourteen,* or *twenty-four.*

fore (*noun, adj.*)   situated near the front

forth (*adv.*)   onward in time, place, or order

fourth (*noun, adj.*)   number

forward (*verb*)	to send on to another address
(*adj.*)	bold; progressive
(*adv.*)	moving toward the front
foreword (*noun*)	introduction to a book; preface

Examples:
Move forward so you can hear the speaker.
The foreword to a book is sometimes called the preface.

grate (*verb*)	to shred; to annoy or irritate
(*noun*)	a metal grill
grateful (*adj.*)	appreciative
great (*adj.*)	large; significant; excellent; powerful; skillful; first-rate

Examples:
Her negative attitude grates on my nerves.
Winning the prize was a great achievement.

| **it's** | contraction of *it is* |
| **its** | possessive form of *it* |

Examples:
It's a nice day today.
The bush has all of its new buds.

| **knew** (*verb*) | past tense *of know* |
| **new** (*adj.*) | not old |

Examples:
The student knew the correct answer.
His new car is this year's model.

know (*verb*)	to understand
no (*adv.*)	a negative response
(*adj.*)	not any; not one

Examples:
You would know the work if you had studied.
Having no money means that you are poor.

| **pain** (*noun*) | suffering |
| **pane** (*noun*) | a panel of glass |

Examples:
A cut finger can cause a great deal of pain.
Windows contain panes of glass.

passed (*verb*)		the past tense of to pass—to move ahead
past (*noun*)		time before the present
	(*prep.*)	beyond
	(*adj.*)	no longer current

> **Examples:**
> I passed the exam and moved to the next grade.
> I was past the exit before I noticed that I had missed it.

patience (*noun*)	calm endurance; tolerant understanding
patients (*noun*)	persons under medical treatment

> **Examples:**
> Waiting for someone usually takes patience.
> Patients in hospitals often are very ill.

peace (*noun*)	absence of war, calm
piece (*noun*)	a portion, a part

> **Examples:**
> Peace came when the war was over.
> His piece of cake was huge.

plain (*adj.*)		simple; ordinary; unattractive; clear
	(*noun*)	a flat, treeless land region
plane (*noun*)		an aircraft; a flat, level surface; a carpenter's tool for levelling wood; a level of development

> **Examples:**
> The flat plain stretched for miles without a tree.
> I used a plane to make the wood smooth.

presence (*noun*)		the state of being present; a person's manner
presents (*noun*)		gifts
	(*verb*)	(third person singular) to introduce; to give a gift

> **Examples:**
> The presence of the teacher kept the students quiet.
> Presents are given on birthdays.

principal (*adj.*)		most important; chief; main
	(*noun*)	the head of a school; a sum of money
principle (*noun*)		rule or standard

> **Examples:**
> The principal rule is the most important guideline.
> There are principles of conduct to be followed at school.

rain (*noun, verb*)	water falling to earth in drops
reign (*noun, verb*)	a period of rule for a king or queen
rein (*noun*)	a strap attached to a bridle, used to control a horse

raise (*verb*)	to move upward; to awaken; to increase; to collect
(*noun*)	an increase in salary
rays (*noun*)	thin lines or beams of radiation
raze (*verb*)	to tear down or demolish

Examples:

A raise in pay often rewards good work.

The sun's rays contain harmful radiation.

The old building was razed to the ground.

sight (*noun*)	the ability to see; a view
site (*noun*)	the plot of land where something is located; the place of an event
cite (*verb*)	to quote as an authority or example

Examples:

Some people with perfect sight don't see clearly.

The opera house's site is between two theatres.

I can cite my grammar text as my authority.

| **stair** (*noun*) | one of a flight of steps |
| **stare** (*noun, verb*) | a fixed gaze; to look at insistently |

Examples:

Each stair climbed brings you farther up the steps.

A steady gaze can be considered a stare.

stake (*noun*)	a post sharpened at one end to drive into the ground; an interest or concern, especially but not restricted to financial
(*verb*)	to attach or support; to set limits with a stake
steak (*noun*)	a cut of meat, usually beef

Examples:

My stake in the profits amounted to a quarter share.

I like my steak well done and thick.

| **stationary** (*adj.*) | standing still |
| **stationery** (*noun*) | writing paper and envelopes |

Examples:

Anything that is stationary does not move.

Stationery can be written upon.

they're	contraction of *they are*
their	possessive
there	at that place

Examples:
They're a happy couple.
This antique is their prized possession.
I'll meet you over there, behind the store.

to (*prep.*)	in a direction toward
to (+ *verb*)	the infinitive form of a verb
too (*adv.*)	also; excessively; very
two (*noun*)	number

Examples:
Go to school.
To see is to believe.
I, too, am going to the party.
Two is one more than one.

vain (*adj.*)	conceited; unsuccessful
vane (*noun*)	a plate of wood or metal, often in the shape of a rooster, that pivots to indicate the direction of the wind; the weblike part of a feather
vein (*noun*)	a blood vessel; the branching framework of a leaf; an occurrence of an ore; a strip of colour; a streak; a transient attitude

Examples:
A vain person spends much time in front of a mirror.
The vane on the roof tells the wind direction.
Veins in your body contain blood.

waist (*noun*)	the middle portion of a body, garment, or object
waste (*verb*)	to use thoughtlessly or carelessly
(*noun*)	objects discarded as useless

Examples:
A belt around your waist holds your pants up.
Excess packaging contains much waste.

wait (*verb*)	to remain inactive
weight (*noun*)	the measure of the heaviness of an object

Examples:
Remain here and wait for my arrival.
My weight goes up every time I eat.

ware (*noun*)	an article of commerce	
wear (*verb*)	to have on	
(*noun*)	deterioration as a result of use	
where (*adv.*)	at or in what place	

Examples:
You can sell your wares at the flea market.
What clothes will you wear?
He asked where the museum could be found.

weather (*noun*)	atmospheric conditions
whether (*conj.*)	if it is the case that

Examples:
The weather report calls for rain.
She will go whether I go or not.

whole (*adj.*)	complete
hole (*noun*)	an opening

Examples:
A pie is whole before it is sliced and served.
Holes in the road need to be filled in.

who's	contraction of *who is*
whose	possessive

Examples:
Who's going for pizza?
Whose garbage can is blocking the driveway?

wood (*noun*)	the tough tissue from trees
would (*verb*)	past tense of *will*

Examples:
Most paper is made from wood fibre.
He would go, he said, if he could find a ride.

write (*verb*)	to form letters and words; to compose
right (*adj.*)	conforming to justice, law, or morality; correct; toward a conservative political point of view
(*noun*)	that which is just, morally good, legal, or proper; a direction; a political group whose policies are conservative
(*adv.*)	directly; well; completely; immediately
rite (*noun*)	a traditional, solemn, and often religious ceremony

> Examples:
> Write a letter to your aunt.
> You should always try to do what is right.
> Last rites were said over the dying person.

yoke (*noun*)		a harness fastening two or more animals together; a form of bondage
yolk (*noun*)		the yellow of an egg

> Examples:
> Animals in a team are joined by a yoke.
> Some diners like their eggs cooked without the yolks broken.

you're		contraction of *you are*
your		possessive

> Examples:
> You're my best friend.
> Take your gift to the party.

Words That Sound or Look Almost Alike

Some words are often confused with other words that sound or look almost the same. Learning to spell these words correctly involves a careful study of pronunciations along with meanings.

	Pronunciation	**Meaning**
accept	*a* as in *pat*	*verb:* to receive; to admit; to regard as true or right
except	the first *e* as in *pet*	*prep.:* other than; but; only

> Examples:
> I accepted the parcel from the courier.
> Everyone was there except the two of us.

access	*a* as in *pat*	*noun:* a means of approaching; the right to enter or make use of
excess	the first *e* as in *pet*	*noun:* a quantity or amount beyond what is required

> Examples:
> Access to the files will provide you with information.
> Overeating is an unnecessary excess.

advice	Pronounce *-ice* like the word *ice*.	*noun:* opinion as to what should be done about a problem
advise	Pronounce *-ise* like *eyes*.	*verb:* to suggest; to counsel the word

Examples:

My best advice is to accept the offer.

I advise you to do what is right.

| affect | *a* as in *about* | *verb:* to influence |
| effect | the first *e* as the *e* in *pet* or *i* in *pit* | *noun:* result
verb: to bring about a result |

Examples:

I can affect his decision with my advice.

The effect of the rain was to cancel the game.

| allusion | *a* as in *about* | *noun:* an indirect reference |
| illusion | the first *i* as in *pit* | *noun:* a mistaken concept or belief |

Examples:

An allusion was made to my great intelligence.

It is an illusion to think you will get rich without working.

| breath | *ea* as the *e* in *pet* | *noun:* the air that is inhaled or exhaled in breathing |
| breathe | the *ea* as the *e* in *be* | *verb:* to inhale and exhale air |

Examples:

You can see your breath on the window on a cold day.

Breathe deeply and inhale the clean country air.

| clothes | *o* as the *oe* in *toe* | *noun:* garments; wearing apparel |
| cloths | *o* as the *aw* in *paw* | *noun:* pieces of fabric |

Examples:

The clothes you are wearing are fashionable.

Pieces of cloth can be torn from the fabric to make rags.

conscience	kŏn' shince (two syllables)	*noun:* recognition of right and wrong
conscientious	kŏn shē en' shəs (four syllables)	*adj.:* careful; thorough
conscious	kŏn' shəs (two syllables)	*adj.:* awake; aware of one's own existence

Examples:

My conscience told me to do the right thing.

I conscientiously performed my duty to the best of my ability.

She was conscious of the fact that he was behind her.

| costume | *o* as in *pot, u* as the *ou* in *you* | *noun:* a special style of dress for a particular occasion |
| custom | *u* as in *cut, o* as in *gallop* | *noun:* a common tradition |

Examples:

The costume he wore reflected his Ukrainian heritage.

It is our custom to wash our hands before eating.

council counsel	} *ou* as in *out*	*noun:* a group that governs *verb:* to give advice *noun:* a lawyer; advice
consul	*o* as in *pot*	*noun:* a governmental official in the foreign service

Examples:

The town council passed a bylaw.

Good counsel is advice well received.

Canada has a consul in many foreign countries.

desert	di zurt' *i* as in *pit*	*verb:* to abandon *noun:* something deserved (often plural)
	dez' ert the first *e* as in *pet*	*noun:* barren land
dessert	di zurt' *i* as in *pit*	*noun:* last part of a meal, often a sweet

Examples:

The desert is usually a hot, arid place.

He got his just deserts.

Our family usually eats dessert following dinner.

diner	*i* as the *ie* in *pie*	*noun:* a person eating dinner; a restaurant with a long counter and booths
dinner	*i* as in *pit*	*noun:* chief meal of the day

Examples:

A diner is a place where meals are served.

Dinner is usually eaten in the early evening.

emigrate emigrant	} *e* as in *pet*	*verb:* leave one's country or region to settle in another *noun:* someone who leaves a country to settle in another country
immigrate immigrant	} the first *i* as in *pit*	*verb:* to come into a country *noun:* someone who enters a country to settle there

Examples:

Many people decided to emigrate from Ireland during the famine.

Immigrants to our country bring valuable skills.

farther	*a* as in *father*	*adj., adv.:* greater physical or measurable distance
further	*u* as in *urge*	*adj., adv.:* greater mental distance; more distant in time or degree; additional

Examples:
Montreal is farther than Toronto from Windsor.
We drew further apart in our approach to the problem.

local	lo' kəl *a* as in *about*	*adj.:* relating or peculiar to a place
locale	lo kal' *a* as in *pat*	*noun:* a place, scene, or setting, as of a novel

Examples:
Everyone here goes to the local school on the next block.
Our town was the locale for a movie.

moral	mor' al *a* as in *about*	*adj.:* a sense of right and wrong *noun:* the lesson of a story, fable, or event
morale	mo ral' *a* as in *pat*	*noun:* the attitude or spirit of a person or group of people

Examples:
The moral of the story taught us never to cheat.
Their morale was shown by their enthusiasm for their jobs.

personal	per' son al	*adj.:* pertaining to a particular person
personnel	per son nel'	*noun:* the people employed by an organization; an administrative division of an organization concerned with the employees

Examples:
The matter is a personal one between him and me.
Most of the plant's personnel were laid off.

precede	the first *e* as the *i* in *pit*	*verb:* to come before
proceed	the *o* as the *oe* in *toe*	*verb:* to continue

Examples:
You go first and precede me down the hall.
Proceed with the story you started yesterday.

quiet	qui' et *i* as the *ie* in *pie*, *e* as in *pet*	*adj.:* silent *noun:* silence
quit	*i* as in *pit*	*verb:* to give up; to stop
quite	*i* as the *ie* in *pie;* the *e* is silent	*adv.:* somewhat; completely; truly

Examples:

It was a quiet night when no sound could be heard.

Quit what you are doing and start something else.

It is quite true that I am guilty.

receipt	the first *e* as the *i* in *pit*, *ei* as in the *e* in *be;* the *p* is silent	*noun:* a bill marked as paid; the act of receiving something
recipe	the first *e* as in *pet*, the *i* like the *a* in *about* the final *e* as in *be*	*noun:* a formula for preparing a mixture, especially in cooking

Examples:

The receipt for the dinner was marked "paid."

The recipe calls for more chocolate in the cookies.

special	spĕsh' əl	*adj.:* exceptional; distinctive
especially	Notice the extra syllable at the beginning.	*adv.:* particularly

Examples:

She was a special person, one of a kind.

It is especially important to file an income tax return.

than	*a* as in *pat*	*conj.:* used to make a comparison
then	*e* as in *pet*	*adv.:* at that time; in that case

Examples:

She is smarter than I am.

It was then that I made up my mind.

thorough	the first *o* as the *u* in *urge*, *ou* as the *oe* in *toe*	*adj.:* all that is needed; fully done
though	*ou* as the *oe* in *toe*	*conj.:* despite the fact
thought	*ou* as the *aw* in *paw*	*verb:* past tense of "to think"
through	*ou* as the *oo* in boot	*prep.* used to indicate entrance at one side and exit from the other; finished
threw	sounds like *through*	*verb:* past tense of "to throw"

Note: *Thru* is only an informal spelling for the word *through*. Do not use it in formal writing.

> Examples:
> The thorough investigation found a hidden clue.
> It's not true, though, that I told a lie.
> He thought of the answer before he spoke.
> Go through that exit to get outside.
> He threw the ball as far as he could.

Words That Sound or Look Almost Alike: *sit/set; rise/raise; lie/lay*

These six verbs are among the most troublesome in English because each is similar in sound, spelling, and meaning to another verb. Since they are all irregular verbs, students must be careful to learn to spell the principal parts correctly. The key to learning how to use the verbs *sit, rise,* and *lie* is to remember that these are actions the subject can do without any help; no other person or thing has to be included in the sentence. When you use the verbs *set, raise,* and *lay* in a sentence, the actions of these verbs are done to other persons or objects; these persons or things have to be included directly in the sentence. For example, when you use the verb *to sit,* all you need is a subject and a form of the verb:

I sit.

When you use the verb to *set*, however, you need a subject, a form of the verb, and an object.

I set the glass on the table.

The subject *I* and the verb *set* are followed by the object *glass,* which is what the subject set on the table.

sit:	to take a sitting position *never* takes an object	**set:**	to place something into position *always* takes an object
Present:	I *sit.*		I *set the glass* down.
Present participle:	I *am sitting.*		I *am setting the glass* down.
Past:	I *sat.*		I *set the glass* down.
Past participle:	I *have sat.*		I *have set the glass* down.
rise:	to stand up; to move upward *never* takes an object	**raise:**	to make something move up or grow; *always* takes an object
Present:	I *rise.*		I *raise the flag.*
Present participle:	The sun *is rising.*		I *am raising the flag.*
Past:	He *rose* at eight o'clock.		I *raised the flag.*
Past participle:	I *have risen early* today.		I *have raised the flag.*

The verbs *lie* and *lay* are easily confused because two of their principal parts have the same spelling. It takes concentration to learn to use these two verbs correctly.

	lie: to recline *never* takes an object	**lay:** to put; *always* takes an object
Present:	I *lie* down.	I *lay the pen down.*
Present participle:	I *am lying* down.	I *am laying the pen* down.
Past:	Yesterday I *lay* down.	I *laid the pen* down.
Past participle:	I *have lain* down.	I *have laid the pen* down.

The verb *lie* can also be a regular verb meaning "to tell an untruth." The principal parts of this verb are *lie, lying, lied, has lied*.

Words That Sound or Look Almost Alike: *choose/chose; lose/loose; lead/led; die/dye*

These verbs are often misspelled because there is confusion about how to spell the vowel sounds of the verbs. Study the spelling of the principal parts below.

Present	Present Participle	Past	Past Participle
choose	choosing	chose	has chosen
lose	losing	lost	has lost
lead	leading	led	has led
die	dying	died	has died

Notes:

- *Loose* is an adjective meaning "not tightly fitted." Remember, it rhymes with *goose.*
- *Lead* can also be a noun meaning a bluish-grey metal. Remember, it rhymes with *head.*
- *Dye* is another verb meaning "to colour." Its principal parts are *dye, dyeing, dyed, has dyed.*

Words That Sound or Look Almost Alike: *use/used; suppose/supposed*

To use means to bring or put into service; to make use of.

Present:	I *use* my brother's bike to get to school.
Past:	Yesterday, I *used* my father's car.

Use to means *to have as a custom* or *regular practice* in the past. It usually occurs in its past form, *used to:*

I *used to* take the bus downtown, but now I get a ride with my neighbour.

Note, however, that in expressions with the auxiliary *did*, you use the present form:

Did you *use to* take the bus?

A form of *to be* + *used* to means to be familiar with or accustomed to.

I *am used to* walking to school.

To suppose means *to guess*.

Present:	I *suppose* he is trying.
Past:	I *supposed* he was trying.

A form of *to be* + *supposed* to means ought to or should.

Waiters *are supposed to* be courteous.

Many people have difficulty knowing when to choose *used* and *supposed* in their writing because, in speaking, the final *d* is often not clearly heard.

Incorrect:	*I am suppose to be in school today.*
Correct:	*I am supposed to be in school today.*

Appendix B Answer Key to Practices

Unit I: Sentence Skills

Chapter 2: Recognizing Subjects and Verbs

Finding the Subject of a Sentence

PRACTICE 1 (p. 16)

1. The <u>plane</u> landed.
2. <u>Michelle Bates</u> gathered her bags.
3. <u>She</u> was so excited.
4. Strange <u>sounds</u> filled her ears.
5. A <u>mother</u> and her three <u>children</u> shared a lunch.
6. The battered red <u>taxi</u> idled outside.
7. A light <u>rain</u> had fallen recently.

Finding Hidden Subjects

PRACTICE 2 (p. 21)

1. (You) look at ~~a map of South America~~.
2. Where is the ancient <u>city</u> ~~of Chan Chan~~?
3. Here ~~on the coastal desert of northern Peru~~ stand the <u>remains</u> ~~of this city of the kings~~.
4. <u>Chan Chan</u>, ~~once the fabulously wealthy centre of the Chimor~~, is situated ~~in one of the driest, bleakest regions in the world~~.
5. <u>It</u> was the largest pre-Columbian city ~~in South America~~.
6. ~~In the ruins of this city~~, <u>scientists</u> have found fragments to piece together the mystery ~~of the past~~.
7. How could this <u>civilization</u> have survived this hostile environment and become so advanced?

Finding Action Verbs

PRACTICE 3 (p. 22)

1. Some <u>people</u> (collect) very strange objects. (present)
2. One <u>man</u> (saved) the fortunes ~~from fortune cookies~~. (past)
3. A <u>group</u> of people ~~in Alberta~~ often (met) to discuss their spark plug collections. (past)
4. <u>People</u> ~~in Brandon~~ (will gather) many types of ~~barbed wire~~. (future)
5. <u>Collectors</u> (take) pride ~~in the possession of unusual items~~. (present)
6. A <u>collection</u>, ~~like odd rocks or unique automobiles~~, (will let) a person express his or her individuality. (future)
7. <u>Collections</u> (keep) us entertained ~~from childhood to old age~~. (present)

Chapter Review Exercises

Finding Subjects and Verbs in Simple Sentences

PRACTICE 4 (p. 25)

1. <u>Mother</u> and <u>Dad</u> always (blame) me ~~for any trouble with my sister~~.
2. My <u>sister</u>, ~~the most popular girl in her class~~, (is) two years older than I.
3. Yesterday, ~~for instance~~, <u>she</u> (was trying on) her new graduation dress.
4. Helpfully, <u>I</u> (took out) her new shoes and purse ~~for her~~.

5. <u>Margaret</u> instantly (became) furious ~~with me.~~
6. I (was) only (sharing) Margaret's excitement ~~about her new clothes.~~

Chapter 3: Solving Verb Problems

Correcting Unnecessary Shifts in Verb Tense

PRACTICE 1 (p. 33)

Answers will vary. These are sample answers.

1. After I complete that writing course, I will take the required history course.
2. In the beginning of the movie, the action was slow; by the end, I was sitting on the edge of my seat.
3. The textbook gives the rules for writing a works cited page, but it doesn't explain how to use parenthetical references.
4. I was walking in the park when all of a sudden I saw her running toward me.
5. The encyclopedia gave several pages of information about astronomy, but it didn't give anything about black holes.
6. The invitation requested that Juan be at the ceremony and that he attend the banquet as well.
7. That website gives you excellent information, but it is too cluttered.

PRACTICE 2 (pp. 33–34)

Doctor Norman Bethune <u>grew</u> up in Gravenhurst, Ontario. He was educated in Toronto and <u>served</u> as a stretcher bearer in World War I. He contracted tuberculosis and thereafter <u>devoted</u> himself to helping other victims of the disease when he <u>practised</u> surgery in Montreal. He also <u>invented</u> or redesigned twelve medical and surgical instruments. Bethune travelled to Russia in 1935, joined the Communist Party, and <u>went</u> to Spain in 1936, where he organized the first mobile blood transfusion service during the Spanish Civil War. After returning to Canada, he shortly left for overseas again, this time to China, where he helped the Chinese Communists in their fight against Japan. "Spain and China," he <u>wrote,</u> "are part of the same battle." While there, he contracted an infection and died. Mao's essay "In Memory of Norman Bethune," prescribed reading during China's Cultural Revolution, urges all Communists to follow Bethune's example of

selfless dedication to others. Bethune is the best-known Canadian to the Chinese, and many Chinese visit his Canadian birthplace.

Using the Correct Tense

PRACTICE 3 (p. 35)

1. have stopped
2. would have
3. will buy
4. had never been
5. liked
6. will soon be
7. is

Choosing the Right Voice

PRACTICE 4 (p. 40)

1. The Canadian health minister made no policy or funding announcements at the International AIDS Conference in Toronto.
   The active is more appropriate. Others did make policy announcements. Knowing who didn't is important.
2. Microsoft founder Bill Gates gave $650 million (U.S.) to the war against HIV/AIDS.
   The passive is probably just as appropriate as the active here. Bill Gates is famous throughout the world, but the amount that he gave is extraordinary, also.
3. Zimbabwe's foreign minister was allowed into Canada for the international conference despite a ban on visits by senior officials from that country.
   The passive is more appropriate. The doer of the action would be Canadian authorities—too insignificant to even mention. The subject in this sentence, Zimbabwe's foreign minister, is the centre of the controversy here.
4. Former U.S. president Bill Clinton told the audience that a lot of mistakes were made during his presidency, but underfunding AIDS research was not one of them.
   The active is more appropriate. Former U.S. President Bill Clinton is more well known than anyone at this conference, even Bill Gates.

5. Twenty-two thousand delegates and 8000 journalists, exhibitors, volunteers, and staff attended the International AIDS Conference in Toronto in 2006.

   Both active and passive are equally appropriate. The number of attendees is massive, but the event itself is worthy of attention.

6. Many at the conference discussed in great detail the impact that poverty has on HIV and AIDS in developing countries.

   The passive is more appropriate. The topic of discussion is more important than the general population that discussed it. Also, the sentence using active voice above sounds awkward.

7. The importance of the role of media in spreading the word about HIV/AIDS was stressed by actor and activist Richard Gere.

   The active voice is more appropriate. Richard Gere is a celebrity activist. What he said matters less than the fact that he is at the conference in the first place.

Chapter Review Exercises

Solving Problems with Verbs

PRACTICE 5 (p. 42)

1. He ought not to drive so fast. *or* He shouldn't drive so fast.
2. It is essential that Lynn take her dog to the vet.
3. I wish I were a chef.
4. She sang for a huge crowd Saturday night.
5. I was shaken up by the accident. *or* The accident shook me up.
6. The skiers climbed the hill.
7. My father asked me last night to help him build a deck.

Chapter 4: Subject-Verb Agreement

Making the Subject and Verb Agree

PRACTICE 1 (p. 45)

1. cycles
2. amazes
3. vary
4. cheer
5. hope

PRACTICE 2 (p. 46)

1. are
2. move
3. move
4. are
5. are

PRACTICE 3 (p. 47)

1. is
2. has
3. is
4. specifies
5. is
6. are
7. is

PRACTICE 4 (p. 48)

1. is
2. was
3. seem
4. takes
5. has

PRACTICE 5 (p. 48)

1. are
2. is
3. are
4. are
5. is

PRACTICE 6 (p. 49)

1. are
2. are
3. has
4. have
5. claps

PRACTICE 7 (pp. 49–50)

1. do
2. were
3. does
4. do
5. were

Chapter Review Exercises

Making the Subject and Verb Agree

PRACTICE 8 (p. 50)

1. doesn't
2. were
3. doesn't
4. Were
5. doesn't

PRACTICE 9 (p. 50)

1. price, has
2. decision, requires
3. She, doesn't
4. guide or security guard, sees
5. committee, agrees
6. Potato chips and cola, are
7. One, is

Chapter 5: Coordination and Subordination

Recognizing the Comma and Coordinating Conjunction

PRACTICE 1 (pp. 55–56)

1. The <u>audience</u> <u>was packed</u> into the room (, for) this <u>was</u> a man with an international reputation.
2. <u>He</u> <u>could have told</u> about all his successes (, but) instead <u>he</u> <u>spoke</u> about his disappointments.
3. His <u>words</u> <u>were</u> electric (, so) the <u>crowd</u> <u>was</u> attentive.
4. <u>I</u> <u>should have brought</u> a tape recorder (, or) at least <u>I</u> <u>should have taken</u> notes.

Recognizing the Semicolon, Adverbial Conjunction, and Comma

PRACTICE 2 (pp. 58–59)

1. The <u>restaurant</u> <u>is</u> always too crowded on Saturdays (; nevertheless,) <u>it</u> <u>serves</u> the best food in town.
2. The <u>land</u> <u>was</u> not for sale (; however,) the <u>house</u> <u>could be rented</u>.
3. The <u>lawsuit</u> <u>cost</u> the company several million dollars (; consequently,) the <u>company</u> <u>went</u> out of business a short time later.
4. The <u>doctor</u> <u>told</u> him to lose weight (; furthermore,) <u>she</u> <u>insisted</u> he also stop smoking.

Combining Sentences Using Adverbial Conjunctions

PRACTICE 3 (pp. 59–60)

Answers will vary. These are sample answers.

1. People once preferred to write with a pen or pencil; however, the computer has now become a favourite writing tool.
2. Computers provide a powerful way to create and store pieces of writing; furthermore, they make the editing process fast and efficient.
3. Computers have revolutionized today's offices; consequently, no modern business is without them.
4. Computers have become relatively inexpensive; accordingly, most people own a computer.
5. Many children know more about computers than many adults; moreover, many children are teaching adults how to operate computers.
6. Professional writers have become enthusiastic about the use of computers; nonetheless, there are still some writers who will use only a ballpoint pen.
7. We have many technological aids for writing; nevertheless, let us not forget that the source of all our ideas is the human brain.

Recognizing Dependent and Independent Clauses

PRACTICE 4 (pp. 64–65)

1. DC
2. DC
3. IC
4. DC
5. IC
6. DC
7. DC

Combining Sentences Using Subordination

PRACTICE 5 (p. 65)

Answers will vary. These are sample answers.

1. While he was eating breakfast, the results of the election came over the radio.
2. Simon gave up his plan to launch a dot-com company because he felt it was too risky.
3. I will see my teacher tonight, as she is speaking at the university this evening.

4. The designer hoped for a promotion, although not one person in the department was promoted last year.

5. Since the designer hoped for a promotion, she made sure all her work was done accurately and on time.

Combining Sentences Using a Relative Pronoun

PRACTICE 6 (p. 68)

Answers will vary. These are sample answers.

1. The chemistry lab that I attend is two hours long.
2. The student assistant who is standing by the door is very knowledgeable.
3. The equipment that was purchased last year will make possible some important new research.

Recognizing Restrictive and Nonrestrictive Clauses

PRACTICE 7 (p. 69)

1. Canada's first census, which was taken in 1667, showed 3215 non-Native inhabitants in 668 families.
2. Most of the families who lived near the St. Lawrence River were French Canadians.
3. By the time of Confederation, the population of the country had risen to 3 463 000, which was an increase of 1077 percent over 200 years.
4. If the population of Canada, which is about 30 000 000 persons now, increases by a similar percentage over the next 150 or so years, we'll have a population of 280 200 000 by the year 2167.
5. Where do you think we will we put everyone who lives in Canada then?

Chapter Review Exercises

Combining Sentences Using Coordination and Subordination

PRACTICE 8 (p. 71)

Answers will vary. This is a sample paragraph.

The wind is strong; the waves are choppy and growing larger. I paddle my kayak harder, but my arms are getting tired. As the energy drains from them, they grow limp and heavy. The other side of the harbour seems distant. The glow of the setting sun is behind me, spreading orange and purple fingers across the sky. The wall of rocks that lies offshore picks up the last light of the setting sun, becoming a silver beacon. I focus on that wall and paddle harder. The sea smashes against my bow, pushing me away from shore. As flecks of spray hit my face, I taste the salt on my lips. With that taste of the sea, the beauty of the sea and shore strikes me. I am distracted from my labour and absorbed by the world around me. As my kayak finally glides past the rocks to the sheltered beach beyond, I am exhilarated and exhausted.

Chapter 6: Correcting Fragments

Understanding Fragments

PRACTICE 1 (pp. 77–78)

1. a. Add a subject
2. b. Add a verb
3. c. Add a subject and a verb
4. b. Add a verb
5. b. Add a verb
6. a. Add a subject
7. d. Add or delete words to express a complete thought.

Turning Fragments into Sentences

PRACTICE 2 (p. 79)

Answers will vary. These are sample answers.

1. The otter returned to the river.
2. A bird on the oak branch sang.
3. The river flowed between the island and the mainland.
4. The hawk, in a soaring motion, flew into the sky.
5. The fishing boats on the lake glided over the water.
6. The loon dropped like a stone into the water.
7. Because the fisherman put the net away, the fish were safe at last.

PRACTICE 3 (pp. 79–80)

1. As long as it's a windy day, we'll be able to fly the kite.
2. Into the forest, armed with a machine gun, the fugitive dashed.
3. complete
4. The college student jogged along a deserted and dusty road.
5. The meadow below is where the deer and the antelope play.

6. The groundhog was run over by three different cars.
7. complete

Identifying Phrases

PRACTICE 4 (pp. 81–82)

1. infinitive
2. infinitive
3. prepositional
4. prepositional
5. noun
6. noun
7. prepositional

PRACTICE 5 (p. 82)

1. prepositional
2. infinitive
3. prepositional
4. noun
5. verb
6. prepositional
7. infinitive
8. verb
9. infinitive
10. prepositional

Correcting the Fragment That Contains a Participle

PRACTICE 6 (p. 84)

Answers will vary. These are sample answers.
1. a. He is climbing in the Rockies.
   b. He climbs in the Rockies.
   c. Climbing in the Rockies, he left his stereo behind.
   d. Climbing in the Rockies is the thing to do.
2. a. He is playing video games.
   b. He plays video games.
   c. Playing video games, he didn't hear the robbers.
   d. Playing video games is time-consuming.
3. a. She is going clubbing on Tuesdays.
   b. She goes clubbing on Tuesdays.
   c. Going clubbing on Tuesdays, she met her best friend.
   d. Going clubbing on Tuesdays is tiring.

Recognizing Fragments

PRACTICE 7 (pp. 84–85)

1. complete
2. fragment
3. fragment
4. fragment
5. complete
6. fragment
7. complete
8. fragment
9. fragment
10. fragment

Editing for Fragments

PRACTICE 8 (p. 85)

Fragments:

Which took the game to 5–3 for Italy.
But 10 minutes before the end of extra time.
For head-butting Marco Materazzi.
And had insulted both his mother and his sister.
Partying with abandon.
Because he didn't take the moral high road.
While millions of fans watched his every move.

Sample corrected paragraph (answers will vary):
Soccer's World Cup in 2006 was won by Italy for the first time in 24 years, but it is public disgrace for which the game will be remembered by the world. By half time, the final game between Italy and France was tied 1–1. After 120 minutes, the game was still tied. The final victory depended on the penalty shootout, which took the game to 5–3 for Italy. But 10 minutes before the end of extra time, France's illustrious captain, Zinedine Zidane, was expelled for head-butting Marco Materazzi. Apparently, Marco had called him a terrorist and had insulted both his mother and his sister. Was this a deliberate, desperate, and cheap attempt to achieve final victory in what had become a gruelling final game? Celebrations by Italians around the world were unstoppable. They partied with abandon. But soccer scandal continues to loom over the Italian team. Zinedine Zidane exited from his last World Cup under an umbrella of shame

because he didn't take the moral high road while millions of fans watched his every move.

Chapter 7: Correcting Run-Ons

Correcting Run-Ons

PRACTICE 1 (pp. 91–93)

Answers will vary. These are sample answers.

1. Simple: (a) Five-year-old Davie asked Grandpa for an iPod for his birthday. He started crying because Grandpa didn't know what that was.

   Compound: (b) Five-year-old Davie asked Grandpa for an iPod for his birthday, but he started crying because Grandpa didn't know what that was.

   (c) Five-year-old Davie asked Grandpa for an iPod for his birthday; however, he started crying because Grandpa didn't know what that was.

   Complex: (d) When five-year-old Davie asked Grandpa for an iPod for his birthday, he started crying because Grandpa didn't know what that was.

2. Simple: (a) Many people are opposed to gambling in all its forms. They will not even buy a lottery ticket.

   Compound: (b) Many people are opposed to gambling in all its forms, so they will not even buy a lottery ticket.

   (c) Many people are opposed to gambling in all its forms; indeed, they will not even buy a lottery ticket.

   Complex: (d) Since many people are opposed to gambling in all its forms, they will not even buy a lottery ticket.

3. Simple: (a) Hockey may be Canada's national sport. The game can be quite brutal.

   Compound: (b) Hockey may be Canada's national sport, but the game can be quite brutal.

   (c) Hockey may be Canada's national sport; however, the game can be quite brutal.

   Complex: (d) Although the game can be quite brutal, hockey may be Canada's national sport.

4. Simple: (a) Many young people manage to travel. They find ways to do it cheaply.

   Compound: (b) Many young people manage to travel, for they find ways to do it cheaply.

   (c) Many young people manage to travel; they find ways to do it cheaply.

   Complex: (d) Many young people manage to travel because they find ways to do it cheaply.

5. Simple: (a) The need for a proper diet is important in any health program. All the junk food on the grocery shelves makes it hard to be consistent.

   Compound: (b) The need for a proper diet is important in any health program, yet all the junk food on the grocery shelves makes it hard to be consistent.

   (c) The need for a proper diet is important in any health program; however, all the junk food on the grocery shelves makes it hard to be consistent.

   Complex: (d) Even though the need for a proper diet is important in any health program, all the junk food on the grocery shelves makes it hard to be consistent.

PRACTICE 2 (pp. 94–96)

Answers will vary. These are sample answers.

1. Simple: (a) The airline has begun its new route to the islands. Everyone is looking forward to flying there.

   Compound: (b) The airline has begun its new route to the islands, so everyone is looking forward to flying there.

   (c) The airline has begun its new route to the islands; consequently, everyone is looking forward to flying there.

   Complex: (d) Ever since the airline began its new route to the islands, everyone has been looking forward to flying there.

2. Simple: (a) The movie begins at nine o'clock. Let's have dinner before the show.

   Compound: (b) The movie begins at nine o'clock, so let's have dinner before the show.

   (c) The movie begins at nine o'clock; therefore, let's have dinner before the show.

   Complex: (d) Since the movie begins at nine o'clock, let's have dinner before the show.

3. Simple: (a) The studio audience screamed at the contestant. They wanted her to try for the big prize.

   Compound: (b) The studio audience screamed at the contestant, for they wanted her to try for the big prize.

   (c) The studio audience screamed at the contestant; they wanted her to try for the big prize.

Complex: (d) The studio audience screamed at the contestant because they wanted her to try for the big prize.

4. Simple: (a) Maya needs new shoes. She is running in the marathon.
   Compound: (b) Maya needs new shoes, for she is running in the marathon.
   (c) Maya needs new shoes; she is running in the marathon.
   Complex: (d) Since she is running in the marathon, Maya needs new shoes.

5. Simple: (a) My actor friend grabbed my arm. She wanted to tell me about her new part in the movie.
   Compound: (b) My actor friend grabbed my arm; she wanted to tell me about her new part in the movie.
   (c) My actor friend grabbed my arm, for she wanted to tell me about her new part in the movie.
   Complex: (d) My actor friend grabbed my arm because she wanted to tell me about her new part in the movie.

Editing for Run-Ons

PRACTICE 3 (p. 96)

Every sentence in the paragraph is a run-on sentence. Sample corrected paragraph (answers will vary):

Mythology is the study of myths, and myths are known as the oldest form of literature. The oldest myths are creation myths. Cultures from around the world have their own creation myths. All of them are amazingly similar despite the vast geographical distances between these cultures and the fact that there are no known ways in which communication could have taken place between certain ones. Details of these myths change from one culture to the next; however, various themes of the myths remain the same. For example, although characters (most of the time, but not all of the time) take on new names from one culture to another, every culture refers to the existence of a creator. Also, the number of gods differs from one mythology to another; nevertheless, every mythology has at least one god or one heroic figure in it. All in all, myths are incredible stories that, in many cases, have lasted thousands of years. No matter where they come from and what they are about, they bear striking similarities from one culture to another, and they all share a wisdom about something that never changes: our human nature.

PRACTICE 4 (pp. 96–97)

Every sentence in the paragraph is a run-on sentence. Sample corrected paragraph (answers will vary):

Sigmund Freud and Carl G. Jung were both psychiatrists who have had a great deal of influence on the study of psychology to this day. For example, each psychiatrist is famous for his own model of the human psyche. In Freud's model, there are three main parts. They are the ego, the id, and the superego. In Jung's model, there are also three main parts: the conscious, the personal unconscious, and the collective unconscious. Freud (Jung's teacher and subsequent collaborator until they parted due to a major disagreement in 1912) and Jung both believed that dreams come from the unconscious part of our psyche (for Freud, this meant the id and superego); nevertheless, they disagreed a great deal in the area of dream interpretation.

Chapter 8: Parallel Structure

Making Sentences Parallel

PRACTICE 1 (p. 101)

1. dirty
2. sewing her own clothes
3. willingly explain material more than once

PRACTICE 2 (pp. 101–102)

Answers will vary. These are sample answers.

1. Winter in Edmonton is very windy and bitterly cold.
2. I would prefer fixing an old car to watching television.
3. Alex is a talented athlete, a top student, and even a generous friend.
4. The apartment is crowded and dark.

5. The dancer is slender and graceful.
6. The trees were tall and leafy.
7. My friend loves to play chess, to read science fiction, and to work out at the gym.

PRACTICE 3 (pp. 102–103)

Answers will vary. These are sample answers.
1. The dog had to choose between jumping over the fence or digging a hole underneath it.
2. She was great at swimming, canoeing, and rock climbing.
3. As I looked down the city street, I could see the soft lights from restaurant windows, I could hear the mellow sounds of a nightclub band, and I could sense the carefree moods of people walking by.
4. The singers have been on several road tours, have recorded for two record companies, and have expressed a desire to make a movie someday.
5. They would rather order a pizza than eat home cooking.
6. I explained to the teacher that my car had broken down, my books had been stolen, and my assignment pad had been left at home.
7. That night the prisoner was sick, discouraged, and lonely.

Chapter 9: Pronouns

Chapter Review Exercises

Making Pronouns and Antecedents Agree

PRACTICE 1 (pp. 114–115)

Answers will vary. These are sample answers.
1. The father mailed his son's high school yearbook to him.
2. No one wants his or her income reduced.
3. When a company fails to update its equipment, it often pays a price in the long run.
4. Graduates today have many more options open to them than ever before.
5. Everybody knows his or her own strengths best.
6. All the soccer players put effort into their game.
7. If the campers want to eat quickly, they should help themselves.

Chapter 10: Modifiers: Misplaced and Dangling

Chapter Review Exercises

Revising Misplaced or Dangling Modifiers

PRACTICE 1 (p. 120)

Answers will vary. These are sample answers.
1. Wearing his tuxedo, Victor fed the dog.
2. While we were visiting the Vancouver Aquarium, the otters entertained us.
3. The toddler that ate her breakfast started singing cheerily.
4. A band that we had heard earlier was playing in the park.
5. After running over the hill, I noticed that the farm was visible in the valley below.
6. The truck, which was broken down on the highway, caused a traffic jam for kilometres.
7. I saw three spiders hanging from the ceiling in my bedroom.

Chapter 11: Punctuation

Insert Necessary Commas

PRACTICE 1 (pp. 123–124)

1. Problems with the water supply of Canada, the United States, Europe, and other parts of the world are growing.
2. Water is colourless, tasteless, odourless, and free of calories.
3. You will use on an average day 90 litres of water for flushing, 120 litres for bathing and washing clothes, and 95 litres for other uses.
4. It took 450 litres of water to create the eggs you ate for breakfast, 13 250 litres to obtain the steak you might eat for dinner, and over 200 000 litres to produce the steel used to make your car.
5. The English-Wabigoon river system runs through Grassy Narrows, Ontario, and had become polluted with mercury.

PRACTICE 2 (p. 124)

1. The most overused bodies of water are our rivers, but they continue to serve us daily.

2. Canadian cities often developed next to rivers, and industries followed soon after in the same locations.

3. The people of the industrial age can try to clean the water they use, or they can watch pollution take over.

4. The Great Lakes are showing signs of renewal, yet the struggle against pollution in them must continue.

5. Most people have not been educated about the dangerous state of our water supply, nor are all our members of Parliament fully aware of the problem.

PRACTICE 3 (p. 125)

1. A total solar eclipse, when the moon's shadow blots out the sun completely, is an outstanding cosmic event.

2. Once you see your first solar eclipse, you start looking forward to the next one.

3. However, witnessing this spectacle takes planning and the ability to travel to the best viewing spots.

4. In eastern Turkey, on August 11, 1999, a crowd of astronomers and "eclipse chasers" watched the last total eclipse of the millennium.

5. At the moment of totality, people cheered, clapped, and even cried.

PRACTICE 4 (p. 127)

1. Natural disasters, I believe, have not been historically significant.

2. They have, however, significantly affected the lives of many Canadians.

3. Canada's worst coal mine disaster, at Hillcrest, Alberta, occurred on June 19, 1914.

4. In Springhill, Nova Scotia, furthermore, 424 persons were killed in the mines between 1881 and 1969.

5. Avalanches, storms, and floods, which are natural disasters, have also made their marks on the face of our country.

PRACTICE 5 (p. 127)

1. Honey, I hope you're not planning to wear that hat.
2. I wonder, Samir, if the game has been cancelled.
3. Dad, could I borrow five dollars?
4. Can you help me, Doctor?
5. Ayesha, is that you?

PRACTICE 6 (p. 128)

1. "I'm innocent," he cried, "of all charges against me."
2. He mumbled, "I won't incriminate myself."
3. "I was told," the defendant explained, "to answer every question."
4. "This court," the judge announced, "will be adjourned."
5. "The jury," said Al Tarvin of *The Star*, "was hand-picked."

PRACTICE 7 (p. 128)

1. Kicking, the child was carried off to bed.
2. To Maria, Suzuki was the boss from hell.
3. When you can, come and visit us.
4. Whoever that is, is going to be surprised.
5. Skin cancer seldom kills, doctors say.

Using the Apostrophe

PRACTICE 8 (p. 132)

1. boys'
2. their
3. Moses's or Moses'
4. Antony and Maria's
5. nobody's
6. his
7. 1700's or 1700s
8. It's
9. Vancouver's
10. Wendy's

PRACTICE 9 (pp. 132–133)

1. Cherry's
2. geese's
3. Carol's and Tess's
4. somebody's
5. hers
6. two's
7. can't

Insert Necessary Quotation Marks

PRACTICE 10 (p. 135)

1. "The Hot House" is one of the stories contained in Rosemary Sullivan's *More Stories by Canadian Women.*

2. Nellie McClung said, "I'll never believe I'm dead until I see it in the papers."
3. no quotation marks needed
4. To "diss" is a slang term meaning to show disrespect.
5. She read the article "Whiz Kids" in *The Review*.

Using Semicolons

PRACTICE 11 (pp. 135–136)

1. One of the best ways to remember a vacation is to take numerous photos; one of the best ways to recall the contents of a book is to take notes.
2. The problem of street crime must be solved; otherwise, the number of vigilantes will increase.
3. The meal was composed of bruschetta, an appetizer; roast duck, the house specialty; and lemon mousse, a tart dessert.
4. The bank president was very cordial; however, he would not approve the loan.
5. New methods of production are being used in the factories of Japan; eventually they will be common in this country as well.

Using Colons

PRACTICE 12 (p. 137)

1. Two Canadian-born comedians have achieved great success in the United States: Jim Carrey and Mike Myers.
2. The official has one major flaw in his personality: greed.
3. no colons needed
4. The college offers four courses in English literature: Romantic Poetry, Shakespeare's Plays, The British Short Story, and The Modern Novel.
5. Arriving at 6:15 in the morning, Marlene brought me a sausage-and-cheese pizza, some ginger ale, and a litre of ice cream.

Using Dashes or Parentheses

PRACTICE 13 (p. 139)

1. Herbert Simon is—and I don't think this is an exaggeration—a genius.
2. George Eliot (her real name was Mary Ann Evans) wrote Silas Marner.

3. You should—in fact I insist—see a doctor.
4. Health Canada's website has suggestions to help smokers quit (visit www.infotobacco.com).
5. Mass media (television, radio, movies, magazines, and newspapers) are able to transmit information over a wide range and to a large number of people.

Chapter Review Exercises

Punctuation Overview

PRACTICE 14 (pp. 139–140)

1. To measure crime, sociologists have used three different techniques: official statistics, victimization surveys, and self-report studies.
2. "David" is one of the best-loved poems of Earle Birney.
3. That show uses one thing I hate: a laugh track.
4. Farley Mowat wrote numerous books for adults; however, he also wrote very popular books for children.
5. Tuberculosis (also known as consumption) has been nearly eliminated by medical science.
6. The Victorian period (1837–1901) saw a rapid expansion in industry.

PRACTICE 15 (p. 140)

1. Many young people have two feelings about science and technology: awe and fear.
2. Mr. Doyle, the realtor; Mrs. Tong, the bank officer; and Ivan Petroff, the lawyer, are the three people to help work out the real-estate transaction.
3. The book was entitled *English Literature: The Victorian Age*.
4. "My computer," she said, "has been crashing all day."
5. She brought a bathing suit, a towel, sunglasses, and several books to the beach. (no colon after brought)
6. The meeting to discuss a pay increase—I'll believe it when I see it—has been rescheduled for Friday.
7. The complex lab experiment has these two major problems: too many difficult calculations and too many variables.

Chapter 12: Capitalization

Capitalization

PRACTICE 1 (pp. 145–146)

1. Italian
2. Canadian Rockies
3. Bible
4. University of Alberta
5. Hallowe'en
6. Bell Canada, Friday, Winnipeg, Manitoba
7. Cobalt-60, Canadian, Dr. Donald Green
8. Why
9. Canadian Auto Workers
10. *Women of the Klondike,* North

Chapter 13: Unit I Review: Using All You Have Learned

Identifying Parts of Speech

PRACTICE 1 (p. 148)

2. constant: adjective modifying the noun source
3. of: preposition, which starts the prepositional phrase of creativity and inspiration
4. and: coordinating conjunction (one of the FANBOYS) joining two items
5. him: pronoun in the objective case
6. inspired: action verb in the past tense
7. throughout: preposition, which starts the prepositional phrase throughout his life
8. his: possessive adjective modifying the noun ideas
9. was: helping verb to be in the past tense
10. when: subordinate conjunction that begins a dependent clause
11. often: adverb modifying the past tense verb led
12. the: definite article
13. right: adjective modifying the noun direction
14. had: past tense of the irregular action verb to have
15. impending: adjective modifying the noun death
16. become: past participle of the irregular action verb to become
17. a: indefinite article
18. symbol: common noun
19. properly: adverb modifying the verb understood
20. only: adverb modifying from his inner experiences
21. outer: adjective modifying the noun world
22. for: preposition, which begins the prepositional phrase for him
23. he: pronoun in the subjective case
24. could: modal auxiliary (helping verb)
25. happenings: common abstract noun

Editing Sentences for Errors

PRACTICE 2 (pp. 148–149)

These are sample answers. There is more than one way to correct many of these sentences.

1. Roma (also known as Gypsies or Romany Gypsies) now are living in many countries of the world.
2. The international community of scientists agrees that these Roma originally came from India thousands of years ago.
3. After the original Roma people left India, they went to Persia; there they divided into groups.
4. One branch of Roma went west to Europe, while the other group decided to go east.
5. In the Middle Ages … Little Egypt.
6. *C*
7. Today, Roma families may be found from Canada to Chile, living much as their ancestors did thousands of years ago.

PRACTICE 3 (pp. 149–150)

These are sample answers. There is more than one way to correct many of these sentences below.

1. The laser beam, a miracle of modern science, already has many practical uses in today's world.
2. Laser beams are narrow, highly concentrated beams of light that burn brighter than the light of the sun.
3. Scientists have found many possible military uses for the laser, but they are hoping these can be converted into constructive uses.
4. *C*
5. The possibility of making a laser was first described in 1958, and two years later, in California, the first laser beam was created.
6. Since they are so precise, laser beams are used in medicine to help make a specific diagnosis and

to perform operations such as repairing delicate retinas and removing cancerous tumours.

7. The future uses of the laser seem endless, and it is up to us to decide whether we want to use this invention for war or for peaceful purposes.

Unit III: The Writing Process

Chapter 19: The Paragraph

Finding the Topic Sentence of a Paragraph

PRACTICE 1 (p. 202)

1. Love is a crazy, complicated affair, made trickier by the tangle of superstitions that go along with it.
2. The brain is one of the most remarkable organs, a part of the body that we have only begun to investigate.

Finding the Topic in the Topic Sentence

PRACTICE 2 (pp. 202–203)

1. Remodelling an old house
2. College work and high school work
3. A well-made suit
4. Growing up near a museum
5. My favourite room in the house
6. A student who goes to school full-time and also works part-time
7. The expense of skiing
8. The change that had come over my friend
9. Current tax laws
10. Greek restaurants

Finding the Controlling Idea

PRACTICE 3 (pp. 203–204)

1. T: vigorous exercise CI: reduces stress
2. T: St. John's and Corner Brook CI: differ
3. T: wonder foods CI: less than wonderful
4. T: athletic scholarships available to women CI: numbers increasing
5. T: caffeine CI: adverse effects
6. T: Madame Benoît CI: amusing personality
7. T: computers CI: will make newspapers obsolete

Avoid Restating the Topic Sentence

PRACTICE 4 (pp. 212–213)

1. a. SD   b. R   c. SD   d. SD
2. a. SD   b. SD   c. R   d. SD

Chapter 20: The Essay

Recognizing the Thesis Statement

PRACTICE 1 (pp. 225–226)

1. thesis
2. title
3. fact
4. thesis
5. title
6. fact
7. fact

Unit IV: Writing Strategies for the Paragraph and the Essay

Chapter 26: Cause and Effect

Looking for the Causal Relationship

PRACTICE 1 (pp. 301–302)

1. T   5. C
2. C   6. T
3. T   7. C
4. C

Separating the Cause from the Effect

PRACTICE 2 (pp. 302–303)

1. a. C   b. C   c. E   d. E   e. C   f. E
2. a. C   b. C   c. E   d. E   e. C   f. C

Chapter 27: Comparison and/or Contrast

Evaluating the Two-Part Topic

PRACTICE 1 (p. 315)

Answers could vary depending on the purpose of the paragraph.

3. too broad   5. too broad
4. suitable   6. too broad

Recognizing the Two Methods

PRACTICE 2 (p. 318)

1. block; differences
2. point-by-point; similarities

Chapter 28: Process

Coherence: Order in Logical Sequence

PRACTICE 1 (p. 326)

7, 5, 1, 8, 2, 6, 3, 9, 4

Chapter 29: Description

Coherence: Putting Details in Spatial Order

PRACTICE 1 (pp. 339–340)

1. 4, 2, 3, 1, 5
2. 2, 3, 1, 4

Chapter 32: Narration

Coherence: Placing Details in Order of Time Sequence

PRACTICE 1 (pp. 366–367)

2. 4, 5, 1, 6, 2, 3

Index

Description
    clauses in, 54–55
    coherence: putting details in spatial order,
        338–340
    defined, 334
    descriptive essay, writing, 341–342, 344
    dominant impressions, 334–336
    good writing skills and use of, 334
    introductory paragraph use of, 230
    model essay: A Monumental Experience,
        342–343
    model paragraph: A Day in the Life (I) and (II), 337
    model paragraph: Delicatessen Decor, 335,
        338, 339
    model paragraph: Mother Fortress (MacLeod),
        340–341
    objective/subjective, 335
    order of details, 334
    paragraphs, developing and writing, 335, 340–341
    of places or people, 336
    sensory images, using, 334, 338
    specific details, using, 334, 338–340
    Steps for Writing the Descriptive Paragraph, 340
    term in essay questions, 183
    vague dominant impressions, revising, 336–337
    Working Together: The Hunt for a Roommate, 345
Desert, 448
Dessert, 448
Diagramming ideas, 191–193
Dialogue, 76, 128
Dictionary, 137, 138, 158, 163, 241, 347
Die/dye, 452
Digital object identifier (DOI), 269
Diner, 448
Diner, 448
Directional process, 324–325, 328, 330–332
Direct questions and answers, 179–180, 181
Distinct categories, 355, 357–358
Documentation. *See also* APA style of documentation;
        MLA style of documentation
    acknowledging the author, 172, 266, 268
    connection between internal and end, 266
    defined, 265
    end (list of sources), 265, 266, 268–269, 280
    internal, 176, 265, 266, 267–268, 270–271
    plagiarism, avoiding, 167, 172–173
    questions for analysis, 283
    of research papers, 258
    of URLs, 269, 273
    Working Together: Documenting Sources, 283
DOI (digital object identifier), 269

Dominant impression, 334–337
Dreamwork for the Soul (Guiley), 148

"The Economic Cost of Depression" (Lamphier), 163,
        399–403
Editing. *See also* Revising and editing
    for consistency, 246
    for fragments, 85, 88
    paragraphs for errors, 152–154
    for punctuation, 140–141, 253
    for repetitious wording, 244
    and revising, difference between, 249
    rough drafts, 196–197
    for run-ons, 96–98
    sentences for errors, 147, 148–152
Effect, 447
Emigrant, 448
Emigrate, 448
Emotions, role in writing, 190–191, 287
End documentation, 265, 266, 268–269, 272–273,
        280, 282
Epstein, Richard L., *The Pocket Guide to Critical
        Thinking*, 290
"Error blindness," 250
Especially, 450
Essay questions
    answering in form of thesis statement, 183–185
    example of, 182
    formulating, 186
    frequently used terms in (method of development),
        182–183
    timed in-class, strategies for answering, 181–182
    Working Together: Formulating Essay
        Questions, 186
Essay writing
    answering questions and, 179–180
    argumentation essays, 294, 295–296, 297
    body, 220
    cause and effect essays, 305–306, 307–308
    classification essays, 359, 362
    compare and/or contrast essays, 320, 322–323
    components of an essay, 219–220, 224 (*See
        also* Concluding paragraphs; Introductory
        paragraph; Thesis statement)
    conclusion and concluding paragraphs, 219,
        220, 221
    definition essays, 350–351, 353–354
    descriptive essays, 341–342, 344
    final stages (*see* Revising and editing)
    introduction and introductory paragraphs, 219,
        220, 221